PORTRAIT

⇥OF A⇤

NOVEL

ALSO BY MICHAEL GORRA

The Bells in Their Silence: Travels through Germany
After Empire: Scott, Naipaul, Rushdie
The English Novel at Mid-Century: From the Leaning Tower

EDITED BY MICHAEL GORRA

As I Lay Dying by William Faulkner (Norton Critical Edition)
The Portable Conrad

Henry James. By Abbot H. Thayer. Crayon on paper, 1881.

Portrait

⇥ OF A ⇤

Novel

Henry James and the Making of
an American Masterpiece

MICHAEL GORRA

LIVERIGHT PUBLISHING CORPORATION

A Division of W. W. Norton & Company

New York • London

For information about permission to
reproduce selections from this book,
write to Permissions, Liveright Publishing Corporation,
a division of W. W. Norton & Company, Inc.,
500 Fifth Avenue, New York, NY 10110

For information about special discounts for bulk
purchases, please contact W. W. Norton Special Sales at
specialsales@wwnorton.com or 800-233-4830

Manufacturing by RR Donnelley, Harrisonburg
Book design by Ellen Cipriano
Production manager: Devon Zahn

Library of Congress Cataloging-in-Publication Data

Gorra, Michael Edward.
Portrait of a novel : Henry James and the making
of an American masterpiece / Michael Gorra. — 1st ed.
p. cm.
Includes bibliographical references and index.
ISBN 978-0-87140-408-4 (hardcover)
1. James, Henry, 1843–1916. 2. Authors, American—19th century—
Biography. 3. Authors, American—20th century—Biography.
4. James, Henry, 1843–1916. Portrait of a lady. 5. American fiction—
European influences. I. Title. II. Title: Henry James
and the making of an American masterpiece.
PS2123.G68 2012
813'.4—dc23
[B]
2012013838

Liveright Publishing Corporation
500 Fifth Avenue, New York, N.Y. 10110
www.wwnorton.com

W. W. Norton & Company Ltd.
Castle House, 75/76 Wells Street, London W1T 3QT

2 3 4 5 6 7 8 9 0

FOR MIRIAM

CONTENTS

PART ONE

A PREPARATION FOR CULTURE

PART TWO

THE MARRIAGE PLOT

PART THREE

ITALIAN JOURNEYS

PART FOUR

SEX AND SERIALS, THE CONTINENT AND THE CRITICS

Part Five

PUTTING OUT THE LIGHTS

PROLOGUE

AN OLD MAN IN RYE

MANY YEARS LATER he would remember the way the book had begun. He was old then, and in England, at home in the place he had made for himself, a eighteenth-century brick building called Lamb House in the small Sussex town of Rye. It was a marsh country once known for its shipwrecks and smugglers, thirty miles down the Channel from Dover, and with the town itself resting on top of a hill. Centuries before, it had been directly on the water, but now the coastline had changed, the harbor had silted up, and the flecked blue of the sea lay at a distance of two miles. The ancient port remained charming but had lost its purpose, and the town itself had become an attractive spot for a genteel retirement. It was an odd place for an American novelist, and an odder one for a man whose habits were entirely urban: a figure of clubs and cabs, of dinner parties and first nights. But then he had rarely done the expected thing. He was a famous man, with elaborate manners, and kind; and yet someone whose eyes could drill your spine with their knowledge. Famous—but now little-read, as his royalty figures all too often reminded him. Sometimes he joked about how little his books brought in. His friend Edith Wharton might sell enough to buy a new automobile, but his own checks, he claimed, would only cover the cost of a wheelbarrow.

He had lived in Europe for thirty years—he had taken possession of it, inhaled it, appropriated it. It had been the great adventure of his life. Or rather his expatriation had made other adventures possible, the adventure contained in the litter of printed sheets on his desk. His literary agent had taken two copies of one of his early novels and cut their bindings, slicing the pages free, and had then pasted each one onto a larger sheet. That gave him a single unbound copy with a few inches of white space on all sides, plenty of room to scrawl. He dipped his pen and blackened half a line of type, wrote four words in the margin and drew a circle around them, with a faint thread of ink tethering them to their place in his paragraph. He blotted two more lines, italicized a word of dialogue, turned "I am" into "I'm." Another line gone, but this time a new one replaced it, and his characters no longer "rejoined" in answer to each other's speech; instead they "returned." Now and then, he revised his first revision. The pen sliced, it cut and it qualified, and sometimes it discovered so many ineptitudes that his quarto sheet became an illegible tangle of lines and arrows. The compositors, he knew, had already complained about such pages, and he put them aside to be typed.

Most nineteenth-century novelists touched up their work in the months between its first publication in a magazine and its appearance as a bound volume. A serial installment might have been rushed to make a deadline or trimmed to match the space, and its opening chapters were usually in print long before the book was finished. But Henry James took the business of revision much further than that. He lived in a world of second thoughts, and in the early years of his career he treated his proofs as but a clean copy, something little better than a draft to scribble over. The pieces a magazine had already printed often got the same treatment. A story from the *Atlantic* or *Harper's* might be revised for an American collection, and overhauled again for an English one. He believed that almost every sentence could stand a little work, and could hardly bear to reread his earlier things except with a pen in his hand, making changes as he went. One of his best stories, "The Middle Years" (1893), gives that habit to its main character, a novelist called Dencombe, who in the story's first pages reworks an advance copy of his latest book. Only this time the new work seems good, and he marks it up with a sense of promise. It makes him realize what he might yet do, and he longs for the chance to grow into a magnificent "last manner." But Dencombe is also a sick man and he dies before can he grab it.

His creator had better luck. James had made the character die at fifty, but he himself was now sixty-three, and in the spring and summer of 1906 he lived in a season of second chances. The sheets on his desk were from a book he had published in 1881, a quarter of a century ago: *The Portrait of a Lady*, the novel in which, after a period of careful apprenticeship, he had first allowed his imagination full stretch. He didn't think it was his best book—he preferred *The Ambassadors* (1903), a bittersweet comedy about a group of Americans in Paris—but still it was the one from which he "would pretend to date." The novel told the story of a girl named Isabel Archer; a girl who claims she's fond of her freedom but who stands just the same, after the death of her spendthrift father, on the verge of marriage to a New England mill owner. Then she suffers a fairy-tale rescue at the hands of an aunt. Taken to Europe and furnished with an unexpected inheritance, Isabel finds what looks at first like an ever-expanding field in which to exercise her own sense of independence. At first. For she will soon make the mistake of her young life, and her mixture of "curiosity and fastidiousness," brittle intelligence and inflated confidence, would make her an easy mark for the reader's criticism if she were not, as James wrote, meant to awaken our sense of tenderness instead.

The Portrait of a Lady was Henry James's first true success, and though as a young man he had made fun of the idea of the Great American Novel, greatness had always been on his mind. He had taken pains with the book, and it had changed his reputation. It had made him important enough to be attacked on all sides, and now it was to have a new life. In 1904, James had gone back to the United States, making his first visit in twenty-one years. He saw the places where he'd grown up, in New York and Newport and Boston. He gave lectures and gossiped with old friends and was both fascinated and appalled by the way the country had changed, by skyscrapers and a new American language that he barely recognized as his own, so different was its slang and pronunciation. He went to Florida and California and to the battlefields of the Civil War, in which he had not fought, and brought home a mind of gathered impressions that he began to turn into a travel book called *The American Scene*. But he also matured another plan along the way, arranging with the help of his agent, J. B. Pinker, for the publication by Scribner of a definitive edition of his work; an edition "selective as well as collective; I want to quietly disown a few things." The early books that had made his name—stories like *Daisy Miller*, novels like *The American* or *The Portrait of a Lady* itself—would have their surfaces rubbed over, their style nudged or even kicked into line with that of his later work. And to each novel or collection of tales James planned to add a "frank critical" preface; prefaces that now stand, and that to the *Portrait* in particular, among the most idiosyncratic, and greatest, of his achievements.

Today, *The Portrait of a Lady* appears to look backward and forward at once, offering a Janus-faced lens on the history of the novel itself. It is the link between George Eliot and Virginia Woolf, the bridge across which Victorian fiction stepped over into modernism. James used his heroine to crystallize one of his period's central concerns, that of what George Eliot herself had described as the "delicate vessels" of female experience. Isabel's story touched the limits of what could and couldn't be said about sex in the Anglo-American fiction of the period, and James also flouted the conventions of his era by risking an ending that was both unhappy and open; the novel's final pages leave her fate more unsettled than ever. Moreover, the book challenged its readers' assumptions about the nature of fictional events. In James's hands the drama of the interior life took on the thrill that other writers might find in "the surprise of a caravan or the identification of a pirate," and the result was the most searching account of the moment-by-moment flow of consciousness that any novelist had yet attempted.

But the book looks two ways in another sense as well, not temporally but spatially. In 1888, James told his brother, the Harvard philosopher William James, that he wanted to make it impossible for his readers to know whether he was "an American writing about England or an Englishman writing about America." Sometimes he managed the trick and sometimes he didn't, but one mark of his overall success lies in the different contexts within which his work is now read. That's especially true of *The Portrait of a Lady*. It appears as often in discussions of the Victorian novel as it does in those of American literature, and rightfully so. For its richly suggestive picture of what it is to be an American depends, paradoxically, on the way it uses both its European setting and the thematics of European fiction—the marriage plot, the novel of adultery—to mount a critique of American exceptionalism.

In this book I will tell that novel's story. Most people don't read criticism, not beyond the length of a review. They read narrative—that's why biography is so popular. But *Portrait of a Novel* is not a biography as such, and it offers the tale not of a life but of a work. It shows how Henry James created Isabel Archer's portrait, and to what end: tells not only what happens in the book itself but also the story of how James came to write it and what happened to him while he was doing so; of the book's relation to the major fiction of the decades around it, and of how it was published and received and then, many years later, revised.

One part of my tale offers a picture of James's career between 1878 and 1884, the years for which his own *Portrait* provides a fulcrum. At the start of that period he wrote *Daisy Miller*, an account of a high-spirited and impossibly well-dressed American girl. Men cluster wherever she goes, but Daisy doesn't understand that in Italy she can't flirt with the same freedom as at home in Schenectady, and she will pay for that misunderstanding with her life. Some readers found the story a celebration of American innocence, others an attack on the purity of American women; and it remained James's best-known work long after he had written greater things. At the end of this time he published "The Art of Fiction," a sharply worded essay that began as a knife-cut in the literary debates of his period, but which endures as a major theoretical statement. In between, James not only wrote his first full-length masterpiece but also returned twice to America from his home in London, buried both his parents, and settled his choice of a European residence once and for all. He confirmed the choices he had already made: of the Old World, of his art, and of what he always presented as his consequent decision not to marry.

That decision was one he found himself insisting upon in the early

1880s, even as he made Isabel turn down one proposal after another. Yet there are other ways to think of it, and one element in my story is an account of James's own sexuality. Nobody now doubts the directions of his sexual leanings. His deepest erotic longings were for men, and at a certain point in his life he came to understand that. The precise date of that point has, however, proved impossible to fix, and nobody actually knows if he ever acted upon a physical desire. He burned most of the letters he received, hoped others would burn his, and his stories often depend on the things his characters cannot quite manage to say to each another. His work presents us with a paradox: this apparently celibate writer nevertheless kicked harder than any of his Anglophone contemporaries at the period's conventional distinction between "that which people know" about the sexual life, and that which on the page "they agree to admit that they know."

I will describe the writing of the novel itself, defining James's plans and progress and reconstructing the rhythms of his working life. In doing so I give special attention to the places of the writing—to his work in London, Florence, and Venice, and his settings in the Thames Valley, Florence, and Rome. So I have walked through the Tuscan capital with a nineteenth-century guidebook in my hand, mapping out the various places in which James stayed, and visiting the villa in which he located some of his characters; working throughout to define the difference between those actual places and the uses he made of them. Another part of the tale provides an account of the novel's publication—its serialization on both sides of the Atlantic, its reception and sales—and locates the book within the institutions of the Victorian novel as a whole. Throughout, I alternate sections on the novel with others that place James and his work in their moment, a dialectical structure that allows the fiction itself to suggest just when to pick up on certain issues in the writer's own life; when James takes his characters to Italy, I will take him there too. But above all I will tell the story that the novel tells, watching Isabel Archer make the choices she has insisted upon making, and using my commentary on its plot to carry the burden of argument, as the best movie criticism often does. One of the things Isabel learns is that her field of action is not free, has never been free. The decisions of others have always impinged upon her own, and her belated recognition of those constraints—of the limits placed on her Emersonian self-reliance—has been described as an American version of *Paradise Lost*.

The novel began its serial run in October 1880, appearing in both the *Atlantic Monthly* and in Britain's *Macmillan's Magazine*, and had its first book publication in the fall of the following year. James always dreamed of a good market, and was almost always disappointed. Only a few of his shorter works were bestsellers, but not even *Daisy Miller* or *The Turn of the Screw* (1898) could rival the appeal of Dickens or Mark Twain. By his own measure, though, *The Portrait of a Lady* was a commercial success, selling over 5,500 copies in five American printings during its first year, and it remains today the most popular of his novels.

Most current printings use the text of what James called the New York Edition—the novel as he revised it in the summer of 1906, and in which the language has a physicality that he could not summon in 1880–81. In revision even so innocuous an object as a narrow Manhattan house becomes "a wedge of brown stone violently driven into Fifty-third Street," and that pungent metaphoric power is especially important in James's treatment of Isabel's emotional life; so much so, indeed, that some readers see the revised *Portrait* as a very different book than the one James first published. For my classes I order the New York Edition. Here, however, my emphasis on the book's development has led me back to the text of 1881, now most readily available in the Library of America edition of James's *Novels: 1881–1886*. I do, however, make constant reference to his revisions. They too are a part of this book's story, and looking at them will give me the chance, in however telescoped a manner, to follow out the later years of his life and career.

It was a long career, some fifty years from start to finish, and just as the book we most often read is not precisely the one James initially wrote, so the author we usually visualize isn't quite the same man as the one who in the spring of 1880 began to write that novel in a Florence hotel room. The writer of 1906 has become known as "The Master," a name used even in his own lifetime by a few of his younger disciples. He was clean-shaven and bald, with a massive, egg-shaped head and a body to match. He wore pince-nez and his eyes were heavy-lidded, creased at the corners, and bagged. That James is the hero of a thousand anecdotes and the subject of almost as many photographs; and he sat as well for a great portrait by his friend John Singer Sargent. He carries such imaginative weight that it can be difficult to recover a clear image of his earlier self. That increasingly confident young writer wore a full beard, and his habits were not yet sedentary. He could manage a horse, and in his early manhood enjoyed days of strenuous hiking in the Alps. He knew how to fence, worked out with dumbbells, liked peaches and Bass Ale, and though by 1880 most of his walks were on city streets, he spent the New Year at a Yorkshire ball where, as he wrote to his sister Alice, he found "the British maiden . . . a good solid weight to whirl in the mazes." His prose was tart and vigorous, and he found it hard to restrain the excitement with which he wrote to his parents about an evening with a prime minister or an earl.

In the fall of 1879, James published a short critical biography of Nathaniel Hawthorne. He thought his predecessor had been limited by his time and place, and yet he also valued him above all other American writers, and described *The Scarlet Letter* in particular as touched by the peculiar charm "which we find in an artist's work the first time he has touched his highest mark—a sort of straightness and naturalness of execution." That is the mark Henry James reached with *The Portrait of a Lady*.

In the spring of 1906 he spent his mornings at work on the southern chapters of *The American Scene*, evoking the "swarming . . . pretty girls" of Savannah and the "vacancy" of Charleston, a city that seemed to him still exhausted by the battles of the Civil War. Almost every corner of Lamb House gave him a spot in which to write, but in warm weather James's favorite was a place called the Garden Room. It was detached from the house itself, a studio that he entered from his acre of walled garden; indeed one end of it formed a part of that wall, and was lit by a bow window that overhung the street. Unfortunately it no longer stands. A German bomb took it out in 1940, and in visiting Lamb House today—it is now owned by the National Trust—I could only find its brick outline on the grass. Photographs show the room as uncluttered, almost cleared for action, with a couch pushed up under the window, and bookcases against the walls. It was big enough, and open enough, for James to pace, his left thumb tucked in his waistcoat armhole, his hesitant and at times stammering voice gaining in assurance as it rolled from sentence to sentence.

As he talked, his words would be answered by the sputter and clack of a Remington typewriter. For he shared the room with a young woman from a London secretarial agency, whom he had hired, at 25s. per week, to take down his dictation. The particular young woman of 1906 did not stay long, and her name hasn't come down to us; perhaps she didn't like the work, or found the town too dull. James had been dictating for almost a decade, starting the practice somewhere in the middle of *What Maisie Knew* (1897). Thirty years of his own almost illegible penmanship had cramped his hand, and he now saved it as much as he could. Dictation made concision impossible, and the speaking voice led him into syntactic complications of which he had once been innocent. But he liked having a clean page on which to revise, and by now the typewriter's noise provided an aid to concentration. So did the occasional cigarette.

That was the morning, that gathering up of the American South— three disciplined hours that began around ten. Then lunch and a walk up and down Rye's grassy cobbled streets, a few hours to cover a few miles, his way broken by the small talk of a small town, a chat with neighbors, a greeting to the fishmonger, sometimes a stop for tea at the local golf club; he didn't play but had joined anyway. Everywhere one turns in Rye the beaky peal of gulls hangs in the air, and when James had first visited ten years before, the sound must have made him feel at home, a reminder of the Newport where he had spent his teens. He had rented Lamb House in 1897 and bought it two years later, moving back and forth between the coast and his South Kensington flat; eventually he let the flat go and made do with a room at his club. The house sat—sits—on a curve at the crest of what James called the town's "mildly pyramidal hill," with its front door facing down West Street to the churchyard of St. Mary the Virgin, a minute's walk away; a turn to the left let him amble down to the shops of the High Street. It is a large place, three stories of worn brick with a wide entry hall, the kitchen in a wing off the back, and a set of servants' bedrooms on the top floor; James might sometimes plead poverty but he kept five of them, his secretary not included. He could never have afforded such a place in central London, and he noted with pride that in an earlier age George II had once spent the night.

He himself had few houseguests in the spring and summer of 1906, though in June he gave a bed to the Wisconsin-born Hamlin Garland, whose *Main-Travelled Roads* (1891) is even now read for its unsparing account of midwestern farm life. Garland remembered that they talked late about Hardy and Kipling; James was fond of the latter but suspected his "extraordinary precocity was perhaps at its real end." Yet Garland also noted that James seemed "wistfully an American feeling his expatriation," and his most substantial contacts with the outside world were indeed by letter, many of them still written by hand. He sent a note of congratulations to his friend A. C. Benson, a Cambridge don who had just published a book on the Victorian essayist Walter Pater, and wrote often to the sculptor Hendrik Andersen, on whom he lavished an unrequited longing. Other letters went to his brother William, who was lecturing at Stanford that spring when the San Francisco earthquake hit. The philosopher had been lying in bed when, as he wrote to Sussex, the "room began to sway . . . it went *crescendo* and reached *fortissimo* in about 20 seconds . . . bureau over, everything on the floor, crashing, crashing." The novelist sent a feverish letter of thanksgiving for his brother's safety, but William himself had enjoyed it all, and was surprised by his sibling's concern.

James's most frequent correspondent, however, was his agent Pinker, a former magazine editor whose agency was one of London's first; his other clients included both Joseph Conrad and H. G. Wells. James peppered him with short notes of thanks for royalty checks, and longer ones about the new edition. He did not, for example, like the idea of illustrations; he had never liked having his characters turned into pictures for the magazines. But he had just enjoyed two sessions with a young American photographer, Alvin

Langdon Coburn, and now began to warm to the idea of using a single image at the head of each volume. On June 10, he wrote of the progress he was making with the *Portrait*'s revisions—he was three-fifths of the way through, and wondered about sending what he'd finished to Scribner, so they could begin to set it in type. Still, it had all taken longer than he had expected; his revisions were so extensive that much of it needed to be typed. Yet it was worth it. He had "hugely *improved* the book—& I mean this not only for myself, but for the public." James sent in a second and final batch of copy at the end of July, and the work's great preface followed in the dry sunshine of mid-August.

He wrote most of his letters at night and upstairs, in what was named the Green Room: a paneled study, its walls tight-packed with photographs, to which the Remington was moved each winter. Yet the time from five until eight can be a little eternity, and in those hours Henry James sat down to his revisions. We don't know just where he would have done this, but the weather was warm and so let me place him in the Garden Room, in the slow care and pleasure of this new chance. A picture taken that year by a nephew shows him at a table there, wearing a bow tie and his invariable winged collar, and with a steel pen in his hand. There's a tiled hearth behind him, and he has a bit of a pout, as though impatient at having to hold his pose. Take the photographer away, however, and then imagine the half-smile that comes over his face as he rolls the pen in his fingers. There is an hour before dinner, and the pen scratches and circles, each sheet marked by a delta of wavy lines, each stream attached to a small lake of new words. He is near the end, and he blackens out a phrase, allows his heroine a sentence of struggling comprehension, until at last he is pleased, and knows that the book has repaid his time and his trouble. He has mended some infelicities; he has stretched the fibers of his prose and rewoven the parts that seemed thin. But it had been well made from the start—not like *The American*, with its hidden murder and grand renunciations, a book whose lurid plot he wishes he could change.

The Portrait of a Lady gave him no such difficulties. Yet once he had packed up its pages and begun to talk his way through its preface, James did find a sense of mystery in recovering the days of its origin. He would sit in thought while his amanuensis waited at her keys. Then he was on his feet and the past was in his hands. First came Florence in the spring, where he had worked in a room over the Arno, with the Ponte Vecchio virtually at his feet. The following year he went to Venice, and he remembered going to his waterfront window each time he was stalled for a phrase, as though the right word might lie in the waves outside. Even in Rye, James was drawn to the window, and sometimes paused in mid-sentence to speak to a friend on the sidewalk. In Venice he had brought the book near its close, and whole pages made him see its quays once more, and hear its voices calling across the water. He summoned ghosts as he walked, the ghosts of Ivan Turgenev and George Eliot, the great predecessors who appeared in his mind as sponsors. From the Russian he took a sense of the precedence of character over plot, a belief that story wasn't an end in itself but instead a way to show his people. George Eliot gave him something else, an understanding of the particular characters to whom those plots might happen, and such figures as *Middlemarch*'s Dorothea Brooke had served as a model for his own.

He paces, pauses, and a sentence floats on the air, a memory of the "single small cornerstone" with which he had begun, "the conception of a certain young woman affronting her destiny." His heroine had stood there alone in his mind, unsupported at first by friends or family or any shred of a narrative. And then one morning he woke up in possession of his other characters, a suite of attendants with whom to surround her, and Henry James set himself to the job of "organising an ado about Isabel Archer."

PART ONE

A PREPARATION FOR CULTURE

The English Home. By Alvin Langdon Coburn, ca. 1907. Frontispiece to Vol. 1 of
The Portrait of a Lady in the New York Edition. Gelatin silver print.

1.

THE GIRL IN THE DOORWAY

S O THE YEARS dissolve and there she stands, a "tall girl in a black dress," ready in the novel's first pages to walk through a door and onto the lawn of an English country house. A door is a door, and we don't need to see it symbolically to know that the act of walking through one can be momentous—a moment of passage, of transition. This particular door provides a frame in which the girl stands as if for her portrait indeed. It defines the space around her, it isolates her and makes her into a picture even as she pauses, before stepping onto the stage of her life, to look out at the scene before her, at the shade trees and the carpet of turf and the hill running down to the Thames. We look at her there, and we're not the only ones to do so. For the curious thing about this book is that James doesn't begin with his heroine. She first appears in the opening lines of the second chapter, and the novel itself starts with a conversation on that lawn between three men.

One of them owns this house, the four-hundred-year-old Gardencourt. He is "a shrewd American banker" named Daniel Touchett: an old man who has spent his career in England and will die there, so old now that he hardly ever leaves his chair. One of the others is his invalid son, Ralph, a consumptive whom James will use as the reader's friend, with his perceptions guiding our own. The last of them is a neighbor called Lord Warburton, a man of such brilliant fortune that he seems exempt from the normal conditions of life. The younger men pace the lawn and the old man sits, and they speak of the imminent arrival of the banker's wife from America, of the cryptic telegram in which she has announced that she's "discovered a niece" and is bringing the girl back with her. Mrs. Touchett has described the girl as "quite independent," and yet what, Ralph wonders, does that mean? Is her independence financial, or moral, or does she simply like to have her own way? They continue to speculate, their curiosity piqued, and Mr. Touchett warns Lord Warburton against falling in love with her. And the effect of their interest is to make us interested too. Their questions become ours, and when Isabel Archer steps through that door, she will find a hum of expectation prepared for her.

We could say, crudely, that they're talking about girls, and that James invites us to go along with them, to let our gaze follow theirs. Such a reading can't be the whole truth, however, for Isabel has been standing in the doorway for a few minutes before her cousin notices her. She arrives before they know it, she watches them before they can watch her, and her appearance takes them by surprise. That door may provide a frame, but it's one into which she has put herself and that she can break at will, as she does in stepping forward to pick up Ralph's little terrier, whose barks provide her first greeting. But her position suggests something else as well, and I can't look at her there without recalling a few famous lines from James's preface to the novel.

Novelists love describing their own work with metaphors drawn from the building trades, and when in the summer of 1906 James set out to explore the origins of *The Portrait of a Lady*, he defined the book as a "square and spacious house," a carefully proportioned affair of vaults and arches and brick piled upon brick. Such imagery is simple enough; so simple, in fact, that James didn't stop with it. For in writing he also found that he wanted, if not precisely to justify his choice of a subject, then at least to explain how he had kept a long novel about a "mere slim shade" of a girl from seeming thin. That explanation has many parts, and I will return to it later in this book. What concerns us now is the extended architectural metaphor in which James defined the scope and ambition of fiction itself.

In my father's house there are many mansions. So at least the New

Testament tells us, and James lifted that image to describe what he calls the house of fiction, a building that has "not one window, but a million—a number of possible windows not to be reckoned, rather," from which one may peer out at the "spreading field, the human scene." The individual novelist stands within that house as within a library, tight-packed with his fellows. All human life lies outside, and there's no saying on what part of that varied landscape a particular window may open. All subjects are possible, all legitimate, and the whole trick is to find that subject's appropriate form, the particular opening, whether "broad or balconied or slit-like" that will give the best view. Because there is only one right way to treat each of those subjects, and James himself was never shy about noting the places in his own work where the sash doesn't fit or the panes are too small.

In every window stands a watcher, "the consciousness of the artist" who must make some meaning from the scene outside, and we can imagine ourselves as reading that scene over the writer's shoulder, our eyes following his. We might even think of Isabel as making up a story about the men she sees on the lawn, the world she is about to join; perhaps her very position is what gave her creator that metaphor in the first place. Of course, by the time she appears, James has already cut his window, given it shape and scale and definition, and done so with the book's opening sentence: "Under certain circumstances there are few hours in life more agreeable than the hour dedicated to the ceremony known as afternoon tea." First lines are always important, but they don't always do the same job. One of the most famous beginnings in English fiction is that of *Pride and Prejudice*—"It is a truth universally acknowledged, that a single man in possession of a good fortune, must be in want of a wife." The ironies of Austen's sentence serve to announce both style and theme: a truth acknowledged by whom, and in what sense "in want?" James's words establish a mood and make a world. "Under certain circumstances"—that is, under circumstances like these. The diction may be fussily discriminating, but that's precisely why the sentence seems to make us step ourselves into this space of cultivated leisure, into the lovely middle of a summer afternoon.

The details he chooses only work to increase that sense of leisure. Mr.

Touchett may have been a banker, yet still the three men are separated by age and class and illness from the bustle of the commercial world; they have the time and freedom to enjoy the shadows on the grass. The lawn has been furnished with rugs and chairs, as though it were a room all hung around with landscapes, with pictures of garden and house and river. It is a place of comfort and ease, and the book itself seems as fully designed for the reader's own comfort as the world in which its characters live. So Isabel can't help herself when Ralph murmurs Warburton's name to her as they walk across the lawn. "Oh, I hoped there would be a lord," she says, "it's just like a novel!" For she has now stepped inside her own story, one that comes with a lord and a country house, a ghost, and even a palace in Rome, with everything one wants a certain kind of novel to have. It's a gesture that welds Isabel's love of the props and furniture of fiction to her Anglophilia, a gesture that serves to license such guilty pleasures of our own.

But the future will not be one of tea parties; not only. The men on the lawn talk of health, and money, and marriage. Then Mr. Touchett strikes a curious note—he announces his belief that "there will be great changes; and not all for the better." It's the kind of thing old men say, and not something in which we should try to find a social or political meaning. It does, however, tell us something about *The Portrait of a Lady* as a whole. Isabel may see herself as having stepped inside a novel, but not all novels end well.

The girl is full of questions, her speech darting from dogs to the date of Gardencourt and on to old family quarrels. She settles on nothing except to declare her love of her own liberty, and though her spontaneity doesn't precisely jar with this cozily accustomed world, it does at least refresh it. Whatever she says proves enough, though, and at the end of the book's second chapter, Warburton will turn to Ralph and say that Isabel fits his idea—his ideal—of an interesting woman. Yet why? Many of the novel's first reviewers complained that these opening chapters don't give us a decided sense of Isabel's character. It's true that James does without the kind of clear omniscient statement that we find, for example, at the start of *Middlemarch*: "Miss Brooke had that kind of beauty which seems to be thrown into relief by poor dress." All Dorothea's sensuous asceticism is in that sentence, but about Isabel we're only told that at first she looks pretty; later, that "nineteen persons out of twenty" will find her older sister prettier. The twentieth will think the others all fools. Our initial impression isn't of Isabel in herself, but rather of other people's reactions to her, and James means for our interest to mimic Warburton's, even before telling us anything much about her. Some readers resist this, young women in particular. Few young men do. Nevertheless, she will for many pages seem elusive, a figure not easy to sum up or to know.

Having introduced her, moreover, James then moves away once more, as though he can only approach her indirectly. He begins his third chapter with an account of what he calls Mrs. Touchett's "many oddities," above all her decision to "rescue disagreement from the vulgar realm of accident" by separating from her husband. She spends most of the year in Florence, and comes to England for just one month each summer, while requiring Ralph to travel down to Italy in the spring. Both stiff-backed and quirky, she sees nothing irregular in her marriage, and never revisits a decision. Now and then she crosses the Atlantic to inspect her American investments, and on one such trip, four months before the book's opening scene at Gardencourt, she finds herself walking through an old house in Albany, a building from which all the life appears to have faded; a house of many rooms and two front entrances, one of them permanently bolted. In one of those rooms a newly orphaned girl sits reading—she can hear the visitor tapping her way through the house, and at first wonders if the old woman has come to buy it. Isabel thinks her visitor's manners are strange, but her own are not much better, for all she can say when she realizes the truth is "You must be our crazy Aunt Lydia." Still, that candor serves her well, for just an hour later Mrs. Touchett has promised to take her to Italy.

The book has begun *in medias res*, with James then backing up to tell us what's led to its opening scene. An anonymous 1881 reviewer for the the *New York Sun* wrote that the novel's very material compelled a smooth perfection of form, that the sophistication of James's social world required

a sophistication of style that betrayed "no mark of graving tool or bur-
nisher." And in terms of James's own performance, nothing about these
opening chapters seems more remarkable than the understated ease with
which he slips back through time, the gears of his retrospective narrative
meshing silently. He reaches the past through a form of digression. He enu-
merates Mrs. Touchett's oddities one by one, until he reaches the latest of
them, the fact that she has "taken up her niece," a young woman whose own
tastes and history he then moves to define. Isabel's life has been a happy
one, despite her mother's early death, and the more recent one of her father.
She has traveled, she has never been in want, and though her reputation
for intelligence has probably driven a few suitors away, she hasn't lacked
for either flattery or flowers. As a girl, she had lived through the Civil War
in a passion of excitement, exalted by the valor of both armies; for she is a
creature of contradictions and curiosity both, and loves above all to sense
a "continuity between the movements of her own heart and the agitations
of the world." Yet she also knows how little she understands about that
world, and suspects she has too little acquaintance with unpleasant things.
Her reading, after all, has made her think that the unpleasant might be a
source of interest and maybe even instruction.

Most of James's 1906 revisions to the novel's first chapters were not
of much substance. He tweaked some adjectives, and where Isabel in 1881
had never met anyone "so entertaining" as her aunt, in the New York Edition no one before had "so held her." Only one change really affects our
understanding of her character. James's first version allows her a "glimpse
of contemporary aesthetics," but in the revision he specifies her taste: the
music of Charles Gounod, the poetry of Robert Browning, and the fiction
of George Eliot. In the first edition such references would have seemed
modish, but by 1906 those figures had established a claim to permanence,
and their names fix Isabel in her moment. James provides just one date in
the novel—November 1876—but it's possible from that to place everything else, to say with confidence that Isabel first meets her aunt in the late
winter of 1871. That's too soon for her to be reading *Middlemarch*, let alone
Daniel Deronda, books that James himself had on his mind as he wrote. Still,

if Flaubert's Emma Bovary can be spoiled by her reading of romantic fiction, why shouldn't an ardent American teen have had her head spun by the moralized everyday yearnings of *The Mill on the Floss?*

Mrs. Touchett finds her in a room called the "office" that is, properly speaking, the foyer to the house's locked entrance. Isabel knows that its still and silent door opens onto the street, but she has never had the desire to fling it wide. Doing so would interfere "with her theory that there was a strange, unseen place on the other side," a realm both of terror and delight. This is one of the first things James tells us about the shape of her inner life—that she both fears and enjoys the unknown. Sometimes she welcomes it, and when Mrs. Touchett offers to take her to Italy, Isabel says she would promise "almost anything" to be able to go. Or maybe we should say that she might refuse almost anything. Later that day she has a second visitor, the owner of a Massachusetts cotton mill named Caspar Goodwood, whose "physiognomy had an air of requesting your attention." She has known him a year and thinks him the finest of men; she expects his visit and even suspects its purpose. But he leaves defeated, and the curious thing is that James doesn't need to step inside Isabel's mind to make her refusal of his proposal seem convincing. We simply believe it—and believe, moreover, that Mrs. Touchett's offer is only its proximate cause. Her aunt gives Isabel the excuse she already wants, but her reasons run deeper and we accept her decision without finding it capricious. It is unexplained but not unmotivated, and indeed this shying away from that strange, unseen place called marriage may at this moment be inexplicable even to herself.

Ralph says that Isabel has a "general air of being some one in particular," and James's acount of her Albany life goes some way toward specifying just who. He has started with an image, with a girl who makes a sharp but literally sketchy impression, and then layers one moment upon another, a picture not in space but in time, touch added to touch, tint upon tint. Isabel's portrait will develop slowly, emerging chapter by chapter; George Eliot may give us a firm sense of Dorothea Brooke in a line, but this woman will not be clear until the end. And perhaps not even then. Some part of her character will remain enigmatic, and in this James's work does indeed resemble a painting. Even in the greatest portraits we find a gate we cannot open. There is always a limit to what we can know of the sitter, to how far we can read the soul in the face; the *Mona Lisa*'s smile provides but the most obvious example. Isabel's inner life is as fully dramatized as that of anyone in the nineteenth-century novel, but James will at certain crucial points maintain this early refusal to enter her consciousness.

Here that refusal has something to do with the tension between Ralph's words about the "general" and the "particular," a tension also posed by the book's peculiar title; peculiar for a time in which novelists most often found their titles in proper names and gave their work the form of biography. James will provide that biography, and yet he resists the temptation to call the book *Isabel Archer*. His picture may be definitive—*the* portrait—but its subject has something generic about her. *A* lady, maybe any lady. Think for comparison of Joyce's title, which reverses the articles—*A Portrait of the Artist as a Young Man*. The Irish writer offers a portrait of this particular artist, but he suggests that it's only one of many possible versions, that he could make a different image. Of course, James's title also suggests Isabel's social role and category. A "lady" is not born but made, the product of her own training and other people's perception; indeed of convention itself.

Isabel is just twenty-one when the novel begins, and she will need to grow beyond the sense of undefined potential with which she steps onto the lawn. A lady is what she needs to *become*, and we can understand the terms of that becoming by juxtaposing the nouns of James's title to another pair of words, to "girl" on the one hand and "study" on the other. Those words belong to *Daisy Miller*, which bears "A Study" as its subtitle, and in a certain sense neither a girl nor a study can stand as a completed work. A study is but a quick preliminary drawing, an indication of line and shadow. The term suggests both process and preparation, a stop on the way to a more finished product, and yet it can also seem dismissive. Studies may be quick and slapdash, they have the charm of the not-yet-formed, and as such the word fits James's eponymous heroine, a girl who is left incomplete by her death. The people around her see Daisy as "artless," and a girl is in a way the product of nature. But most girls grow up, and a study may in time give way to a work of greater polish.

When Isabel steps onto the lawn at Gardencourt, she is simply an American girl, a term that in itself suggests a person ever-developing but as yet unfinished. A girl is not a lady—not yet, in some cases not ever. That, however, is what Isabel becomes, and despite James's use of the indefinite article, a portrait is finally the picture of a specific person. Isabel will need to earn her claim to particularity, but by the end of the novel she appears as the definitive version of her type. For in her grace and poise and even, James suggests, in the way she bears her sadness, Isabel Archer will stand as what a lady should be.

2.

A NATIVE OF NO COUNTRY

A T THE END of the 1860s the Royal Mail steamship *China* made a regular circuit between Liverpool and New York under the command of E. M. Hockley. At 1,500 tons the ship wasn't a large one, and she tossed and rolled even on a passage of relative calm; though for her period she was quick enough. A manifest handed in on her May 1868 arrival in New York suggests that along with the mail the *China* carried about 70 passengers. Few of them were immigrants, most were American citizens, and 15 of them listed their occupation as "gentleman," though a Mr. George C. Power defined himself as a "miser" and the teenaged Thomas Scarby was a jockey. The young man who boarded the *China* in New York in February 1869 had published a dozen stories, but he too would have put himself down as a "gentleman." He was twenty-five years old, and after a ten-day passage he disembarked in Liverpool, where he celebrated his arrival with a cup of tea and promptly wrote to his parents. He had been taken to Europe as a child, but this was his first visit as an adult: a stay of fourteen months that would take him through England and France and down into Italy. They are the months in which the figure we know as Henry James becomes recognizably himself, the months in which he began to inhabit the transatlantic world he would make so distinctively his own.

Yet nobody is without antecedents, and least of all Henry James. Part of what made this time so important, in fact, is that it gave him his first sustained period away from his family, and if we want to understand him, we will need some account of the people, places, and events of his early life. He was a second son, and had been born in New York on 15 April 1843, at his parents' house on Washington Place. The street runs for a few blocks west from Broadway to Washington Square, and was then quietly fashionable. Or at least it was for the moment. Manhattan's grid pattern already defined its layout, but as late as 1840 there were unbuilt streets within a few blocks of James' birthplace, and only a few spindles of development went up as far as 30th Street. The city's growth was already unstoppable, however, and the census of 1840 put New York's population at 312,000, fully 100,000 more than it had been in 1830. In 1850 it broke half a million, and by the time of James's birth the fashion had for fifty years been moving steadily uptown, from the Battery to the Bowery to Lafayette Place; even Washington Square itself would soon enough seem outmoded.

He was just fifteen months younger than his brother William, but the gap looked determinative. The older boy appeared to be "always round the corner and out of sight," and in childhood the two were scarcely ever in step. Nor was William's priority limited to age. No other American family has produced two such minds in the same generation, and their relationship has been obsessively analyzed; I use that last word advisedly, while recognizing that the obsession doesn't figure as heavily in William's biographies as it does in Henry's. Leon Edel has read the pair in terms of the relations of Jacob and Esau, a sibling rivalry in which the younger eventually outdoes his elder; more recent accounts see Henry as following after his brother in a haze of homoerotic desire. And there is evidence for all of it. Henry established himself as the rising star of the *Atlantic Monthly* while William was still suffering from one spasm of professional uncertainty after another. The future author of *The Varieties of Religious Experience* didn't publish his own first book until 1890, but early on he seized the right to criticize. Their relations became tender with age, and yet William never lost his sense of competition; the more wavering his own path, the more faults he found with Henry's steady application. As for the question of desire, much can and has been made of a letter Henry wrote from London on William's marriage in 1878, in which he described his own absence from the ceremony in terms of being "divorced from you."

I would tell a different story, albeit one that does stress William's earlier birth. But to understand it we need to look at their parents, and in particular at their father. Henry James, Sr., had been born in Albany in 1811, a city where his own father had made a fortune. An Irish Protestant immigrant, the first William James had begun by importing everything from rum to window glass, before moving on to banking and real estate. He eventually owned the land that would become the downtown of Syracuse, a city that developed around the saltworks he founded, and he had thirteen children by three wives. The James family lived in great comfort—but also, in Henry Sr.'s case, in great pain. At thirteen he was so badly burned in trying to put out a fire that he lay bedridden for years, and finally lost a leg. He became an adept user of his day's prostheses, with his cork leg stumping along a sidewalk. But he did need sidewalks, and that meant that the family life he later established with Mary Walsh—they married in 1840—was therefore an urban one. At seventeen he entered Union College, and his career there was so marked by extravagance that his father cut down his share of his estate. Henry Sr. broke that will in court, and is said to have murmured "Leisured for life" at the judgment that gave him an income usually estimated at $10,000 a year in the dollars of his time.

What he did with that leisure was to become one of the most incoherent of American religious thinkers. He went to divinity school, dropped out, abandoned Calvinism and returned to it, traveled, drank, swore allegiance first to the Swedish mystic Emanuel Swedenborg and then to the French social philosopher Charles Fourier. In 1844 he suffered a breakdown that he described as a great "vastation," produced by the sense that there was "some damned shape squatting invisible to me within the precincts of the room." His recovery took two years, but he then found what was, for him, a stable faith, one that matched his belief in the literal divinity of humankind with a bitter condemnation of anyone so foolish as to worship a God of punishment. He had a talent for aphorism but could not carry an argument; his many books went unread. In an America that already worshiped business, he was an anomaly, a man without an office, and even his children found his position strange. It didn't help that he answered their questions about what he "was" by telling them to "Say I'm a philosopher, . . . say I'm a lover of my kind, . . . or, best of all, just say I'm a Student."

The elder Henry James found his true career in the peculiar education he constructed for his children. Eventually, there were five of them—two more boys, Wilky and Bob, and at last a solitary daughter, Alice. His own quest for answers had made him take his family abroad soon after Henry's birth; they were in England when the "vastation" hit. They soon came home, but after a decade of New York he was ready in 1855 to go again, only this time to Switzerland and in search of schools. He followed the rumors of progressive education wherever they led, and sometimes moved his children from one establishment to another for the sake of change alone. In New York the older boys went to ten schools in eight years, and in Europe they quickly retreated from Geneva to Paris to Boulogne. James gives Isabel a version of this upbringing, describing her as having neither a settled home nor a coherent education. But he adds that Isabel herself would dispute that description, and believed that her own "opportunities had been abundant." Still, the results could be comical, and in 1859 his parents decided that "Harry" was too fond of books and sent him to an engineering school instead.

In all this the father consulted his own preferences, but in the late 1850s he began to heed William's desires as well. Henry was a quiet boy, with a marked stammer, and happiest when left alone. William was energy embodied, and his plans and ambitions seemed to change by the week. He craved a more systematic education than the family practice had as yet allowed, he was interested in science, he wanted to be an artist, and the Jameses returned from Europe not once, but twice so that he could work in the Newport, Rhode Island, studio of the painter William Morris Hunt. All told, the family was abroad from 1855 to 1858, and again between 1859 and 1860. Those years gave the future novelist so decided a command of French that his English would later be convicted of Gallicisms. More important, that experience reinforced the family's sense of isolation from the central experiences of American life. They lived apart from the turmoil of the years before the Civil War, estranged from the defining issues of their nation and their day. The Jameses learned of Bloody Kansas or John Brown's raid on Harper's Ferry only from outdated newspapers, and the young Henry never quite got over that sense of disengagement from public life. Years later he wrote that their expatriation left them "interested in almost nothing but each other," and his words give some point to William's 1889 statement that the novelist was "a native of the James family, and has no other country."

That country had a most irregular landscape. Henry remembered that they "breathed inconsistency and ate and drank contradictions." The enveloping clouds of parental concern hung heavy and low, but their father changed his mind so often that the children's world sometimes seemed to shift its shape, and they might be told that the canyons suddenly at their feet had been put there in their own best interests. Not that that world looked the same to everyone who lived in it. Most observers thought Mary James was far more conventional than either her husband or their children; a benign but passive presence, and so fully subsumed by motherhood that no biographer has yet been able to separate her from that role. And the terrain that Alice had to negotiate looked especially trackless and strange. Her father believed that women had their lives in a separate and subordinate sphere, and she did not share her brothers' education. She was taught instead at home, and spent her adult life as an invalid, the victim of indefinable ailments that kept her in bed for years at a time, apparently unable to walk. Yet she had a caustic tongue, which her brothers enjoyed, even if Henry also found himself disturbed, after her 1892 death from breast cancer, by the frank and intimate pain of the diary she left behind.

Alice's future would forever be on hold, but by the time the family came back to America in 1860, the question of a career had become pressing for her two oldest brothers. Their father rejected the idea of college—it was narrowing, a restriction of the mind's free motion. He wanted his children to proceed by mistakes, to experiment with careers, not choose one; an interesting life was enough, it needn't be "paying" as well. But his fortune wasn't large enough to give his children the same freedom that he had had. Choice was required, and at this point a barrier fell between the older boys and their younger brothers. On their return the family settled in Newport, but Wilky and Bob were sent away to the new Concord Academy, whose curriculum stood for their father's latest thing—a fusion of Abolition and Transcendentalism. William painted, and Henry looked on, reading quietly in a corner of Hunt's studio, where the other pupils included John La Farge. The New York–born La Farge is now remembered for his stained glass above all, but his 1862 portrait of the writer is the best early one, and shows the young James in full-lipped and moody profile.

Newport had by the middle of the century become the most stylish of summer resorts, though by the standards of the century's end both the fortunes and the houses were modest. But the town with its shipyards and close-packed eighteenth-century streets had its own independent life as well. It had been a center of fine cabinetmaking and was the site of both the first synagogue and the oldest lending library in America; a port city with its own traditions, and its own old families. James's best friend in town belonged to one of them. He was a boy named Thomas Sergeant Perry, whose grandfather Oliver Hazard Perry had been a hero of the War of 1812, defeating a British squadron in the Battle of Lake Erie. Perry would later teach at Harvard and become a noted critic, and in his teens he gave the young Henry James someone to talk to about novels; someone, moreover, who knew things that James didn't. For Perry was a passionate reader of American literature, and introduced his friend to the works of Hawthorne.

When the Civil War began, Henry Sr. did not at first support it. He had backed Lincoln in the 1860 election, yet thought the president's initial war aims—restoration of the *status quo ante*—too limited to be worth dying for, and spoke of having to keep "a firm grasp upon the coat tails of my Willy and Henry, who both vituperate me" because he wouldn't let them enlist. Perhaps they did not try very hard. William at this period began to suffer from eye strain. He left Hunt's studio and persuaded his father to let him enter the Lawrence Scientific School at Harvard, where he worked with the Swiss geologist Louis Agassiz. He enrolled there in the fall of 1861, just a few months after the war's start. Two years later he switched over to the medical school, and then interrupted that study as well to join Agassiz on an expedition in the Amazon. He finally earned his M.D. in 1869, though he never practiced, and years later wrote that civic life needed to find a sense of collective purpose in what he called the "moral equivalent of war."

His two youngest brothers did not need that equivalent. Wilky was bigger and more athletic than his elders, Bob had an inborn sense of aggression, and their school had made them militant. Wilky joined up at seventeen, and Bob was even younger. They each gained commissions in the Union's new regiments of black soldiers, and Wilky was badly wounded in the 1863 assault on Fort Wagner in South Carolina; the battle is commemorated in Augustus Saint-Gaudens's bas-relief in honor of the 54th Massachusetts Infantry, across the street from the State House in Boston. He never fully recovered from his wounds, and died in 1883, before he reached forty. His father shuddered at what he called the sight of "so much manhood so suddenly achieved." But he was proud to have some sons in uniform, now that Abolition had become central to Lincoln's purpose; and Bob would always believe that the two of them had been discarded.

Henry had a peculiar war. In October 1861 he joined a volunteer crew in helping to put out a Newport fire. There were many hands on the pumps, men working in too-close quarters, and as James frantically tried to ensure the water's steady flow, he found that "I had done myself, in the face of a shabby conflagration, a horrid even if an obscure hurt." Yet this account has a number of uncertainties about it. In the later 1860s, Henry's bad back became a family byword, and Edel speculates that he may have suffered a slipped disc. Immediately after the fire, however, he went up to Boston; whatever damage he had suffered was clearly not incapacitating. By the next year the pain had kicked up, although a doctor found no trace of physical injury. Edel adds, however, that the hurt was "exacerbated by the tensions" of the war, and in his autobiography James himself puts the trouble earlier, associating it with the start of combat "during the soft spring of

'61." He writes there of a "passage of personal history" that seemed to have a close and yet inexpressible connection with the war itself, and other critics have seen that passage as a psychic and not a physical one: an instant of self-examination that revealed how fully he shrank from doing the expected masculine thing. His survival depended, and not just in a bodily sense, on accepting his place on the margins. Still, in 1863 he did appear before the Rhode Island Board of Enrolment; he received an exemption, apparently because of his back. His physical troubles were real, and they did get worse. In 1880 he told a friend that a "muscular weakness of his spine" meant that he had to lie down for several hours each day. Yet in thinking of him at the time of the Civil War it's hard not to see those problems—it would have been hard for *him* not to see them—in the terms one of his characters uses to describe Ralph Touchett: "Fortunately he has got a consumption; I say fortunately, because it gives him something to do. His consumption is his career; it's a kind of position."

In the fall of 1862, James made an attempt at another métier. Shortly after that September's slaughter at Antietam he enrolled for a year at Harvard Law School, which then occupied but a single building at the edge of the Yard. His memoirs describe the place in metaphoric terms, as though attendance were an equivalent of military service, and he even suggests that for him the campus was "tented field enough." At the end of his life he spoke with deep admiration of Walt Whitman, who spent the war as a nurse in military hospitals; James visited such hospitals in Rhode Island, but could offer only a helpless goodwill and a bit of pocket money. He mourned the death in battle of two cousins, and read and reread his brothers' letters home, but his own record was one of "seeing, sharing, envying, applauding, pitying, all from too far-off." He never had to prove himself as they did, and he never lost his "sense of what I missed." There is more regret than guilt here, I think, but a regret that depends upon an awareness of his own limitations. In 1884 his friend Oliver Wendell Holmes, Jr., who had received one of his three wounds at Antietam, gave a Memorial Day speech in which he claimed that "through our great good fortune, in our youth our hearts were touched with fire." Henry had only worked the pump, and

it wasn't that kind of fire anyway; no metaphor could make it so. As the
war ended, he and William each looked set for a career as an invalid, with
their different troubles of backs and eyes, and in William's case a species of
depression. Henry's health would be rescued by his travels and expatriation. William's would take longer, and his recovery came only with the marriage he both wanted and resisted.

And yet in these years James did make a start at something. In 1864 he
knew the pleasure of holding in his hand a dozen greenbacks, payment for an
essay in the *North American Review*—his first piece of professional writing.

James began to write in his teens. The first record we have of it comes
in an 1860 letter from Wilky to their Newport friend Perry, in which he
noted that "Harry has become an author I believe, for he keeps his door
locked all day long, & a little while ago I got a peep in his room, and saw
some poetical looking manuscripts lying on the table." James himself would
soon claim that in these "secret employments" he was a stranger to no style,
and we can imagine him as engaged in pastiche, training himself by imitat-
ing one kind of work after another; indeed, as late as 1878, and with half a
dozen books behind him, he described himself as still going through a conscious process of evolution, one slow and deliberate step after another. He
knew when he entered law school that he wanted a literary career, and spent
as much time as he could reading Sainte-Beuve rather than Blackstone. In
fact, as he wrote to Perry, his ambition then was to do for English literature what that shrewdly omnivorous French critic had done for his own. As
indeed he would—no novelist, in any language, has left a more important
body of criticism.

In his autobiography James recalled a moment in childhood when he
went with his father to an uncle's estate on the Hudson. There was a cousin
of his own age there, a girl named Marie who refused to go to bed when she
was told. "Come now, my dear," his aunt said, "don't make a scene—I *insist*
on your not making a scene." Immediately the boy began to read a world

into that phrase—to understand that life itself was a series of scenes, and "we could make them or not as we chose." His aunt's words stuck because they had made it a scene even without the little girl's help, and in time James would himself develop what he called a "*scenic* method" of novelistic construction. His books never simply flow or meander, but are instead built around a series of carefully prepared dramatic incidents. Some of them are conversations for which his characters might themselves prepare, knowing that a scene in Marie's sense is imminent. Others are moments of recognition, or else tableaux that James drew with an eye to their effect on the reader, as in the *Portrait*'s opening chapter.

The scenes he himself made were largely on paper. But his life did have its episodes of understated drama, and an important one opened in North Conway, New Hampshire, in the summer of 1865; a scene whose central figure would influence the whole course of his future work. James's favorite cousin was a young woman called Minny Temple, the daughter of his father's sister. She was an orphan and lived with her paternal relations, but they too were in Newport and he saw her often. Henry found her full of a vivid life, playful and possessed of a rare intellectual grace. His sister Alice was reserved, as tightly wound as her own plaited hair; Minny's temperament was in contrast as open as a window in summer, and "afraid of nothing she might come to by living with enough sincerity and enough wonder." She believed that a distant chance of the best thing was preferable to a certainty of the second-best, she had a talent for uncomfortable questions, and the rest of Henry's family weren't sure they liked her. Minny was no respecter of persons. She was irritated by her uncle's attitude toward women, and feared that he disliked her "for what he called my *pride and conceit.*" Alice was suspicious of any young woman of whom her brothers appeared fond, and though William's most recent biographer suggests he was drawn to her, he also at times proved hostile. The truth is that Minny was very much like him, and in spite of her charm she yearned for a sense of certainty. She had an earnestness that was too full of doubt to be sanctimonious, and used her letters as an occasion for self-scrutiny in a way that her more guarded cousins did not. She was maybe a bit spiky, and certainly she could shock; a picture of 1861 shows her with hair cropped short like a boy's.

She spent the summer of 1865 in the White Mountains with her sisters, and Henry decided to join her there. He was twenty-two that year and Minny just twenty, but she drew others around her as well—two young army officers from Boston who were already on the way to eminence. One of them was a lawyer named John Gray, a man with an angular jaw and dark insistent eyes. He would found the most Brahminical of old Boston law firms, and eventually became the dean of Harvard Law School. The other was a family friend whom I have already mentioned, the twenty-four-year-old Lieutenant Colonel Holmes—a tall man who later wore the handlebars of a matinee villain. Henry was slighter than either of them in both build and height; he had a characteristic way of tilting his head a bit to the left, and parted his hair in the middle. Picture them there: the windy hump of Mt. Washington sits in the distance, and on the lawn of a wood-framed New England house, the young people sit and talk. To the soldiers it must all seem strange, an atmosphere of lemonade and muslin after years of blood and bullets. But the summer breeze is pregnant with futurity, and James would remember that their conversation was full to the brim with freedom. They spoke as though they were all fresh-faced, and yet in a way that it would be crude to call innocent.

Day passes day, the evenings begin to demand a shawl, and a few early leaves flush red. In James's memory they form "the most delightful loose band conceivable," but of course there are tensions. The future justice prefers girls who aren't so intellectually demanding. Minny thinks he's arrogant, and at first she finds Gray a bit stiff. Still, she appears to hold the young men hostage, and in James's mind the summer's drama lies in the fact that she cares nothing at all about the flutter around her. But there is another drama here too, and if in memory he made a scene around Minny, we ourselves can make one around him, one that lies in James's own contemplation of the other men, in the contrast he cannot help drawing. They are men of mind and yet also men of action, with a kind of glitter "that I had no acquisition whatever to match." He listens to their stories, but can't join in them, and probably his own experience had best remain unspoken. The war has touched and tested them, they have survived the nation's great questions, while he—he had published a few book reviews and two pieces of short fiction.

One of them, true, had appeared that spring in the *Atlantic Monthly;* though only eight years old, the magazine already provided a mark of high-toned aspiration and achievement. Yet "The Story of a Year" defines the same limit to James's knowledge as did that North Conway summer. It begins with the engagement of John Ford and Elizabeth Crowe, but when the young man's regiment calls him up, the tale refuses to follow him into battle. Its concern lies instead with the girl Lieutenant Ford has left behind, with the period's "unwritten history . . . the reverse of the picture," and above all with the new relations she forms in his absence. It is not, in truth, a very good story. Nevertheless, its suggestion that life doesn't stop when the hero goes away does point to the young author's developing sense of realism.

So would his conversations with an editor who joined the *Atlantic* in the following year. William Dean Howells was the son of an Ohio printer, and six years older than James. He was old enough to have helped in Lincoln's 1860 campaign, and was rewarded with the job of American consul in Venice; an experience he turned into an open-hearted account of Italian manners called *Venetian Life.* When he returned to the States, he joined the staff of a new political weekly called *The Nation,* where James was already a contributor, before moving in 1866 to Cambridge and a position as the publisher J. T. Fields's assistant on the *Atlantic.* Howells was portly, with a soup-strainer mustache, and self-consciously a family man. He saw the writer as a middle-class professional, a responsible citizen like a doctor or a lawyer, and would soon become a creature of tuition bills and summer vacations. Howells recognized James's ability from the start, but what James remembered above all was that he had "published me at once—and paid me," money less important in itself than as a promise of his own future independence.

The James family had moved up from Newport to Boston in 1864, and then over the river to Cambridge in 1866. Henry Sr. took a large house in Quincy Street, just across from that of Harvard's president, and on the site of what is today the university's faculty club. He had many years left, but his own travels were over, and the address would hold until the death of Mary James in 1882. William's long career at Harvard would probably not have been possible without that move; he may have drawn the family north in his path, but he didn't start teaching until 1873 and remained largely under his parents' roof until his marriage. From Henry's point of view, however, the most important consequence of the move might well have been his growing friendship with Howells.

Neither of them could remember when they first met, but it was probably just after the *Atlantic* had accepted another story about the war's home front, this one called "Poor Richard." Howells had told the reluctant Fields to take it, and everything else the author might produce, though he also believed that James's very artfulness meant he would have to create his own audience. Of course, Howells himself would help with that. He took over from Fields in 1871, and as the *Atlantic*'s editor for the next decade published a number of James's stories and five serialized novels, culminating with *The Portrait of a Lady* itself. About Howells's own fiction James would for many years remain ambivalent. He liked his prose and yet thought he needed a larger subject, that he was too absorbed by his American world. But he admired the picture of city life and social unrest in the other writer's best book, *A Hazard of New Fortunes* (1890), and recognized that he could not match its Balzacian range.

In December 1866, Howells wrote to a friend that the evening before, the two young men had talked for hours about their own aesthetic principles, and in a memoir left unfinished at his death in 1920 he noted that "we seem to have been presently always together." James had had literary friendships before, but this one was different, an elective affinity between adults, in which his family and their connections had played no part. And like most friendships, it developed habits. There were a series of what Howells recalled as long aimless walks through the Cambridge streets by night, and daytime wanderings in the woods around Fresh Pond. A few years later they spent an afternoon on that small lake, Howells rowing, while James told him the story of *Roderick Hudson*, the book about an American sculptor in Rome that the editor had bought for the *Atlantic*. Two or three evenings a week they met at the older man's Sacramento Street home, and "sat reading our stuff to each other." Yet though each of them remembered the fact of those talks, their substance went unrecorded, and I would give a good deal for the kind of oral history that we find today in accounts of moviemaking—that testimony to the act of collaboration in which the cinematographer talks about the director, who answers with an anecdote about an actress.

For their conversation was a collaboration indeed, and one that we can only recapture by reading what they wrote to and about each either for the next half-century. They would have spoken of Dickens, who visited Boston in 1867, leaving James with a memory of the Englishman's all-consuming eyes, and probably they spoke about audience: about what American readers wanted and how they might be nudged into wanting something else. Neither of them liked the multiplotted novel of the Victorians, the twisted strands of seemingly divergent narratives that make up a book like *David Copperfield*. They wanted instead to tell a single story, and to make that story's ending grow directly out of its characters, rather than be imposed through the deus ex machina of sudden or startling events. So as they walked along the Charles, they would have talked about plot, or rather about what their critics called plotlessness; years later, Thomas Hardy would contrast his own kind of forcefully knotted fiction to that of Howells in particular. Above all, they spoke of the need for a distinctively American realism. They both admired the recently dead Hawthorne, but nevertheless wanted to tamp down the metaphysical conceits on which his work relied. They similarly ruled against the kind of sentimental fiction that, for readers today, is exemplified by the death scenes in *Uncle Tom's Cabin*. Such books were enormously popular, and there was a trace of misogyny in the way they thought about such writers as Elizabeth Stoddard or even Harriet Beecher Stowe herself. But they took more from such novels than they would have

been willing to admit; with James it shows in the way he idealizes his heroines, idealizes them so fully that he has to knock back a chaser of irony too.

Howells was never as much of a spectator as James, and he was in
aesthetic terms by far the more conservative; he no more allowed himself
James's sense of ambiguity than he did the violent operatic grandeur of
Hardy. He believed the American novel needed to recognize what he called
the "smiling aspects" of life, and later opposed his own kind of realism to
the naturalism of Émile Zola and such American followers as Frank Norris.
As an editor, he tried to cajole his friend into providing the happy endings
he thought their readers required. James fobbed him off with the charming
but inconsequential *Europeans* (1878), which finishes with a handful of marriages while refusing to let the most interesting of its possible unions come
off. They did not agree about everything, but between them they created an
American novel of manners, the novel of our eastern seaboard.

The best of James's early pieces is probably "The Romance of Certain
Old Clothes," a tale of sibling rivalry decked out as a ghost story.
His work in the 1860s has often been read as a transparent indication of his
own psychic state; and perhaps inevitably so, given its often clumsy narrative machinery. This story is different, both cold-blooded and playful in the
revenge it allows a younger sister to take upon her elder; as though James
winkingly knew precisely what he was up to. In truth, however, none of
his apprentice fiction would have survived without the warrant of his later
career. His ferociously capable criticism is a different matter, and scholars
of Dickens and George Eliot among others still need to consider his early
pieces on them. In these years he could most often be found at his parents'
house in Quincy Street. He was publishing regularly but not making enough
to live on, and one detail in Howells's memories strikes a curious note.
James often knocked at their door on Sunday evenings, around suppertime,
but "he joined us only in spirit," for he took nothing except a digestive bis-
cuit which had been prescribed for him, and which he didn't eat so much as
crumble. In the later 1860s he suffered from what Howells understood to be

indigestion. It was in fact a prolonged period of constipation, and one that James believed made his back troubles worse. The biscuits did not help, and at times he seems to have felt both hungry and surfeited, reluctant to eat lest he exacerbate the difficulty.

We cannot prescribe at a distance—cannot determine the proportion of the psychological and the physical in the postwar disorders of both Henry and William James. They each craved and yet resisted an adult life, and in this there was a marked contrast with their younger brothers. Using their father's capital, Wilky and Bob attempted after the war to grow cotton in Florida, hiring freed slaves as a labor force. They paid them fairly, but they had no experience of farming, and moreover encountered the forerunners of the Ku Klux Klan. Eventually they both moved to the Midwest, settling and marrying in Milwaukee. In the spring of 1867, William went to Europe, where he tried out a series of Teutonic spas and, more consequentially, began his love affair with German academic life. Their friend Perry was also abroad, and Henry's letters to him are full of a longing for travel. On the one hand, that longing is professional—he thought he needed a few years in England before he could work as he wanted. But he also had a more primitive desire for escape, for the Paris that haunted his imagination. William came back—and then, with much complication and delay, it was Henry's turn. His parents thought he was traveling for his health, and so he was; but not for his bodily ailments alone.

James's friendship with Minny Temple had endured and deepened in the years since that New Hampshire summer. He was not *in* love with her, not in any physical sense, but he did love her. He found her a necessary presence, and her frank, playful independence already provided an inspiration. Yet that independence wore a curb, for she now lived with a married sister; not quite a poor relation, but not her own mistress either. And there was something more. In 1868 she was diagnosed with tuberculosis, the disease that had killed her parents. She had never cared much for the marriage market, but now that shop looked closed to her. In the *Portrait*, however, James took the idea of cousins marrying seriously enough to make Ralph reject it as a bad idea, and to argue as well that people in his stage "of pulmonary weakness had better not marry at all." Those words might have their origin in a letter Minny sent James in June 1869, when he was already in Switzerland. "I wish I were there too," she wrote, and then added that "if you were not my cousin I would write to ask you to marry me and take me with you, but as it is it wouldn't do." Yet Minny could write that way precisely because such questions were not at issue between them. She struggled against her illness through a fiction not of love but of travel, of a health-giving voyage to the warm south; in the same letter she sketched a plan to get herself to Rome, and wondered if he would be there to meet her. James conspired with her in telling that story, and in his autobiography remembered that in their leave-taking they kept at bay the significance of her periodic hemorrhages. Those memoirs were written, however, with the blurry hindsight of over forty years, and it's more accurate to say that Minny helped him not to know. She was more open in writing to John Gray, with whom she had developed a rich friendship. James's autobiography aside, most of what we know about her comes in fact from the letters Gray preserved, letters that make a black comedy out of her different doctors' prescriptions.

Henry James went to England, and to Paris. He hiked through Switzerland and traveled down into Italy, to Venice and Florence and then Rome, where he found himself "reeling & moaning thro' the streets in a fever of enjoyment." None of the letters he wrote to his cousin have survived, and the truth is that during his first ten months abroad he does not seem to have thought much about her; in writing to Quincy Street he mentions her but rarely. Perhaps his emotional landscape changed with his physical one; perhaps he took her affection for granted. Still, he read with pleasure of her plans for a trip to California, and wrote to Cambridge of his disappointment when the project fell through. In February 1870 he went back to England, to the spa town of Malvern in Worcestershire. There he learned that she had suffered a series of new hemorrhages and felt glad he had just sent her a letter. Now the envelopes from home began to carry their load of bad news, though it took some time for him to register its weight. On March 19 he wrote to his father that there was "somehow too much of Minny to disappear" just yet, and noted his plans to write her once more, as if making up his arrears.

But by that time her body was cold. She died on March 8, 1870; she was just twenty-four. The letters James sent on getting the news carry all the volubility of grief, and have been obsessively read by his biographers. He wrote to his parents within hours that it was all "more strange and painful than I can find words to express." Mrs. James's last account of Minny hadn't prepared him for the thought of that "poor struggling suffering *dying* creature," the girl who now survived only in memory—and yet given her suffering, who "would have her back to die more painfully?" Death is a release; so far, so Victorian. James also spoke, however, about her trouble in reconciling herself to the social world around her and suggests that her release wasn't from a medical condition only. He dropped the letter and took it up again in the evening, claiming that he seemed already to have accepted her death, and yet wishing too that they had been in closer touch during these last months. But he also returned to his sense of the difficulties she would have faced in any future life, and in writing to William a few days later he struck that note once more. Minny was a victim of her own intelligence, and unlikely ever to have found happinesss. Nevertheless, she had taught him so much about the "reach & quality & capacity of human nature," and he went on to evoke her strenuous, exacting presence for a dozen manuscript pages. But at the end of it all he still had to accept that no matter how long he might "sit spinning my sentences she is *dead*." Nothing changed that, and he recognized then that he was trying to fight off his knowledge, to change her death from hard fact into the most billowy of ideas.

Edgar Allan Poe wrote, punningly, that "the death of a beautiful woman, is unquestionably the most poetical topic in the world," and many readers have found something ghoulish in James's loggorhea, in the speed with which he reconciled himself to Minny's loss. The fullest account of their relationship can be found in Lyndall Gordon's *Private Life of Henry James,* which suggests that James's inattention during his year away contributed to a loss of spirits that hastened her along. He was too fully absorbed by his own illness, too self-absorbed to commit himself to her plan of meeting in Rome. She turned her face to the wall. That reading owes too much to the plot of James's own *Wings of the Dove* (1902) to be entirely persuasive, and yet that novel does in itself suggest a retrospective recognition of his own limitations, his own inability to sense the depths of another person's need. I would stress something else about those letters. They resemble nothing so much as his later notebooks: notebooks in which, once given a nubbin of anecdote, he plots out such masterpieces as "Brooksmith" or "The Real Thing" in a few rapid moments, imagining characters and sketching possibilities. Wish away Minny's consumption and there would be problems still. What would she do, and how would she live? Her unlived future goes on in his head. These letters are ghoulish only if that means they are written by a novelist, by someone whose job is to turn life into narrative.

3.

A SUPERSTITIOUS VALUATION

JAMES TOOK MINNY'S death as marking an end to youth, but for him these years formed a crux in other ways as well. In 1860 he had written to Perry from Bonn that if his family's future lay in America, then it was about time they began to live there—"the more I see of this estrangement of American youngsters from the land of their birth, the less I believe in it." That precocious generalization makes me smile; the "more" he had seen was very largely the example of his own siblings. Still, it does speak to a sense of disquiet. Expatriation made one interesting, but it also marked one off, and it remained unnerving even when he began to take his own steps toward it. Yet that literally unsettling quality wasn't something he thought he could avoid. James would in any case have leaned toward Europe, toward its cities and art and the pleasures of its perfected landscape, but the Continent also presented him with a problem he thought he had to face. No European novelist, he wrote in an 1881 notebook, "is obliged to deal in the least with America." No one would call him incomplete for ignoring it. He believed, however, that every American writer did have to take account of Europe, and while he suspected that the balance might shift, that American culture might someday become a necessary fact of European life, he saw that situation as fixed for his lifetime.

It was fixed, moreover, in a way that pressed upon his own generation in a different way than it had upon their predecessors. Hawthorne had done without Europe until he was fifty. He didn't cross the Atlantic until his college friend Franklin Pierce was elected president in 1852, and gave him an appointment as the American consul in Liverpool. It had been an opportunity, not a necessity, and he had already done his most important work when he sailed. In fact, Hawthorne's needs had been of a very different kind, for he belonged to a generation in whose formative years the books and standards and tastes had all come from abroad, and one that had in consequence to declare its own sense of self-reliance. It had to cultivate a sense of cultural difference, one that the nation's very isolation had helped bring to maturity; in the days before steamships, when travel was still uncomfortable and slow, Hawthorne and his contemporaries could even believe that their own insularity might help keep them honest. James had both the luxury and the burden of a different aesthetic. He thought the future of American literature lay not in autonomy as such, but rather in the fact that "we can deal freely with forms of civilization not our own, can pick and choose and assimilate." In that, at least, he was at an advantage. Europeans were too bound by their own national traditions, but "to be an American is an excellent preparation for culture."

The difficulty lay in knowing how to weigh those choices. In the early months of 1872, James was living once more at his parents' house in Cambridge and seemed for the moment to have stalled. He tried to keep busy with reviews, but he wasn't writing much fiction, and he already knew that his future life lay elsewhere; he could console himself only by thinking that at least he wasn't with his younger brothers in Wisconsin. His most regular correspondent that winter was Charles Eliot Norton, who as the editor of the *North American Review* had handed him the first money he ever earned. Norton was a translator of Dante who in 1875 became Harvard's initial professor of art history, and in the early 1870s he had used his private fortune to set himself up for a year of study in Dresden. In February 1872, James wrote him a gossipy letter from Cambridge, full of news about the latest books and lectures, including the fact that "Wendell Holmes . . . my brother, & various other long-headed youths have combined to form a metaphysical club"; a club that touched off that distinctively American philosophy called pragmatism. For our purposes, however, the most interesting part of the letter is a seemingly casual sentence about his own longing for travel: "It's a complex fate, being an American, & one of the responsibilities it entails is fighting against a superstitious valuation of Europe." James's tone here seems at once playful and anxious. He knows he exaggerates the merits of life abroad, and yet dreams of "moonshiny" plans for getting there, as though he had already realized that defining those complexities would become the business of his life.

Later that spring he got his chance. His parents decided that what had worked for their older sons might work for their invalid daughter as well, and yet Alice couldn't travel alone. She would need both a chaperone and a protector; their aunt, Catherine Walsh, might fill the first role, and James himself took the second. He spent five months as their cicerone, most of it in the Alps, and when they left for home that October, he stayed behind. It was in many ways a changed Continent from the one he had explored just two years before. The Franco-Prussian War had replaced the French Second Empire with a new Third Republic, and the radical democracy of the Paris Commune had been snuffed cold in a series of grotesque reprisals; France would never know another monarch yet remained firmly conservative still. But another empire had now risen, as if in its place—the new German Reich, with Otto von Bismarck as its "Iron Chancellor"—and then there was the afterthought of a fully united Italy. James could when he wanted be a shrewd political analyst, and in writing to William from Paris he noted that beneath the city's "neatness and coquetry, you seem to smell the Commune suppressed, but seething." Usually, though, he let himself look elsewhere, and his work in this period says little about the Continent's political changes beyond noting that in Rome the end of the pope's secular rule meant he could now buy an uncensored newspaper.

Nor did he take much notice of American public life when, under a mix of financial and familial pressure, he returned in the late summer of 1874. He settled in New York, making an attempt at independence in a city to which he felt a sentimental attraction, drawn as he always was to the traces of his personal past. It was an era to which a sharp-edged new writer called Mark Twain had just given a name: the Gilded Age, an age of watered stock and bought elections, of Jay Gould and Boss Tweed. At first, James liked the "rattling big luxurious place," though he also knew what he didn't know, and left the subject of Wall Street alone. In his apartment on East 25th Street he wrote two articles a week, most of them for *The Nation*, notices of books and plays and paintings, and worked his way through the year-long serial of *Roderick Hudson*. After a decade of short stories it was time to move past his apprenticeship—not only to commit himself to a full-length novel, but also to come out in hardcovers. So in 1875, James read the proofs of his first three volumes: *A Passionate Pilgrim*, a collection of stories; a gathering of travel essays called *Transatlantic Sketches*; and the book version of his *Atlantic* serial. It was a smart professional move, but he had come home in part because he thought New York would be less expensive than Italy. It wasn't, and by the time *Roderick Hudson* was moving through the press, he was gone. In October he left America once more, settling at first in Paris and then, after a year, crossing over to the London that would become his home. He would not return to America until after the 1881 publication of *The Portrait of a Lady* itself.

He went for many reasons. He wanted to see paintings and old buildings, and he had found that in New York even a successful writer was an anomaly in a world given over to business. Literature was admired, and journalists had their narrow place, but the writer as such had little social purchase. He went because, though he had known periods of acute loneliness abroad, he was still his own man there, as he was not in America. But he also went because he knew that Europe was where his material lay.

In 1879, James accepted a commission from his London publisher, Macmillan, to write a short book on Hawthorne for a series called "English Men of Letters"; it was their first volume on an American writer. The book he produced records a new generation's attempt to understand its ancestors, and with the exception of *The American Scene*, it offers his most searching account of his native land. Yet though *Hawthorne* remains a founding document in the writing of American literary history, at home James was attacked for what his readers saw as condescension, a criticism inseparable from their knowledge of his decision to live abroad. One passage in particular drew attention. In the preface to *The Marble Faun*, his 1860 story about a pair of American artists in Italy, Hawthorne had noted the difficulty of writing about his homeland, a country in which he pretended to believe "there is no shadow, no antiquity, no mystery, no picturesque and gloomy wrong, nor anything but a common-place prosperity." James lifted that thought, and then extended it in a passage of great comic brilliance, a list of everything that in Hawthorne's day looked absent from the

> . . . texture of American life. . . . No State, in the European sense of the word, and indeed barely a specific national name. No sovereign, no court, no personal loyalty, no aristocracy, no church . . . no palaces, no castles, nor manors, nor old country-houses . . . nor thatched cottages nor ivied ruins; no cathedrals . . . no Oxford . . . no novels, no museums, no pictures, no political society, no sporting class . . . no Epsom nor Ascot!

It's wonderful fun to read *Hawthorne's* list aloud, and James allows that his ingenuity has led him into overstatement. He admits, moreover, that a great deal remains even in a land without thatch or ivy, though just what is itself the American's "secret, his joke, as one may say." And the critic Robert Weisbuch has suggested taking this passage as an example of that joke. For most of James's readers liked the fact that they didn't have to live with those bits of an old European order. The absence of Ascot was for them a positive recommendation, and what was left seemed nothing less than America itself.

That list did, however, give a warrant to those who saw James as dismissive of American life, and in reading we have to remember that no matter how perceptive his criticism is about other writers, it usually says more about his own ambition and practice. So let me shift the terms. It's not simply that America lacks the things he lists, but rather that such institutions and practices provide the novelist with his fabric, or at least the kind of novelist that James himself wanted to be. They make up the world of Austen and Balzac—the buzz of implication, of half-expressed meanings, that both characters and readers alike must learn to hear. The limitations James found in American life were limitations above all in the material it offered for the novel. "It takes a great deal of history to produce a little literature," and in America the deposit of that history was still so thin "that we very soon touch the hard substratum of nature," a place where the air itself looks new.

Other kinds of fiction were possible. For much of the nineteenth century the country's most important storytellers thought of themselves as writing not novels in the English sense of the term but rather what they called romances; as though the exceptionalism of the American condition operated even in the realm of prose. The difference is far from absolute, but still there is a distinction to make. One classic account suggests that while the novel sets its characters in some plausible and closely described relation to their world, the romance works in contrast to endow its people with a sense of mystery. The social background in such works may remain abstract, the characters are often flatly emblematic, and the writer's emphasis falls instead upon an often astonishing plot that serves as the vehicle for an overarching symbolic truth. Hawthorne himself is the best example here. In James's words, he had "asked but little of his *milieu*" and had used that very thinness to heighten his narratives. For once that Old World clutter was cleared away, his characters had accordingly appeared as giants, isolated on the granite platforms of their moral dramas. Often they were outcasts. Think of Hester Prynne in *The Scarlet Letter*, with her lonely hut at the edge of town; think too of Melville's Ahab, or even of Huckleberry Finn. Then recall the busy village life of Austen's *Emma*.

James himself would always feel the pull of romance, with its appeal to an ideal essence, and it reasserted itself late in his career in such tales of the blighted heart as "The Beast in the Jungle." Still, he needed the thickened air of history. He needed its baggage and furniture, he wanted its Louis Quinze, and in his own overvaluation of Europe he associated history itself with abroad, as something America couldn't give him. Later he would wonder if that had been a mistake, and encouraged Edith Wharton to "do New York," to take up the chance he had missed. Missed, perhaps, because of the way his father had removed his children from American life; the more rooted

Howells found that Boston had texture enough. But this is too simple. It's not just that James discovered his material in that furniture, but rather that he discovered it in the American encounter with a world of chestnut commodes and silver salvers. He found his material in dramatizing the collision of an American sensibility with all that made the Old World old.

Some of that would come in travel writing—there was a market for essays with titles like "Roman Rides"—and some in criticism, presenting the works of European masters to an American audience. Most of it took the form of fiction, however, like the long story called "Travelling Companions" that James published in the *Atlantic* at the end of 1870, a tale of courtship conducted against a touristic experience of Italy. It wasn't the first piece he had set in Europe, but it was the first he wrote about the adventures there of people like him, and on reading it his publisher's wife, Annie Fields, noted in her diary that she wept as she finished it, "not from the sweet low pathos of the tale . . . but from the knowledge of the writer's success." Other stories followed. In "A Passionate Pilgrim," an American claimant to an English estate learns that the Old World cannot give him a home, and in "Madame de Mauves," James offered his first sustained look at a transatlantic marriage, an account of an American woman's recoil from her husband's moral universe. He would eventually grow tired of what became known as the "international theme," and in the years after the *Portrait* he even abandoned it for a while. Yet he came back to it in such late masterpieces as *The Ambassadors*, and his encounter with the world that *Hawthorne's* shopping list so merrily evokes would prove decisive. It is what made him Henry James.

James's experiences in England, Paris, and Italy will carry much of this narrative, in its later chapters especially. We will watch as he learns, in the 1870s and early 1880s, to define the terms of a life that is both American and European at once. So rather than chronicle his movements here, I'll instead offer a series of vignettes as a way to evoke his early years abroad. There are three of them—three sketches, three cities, and three encounters with minds as large as his own.

Henry and William in Florence, November 1873. James had been in Tuscany for a month when his older brother came to join him; William had begun to teach physiology at Harvard that spring, but almost immediately asked for a leave. They stayed at the Hôtel d'Europe, a few steps away from the river at the foot of the via Tornabuoni—then as now the home of the city's most fashionable shops—and bombarded Quincy Street with reports on each other's well-being. Henry wrote that on some days his brother had "the appearance, the manner, and almost the activity of perfect health." William was not so encouraging—he thought Henry seemed liverish. Their hotel was full of people they knew, but William found Florence itself rather dusky and small. He couldn't quite shed the spirit of Cambridge, and admitted that the city's dirt and slime filled him with horror. Still, he did recognize that Henry was very much at home—perhaps, indeed, too much so—and "could do more work than at any previous time."

They visited Fiesole, they walked through the galleries of the Palazzo Pitti, and one morning William sat over a letter to their sister Alice and wrote sadly about the "set of desultory years behind" him. He wanted some solid practical task, some work he might make his own, but he didn't yet know just what it might be; and meanwhile his younger brother was across the room, driving his quill through the last pages of an article on Turgenev. William knew that Henry now lived for his work, but he was so impatient with his own inability to settle that he leaned on his brother to come home and take some job of editorial drudgery, telling him that a novelist's life was abnormal "as a matter of mental hygiene." He liked to impose his own uncertainties on everyone around him, and reveled in evoking the dreariness he saw as his brother's necessary American fate. But his words, as always, had their power. Henry did come home, as we have seen. He tried New York—and left.

With Ivan Turgenev in Paris, 1875–76. James's article in praise of the Russian novelist appeared in the *North American Review* for April 1874, and the older man responded by inviting the American to call on him; they met in the late fall of 1875, soon after James had arrived in Paris. Turgenev was in his late fifties, and by now visited Russia only briefly each summer, splitting the rest of his time between France and Baden-Baden. He was tall and bearded and had once been a figure of enormous physical vigor, though now both his strength and his best work were behind him. The lyrical country scenes of *A Nest of Gentlefolk* had appeared in 1859, and *Fathers and Sons* in 1862, with its picture of the nihilist physician Bazarov; while the apparently artless *Sportsman's Sketches* lay even further back. Still, that 1852 volume had done two great things. Its seemingly documentary account of the hardships of peasant life had established a new aesthetic for the short story, and it had played an important role in the change of hearts and minds that led to the 1861 emancipation of Russia's serfs.

To the young James, however, what mattered wasn't Turgenev's liberalism so much as the delicacy and finish of his work. They met in the house Turgenev shared with the opera singer Pauline Viardot and her husband in the rue de Douai, just below the Place Pigalle. At that first meeting they talked for two hours, and before the year was out the Russian gave the young man a rare mark of his esteem: he introduced him to the circle of French writers with whom he gathered on Sundays at the flat of Gustave Flaubert. There James met Émile Zola, flush with the success and the suppression alike of *L'Assommoir*, his frank, unsparing novel about the family of a Paris laundress; there too he met the then-unknown Guy de Maupassant. It wasn't a world in which he felt entirely at home, and though he wasn't shocked by the sexual license of their talk, he was by the fierceness of French literary quarrels. Nevertheless, the influence of Flaubert's *cénacle* proved decisive, and James was moreover the only important writer in English to see it from within.

In his essay James noted that Turgenev's characters all seemed to be portraits, and one rainy afternoon in the rue de Douai the Russian told him that everything in his stories was indeed drawn from some particular person he had seen or known. He never consciously added anything to them, but instead tried only to offer a faithful picture, for he distrusted invention and believed that there was beauty and strangeness enough in the real. Thirty years later James put that conversation into his preface to the *Portrait*, remembering Turgenev's inspiriting claim that his characters seemed to hover "before him, soliciting him . . . interesting him and appealing to him just as they were and by what they were." Plot was to him an irrelevance—it got in the way of the truth, of the emotional logic that governed his people. The business of writing lay not in making his characters "do" anything, but rather in discovering a situation that would allow them to reveal themselves. For him, that was story enough; but as he ruefully told the younger writer, it might not be for one's readers.

The Two Henrys: London, February 1880. Henry Adams came over to London that winter, renewing his acquaintance with the city where his father had been the American minister during the Civil War, a diplomat charged with keeping Britain from recognizing the Confederacy. The young Adams had spent that war as his father's private secretary and in the intervening years had split his time between Washington and Boston, where he both edited the *North American Review* and taught medieval history at Harvard. By now, however, he had given up on teaching, and in the summer of 1879 he crossed the Atlantic to gather materials for what would become his masterly nine-volume history of the United States in the early years of the nineteenth century. He went to France and to Spain; he hired copyists to transcribe state papers in Paris and Madrid. For Adams was a rich man, made so not only through inheritance but also by his marriage to the razor-tongued Clover Hooper.

The two men had known each other for a decade, and in 1870, James had described his slightly older counterpart as a "youth of genius and enthusiasm—or at least of talent and energy." Adams's temperament was as dry as gin, and James did not at first like him. But he soon grew fond of the couple, and even in a London where he had known an enormous social success, he enjoyed having some American confidants. They saw each other regularly in Paris throughout the fall of 1879, and in that London winter Clover noted that the novelist came "in every day at dusk and sits chattering by our fire." Sometimes he went so far as to invite himself to dinner. That season he was finishing his work on *Washington Square*, a short novel about a father's thwarting of his daughter's hopes. In February he sent off a review of Zola's "unutterably filthy" novel about prostitution, *Nana*—

a review in which he never quite names the source of that filth—and on the twenty-second he went to spend his Sunday afternoon at the Adamses'. They had taken a house just off St. James's Park, on a little street halfway between Buckingham Palace and Parliament, and the novelist sat talking with Clover while his host wrote a letter to his former student Henry Cabot Lodge. Adams's words are full of happy spleen on the subject of Paris, a city he thought "a fraud and a snare," but he moved on to speculate about the coming presidential race, and then closed the page by looking up and noticing the other man in the room. "Harry James," he told Lodge, "is standing on the hearth-rug, with his hands under his coat-tails. . . . I am going out in five minutes to make some calls on perfectly uninteresting people."

Later that day James wrote to their mutual friend Lizzie Boott about his plans to take a working vacation in Italy; he expected to see her in Florence, where she lived with her father in a villa just outside the city gates. The Adamses, he reported, were "not at all crazy" about London, and yet thought him unnatural in wanting to leave it so soon after their own arrival; James thought they were a bit homesick. But he then switched subjects to note the fury with which the American press had greeted his book about Hawthorne. The reviews admired its handling of the fiction; they execrated its account of America. Probably he should have anticipated that reaction. He had argued in the book itself that his countrymen believed that every other nation was part of a "conspiracy to undervalue them," and now it must have seemed to them as if an American had joined in that pact. Inaccurate, narrow, crude, sneering, and above all unpatriotic, a book that could only feed the English incomprehension of America—so it was described, and even Howells had had some reservations about it.

It wasn't the first controversy James's work had caused, however, and probably *Hawthorne* wouldn't have been so harshly received without the example of *Daisy Miller* the year before. That story of a New York girl's indiscretions in Europe had also gotten its first publication in Britain. A Philadelphia monthly had earlier rejected it, finding it a libel on American femininity; for Daisy dies, in Rome, of malaria and a compromised reputation alike, after she is seen out walking with an Italian. Most readers loved it, though, and the behavior of the title character was discussed as though she were real. People took sides at the dinner table, either for or against her, and with her open pleasure in what she called "gentlemen's society," Daisy became a flashpoint for all that the *bien élevé* didn't like about their own country. Yet how far should one go in criticizing her? *Harper's* argued that Daisy wasn't "fast," but only ignorant. Any genuine reprobate would have known not to speak so frankly, and those who recognized the accuracy with which James had captured a particular American type should also recognize that their repudiation of her was unjust; they were indulging in the same kind of innuendo as the characters whose gossip had destroyed her good name.

James himself eventually dismissed the tale as slight, and in a later story, "Pandora," he even joked about making a German diplomat read it as a guide to American manners. Nevertheless, it gave him his first real taste of fame. What it didn't provide was money, not directly. In those days before international copyright the tale was pirated in America, and James got almost nothing from its quickly sold 20,000 copies. Every reader of the major British and American magazines now knew his name, however, and he quickly established his brand by following *Daisy Miller* with such briskly written comedies about the social relations of America and Europe as "An International Episode" and "The Pension Beaurepas." Still, that success brought its troubles. James might be too brilliant to ignore, but his strictures on the provinciality of American life made him suspect to a public that remained anxious about their country's place in the world. In April 1880, Clover Adams wrote to her father that it was "high time Harry James was ordered home by his family. . . . He had better go to Cheyenne and run a hog ranch." She knew the criticism of him was silly, but still he must have seemed in danger of losing the American tone. By that time, however, James himself was no longer in London. He had crossed the Channel at Folkestone, waiting five days for a calm sea, and then passed through Paris and Turin on his way to Florence, where he thought to rest for a few weeks before settling down to work on what he called a "big" novel.

. . .

If the 1875 publication of his first books represented an end to his apprenticeship, then James's plans for the novel he had decided to call *The Portrait of a Lady* were something else—a frank bid for mastery. We first hear of the project in an October 1876 letter to Howells. James was busy with *The American*, whose protagonist was the emblematically named Christopher Newman, but he recognized the financial necessity of always having a serial running somewhere, and he didn't believe the *Atlantic* could handle them all. He was negotiating instead with *Scribner's*, a magazine he did not like, to write a novel about what he called an *Americana*, whose adventures in Europe would be a counterpart to Newman's. The *Scribner's* plan fell through, however, and James then offered the book to Howells, noting early the next year that he was willing to wait until the *Atlantic* could give him the space he wanted. The project would be "the portrait of the character and recital of the adventures of a woman—a great swell, psychologically; a *grand nature*—accompanied with many developments."

James's tone is ironic but the ambition is real, even if it would be another three years before he felt entirely free to pursue it. He did begin the story, that much is sure, and in April 1878 offered to show some of it to Macmillan. But nobody today knows just how far he then got, or just how closely this lost ur-*Portrait* resembles the opening moments of the book we now read. Those notes to Howells aside, his letters give no details of its narrative, but in May 1877 he wrote to his mother that he planned a novel "to which the American shall be as water unto wine." Later he had to add that *The Europeans*, which William found thin, was not the book he meant. William was always his most formidable critic, though often his least accurate one. He had an uncanny ability to find the flaws in his brother's earliest and most conventional stories, but his own belief that novels were no more than an amusement meant that he objected to what was most original about James's later work. Still, the novelist recognized the logic of William's demand for something larger, and with a clear sense of his own development, he now felt ready to work on a greater scale.

In August 1879 he finally gave Howells the book's title, and that summer he also contracted for the novel's serial publication on both sides of the ocean. It would appear simultaneously, a few chapters each month, in *Macmillan's* and the *Atlantic*. Yet still he delayed, even after the magazines had gone through the delicate business of adjusting their schedules around each other. Both *Roderick Hudson* and *The American* had been critical triumphs. Readers already saw him as one of the most esteemed of all American novelists, and certainly as the most challenging; a writer whose predilection for unhappy endings provoked discussions about just what a novel should be. Nevertheless, his books did not sell; Frederick Macmillan even apologized to him for the small size of his checks. So James felt at once in need of the success he thought his *Americana* would bring, and yet forced to delay because he could not yet afford the unbroken stretch of time he would need for it. He wrote both *Hawthorne* and a minor, six-month serial called *Confidence;* he wrote stories and art criticism, a piece on the Comédie Française, and another on the reopening of Parliament. He put off the big novel's start, as he did a planned trip to Italy; it's almost as though the two were inseparable, as though he could not imagine starting this particular book in any other place. Instead he worked to give himself as much room as he could, and in the winter of 1880 he quickly produced *Washington Square*, a book whose epigrammatic spark seems to me unmatched in his *oeuvre*.

And then he had enough—a solid bank balance to see him through what he knew would be a long and careful piece of work. He could afford to take the time he needed. James reached Florence on March 28, and then paused once more, traveling south to Naples to visit a Russian friend, an acolyte of Richard Wagner's named Paul Zhukovsky. But he soon came back to Florence, and there, in an unusually rainy spring, he took up his old beginning, and in an "open window overlooking the yellow Arno" started off on the book that would ensure his literary permanence.

4.

ALONG THE THAMES

With nine months of work on the *Portrait* behind him, James left London in December 1880 to spend the holidays in the West Country. Christmas Day found him at Plymouth, one of England's largest military bases, where his host was the garrison's commander, an Anglo-Irish general called Pakenham. He made the acquaintance of a naval captain, who invited him out for breakfast on an old-fashioned ship-of-the-line, and then on the twenty-seventh he moved further down the coast, into Cornwall. The air was mild and warm, and James enjoyed its "far-away-from-London quality." Yet a steady rain kept him largely indoors, and one night when a gale set the windows awash, he sat down to write a letter to his Cambridge friend Grace Norton.

She was nine years his senior, and had a talent for probing questions; as fits someone who would later become known for her own work on Montaigne. Much of her life was spent in the shadow of her widowed brother Charles, traveling with him and helping to care for his children at the family's Shady Hill estate. She had the more penetrating mind, however, and James wrote to her with special frequency throughout the first decade of his expatriation; his letters to her are among the warmest and most confidential he ever sent to anyone outside his immediate family. That of December 28 is no exception. Their correspondence had lately turned on the issue of marriage. James's friends and relatives in America were eager to settle him into family life, and he found himself having gently to deflect the question. He also thanked her, however, for her kind words about his new novel, whose opening chapters she had just read in the *Atlantic*, and the meat of his letter was a reply to a specific question. She was, James wrote, both right and wrong to take Minny Temple as the original of Isabel Archer. He admitted that he had had his cousin in mind, that he had given Isabel an "infusion . . . of her remarkable nature." Still, he cautioned against taking the character as a direct portrait, for "Poor Minny was essentially *incomplete*, and I have tried to make my young woman more rounded, more finished." Her tuberculosis had kept her from becoming the person she might have been, and yet for James her incompleteness wasn't only that of early death, of a teleology that falsified her nature. For in life, as he added, we are all incomplete, and our days are a chaos of contingencies. They do not in themselves possess an intrinsic meaning, a necessary form, but must be *made* to mean, and it's the writer's job to fill his subjects out, "to justify them, as it were": to depict some final state or being toward which the unimpeded self might tend.

On the evening of Isabel's arrival at Gardencourt, Ralph asks his mother what she means to do with her. Mrs. Touchett has a ready answer: a Paris wardrobe, and Florence in the autumn. Of course, the question belongs to James as well. In the novel's preface he depicts himself as asking what *he* will do with her, and his own answer at first resembles Mrs. Touchett's. He'll take her to Europe; that will be the starting point for her adventures. Ralph isn't satisfied with his mother's reply, though, and he soon modifies his question to ask what Isabel is "going to do with herself." With most women, he thinks, that issue doesn't arise; they simply wait for the man who will "furnish them with a destiny." Isabel, however, gives him the impression that she has "intentions of her own." She may be incomplete, but it doesn't seem to him as if the ordinary terms of a woman's life will be able to contain her. And yet what is it open for her to become?

In his preface James writes that the germ of the novel lay in his sense of a single character, a young woman who "stood there in perfect isolation" and to whom everything else would need to be added: setting, plot, other people, the whole body of relations that would lead her to a full recognition of her own situation. I recognize the general truth of James's belief that we are all of us unfinished, but still there's a special charge in his sense of Minny's torn-out page. He adds in the preface that he saw the character as "affronting her destiny," and Isabel will indeed come to face her future. But that verb—not confront, but affront—gains an extra force if we see Minny as having provided a model, and James himself offers an affront to his cousin's destiny, a slap across its face; an affront that consists of trying to imagine just who she might with Isabel's chances have become. Indeed, it's precisely because the character remains so closely tied to James's memory that Isabel cannot be an exact portrait. Minny's thread was cut so short that there is, paradoxically, more room for growth, for James's own portrait to diverge from the figure Grace Norton remembered. The sumptuously dressed great lady of the book's later chapters owes little to the hemorrhaging girl complaining about her sickroom regimen of "gruel and silence."

Still, James's imagination of Isabel's career is, in one sense, an extrapolation from Minny's family circumstances. In 1906 he wrote to his agent, J. B. Pinker, suggesting a subject for the photographic frontispiece to the revised edition of the novel: "a view of the English country house (Hardwicke, near Pangbourne, on the Thames) which I had vaguely and approximately in mind, years ago, for the opening of the *Portrait*." The place belonged to a Member of Parliament named Charles Rose, whom James had known since his early days in England; they were contemporaries, and in writing to Pinker, James remembered that he had once stayed there with him. An image of that house did indeed become the novel's frontispiece, but the details of any trip that James himself made to Hardwick Court (without a final *e*) are now irrecoverable. No correspondence with Rose survives, and James nowhere else mentions the place. Still, let me posit a visit at some point in the second half of 1877. That was the year Rose took up residence, leasing the estate at first and then later buying it, and in a letter James mentions dining with him in London that June. He had been in Britain for only a few months and had had few country invitations as yet, but this one would be apt to follow, and the house was close enough to the city to let him go down for just a single night.

It is a Tudor building, "a good deal bruised and defaced in Cromwell's

wars," and some forty miles upstream from London; the words come from
the novel, but the facts are confirmed by architectural historian Nikolaus
Pevsner, and both writers note the irregularity of its bricks and gables. The
house sits on a low rise above the water, with a steep hill rising directly
behind, and its view across the river to the hedged fields beyond is little
changed from what it would have been in James's day. I spent a summer
morning there, driving from Oxford though one impeccable village after
another, swooping at last downhill into Whitchurch-on-Thames, and turning into a narrow lane just before I reached the river. The house was a mile
on, and the fields along the way were filled not with sheep or cows but with
hundreds of spitting long-necked llamas; a neighbor's farm. Then a set of
open gates, a parking space next to the manor office, a friendly greeting.
Hardwick still belongs to the Rose family, though the current owner was
absent, and the estate's manager showed me over the house and grounds:
the library with its elaborately plastered ceiling from the time of Elizabeth
I, the spot where the Roundhead cannonballs had hit, the direction from
which carriages would once have approached. The warm brick of the house
itself is surrounded by graveled walks, avenues of old trees channel one's
vision down to the water, and there is indeed a great spread of lawn on
which one can imagine having tea. The Thames runs placidly here, and
in the novel's early chapters James describes Ralph and Isabel as spending
some of their time in a rowboat; a 1906 article in *Country Life* claims, in fact,
that there is "no more beautiful reach of the river than that upon which the
Hardwick terraces look down."

It isn't a grand place—not a power house, not a place of lordly display.
And yet it is a striking one, this substantial family home, with its thousand
acres of mixed farming and timber, close to London but marked with an
enduring sense of privacy. Other estates along the Thames have a description and a history that can match it, including the larger Mapledurham just
downstream, whose grounds one can now rent for weddings. But James
had a particular reason for drawing upon Hardwick, quite aside from the
attractions of the house itself. Minny Temple's mother had been a James,
the sister of the novelist's father. She was the writer's first cousin on her

mother's side. And Charles Rose, a London banker turned country squire, was her first cousin on her father's.

Let me trace the geneology. The Temples came from Rutland, Vermont—Daniel Touchett's hometown. Robert Temple married Catherine James; they had six children, Minny among them. In 1843, Robert's sister Charlotte married a Scottish-born Montreal lawyer named John Rose, who over the next twenty years became one of Canada's most successful financiers. Rose returned to Britain in 1869 and set up a merchant bank that specialized in railroads, the era's most consistently lucrative investment; he also served as an unofficial representative of the Canadian government and was made a baronet in 1872. James liked the Rose children, but kept his distance from the formidable woman he called "Aunt Charlotte," refusing several invitations to stay at Loseley Park, the much grander place in Surrey, closer to London and not on the water, that the Rose parents were then renting. He finally saw it only in July of 1880, as he was reading proof on the *Portrait*'s opening serial installments. Nevertheless, he knew Loseley by reputation already, and gave Gardencourt both its picture gallery and its ghost; Hardwick has neither.

For our purposes, however, the real interest lies in the figure of Sir John—not the historical person, but the man seen in terms of his family position. He is the uncle by marriage whom Minny Temple would have visited if she had ever been well enough to travel. The situation into which Isabel steps has a much closer resemblance to that of James's own extended family than most scholars have noted, even though, as people, the Roses have almost nothing in common with the Touchetts. Family tradition holds that Charles Rose served as the model for Mr. Toad in Kenneth Grahame's *The Wind in the Willows* (1908), while the *Dictionary of National Biography* describes his father as dying of a "heart attack brought on by the excitement of shooting a stag." It's hard to imagine the shrewd but modest Daniel Touchett doing that, and the character owes less to Sir John Rose than to an American banker named Russell Sturgis, a member of an old Salem family who in Britain became a director of Barings Bank. The Sturgises did have a house on the river, albeit one closer to London, and Italianate rather than

Tudor; James spent some of his Christmases with them, and their son Howard became one of his closest friends. The figure of Mr. Touchett isn't so
much a composite as a laminate, in which James has glued the temperament
of one financier to the family of another. But it's time to leave the paral-
lels between Minny and Isabel behind us. Or rather to note that Isabel also
owes something to James himself, who in Europe had successfully affronted
the invalid's destiny that in his parents' America had seemed to await him.
She is both cousins made well, while all that was ill and infirm about both
Minny and Henry too is placed in the novel on the frail shoulders of Ralph
Touchett.

Ralph finds himself after Harvard and Oxford sitting lazily upon a stool
at his father's bank. He is a spectator, devoted to the ironic appreciation of the world around him, and even before his disease sets in, it seems to
the people he knows as if he will be "shut out from a career." Then his lungs
begin to go, and he resembles Minny in at first viewing his illness as that
of "an uninteresting . . . person with whom he had nothing in common."
The picture of Ralph in the novel's early chapters is almost as detailed as
that of Isabel herself, and part of the impression she makes on us comes
from Ralph's sense that she has changed his own life. Let's therefore ask the
same question of him that he does of his mother: what will he do with her?
Ralph is willing enough to fall in love, but he believes it must be a passive
experience, and a silent one. Illness has confirmed his habit of watching,
and the richest entertainment he can now imagine lies in the "conscious
observation of a lovely woman." So Isabel's presence comes as a kind of
gift—as though, he thinks, he had gotten a Titian in the mail, or had the key
to some great building thrust into his hand. Still, he recognizes that so far he
has only "looked in at the windows." The door to her inner being remains
locked, and perhaps the house isn't yet ready for viewing, the furniture still
being moved from place to place. The curious thing is that James also uses
the language of architecture to define Isabel's attitude toward Ralph. She
wants to see the life hidden behind his joking façade, "to pass through the

ante-room . . . and enter the private apartments." Almost everyone who reads *The Portrait of a Lady* sees Ralph and Isabel as one of fiction's great might-have-beens, and the consonance in the language with which they think of one another confirms their essential harmony.

On the night of her arrival the two of them walk by candlelight through Gardencourt's picture gallery, and when Isabel asks if the house has a ghost, Ralph replies that it does: a ghost that she will not be able to see. No "young, happy, innocent person" ever has, only those who have known misery; he himself saw it long ago and hopes she never will. Over the next weeks—the next chapters—they grow increasingly close, taking long drives through a countryside of hedgerows and common, parkland and thatched cottage, and she soon falls in love with Gardencourt's sense of order and seclusion. It is a place where "in the thick mild air all shrillness dropped out of conversation." Nothing much happens in the chapters that follow Isabel's arrival in Britain. There are no major developments in the plot, and some readers complain that here the book moves slowly. But these chapters do allow us to learn our way around James's characters, to form a sense of their habitual life, and they give the novel a sense of space that it will keep until the end.

Or perhaps we could say that nothing much happens except talk. One afternoon Lord Warburton drives over for an impromptu overnight visit. Isabel had thought him pleasant on the day of her arrival, but now she finds him delightful, as though he quickened her sense of life's pleasure. He stays on for a second night, when the party lingers in the drawing room until Mrs. Touchett rises and announces that it's time to wish the gentlemen good night. Isabel is at first puzzled. She wonders aloud if she need go up, and that forces her aunt to be explicit. We are no longer in Albany, she says; you cannot, here, sit unchaperoned in the company of a man to whom you are not related. Ralph protests, but Isabel acquiesces, and when she follows her aunt upstairs tells her that she will "always want to know the things one shouldn't do." So as to do them? her aunt asks, uncertain of an American girl's limits. Yet Isabel is not so simple: "So as to choose."

Those words end a chapter, and there is a sense of drama in their placement; there's much more at stake in this conversation than bedtime.

"Whoso would be a man must be a noncomformist," Emerson writes in "Self-Reliance," and adds that if you "always scorn appearances . . . you always may." Isabel won't go as far as either Emerson suggests or Mrs. Touchett fears, but this new kind of young woman does want the freedom to determine the degree of her own conformity. She needs to know the limits of propriety—needs to know other people's rules in order to make her own. She reserves the right to shape her own life, and at this moment she more closely resembles the ambitious young men of the nineteenth-century novel than she does most other fictional members of her sex. Heroines are often rooted in the place where they grew up; George Eliot's Dorothea provides an example. Those young men, however, have usually moved from the provinces to the city, stepping into a larger world in which they must carve their own path; so Rastignac in Balzac's *Père Goriot* declares war on society, knowing that's the best way to reach its top. The self for these characters is defined by ambition, which is often worldly enough—money, fame, power. Isabel's own ambition is less violent and yet perhaps more daring. It isn't just the freedom to name the terms on which she will meet the world. No, she wants the freedom, in Emerson's words, to be self-sufficing, and her ambition will define itself in terms of a radical autonomy, a cultivation of individual identity in which her very sense of self comes to stand as the chief object of her own desire.

At the same time, however, we need to look at the particular thing that prompts Isabel's declaration of her freedom to choose. It is a social practice of the Old World, something unknown in Albany, and while she doesn't reject it outright she does suggest that she has the liberty to observe it or not. In itself, it has no necessary hold upon her. Her ambition, that is, takes a peculiarly American form, and to understand it we will need to look at another character as well. Isabel's best friend is a newspaper correspondent named Henrietta Stackpole, who specializes in chatty opinionated travel essays. Isabel sees her limitations—Henrietta has no sense of discretion, and remains so closely in step with her public as never to go beyond the obvious. Nevertheless, she admires her energy and assurance, taking her as "proof that a woman might suffice to herself and be happy." Now Henrietta has come to England, and Isabel asks to invite her down. James thought he had botched his reporter, writing in his preface that her place in the book was greater than her purpose, and even in 1880 he admitted, in a letter to Howells, that most readers would find her true-blue patriotism a bit overdone. Yet Henrietta is more important than her creator himself seems to realize, and her arrival at Gardencourt allows James to qualify his sense of the particular strain in American identity that is reflected in Isabel's desire to choose.

Henrietta's sense of self-reliance has one limit. Almost the first thing she says is that England makes her feel cramped, and she soon falls into an argument with Mrs. Touchett. We have different points of view, Isabel's aunt says: "I like to be treated as an individual; you like to be treated as a 'party.'" Henrietta denies this—she wants, she claims, to be treated as an American lady. Yet she has indeed spoken of traveling with a "party" she met on the steamer, a lovely group from Little Rock, and however comically handled, their dispute points to an ideological crack in the center of American life. For how can anyone be somebody in particular in a land of certain self-evident truths—how much can any one individual be allowed to stand out? On the one hand, we share a belief in a republican egalitarianism; we are all created equal. On the other, we each have the freedom to pursue our own individual happiness, a freedom that quickly produces both a fierce sense of competition and the social divisions that rise from it.

Tocqueville among others had explored that tension, and in James's day such issues were a staple of the magazines for which he wrote, with writers asking on what grounds, if any, a sense of individual distinction might rest. The historian Francis Parkman, for example, wondered in 1878 about the ever-uncertain role of the "cultivated" in a polity split between "an ignorant proletariat and a half-taught plutocracy." Still, the implicit three-way debate between Isabel, Henrietta, and Mrs. Touchett cuts more sharply than that. It is, above all, a dispute about the nature and limits of desire. Tocqueville had warned that individualism might undercut any sense of a public good, and when pushed to an extreme, the pursuit of personal freedom that stands as an integral part of American identity does indeed end by putting one at odds with the nation as a whole. There's nothing more American than wanting to choose, and the most American thing of all is to insist upon choice, upon one's right to break the social compact. From that Henrietta draws back. Self-reliance cannot go unfettered and choice has its limits; limits that mark out one kind of American identity, sacrificing individual eminence to purchase a Main Street cohesion.

James's conception of Henrietta as a secondary figure here keeps him from engaging with these issues as fully as he might; later chapters have deeper things to say about the terms of American identity. But let me suggest one of the ways in which he tries to finesse them. Isabel thinks of Ralph as a "cosmopolitan," someone marked by a culture that transcends linguistic and national borders. Henrietta merely calls him "alienated," and asks if he thinks it right to give up his country—to live abroad, and with foreign manners. His answer is quite simple, and speaks, perhaps, for James as well. He tells her that he can no more give up his country "than one gives up one's grandmother. It's antecedent to choice." He doesn't stop being an American just because Oxford has swallowed up Harvard, and in one sense he might even be more of one. Isabel finds a deep appeal in Gardencourt's sense of "well-ordered privacy," but the pleasure she takes in it is conditioned by her national origin. Her own antecedents lie elsewhere, and so the Continent is indeed a choice, a background against which, as an American, she can move freely, a place that conduces to the sense—perhaps the illusion—of liberty on which she depends and by which she lives. James himself had spent a decade in making that place his own by the time he sat down to tell her story in his hotel room overlooking the Arno. He had tested its attractions, and had even given his homeland one last try before making a final declaration of independence. In settling in the Old World he had, paradoxically, left his past behind, and for Isabel Archer, as indeed for James himself, the consummation of her utterly American desire to choose will be to elect a European home.

PART TWO

THE MARRIAGE PLOT

A Vista. By Alvin Langdon Coburn, ca. 1913. Photogravure print.

5.

HER EMPTY CHAIR

JAMES HAD BEEN at work on the *Portrait* for a month in the Tuscan spring of 1880 when he paused, on the 14th of May, to send a letter of congratulations to a friend in London, a banker named John Cross. "I have just heard of your marriage," he wrote, and offered a "word of very friendly sympathy on the occasion—which I beg you to communicate, in the most deferential form, to your illustrious wife." Sympathy and deference—the words may be ironic, but they still suggest that the forty-year-old Cross had done something startling, and maybe even scary. For his new wife was almost twenty years his senior, and illustrious indeed. She was the most learned imaginative writer in Britain and the country's greatest living novelist, the woman known under the pen name of George Eliot.

The James family had been reading George Eliot's work ever since the 1859 publication of her first novel, *Adam Bede*, the story of a rural hierarchy disrupted by a love affair that cuts across the lines of class. Its author had shown them the parsonages and manor houses of Jane Austen, but she also depicted the broken-down cottages and farmhouse kitchens that Austen left out; and her calm meditative voice treated her characters with a sympathy that she made both an aesthetic principle and a moral duty. Nor was George Eliot content with making the English countryside her own. Both *Adam Bede* and its successor, *The Mill on the Floss*, were among the bestsellers of their day, but she then turned to the past, to Renaissance Florence, and in *Romola* had brought the city of Savonarola onto the page. It was the most brilliant if not the best of Victorian historical novels, and perhaps the most lucrative; her publishers had paid an astonishing £7,000 for the serial rights.

Indeed, James ended his note to Cross with the wish that he could enclose a view of the Arno, "which your wife knows so well and which she has helped to make me know." That was only the beginning of what he had learned from her, however, and in their letters both he and his brother William had argued about, and argued with, her later *Middlemarch*. William found himself "aghast at [its] tremenj'us intellectual power," and Henry worried that his older sibling would find his own praise of it stingy. His admiration was never unmixed, and he published pointedly critical accounts of both *Middlemarch* and *Daniel Deronda*, books that to him marked the limits of old-fashioned English storytelling. Nevertheless, he admired George Eliot above all other British novelists. He went to school on her as he did on Turgenev or Balzac, and as he did not on Dickens. Her work shaped his, and to understand him we need to understand both what he took from her and what he resisted.

He knew her work intimately—her work, but not the woman herself. What he did know, what everybody knew, was her story. He knew that her marriage to Cross was in a sense her second one: in a sense, because she had never been legally joined to G. H. Lewes, the man with whom the then-little-known Mary Ann Evans began to live in 1854. She was born in 1819 in Warwickshire, where her father managed the estates of one of the county's largest landowners. Robert Evans was proud of his clever daughter, and she received as good an education as possible in an age when women could not yet attend university. It gave her a command of modern languages, and her own hard study added the classical ones; her first books were translations from German. After her father's death she moved to London and in 1851 took a job at the *Westminster Review*, a progressive quarterly where her own essays soon appeared alongside those by writers like John Stuart Mill. G. H. Lewes was another of the *Review*'s contributors, a man who could write anything from a successful play to works of popular science. He had separated from his unfaithful wife, but the peculiarities of Victorian family law kept him from obtaining a divorce. Evans was therefore inviting something more than notoriety when she decided to leave her past behind and to travel with him to Germany, where the man she now called her husband would work on a biography of Goethe. The sexual mores of Weimar were far from constricting, and they could live together openly in a city where such unions had a recognized place; a city where Goethe himself had in fact set the example. In England, though, she was at first cut off from almost everyone she had known before.

Lewes kept his male friends, and many of them became hers as well. But most women now refused to know her, and her brother Isaac broke all contact. In daily life she was always called Mrs. Lewes, but she couldn't publish under either that name or her own. So when she began to write the stories collected as *Scenes of Clerical Life* (1857), she decided to use a pseudonym, and a masculine one at that; at first not even her publisher, the Edinburgh firm of John Blackwood, knew the author's real name. The success of her first books made that secret impossible to keep and in time "George Eliot's" combination of rectitude and genius made the Leweses' world accept them. Even princesses asked for introductions.

Lewes had died in 1878, however, and now she had married a man whom she had until recently called "Nephew." John Cross was not her nephew by blood. He was from a Liverpool banking family, and the Leweses initially knew him through their friendship with his widowed mother. They first met him in Rome, in 1869, and soon learned to rely on him in the practical details of life. He supervised their investments, increasing the already-large sums that her books had earned; he found them their country house in Surrey. John Cross was sternly handsome, and the novelist had turned to him as something like a son after Lewes's death; while he had turned to her as something more than a mother when his own mother died soon thereafter.

James's letter to Cross wasn't his only one about this unexpected union. On that same day he wrote to Quincy Steeet, and after settling some details of family business, he passed on the news. The last time he had seen the new couple, James told his father, Cross had been sitting next to the novelist and reading aloud from Chaucer; "I knew he adored her but I didn't know he desired to unite his 40 years to her 58." But he then added an image that explained the marriage, or at least her side of it. Since Lewes's death she had been "shivering like a person who had had a wall of her house blown off." Lewes had made her career possible. His love had helped her overcome her often crippling self-doubt and had given her the confidence she needed to work. He kept her from seeing any damaging reviews, he made her bargains with publishers, and he held a shield between her and the world, one that at first deflected scandal and later fended off the hazards of fame. Now he was dead, and she had simply "taken Johnny to make up the wall." Later that summer James spoke of the marriage again, this time in a letter to Grace Norton. He had just sent his regrets for a house party to which the pair had also been invited; his monthly deadlines on the *Portrait* had begun to press, and he assumed there would be other opportunities in the future. "Aren't you sorry?" he wrote, "so that I might tell you they were grotesque? I don't think they are, but they are deemed to be." Yet the marriage lasted only seven months. Her health had long been troubled, and weakened by both kidney failure and a throat infection, she died on December 22, 1880.

She was buried on December 29 in London's Highgate Cemetery; James was in the West Country for the holidays, as I noted in my last chapter, and did not go to the funeral. A few weeks later he did, however, pay a visit to Cross, and was invited to sit in the novelist's "empty chair" as he listened to the banker's account of her extraordinary mind, taking in his admission that he had been "a cart-horse yoked to a racer." James's private impression was that Cross would have found the pace impossible to sustain. Nobody then knew just how difficult, though, and years later the story came out that on their honeymoon in Venice he had thrown himself from their hotel room into the Grand Canal; some gondoliers hauled him to safety, and they left the city as soon as he could travel. In his biography of her, Cross noted only that the city's air had made him "thoroughly ill." That book was described by William Gladstone as "a Reticence in three volumes"; nevertheless, the couple lived in apparent harmony for the few months left to them, and the episode remains a mystery.

. . .

W e don't know if James and George Eliot ever wrote to one another. No letters between them have ever been found, though after her marriage she did tell a friend, and with evident pleasure, that "Johnnie had a graceful letter of congratulation from Mr. Henry James." We have a somewhat firmer knowledge of their few recorded meetings. In his May 1880 letter to his father, James speaks of "the last time I went to see her," and one to William from the spring of 1878 records his first Sunday afternoon visit to the Priory, her house in Regent's Park. But we don't know how long a sequence lies bracketed between those dates, how many times he took his cup of tea at the Leweses' regular Sunday at-homes.

The drawing room at the Priory was long and bow-windowed, and underfurnished by the tastes of the times; a room in which many people could stand but not many sit. Lewes kept up a flow of talk, greeting his guests and making people laugh off in the corners, but the novelist herself didn't participate in anything like a general conversation. She sat instead at the room's very center, in a chair across from the fireplace, to which her visitors were led up, one at a time. James's account of his own initial entrée remains evocative: "I had my turn at sitting beside her and being conversed with in a low, but most harmonious tone; and bating a tendency to *aborder* only the highest themes I have no fault to find with her." Every record agrees with his sense of the hushed elevation of the Leweses' household; Dickens wrote to them, only half-jokingly, that he hoped "to attend service."

Nor was he the only one. Almost anyone with a claim to distinction might appear in Regent's Park, and Lewes kept an occasional record of those who did. The painter Edward Burne-Jones came regularly, so did Anthony Trollope, and on one Sunday the guests included both the historian Lord Acton and the military hero Sir Garnet Wolseley, who would later become commander-in-chief of the British army and a friend of James's own. James himself remembered a conversation with the philosopher Herbert Spencer, with whom the young Mary Ann Evans had once been in love. Many of George Eliot's visitors left an account of her talk, and as James did, they noted first the music of her voice, and then the force of her ideas, the details of what she said about Spain or truth or God. Most callers also recorded their impression of her looks. She was famously horse-faced; though they often said she wasn't as plain as they had expected.

About that the young James was only a partial exception. One of the things he most wanted on his first adult trip to England was the chance to meet her, and in May 1869 he got it. Grace Norton was a friend of the older writer's, and brought James along to call. But their visit coincided with a medical emergency. Lewes's son Thornton, who would soon die of tuberculosis of the spine, lay writhing in agony in the drawing room, and James almost immediately went in search of a doctor. Still, he saw enough in those few minutes to describe George Eliot to his father, a description that begins in callow convention and then reverses itself. She had a dull eye and a mouth of crooked teeth, but her speech soon began to charm him with an "underlying world of reserve, knowledge, pride and power," and by the time he left, he thought her the greatest woman he had ever met. Almost ten years later he went with one of the Leweses' country neighbors for a rainy afternoon at their house in Surrey, and in his autobiography turned the moment into an anecdote at his own expense. His friends had sent the two volumes of *The Europeans* ahead, but no one referred to it and he soon realized that the Leweses would be happier alone. At the end of the visit James stood ready to climb into the carriage when Lewes gestured for him to wait, and then appeared at the door with the books in his hand, begging him to "take them away, please, away, away!" James left believing they hadn't connected "book with author, or author with visitor," but in truth they had other things to worry about. Lewes had been ill for months, and in just a few weeks would be dead.

George Eliot probably read some of James's early stories and essays, but I think it's unlikely she read his reviews of her own work. They are just hedged enough to make me suspect that Lewes held them back. In his seventies James wrote with full-throated admiration of the effect her books had had upon him. To read *Middlemarch* was to be soaked through with some sustaining essence, and "we of the faith" went to her not only for the pleasures of narrative but also for lessons in how to live. Yet if the old James had shaken off what he called "the anxieties of circumspection and comparison," the young writer found George Eliot's influence strong enough to feel he had better resist it.

"'Middlemarch' is at once one of the strongest and one of the weakest of English novels." So James began his 1873 review of a novel that he judged both "a treasure-house of details . . . [and] an indifferent whole." He was still not thirty and had yet to publish any significant fiction of his own, but he already had a distinctive line in ambivalence and wasn't shy about rolling it out. George Eliot's panoramic account of an English country town offered too many seemingly separate plots, too many distractions from what he took to be its core. Its center lay in the story of Dorothea Brooke's two marriages, and yet the novel appeared to treat her tale as but one episode among many; the character herself remained of more consequence than the action around her. James admitted that the tight focus he sought would have cost us many of the book's best moments, and he admired its account of the soul-murdering marriage that the young doctor, Lydgate, contracts with the town beauty, Rosamond Vincy. He could not, however, reconcile himself to the way George Eliot had matched Dorothea's story to Lydgate's. She had given the book "two suns . . . each with its independent solar system" of orbiting characters, and yet the two stars rarely touch; the drama of their possible relations never quite catches hold.

James had similar reservations about George Eliot's last novel, *Daniel Deronda*, another book evenly split between two characters who hardly ever meet. One is the beautiful Gwendolen Harleth, who marries for money even while knowing of her husband's mistress and their children, and the other is the title character, a young Englishman who late in the novel discovers his Jewish ancestry. Most readers have followed James in finding Gwendolen the more interesting of the two, but his account of George Eliot's work depends upon something more than a preference for one narrative line over another. James had little interest in the multiplotted novel that stands as the mid-Victorian norm. The slow episodic meander of Dickens or Thackeray may have spelled enchantment to him as a child, but the adult's taste rejected them, and over thirty years after reviewing *Middlemarch* he returned to the burden of his critique in the preface to his own *Tragic Muse*.

In that book James chose, for the first and only time in his career, to run the centrifugal risks of his Victorian predecessors by yoking together two originally separate narratives. He laid one scene in the theater, the other in English parliamentary politics, and worked throughout in the fear that the seam which joined them might not hold, that he might not be able to fuse these disparate lives into a unified composition. Painters had an easier time of it, he thought. The eye can move from point to point in an instant, and so they can give us two pictures in one; he marveled at the way Tintoretto could depict "without loss of authority half a dozen actions separately taking place." But he could not envision so varied a coherence in prose, and in writing about *The Tragic Muse* he worries at the question until it resolves itself in one of his greatest phrases, his necessary if inaccurate description of Victorian fiction as a menagerie of "large loose baggy monsters."

Middlemarch sometimes puts Dorothea aside for many pages at a stretch, and on some of her reappearances the reader does have to work to reconnect her to the rest of the novel. Still, we now find George Eliot's special glory in precisely the spot where James thought her weakest—in the very plurality of her narrative, with its attendant sense of all her characters' missed chances. Nevertheless, his review of *Middlemarch* tells us more about the book than any other contemporary account, and if the best of James's own novels are in contrast marked by what he called the "deep-breathing economy" of a single story, it's because he had what he saw as her own limitations before him. He wrote in conclusion that the book "sets a limit . . . to the development of the old-fashioned English novel." That judgment holds. Members of the following generation like Hardy or James himself drew heavily on George Eliot's work, albeit in very different ways; but in neither case did they imitate her sense of narrative structure.

James's several pieces on her raise other questions as well. In 1866 the very young critic lamented her decision to run the plot of *Adam Bede* on past its climactic pitch, to tie the book off with fifty pages of reconciliation. Anyone could see what would probably happen next—did the novel really have to spell it out? George Eliot made things too easy for us. The ideal reader he wished her pages had implied would be someone engaged enough to deduce it all for himself; an active, inference-drawing reader for whom no meaning need be underlined. This question will return to us when we consider the ending of *The Portrait of a Lady*, and James himself came back to the issue in a later review of Cross's biography. The conclusion of *Adam Bede* exemplified the popular belief that a story should end with "marriages and rescues in the nick of time." Yet such incidents as Hetty Sorrel's reprieve on the scaffold did not belong to nature, "by which I do not mean that they belong to a very happy art."

The American recognized that George Eliot's reliance on such forms of resolution grew from something deeper than mere convention. She thought of herself as a teacher, and believed that what she called "aesthetic teaching" was the highest form of instruction. She also thought, however, that if it ceased "to be purely aesthetic—if it lapses anywhere from the picture to the diagram—it becomes the most offensive." Any lesson she might offer must develop out of the picture itself, rather than precede it. At the end of *Middlemarch*, Dorothea helps another woman at what she believes will be the cost of her own happiness. That moment of charity, however, is not the point of the narrative, but rather its product. It proceeds from the logic of the character's development, and George Eliot's words imply that she would have failed if it looked as though she had worked the other way around. But James thought that she did sometimes lapse, that she stylized her picture of life in order to make it fit her lesson. He saw her as an idealist who had "commissioned herself to be real," and his account points to both the risks and the peculiar genius of her narrative voice, to the often intrusive commentary, usually in the first-person plural, that she offers upon her characters. It is a voice at once earnest and shrewd, not quite omniscient but certainly wiser than any of us in canvassing the choices those characters face. Even as he acknowledged the perils of her style, however, James admired the way that her best work pushed beyond didacticism, and he praised her ability to combine her love of an individual character's "special case" with the force of her "generalizing instinct."

His own books would be different. He thought she gave English fiction a claim to both rigor and respect that it had earlier lacked, but he did not simply want to fill her chair, and hoped his stories would "have less 'brain' than *Middlemarch* but . . . more *form.*" In *The Portrait of a Lady* he found that form by taking George Eliot as a negative example. James gave his own heroine the centrality he felt she deserved, and the novel comes to us without any rival plots or competing points of interest; he never allows our curiosity about Lord Warburton's parliamentary career or Henrietta Stackpole's newspaper to distract us from the subject of the portrait herself. Isabel isn't always onstage, and she isn't the only character whose mind James allows us to enter. But she's what the other characters talk about, even, or especially, when she's off the page.

James's preface to the novel acknowledges what he owed George Eliot, but though he summons her heroines by name he also misquotes a line from *Daniel Deronda.* "In these frail vessels is borne onward through the ages the treasure of human affection"; she had actually written, not "frail," but "delicate." Memory does that, though the slip might also point to James's sense of both his debt and his difference. His early critics, Howells among them, had stressed that debt, linking Isabel to *Deronda*'s Gwendolen Harleth, comparing the difficulties each heroine faces in maintaining her independence of mind and spirit. And both Isabel and Dorothea are liable to the strictures that George Eliot herself laid down in her 1856 essay, "Silly Novels by Lady Novelists." Written before she had ever tried a story of her own, the essay attacks what she calls the "mind and millinery" school of fiction, books in which the heroine dazzles with both her wit and her eyes; a girl whose nose and morals alike remain perfectly straight and fine. James's Isabel has fixed her mind on bravery and beauty and truth. She sees herself as good company, she believes herself a pattern of consistency, and she longs for the chance to display what she never doubts is her own capacity for the heroic. Yet her story is not a silly novel, even if she does at first seem very young. The heroines George Eliot disparages never receive their comeuppance, but James knows that his own protagonist, with her scant knowledge and inflated ideals, would be an easy victim for a "scientific criticism, if she were not intended to awaken . . . an impulse more tender and more purely expectant."

"Scientific" is an Eliotic word, one we can associate with the author who in *Middlemarch* took her metaphors from physiology and optics. "Expectant" is, however, all James, the word of a novelist who asks us to wonder, with Ralph Touchett, about just what Isabel will do.

6.

PROPOSALS

I N T H E O P E N I N G chapter of *Middlemarch*, George Eliot raises the question that shadows almost every heroine of nineteenth-century British fiction: "And how should Dorothea not marry?—a girl so handsome and with such prospects? Nothing could hinder it but her love of extremes." Marriage is the expected fate of young women, or at least of young women in novels, the point toward which all narrative tends. Austen does it, Dickens palms a few cards to make it come right at the end of *Bleak House*, and we all know about *Jane Eyre*. Dorothea will prove no exception, even if her choice of a husband does betray that taste for extremes: a parched scholar, a clergyman more than twice her age. Yet those marriage plots are an English oddity, and don't have anything like the same purchase in the Continental novels that James himself admired. Balzac's women find their careers in adultery. For them as for Emma Bovary a wedding serves only to inaugurate a series of love affairs, and in Turgenev marriage remains ancillary to other longings, to a passion for justice or truth. James was impatient with the Anglo-American expectation that a book's last chapters should provide a grab-bag of "husbands, wives, babies, millions": impatient with both the reader's demand for such treats and the writer's willingness to feed it. That's one reason he admired George Eliot. For Austen's heroines a wedding may stand as an end to experience, but for Dorothea it is only the beginning. She marries for the first time in the book's tenth chapter, and in both that novel and in *Daniel Deronda*, a part of Eliot's greatness lies in charting the inner contours of unions gone wrong, of marriages that should never have been.

James had a different specialty. His early books are often about weddings that don't happen, novels in which nobody ever quite gets to church. And he begins Isabel's story by making her choose to have a story in the first place. She decides to go to Europe with her Aunt Lydia instead of allowing Caspar Goodwood to foreclose her fate. Still, it's not immediately clear that this new plot will be any different than the one she's escaped, and when in the summer of 1906 James paced out the tale of his own intentions, he found himself remembering his difficulty in giving her another kind of narrative. "Millions of presumptuous girls" might affront their destiny each day, and yet what were the possible fates that awaited them? He wanted a heroine who would be the novel's "all-in-all" but that begged the question of what he could make her do. "We women can't go in search of adventures," George Eliot's Gwendolen Harleth had said, can't become explorers or go out to hunt tigers, and when James wrote the *Portrait*, he had *Daniel Deronda* very much on his mind. He knew that Isabel's range of action was circumscribed by her sex, and knew as well that those actions might seem mild in comparison to the masculine world of "flood and field . . . of battle and murder and sudden death." Even a trip to Europe looked tame—an event too familiar to be interesting. Yet James had found a solution, and in his preface the memory of it makes his prose grow tense with excitement. He could fix the problem by placing "the centre of the subject in the young woman's own consciousness," by resting his gaze upon her ever-developing understanding of her relation to herself. Her adventures would lie not in the outward events of her life, but rather in her comprehension of them, in an inner drama that might, to her, seem as enthralling as any tale of pirates or caravans. To her—and to us insofar as James could make us care about her.

James here overstates his own originality. That attention to the unhistoric acts of ordinary life may not have featured heavily in the American romances of Melville or Cooper, but earlier English novelists like Elizabeth Gaskell or George Eliot herself had already put their narrative weight upon the heroine's understanding of her own situation. James here bends American fiction in their direction, and his difference from them in the *Portrait*'s opening chapters is one of degree only. So we come back to a version of that question about Dorothea. Admit, with Ralph Touchett, that Isabel has intentions of her own: still, how should she not marry? She may have sent Goodwood away, but Gardencourt is the start of a new story, and when old Mr. Touchett tells Lord Warburton that he "must not fall in love with my niece," it looks like a command to be broken. But as we hold this thick volume in our hands, we also know that his path, that anyone's path, will not be smooth; we know that the drama will lie in Isabel's resistance to the plot laid down before her.

Of course, Austen gives us many heroines who refuse a suitor or two, and yet none of them seem suspicious of marriage in itself. James's heroine does, and he links her opinion of it to her admiration of the happily self-sufficient Henrietta. Isabel thinks the subject vulgar—vulgar to worry over, to be eager for, or even to think about. She believes "a woman ought to be able to make up her life in singleness, and that it was perfectly possible to be happy without the society of a more or less coarse-minded person of another sex." None of the men in this book can be fairly described as coarse-minded, though James was perfectly capable of creating such figures; Morris Townsend in *Washington Square* is perhaps the best example. The term belongs to Isabel, and points to her conventional understanding of the difference between the sexes. What's less conventional is her apparent willingness to accept the consequences of it: if that's what one thinks about men, then why not stay single indeed? Isabel also believes, however, that "if a certain light should dawn she could give herself completely." Yet she cannot hold that image of surrender steady. It always ends by frightening her, and her belief in that light paradoxically serves as a warning. It reminds her that experience has its costs. For she could give her self—could relinquish not just the body but the soul.

That, however, is the price her society expects her to pay. To Goodwood she at first makes Europe seem a mere postponement of decision, but the new possibilities of this larger world will carry new threats as well. "It's just like a novel," she says as she steps onto the lawn at Gardencourt, as though her life had been written already, and a new episode in that life opens when she drives over with Ralph and his mother for lunch at Lockleigh, the nearest of Lord Warburton's half a dozen houses. She meets his brother, the Vicar, and his two unmarried sisters, and when they wander through the park after lunch, Warburton tells her that he hopes she'll soon pay him a more extended visit. It will be a few chapters yet before he falls to his metaphoric knees, but Isabel has heard such words before and doesn't like them. She turns the subject as quickly as she can and speaks instead of her desire to improve her mind; a mind that Warburton describes as being already "a most formidable instrument."

The scene ends with Warburton murmuring that he will come see her at Gardencourt. Isabel's answer is cold—"Just as you please"—and yet her coldness isn't that of coquetry. It comes instead "from a certain fear." James will make us wait for the sequel—or rather he made his first audience wait. The scene falls near the end of the book's second serial installment, and for readers of the *Atlantic* the proposal lay a full month in the future. Before moving to it, however, we need to clarify the nature of Isabel's fear. Today we usually see it in sexual terms, and for decades now there's been a lively critical conversation about Isabel's apparent timidity in the face of carnal experience. Some readers have even described her as frigid, and the fact that in 1906 James revised a description of her from "cold and stiff" to "cold and dry" would appear to give them a point. Yet that debate has always seemed to me reductive. Many young women of Isabel's background and period feared an experience about which testimony was hard to find, and that was often presented as an obligation of marriage. And while most scholars do favor the novel's later version, an alternate line of criticism has made a strong argument in favor of its first one, its account of Isabel's hesitation to marry in particular. "Cold and dry" may reflect James's changing understanding of his character's situation, but emphasizing Isabel's sexual reticence makes her desire for independence seem but an aspect of her fear. It turns her into something like a "case." I see it the other way around, and take that fear as an incipient political position, an aspect of her prior desire for self-sufficiency. This can doubtless be overstated. Nevertheless, James's account of Isabel's self-conception does in the book's early chapters link her to the "woman question" of Gilded Age America, to a time when professional opportunity and higher education for women had begun, however tentatively, to expand.

I say in the "early chapters" advisedly, for even in the 1881 edition James will move away from such social questions and into a concentration on the drama of Isabel's consciousness. And yet this reading is too broad to stand even there. It may justify her reluctance to marry Caspar Goodwood, whose energy does appear to drain her freedom; but then he if anyone is the source of Isabel's fear. For Lord Warburton we will need a further layer of explanation.

When Henrietta arrives at Gardencourt, she brings along a bit of news: Goodwood too has come to England, and apparently for the sole purpose of renewing his suit. The reporter makes our heroine recognize that she had indeed encouraged him, but she also sees that Isabel herself has changed. James's heroine no longer believes in the necessary truth of her own earlier opinions and yet is more confident than ever in her engagement with the larger world around her. She may not yet know just where she fits in, but she has now begun to see beyond both Albany and America itself. So Henrietta's news gives her a sense of alarm, and sets her to wandering through the park in a funk. Eventually she drops onto a bench, and as she sits there fuming, a servant arrives to hand her a letter. She recognizes the writing as Goodwood's, and James gives us his letter entire. It's our first direct impression of him, and we quickly see that the mill owner's words have force but no logic. They insist, they protest, they assert, and his assertions are all couched in negatives. He does not accept his dismissal, he does not believe he is disagreeable to her, and he now hates America because she isn't in it. "May I not," he writes in conclusion, "come and see you for half-an-hour?" Isabel has just folded his letter when she looks up to find Lord Warburton standing before her.

Proposal scenes in fiction are in themselves a genre, and therefore have rules. The successful ones are usually brief, and almost never give the actual words of concord. Maybe there's a lightning flash, as at the end of *Middlemarch*; maybe we're told, as in Austen, that the characters said just what they should. But Isabel will decline this offer and the scene can therefore take up the entirety of the book's twelfth chapter, ten pages of nervous comedy set on the most splendid of summer afternoons. Lord Warburton doesn't storm like Austen's Mr. Darcy. His manners are at their bashfully perfect best, and he even apologizes for coming down on her with "such a thumper." He recognizes that they have spent barely a full day together, and hopes she won't object to Lockleigh; "some people don't like a moat, you know." But Isabel delights in everything old, and his house—his several houses—are not an issue. Or are they? Lord Warburton has the sweetest voice she has ever heard. She understands that however abrupt his offer there is nothing frivolous about him, and yet doesn't hesitate in asking him to leave her. She promises to write, but she already knows the burden of her letter, knows in the face of every novel she has ever read that the idea of marrying a viscount doesn't correspond to her own image of happiness.

At Lockleigh, Isabel had been afraid of his proposal even before she knew that Caspar Goodwood was in England. The letter she has just received doesn't affect her decision, but it does affect the story she tells about that decision, the explanation she gives herself about just why she cannot marry Lord Warburton. She wonders that "it cost her so little to refuse a great opportunity," and it's true her passions do not seem engaged. The light has not shone, yet though she tells her aunt that she doesn't love the man, she admits to her more congenial uncle that she likes him well enough. So let's bracket emotion, and take seriously something that Warburton himself says: "I'm afraid it's my being an Englishman." Or at least a particular kind of Englishman. Isabel may delight in a moat, but she doesn't want to marry one. She feels no threat from him personally, as she does from Goodwood, but she also has an idea that as "Lord Warburton" he isn't so much a person as a "personage." She has never known a personage, and until now has thought of individual eminence in terms of character, of "what one liked in a gentleman's mind and in his talk." Isabel likes War-

burton's mind—and yet he also looms as a set of possessions and powers
that can't be measured in such familiar terms. She can't forget that he has
a seat in Parliament as Mr. Touchett has one at his own table, she feels his
hereditary force and his 50,000 acres, and she resists the idea of being pulled
into his orbit. The very splendor of his offer seems a confinement, and in
refusing him she stakes a claim to her own autonomous existence. Or as she
says to her uncle, "Imagine one's belonging to an English class"; the whole
point of being an American is that one doesn't.

Three years after finishing *The Portrait of a Lady*, James wrote a piece
called "The Art of Fiction" that both synthesizes and corrects a series of
Victorian assumptions about the nature and purpose of the novel. The
essay makes no single argument but stands rather as a manifesto, a claim
that fiction has the same importance as poetry or painting; a claim that now
seems commonplace but that in James's own day struck some readers as
presumptuous. Fiction was popular but no more than an amusement; not
serious, not improving, and too worldly. So its sterner critics felt, and in
many ways James agreed with them. For the novel—the English novel
in particular—had too often failed to take itself seriously, and in defining
just how it might James produced an essay that has the same high place in
the history of criticism as Sidney's "Defense of Poetry" or Wordsworth's
preface to *Lyrical Ballads*. In his prefaces to the New York Edition, James
would write with greater rigor about some central issues in his own *oeuvre*.
But he never matched the breadth and wit of these early observations about
the form as a whole.

"The Art of Fiction" is endlessly quotable, and I'll return to it in later
chapters, in particular to James's account of Victorian self-censorship. At
this point, however, its most relevant passages are those that touch upon the
"old-fashioned distinction" that some critics of the period made between
"the novel of character and the novel of incident." Yet character itself determines incident, James argues, and every incident serves in turn to illustrate
character. His choice of such an illustration is a woman standing with her
hand upon a table and looking "at you in a certain way." That example does
admittedly betray his own predilections; he finds his character-revealing

incident in a glance, not a courtroom or a sword fight. Still, it allows him to deny that there is any way to separate story from character, and either from what he calls their "treatment," a term we may equate with "form." And he then begins to toy with a reviewer who has used a work of derring-do as a stick with which to beat the kinds of stories in which girls from Boston turn down English dukes for "psychological reasons"—tales that are of course his own.

James's argument here anticipates his exploration, in the preface to *The Portrait of a Lady*, of the particular adventures open to women. He suggests that psychological reasons may stand as subjects in themselves, that the life within has a drama of its own—but then few of us today need to be convinced of that. We have read our Freud, and we have also read our James, and we've learned to take pleasure in following the logic of a character's ever-shifting mood and motivations. Indeed, our whole experience of nineteenth-century fiction, from Austen through George Eliot and beyond, has taught us that there are "few things more exciting than a psychological reason." James knows that Isabel looks both finicky and precipitate, and he asks us not to smile at this American girl, who on receiving an offer from an English peer was inclined to think "she could do better." Not that she has a vision of what that "better" might be. She seems precipitate even to herself, and knows that most women would have accepted Warburton immediately. It even makes her afraid, makes her wonder "Who was she, what was she, that she should hold herself superior?"

And perhaps for the first time in her young life, Isabel lacks an answer, lacks a clear conception of her fate or future happiness. She only knows that this isn't it. Nor is a marriage to Goodwood, though she does believe there's something unfinished between them, an account that must someday be settled. Many readers feel exasperated with Isabel at this point, an exasperation couched in a form that echoes her own question: just who does she think she is? They find her unaccountably arrogant, and yet refusing Lord Warburton does serve to pique our curiosity. We want to know—*she* wants to know—what effect her choice will have. We want to know what such a girl will do for an encore, and agree with her when she tells herself that if she doesn't marry Warburton, then she must do something even greater. Her independence will have to find some more enlightened end. But what?

When Warburton proposes, Isabel recognizes that she has stepped into a scene she has read too many times before. She may not yet understand just what she wants, but she does recognize that this scene's very familiarity stands in itself as a reason to say no. She rejects the plot that other people might write for her, and insists instead that she must be free to choose, free to make her own mistakes. Her choice here may even be the right one, though that doesn't mean it will lead to happiness. For Isabel cannot escape the fate she seems to crave, the fate that waits to test her in the book's 500 remaining pages. Nor can we. However much we may want to live on in that world of green lawns, we have to recognize that James has made a different and less comfortable plot around this particular woman. When after receiving his proposal Isabel asks Lord Warburton for a moment in which to collect her mind, he gives a little sigh and says, "Do you know I am very much afraid of it—of that mind of yours." His words make her blush, and then, with a note in her voice that seems to ask for compassion, she answers. "So am I, my lord!"

7.

AN UNMARRIED MAN

I SABEL ARCHER WAS not the only figure in James's world who needed to explain a reluctance to marry. Her creator found himself in that situation as well, and in the very months he devoted to her story. By the time he finished *The Portrait of a Lady*, James had faced three consequential choices. The first of them was the young man's choice of inaction, his standing aside from the Civil War. The second was his election of a London life, a life abroad. And the third was his decision to remain unmarried, a decision codified in a series of letters he wrote in the fall of 1880, as he worked through the complications of Isabel's own alternatives. Scholars have usually seen those last two decisions in isolation from one another, and in the past they usually concentrated on James's choice of Europe, an interest we can summarize by a glance along the library shelves. *The Pilgrimage of Henry James*, *The Complex Fate*, *The Conquest of London*—these are some representative titles from earlier generations of scholarship. Such critics did not see his expatriation in any single way. Some presented it as a sacrifice and perhaps a mistake, a loss of his American subject and identity. Others saw his cosmopolitan experience as being at one with the modernism of his late work. These positions each have their adherents today, but they are now complicated by an awareness of the novelist's other choice, the one previous eras preferred to elide. Middle-aged bachelors were not rare in James's time. The term wasn't yet a bit of code, and the fact that this one seemed to trail no liaisons behind him allowed our predecessors to present him as wed to the page. They were helped in this by James's own tale of his "obscure hurt," and also by the many spectators in his work, Ralph Touchett included, characters who hold back from an active life. That emphasis suited the still-decorous nature of mid-twentieth-century biography, and it suited too the preferences of the James family, of William's widow and their children, who controlled access to the writer's papers. Oscar Wilde's sex life might be unavoidable, and Flaubert's too. With more reticent subjects much could remain unsaid.

In my prologue I wrote that while we cannot know if James ever acted upon a physical desire, nobody today doubts the shape of his erotic longings. A Venetian travel essay of 1873 speaks of a boy's beauty in terms that James never uses of girls—one urchin has "a smile to make Correggio sigh in his grave. . . . [a] little unlettered Eros of the Adriatic strand." The most powerful moments in his early novel, *Roderick Hudson*, describe the fascination that Roderick's patron Rowland Mallet feels for his protégé, with his attempts to guide and indeed live through the young artist. James's biographer Fred Kaplan argues that the novelist came to a "dim sense" of his own homoerotic desire during his 1875–76 residence in Paris. Yet how dim? He wrote then to his sister that he had developed "a most tender affection" for a new friend, the monied Russian émigré Paul Zhukovsky. "He is much to my taste," James added, "and we have sworn an eternal friendship"—a friendship that nevertheless cooled in ways I'll describe below. Twenty years later he began to fall in love with a series of younger men. The letters he sent them are extravagant not only in their professions of devotion but also in the physicality of their language, their pages of hugs and holding close; and Howells, in an essay left unfinished at his death, referred to them as a "strange exhibition." They confirmed his sense of James's "oddity," an oddity he lacked terms to describe. Still, such "verbal passion," in Kaplan's terms, did not in itself require any physical expression, and the most interesting details remain those of consciousness, the slow dawn of what one had already half-known.

Given that sexual preference, it's crucial to stress that James's decision to remain unmarried was nevertheless a decision, and one that was by no means inevitable. It was a choice, and we can view that choice as inseparable from his decision to live abroad, as different aspects of the same thing. Certainly they were seen that way in his lifetime, albeit in negative form. In 1894, Theodore Roosevelt wrote an essay in which he attacked the "Europeanized" American, whom he defined, with unmistakable reference, as an "undersized . . . man of letters, who flees his country because he . . . cannot play a man's part among men." His private comments were even more brutal, though the two men got on well enough when they shared a table at a White House dinner in 1905. But let me put it in other terms. Don't think of marriage, or of James's apparent lifelong celibacy, or even perhaps of desire. Think rather of the young man's sense that something held fast within him had made him a stranger to much of the world around him. In his 1955 poem "The Importance of Elsewhere," Philip Larkin describes how when living abroad, and lonely, his own oddity had made sense. The different accents around him served to mark out his difference, and paradoxically made him feel welcome. Larkin's peculiarities were those of misanthropy, not sexual identity, but still his lines are relevant. Living elsewhere makes him look merely "separate, not unworkable." The danger lies in going home, where he has no such excuse.

London became James's elsewhere, a place that underwrote his existence. In his fifties he came to believe that loneliness itself was "the deepest thing about one. . . . Deeper about *me,* at any rate," deeper even than his art. But those words were written in the relative isolation of Rye, and written as well to one of the young men in whom he was interested; in this case the journalist Morton Fullerton, a bisexual rake who later became Edith Wharton's lover. During his early years in London, James enjoyed a life full of other people, dining out almost every night and with his weekends spent at house parties that sent him traveling from Scotland to Cornwall and back again. Such a life couldn't supply his every need, but the city was indeed a good place to be a bachelor. Spare men were in demand, and then there was the sociable male world of the clubs—he very quickly became a member of the Reform, and then the Athenaeum. Some people find a kind of license in living abroad; for Christopher Isherwood a few decades later, the Berlin of the Weimar Republic meant boys. But for James it regularized the experience of not having. Living in England separated him from the expectations of his family. It marked him out and objectified his sense of isolation. It normalized his sense of being apart, and he was determined to keep that sustaining sense of difference, noting that though he had become "Londonized" he was not at all Anglicized.

Yet suppose he were to marry? Would he take an English bride, and go even further in giving up his country? Or if he found an American wife, would he not then come home? Such branching questions seem to place him inside one of his own stories, and in his first years abroad James faced a steady run of them. Nor did those questions all come from Quincy Street. In England he was widely viewed as eligible—a man old enough to be steady and yet still willing to dance. In 1878 he wrote to William that another guest at a house party had asked, upon seeing him alone, if "Mrs. James" was fond of London. "Is she? Ask mother." Later that year he added that he believed in marriage almost as much for other people as he didn't believe in it for himself, and announced that he rejoiced in William's marriage "as if it were my own; or rather much more." At other times he joked about his chances. In one letter to his mother he suggested that he might marry a widowed Marchioness—a dowager in her twenties, and pretty—while in another he claimed he had proposed to a woman of eighty, who appeared to think she could do better.

These letters to Quincy Street show us a man at ease with himself. He sees the comedy in other people's assumptions that he must be in want of a wife, and it astonishes us now that they didn't see it too. More than a hundred years later we share the sense of another American abroad, the diplomat E. S. Nadal, who wrote in a 1920 memoir that "of all the men I ever knew [James] was the man whom I could least imagine" as married. Nevertheless, he found himself called upon, in the last months of 1880, to quash the rumor of his own impending wedding. He had thought of going home that fall but canceled his passage under the pressure of work; he now planned to return to America the next year instead, after *The Portrait of a Lady* was finished. But some of his friends "supposed that I put off my journey because I had intentions of marriage here," and there was also talk of a young woman from Bangor. "This last report," as he told his mother, "is a slight mistake."

James's most detailed account of his situation comes in a letter he sent that November to Grace Norton, one written in reply to a letter of her own, now lost; presumably it was part of the great pile of correspondence that he burned at Rye in 1909. She too had heard the rumors, though apparently without crediting them, and James writes to her of his amusement at his world's "generally felt (or expressed) desire" that he should get himself to the altar. But he found it impossible to imagine a conjugal future, though he added that if he were to describe the grounds of his conviction she would think him "dismally theoretic." Isabel too is theoretic, but James's reasons are not his character's. Nor are they so fully developed. One's attitude to marriage, he argues, is a part of one's attitude toward life itself, and if he were to wed, he "should be guilty in my own eyes of an inconsistency—I should pretend to think just a little better of life than I really do." On a first glance that statement looks wise, almost stoic in its elevation, and yet it explains less than it seems to. James doesn't go on to specify the nature of his disenchantment, and instead throws up a distancing barrier of charm. His view of life is sanguine enough, and after all, an "amiable bachelor" has his social uses. Yet I can't quite dismiss his words as a piece of pleasant blinding chatter, and one phrase stops me short. For he adds that his opinion of life, with all its consequences, "doesn't involve any particular injustice to anyone, least of all to myself."

It's always dangerous to draw inferences about a writer's life from his fiction, his fiction from his life. Still, a look at one of James's tales can help us understand the choice he had made, and the possible nature of that injustice. Soon after finishing the *Portrait* he began a series of stories about the lives of writers and artists. Some dealt with the costs of fame, others examined the nature of artistic illusion, and still more probed the relation between life and art, asking how one's actions in one sphere affect one's fortunes in the other. Despite their individual variations, they comprise a unified body of work, and in the history of James's short fiction they fill the years between the international stories of his early career and such late tales of the uncanny as "The Jolly Corner." James may have been suspicious of George Eliot's moralized fables, but he was far from immune to such fables himself, and these middle-period works all have a didactic streak. They draw pictures as a way to explore a set of propositions about art and life and the relation between them, and they have always been taken as parables about James's own work and career. The 1888 "Lesson of the Master" has in particular been read as a tale about his own sense of dedication, for it turns on the advice an older writer gives to a younger one: don't marry, not if you care for your art. And James himself colluded in giving the piece its explanatory force; he did not discourage the younger writers who at the start of the twentieth century began to call him "Master."

For our purposes, however, the most suggestive of these stories is a tale that speaks to its author's sense of a hidden sexual life. Though not necessarily his own; or not only. We will need the details of James's own biography to turn the key of "The Author of 'Beltraffio,'" but its anecdote can be put quickly. The story is told by the American disciple of a writer named Mark Ambient, a novelist whose works preach "the gospel of art . . . a kind of aesthetic war-cry." Yet Ambient's sermon isn't devoted to the quest for formal perfection alone, for he also wants his books to have all the impudence of life itself, and a part of that is the willingness to shock. His models are classical, not Christian, and if his settings are modern, they are also Italian; his pages burn always with the hard gem of Mediterranean sensations. James's narrator soon learns that Mrs. Ambient will not even read her husband's work. She thinks it "most objectionable," and she fears in particular the effect that Ambient might have on their little boy, whom they have nicknamed Dolcino. She tries to keep the child from his father, and calls him away whenever the novelist wants to hold or play with him. Then two things happen. Dolcino grows feverish, and the narrator persuades Mrs. Ambient to read the proofs of her husband's new book. She takes the pages into the sickroom, and then locks the door behind her. For she is so shocked by what she reads that she decides it's better to let the boy die than to be exposed to his father's corrupting force.

James developed his plan for the story in a notebook entry for March 26, 1884, an entry that not only sketches the tale in its entirety, but also provides the bit of fact from which it grew. He got the idea from the critic Edmund Gosse, a new friend but already a confidant. Gosse was a taste-maker who would help bring Ibsen's work to an English audience, and is today best known as the author of *Father and Son* (1907), a book about his break from his father's evangelical beliefs that stands as one of the period's best autobiographies. The anecdote he told James concerned a third writer, a historian of the Italian Renaissance named John Addington Symonds. They had touched on Symonds's aestheticism, and also on his tubercular lungs, which had exiled him to the cold dry air of the Alps. Yet the worst of it, Gosse told him, was that "poor S.'s wife was in no sort of sympathy with what he wrote, disapproving of its tone, thinking his books immoral." Mrs. Symonds did not let a child die, but their friends took the story as a family portrait, and scandalous; and all the more scandalous to those who knew the secret of her disapproval. James himself professed ignorance, and begged Gosse to enlighten him—just what *had* he divined about "the innermost cause of J.A.S.'s discomfort?" Even a postcard would help, he wrote—so long as its wording was "covert." But both that word and the tone of the letter as a whole are so coy that it's hard to believe he did not already know of Symonds's homosexuality.

The terms in which homosexuality was understood changed radically over the course of James's adult life. In 1895 a series of trials ended by send-ing Oscar Wilde to jail on a charge of "gross indecency." The playwright had been at the peak of his success, with *The Importance of Being Earnest* running as the season's great new hit, when he filed a suit for libel against the Marquess of Queensberry, the father of his lover Lord Alfred Doug-las. Queensberry had described him as a "somdomite" [*sic*] and Wilde was unsurprisingly unable to make his case. He was then arrested under a law that made homosexual acts between men illegal. His first criminal trial ended in a hung jury; the second sent him to jail for two years. Those trials are now sometimes taken as the point at which the "homosexual" began to be recognized as a type, a category of person—a category defined by the criminal law. Yet that definition has, paradoxically, proved an important station on the road to our contemporary understanding of homosexuality as an identity, something as central to one's sense of self as one's ethnic inheritance or biological sex; an intermediate stage medicalized the term, viewing it as a psychological disorder. In the early years of James's life, however, homosexuality was seen in terms of practices, not persons: specific actions, in relation to which one might be defined as a "bugger" or a "sodomite." It was understood as a taste, a preference for particular forms of friction, and like all tastes it involved an element of choice. Though *as* a taste it was also a habit, a craving, a vice; perhaps indeed an addiction, like opium or absinthe. The most common adjective in descriptions of such practices was, in fact, "vicious"; use that word and no more need be said.

Tastes can change, however, or be broken; so at least many people in James's period believed, and in 1864 Symonds had married in the hopes that it might change his. It didn't. On his many stays in Venice the historian later enjoyed a long affair with his gondolier, Angelo Fusato, and in recent years he has become an important figure in our developing understanding of Victorian homosexuality. At his death in 1893, Symonds left behind a frank memoir, unpublished until 1984, and two privately printed books. *A Problem in Greek Ethics* (1883) examined same-sex relations in the ancient world that he took as a model, and was circulating from hand to hand in London by the time James wrote "The Author of 'Beltraffio.'" The second book, *A Problem in Modern Ethics* (1891), provided both a rigorous account of current medical knowledge, and a refutation of popular prejudice against what he called "inverts." There were only fifty copies printed, but Gosse had one and James read it almost immediately. He found it impressive, and admired Symonds's bravery. Yet while his sympathy is clear, so too is his sense that he himself would not be joining any "band of the emulous."

So far as we know, James met Symonds just once, during his first year in England, and described him in a letter to William as a "mild cultured man, with the Oxford perfume." The perfume was that of aestheticism and the phrase should have been a giveaway; though not perhaps to William. They were both in Venice in the same spring of 1881—Symonds met Fusato that May—and possibly James heard talk of him then. We do have one letter from the novelist to the historian. James had sent him his own 1882 essay on that city, and in the winter of 1884, just a month before he planned out his story, he wrote in reply to Symonds's (now lost) note of appreciation. He wanted to recognize Symonds's position as one of the few "who love [Venice] as much as I do . . . . for it seemed to me that the victims of a common passion should sometimes exchange a look." The words sound astonishingly blunt. But to hear them that way we have to accept, first, that James knew all, about himself and Symonds too; and second, that he would admit to that knowledge in writing to someone he had met just once. This seems unlikely. James did, however, have a way of shutting his ears to his own double entendres, and one can imagine the bewilderment of the apparently humorless Symonds, a man free of cant and camp alike. There's no record of his reply, and James usually kept his distance from that Oxford perfume, which as the century waned became ever more explicitly linked with homosexuality. He referred to Wilde as an "unclean beast" when they were both in Washington in the winter of 1882, and his later sympathy at the playwright's arrest had a distinct edge. "He was never in the smallest degree interesting to me," he told Gosse, "but this hideous human history has made him so—in a manner." There is in all this a great deal of protective coloration from a man who told his friend Nadal that "a position in society is a legitimate object of ambition."

Let me add one more detail before returning to "The Author of 'Beltraffio.'" In his memoirs Symonds wrote that "being what I am, the great mistake—perhaps the greatest crime of my life, was my marriage." Not that it was entirely a failure. They were happy in their children, and after a time his own sexuality left his wife free of appetites she thought ignoble. Nevertheless, it had been founded on deceit—and he had deceived himself as well as her, for in ignoring the truth of his own passions he had been willing "to accept the second best and to give the second best." It's hard to read those words without recalling something Isabel Archer says about another character near the end of the *Portrait:* "She made a convenience of me." Both her words, and Symonds's own, bring back James's letter to Grace Norton about marriage. He was ever-cautious, he denied himself much, and he knew his world's limits too well to be brave. But he did not commit that particular injustice.

W e never learn just what Mark Ambient's books are like. James gives us no quotations, no plot summaries, no details. There's an obvious dramatic reason for that: how could any novel be so wicked as to make a child's death seem the lesser evil? Better to tantalize us with the thought of what *might* be there, and indeed James teases us in similar ways in almost all of his stories about writers. "The Death of the Lion" concerns a missing manuscript, the eponymous letters of *The Aspern Papers* are burned unread, and every character who figures out "The Figure in the Carpet" dies before revealing its secret. Nor are these puzzles limited to James's stories about artists. He refuses to tell us the source of Chad Newsome's wealth in *The Ambassadors*, doesn't specify the contents of *In the Cage*'s crucial telegram, and never lets us know if the ghosts in *The Turn of the Screw* are really there. Those are the easy examples. More difficult are the tales that depend upon an economy of knowledge, those about the impossibility of ever knowing what happens inside another person. *What was she thinking?*—we've all said those words, whether in outrage, frustration, or bemusement. But really it's the question of James's fiction as a whole. Knowledge in his world remains a scarce resource, and he almost never allows himself the novelist's privilege of shuttling from mind to mind. Even in the third person he restricts himself to the point of view of a single character, a figure who understands as little about the other characters' inner lives as we do of our neighbors'.

The French critic Tzvetan Todorov has suggested that such lacunae are themselves the figure in James's own carpet, that his stories are "always based on the *quest for an absolute and absent cause.*" They depend on the unspoken. In "The Beast in the Jungle," John Marcher's life-determining secret is the simple fact that he has one. It is there, and yet not, has shape but no substance. We call such haunting things "uncanny," a term that Freud defines as the "name for everything that ought to have remained . . . hidden but has come to light." Except with James that light throws shadows, a chiaroscuro in which one's hurt remains obscure, in which secrets are sensed but not shown. In "The Private Life" he imagines a great writer with a literally divided self, a man with two bodies. One of them goes about in public, he dines and talks and is merry. The other stays in his room—where he works. Only in the late "Jolly Corner" does the hidden step into sight, when Spencer Brydon finds himself staring at a ghostly figure who seems to be his own disfigured double, a figure at once like him and unlike, the same and yet different. Such a persistent pattern of the imagination runs deep, so deep that we should hesitate in giving it a name. Still, I think we must—must define it as James's sense of his own buried life, though even then I would pause before limiting it either to or by the word "closet."

That term does, admittedly, work for "The Author of 'Beltraffio,'" a story that seems itself in the closet—the story, and not just its subject. The stakes for which its characters play go beyond the morality of books alone, and their urgency appears inexplicable in terms of the tale itself. Its absent cause isn't Ambient's work but rather Symonds's own sexuality, and the story's power depends upon its reticence, upon its inability to step forth and speak, to tell us what it means. I do not, however, think that we can extend this sense of the closet to James's work as a whole, to say that in all cases its absent cause has that same narrow referent. Or at least not only. In postwar America John Cheever's closeted bisexuality allowed him, in stories like "The Swimmer" and "The Housebreaker of Shady Hill" to analyze the masks and deceptions of suburban life, to see its full measure of sorrow, and yet without making that sexuality in itself his subject. It pierced a window; it was not what he saw in looking through it. So too with Henry James. His own renunciations and solitude allowed him to understand the renunciations of others. It allowed him to portray the mix of anguish and rueful acceptance with which Ralph Touchett regards his invalid's fate. But they are not, or not always, the same thing.

In 1907, James hired a boyishly handsome young woman named Theodora Bosanquet as his typist. She came from a sprawling cultivated family, with links to the Darwins, and was herself a graduate of University College, London. She had also been reading James since her teens, and when the position came open, she abandoned a more remunerative career as an indexer and learned to take dictation; she stayed with him until his death in 1916. In Rye she found rooms near Lamb House but moved back to London during the winter months that James himself spent in town. Probably she knew him as well in his final years as anyone, and indeed she found him his last London home, around the corner from the Chelsea flat that she shared with another young woman. She never married and after James's death worked in war-related ministries, for which she received an MBE; later she wrote a book about the French poet Paul Valéry and was an editor at the progressive weekly *Time and Tide*. Yet she is best remembered for an elegant pamphlet, published by Virginia Woolf at the Hogarth Press, called *Henry James at Work*.

That 1924 essay provides an indispensable account of his methods and character, and in it she notes that though James "loved his friends . . . he was condemned by the law of his being to keep clear of any really entangling net of human affection and exaction." James was lonely, he wanted company and affection, wanted to open his arms wide and then fold them tight, and yet by the time he began to fall for younger men, his habits were so fixed that he could not have changed them if he wished. The first of them, in 1899, was the sculptor Hendrik Andersen. James met him in Rome and tried to advise him on his career, much as Rowland Mallet had done with the eponymous Roderick Hudson. He commissioned work from him, talked him up, wrote often, and invited him repeatedly to Lamb House; Andersen in turn hoped that James might provide some financial support for his own dream of a utopian community. Later there was, as I've said, the caddish

Morton Fullerton, and an astonishingly handsome Anglo-Irishman called Jocelyn Persse; well connected and with an acquiline nose but entirely unintellectual, Persse later said he could never understand why James liked him. The last of them was the popular novelist Hugh Walpole, who years after claimed that he once offered himself to his mentor. But though James may have addressed him in letters as "darlingest Hugh!" he was also reported to have backed away, saying "I can't! I can't!" Another friend, a shrewd French scholar named Urbain Mengin, speculated that James would have had "a horror of the physical act." His very way of grasping another man's arm suggested that "he wasn't capable of this kind of surrender . . . he would never have done this if these gestures had, for him, the slightest suggestion of a pursuit of physical love."

James's life is as massively documented as that of any American writer, but still we find gaps—and have no way to tell if they are in the documents or in the life itself. The biographer Sheldon Novick has claimed that in 1865 James had a brief affair with Oliver Wendell Holmes, Jr. But his argument depends upon a French phrase that James scribbled in his notebooks forty years later, and Novick's interpretation seems, by any standards of evidence, uncertain. James speaks there of "*L'initiation première*," but the initiation to which he refers is very clearly his entry into the life of letters. The phrase belongs to his memories of the Cambridge in which his career began, of the Norton family and the poet James Russell Lowell and of hearing Dickens read on his American tour of 1867. He only mentions Holmes some sentences later, and in a very different context, describing his envy on learning that his friend had left for England. Still, James did sometimes ask for news of the future jurist with a mix of avidity and asperity that he didn't show in writing of others. Novick's argument is unconvincing, but I wouldn't rule out some one-sided and perhaps half-understood attachment. Nor would I insist upon it.

In a 1913 letter to Walpole, James wrote that he didn't "regret a single 'excess' of my responsive youth—I only regret, in my chilled age, certain occasions and possibilities I didn't *embrace*." That language tells us little, however, about either the number or the nature of those excesses, and the scare quotes imply that nothing he did can quite rise to the emphasis of the sentence's last word. Other young men on a European tour found that the Continent offered them the chance for a safely anonymous sexual life; Symonds knew that his gondolier had been kept by other men before him. James would have had such opportunities, but we will never learn if he took them. Yet we do know that he was no prude, however discreet and however abstemious. His fiction hangs upon sexual themes—sexual and not romantic—to a degree unusual for Anglo-American writers of his period. Both *The Golden Bowl* (1904) and *What Maisie Knew* (1897) depend upon adultery. The former describes Maggie Verver's growing awareness of her husband's affair with her own best friend; in the latter, a child of divorce serves as the conduit for a liaison between her stepparents. And *The Awkward Age* (1899) is just one of his many accounts of sexual education: of what, and at what age, one can both know and admit that one knows.

James thought that English writers were often squeamish, the men in particular, and praised the Neapolitan realist Matilde Serao for her frank acknowledgment of physical passion. If he found Zola's concentration on appetite too narrow, he also admired him, and viewed the descriptions of prostitution and lesbianism in *Nana* as both filthy and fascinating in equal measure. In Paris he listened without apparent embarassment to the conversation in Flaubert's circle of disciples and enjoyed shocking Howells by repeating some of it. These are issues to which I'll return. Still, about some parts of his own life we must accept a sense of bafflement. He has never been convincingly linked to another person, and his precise mixture of self-knowledge and self-control, of repression and sublimation, remains a formula that we do not know.

Nevertheless, there is one moment in Gosse's 1922 volume of literary memoirs that tantalizes us with a glimpse of something more. Most of James's friends, Gosse wrote, "supposed that he was mainly a creature of observation and fancy," whose senses remained untouched by the life around him. But he sometimes allowed the doors to open, and on a visit to Rye, as they walked in the garden amid the deepening twilight, Gosse suddenly found himself listening to a story. His host told him, "in profuse and enigmatic language," that he had once stood at dusk on a city street, watching "for the lighting of a lamp in a window on the third storey. And the lamp blazed out, and through bursting tears he strained to see what was behind it, the unapproachable face." James had stayed there for hours, wet from the rain and repeatedly jostled by the hurrying crowd, "and never from behind the lamp was for one moment visible the face." The story ended, and from James's voice Gosse knew that he could ask no questions about it. But for a long time the novelist stood there in silence beside him.

That is all. There is no date, no city specified, no name to that face. The mix of rain and romance will make many readers link it to Paris, but we have no real warrant for doing so. Maybe we think of Paris because of the moment in *The Ambassadors* when Lambert Strether looks up at the window of Chad Newsome's flat, or because Gosse's description corresponds so neatly to the Parisian ending of *The Age of Innocence;* so neatly, in fact, that it makes me wonder if Edith Wharton might have heard the story as well. The most provocative account of this moment belongs to the Irish novelist Colm Tóibín in *The Master*, his superb 2004 fictional account of James's life. Toibin both places that window in Paris and gives its hidden face a name: that of the Russian Paul Zhukovsky. No biographer would take that liberty, and yet the suggestion strikes me as plausible. James first met him in the spring of 1876. Russian émigré society was easy to penetrate, and he found it an "oasis . . . in the midst of this Parisian Babylon." But no one in it drew him as did the rich and elegantly bearded Zhukovsky. He was an amateur painter who had grown up in the Russian imperial court, and his family was close to Turgenev; indeed the acquaintance began with James pumping him for stories about the older writer. The American's letters that spring are full of him. To Quincy Street he wrote that they had sworn an everlasting friendship, and though James suspected his friend was weak, he still found him "sweet and *distingué.*" He was fascinated by Zhukovsky's tales of his months in Venice, but in writing home made sure to insist on his friend's "extreme purity of life," even if that life had been too picturesque to have "formed a positive character for him."

James was smitten enough to make excuses for what he himself saw as Zhukovsky's limitations. The Russian was darkly sensuous and quite clearly homosexual; if ever the young writer was tempted to go beyond the conventional terms of romantic friendship, it was now. That summer, however, Zhukovsky went down to Bayreuth for the opening of Richard Wagner's new Festspielhaus, where the first full production of the *Ring* cycle had its premiere that August. And when the two men met again that fall, something had changed. Zhukovsky now had a new passion, and that November James wrote to his father of a "musical séance" at his friend's apartment, in which he sat from nine until two listening to Wagner transcriptions for piano. James never had much feeling for music, and though he recognized the pianist's talent, he also found himself bored. In that same letter he reiterated a decision he had announced in an earlier note to Quincy Street. He now planned, as we will see in my next chapter, to make his home in London; and later that month he wrote that though Zhukovsky remained charming he was also "a lightweight and a perfect failure."

Maybe this was when James stood one night in that street, watching for that face, and yet knowing that even if he were to see it—even if he could overcome his own reticence and fear enough to come in, come out, of the rain—there would remain a gulf between them. It wasn't just Wagner. It was James's own sense of ambition and purpose. He admired Turgenev and yet soon outgrew the need to sit at his feet; Zhukovsky, in contrast, seemed to him but a dilettante and content to be a disciple. There was no break. James saw him for a few weeks in Paris the next year, and when in 1879 Zhukovsky took a villa at Posillipo on the Bay of Naples, he invited James for a visit. The novelist didn't go to Italy that year but the next spring he went to Florence to begin his work on *The Portrait of a Lady*, and then continued on south to spend a few days with his "peculiar" friend before settling down to his desk. Yet James cut his visit short. Wagner had rented a villa nearby, and took up most of Zhukovsky's time, so that the Russian seemed to be perpetually shuttling from house to house. And there was also his Neapolitan servant, Pepino—in Cosima Wagner's words, a "sturdy, thickset, simple" fellow, whom Zhukovsky had "rescued . . . from the gutter." Pepino had a good voice and the composer enjoyed singing duets with him, but his services weren't limited to waiting at table, and when after two years Zhukovsky finally dismissed him, the Wagners sent him a note of congratulations.

James could no longer insist upon his friend's purity, and in fact wrote to Grace Norton that the mores of Zhukovsky's new world were as "opposed to those of Cambridge as anything could well be—but to describe them would carry me too far." He added that he had declined an invitation to meet the composer, "as I speak no intelligible German and he speaks nothing else." James's sense of the intelligible was high; for the purposes of reading, at least, his German had once approached fluency. To his sister he wrote more frankly. Naples had a "vileness" that took the edge off the beauty of her surroundings, Zhukovsky was a "ridiculous mixture of Nihilism and *bric a brac*," and he himself had recoiled from the "fantastic immoralities" of the people around him. Both Naples and Bayreuth were bywords for license, and Kaplan suggests that James was appalled by the mix of homosexuality and adultery that characterized Wagner's circle. There is, admittedly, a difference between hearing about other people's liaisons and seeing them enacted before you, and even a Henry James who *wasn't* celibate would always have preferred discretion to display. Still, I think James's biographers have overplayed the degree of his shock. He may have objected to Zhukovsky's choice of a lover, but professing his moral revulsion was a useful strategy in writing to Quincy Street; and especially useful for someone insisting that he would never marry. James was on the brink of fame. He left that villa because it was the place in which he could least afford to be seen; perhaps the place in which he could least afford to see himself.

In Boston during the winter of 1881–82 James set down an account of his career to date. Composed with the new sense of mastery that the just-completed *Portrait of a Lady* had given him, this "American Journal" offers a mine of circumstantial details, defining the places he had visited, the people he had known, and what he had written where. It is in many ways more useful than his later memoirs: his clearest statement, in language at once colloquial and elevated, of his ambitions and dreams, of the myth he would make from his choice of the Old World. In summoning up the spring of 1876 he recalled his first meeting with Zhukovsky and then wrote this sentence: "*Non ragioniam di lui—ma guarda e passa.*" It is a line from the *Inferno*, with Dante's plural adjusted to the singular, and the sentence stands as a pained memory and warning alike: "Let's not talk about him— just look and move on." Zhukovsky himself would move ever deeper into Wagner's world and find there the sense of purpose that James thought he lacked. He did the production design for the 1882 premiere of *Parsifal* at Bayreuth, modeling the Grail Hall on the interior of Siena's Duomo, and his sets were still being used in the 1930s. And James traveled on as well, back to Florence and his room at the Hôtel de l'Arno, back to the opening pages of what would become a great novel. There was new work and new friends. In the letter to Alice in which he wrote of Posillipo's immorality, he also spoke of meeting an American writer named Constance Fenimore Woolson, an admirer who had brought him a letter of introduction from one of his many cousins. His relations with her in the years to come would be entirely different from those with Zhukovsky, and even more consequential.

8.

A LONDON LIFE

THE MUSIC HAD bored him, the pianist's fingers shimmering their way through hour after hour of the *Ring* cycle, and that boredom set him off from the other people gathered in Paul Zhukovsky's drawing room. He didn't share their enthusiasms, he wasn't one of them, and perhaps his awareness of the gap between them extended to his sense of Paris itself. In the fall of 1876, James had reached another moment of decision. A year before, he had left America behind, had made his choice of a European life, and appeared to fix himself in France. Now Paris too had begun to seem unworkable. In later years his decision to quit the City of Light for the "murky metropolis" of London would come to have the look of a plan, as if he had simply needed a bit of finishing before settling down in the English capital. Yet though James would indeed write that he had wanted London all along, "and Paris was only a stopgap," his decision was more sudden, and more contingent, than his words suggest.

That July he had left Paris for the summer, traveling at first to Étretat on the Normandy coast. The town had once been a fishing village but had now found a second life as a resort, its visitors drawn by the high white cliffs and natural arches that flanked its little bay. Courbet had already painted them, and in the next decade Monet would make them into icons. James then went south to Biarritz, and crossed briefly into Spain on his first and only visit; he went to a bullfight, and of course turned the experience into an article, telling his readers that "if I sometimes shuddered, I never yawned."

Before leaving Paris, however, he had thought to economize by giving up his apartment just off the rue de Rivoli. He hoped to get it back in the fall, but somebody else had taken it in the meantime, and he soon suffered another blow as well. Since arriving in France he had written a biweekly column for the *New York Tribune* and counted on it to cover half his rent. The best of those pieces on French life still bear reading today, but they weren't gossipy enough to satisfy his editor, and when James asked for a raise, the paper let him go.

His friendship with Zhukovsky wasn't now enough to hold him, and he also felt caught between two different kinds of provinciality. The society of the city's American colony seemed tiresome, and as for the writers he knew? Turgenev excepted, they were the creatures of quarrels he didn't share, of schools and groups and politics in which he remained an outsider. The full tale of his relations with them, with Zola and Flaubert among others, must wait until this book's fourth part, when I'll turn to what James learned from his reading of French fiction. But in 1876 he wrote that "I don't like their wares, and they don't like any others." He thought them parochial, virtually ignorant of anything that wasn't France. Not reading Henry James might still be excusable; not reading George Eliot wasn't.

It would, he thought, be ignoble to remain for the restaurants alone, but really there was nothing else to stay for. He wrote to his father that in imaginative terms Paris had ceased to pay—the language of mental investment was a constant in his letters to Quincy Street—but when he told William that he was thinking of moving to London, he also enjoined him to "*say nothing about it until I decide*" [italics in original]. He must have feared looking irresolute, someone to whom France was as unworkable as New York had been just the year before. James announced the move to Howells in the same letter in which he first mentioned his plans to write about an *Americana*, and he crossed the Channel on December 10. It was a choice he never regretted.

Within two days he had found the serviced flat in Bolton Street, just yards from Piccadilly, where he would live for the next decade. James was careful with money. He could draw on his father's letter-of-credit, but he knew his siblings had cut into the family's capital, and he now did without his parents' help. London's prices seemed a bargain after Paris, though at two and a half guineas a week—a bit more than twelve dollars—his apartment can't be called cheap. He was paying over fifty shillings at a time when many skilled workmen had a weekly wage of just thirty, and twenty years later he took Lamb House for little more than half of what his few rooms had cost. On the other hand, he could afford it: his income for 1876, almost all of it from magazine sales, has been estimated at a bit under $2,800. Moreover the place came furnished, and with breakfast provided; he had no need for a servant of his own.

From one window he could see a narrow wedge of the then-almost-treeless Green Park, and in the entire city there were few more convenient addresses for a man of James's habits. To the north Bolton Street opened after a block into the land of hostesses and dinner parties, into Mayfair and the more bourgeois quarter of Marylebone beyond it. To the south he had the shops of Piccadilly, some of them surviving still, like the epicurean grocer Fortnum & Mason; off it ran the more exclusive Bond Street, with its galleries and goldsmiths. A further walk along Piccadilly carried him past the Royal Academy, at whose annual exhibitions he soon became a regular, and then on toward the National Gallery and the theaters of London's West End. Crossing it from Bolton Street took him by the site of the present-day Ritz and into the gentlemen's world of the clubs in Pall Mall.

Not that that world was yet his. In later years James would have more invitations than he could accept, but he spent his first Christmas in London alone and wrote to reassure his mother that his spirits were high. The weather was "beyond expression vile—a drizzle of sleet upon a background of absolutely *glutinous* fog," but his fire was warm and he delighted in his new subscription to Mudie's, England's largest commercial lending library, from which he could for a nominal sum borrow as many novels as he wished. Though he would not need Mudie's for long. None of his work had yet appeared in Britain, and while he had many acquaintances there, he had as yet no friends. But within two months he would write to his father from the library of the Athenaeum. It was London's most distinguished club—

a fat archbishop was reading in a nearby chair—and frankly intellectual. Nobody got in on birth alone, but James had already become a temporary member, and in 1882, with *The Portrait of a Lady* behind him, he became a permanent one.

In 1948 the critic Lionel Trilling wrote an introduction to James's 1886 *The Princess Casamassima* in which he argued that many nineteenth-century novels work by tracing the career of the "Young Man from the Provinces," an *ingénu* who is both enthralled and disillusioned by the great capital whose life he seeks to enter. Most of Trilling's examples are French—Balzac's *Père Goriot*, Stendhal's *The Red and the Black*—but he also cites both *Great Expectations* and James's own novel. Despite its title, the protagonist of *The Princess Casamassima* is a London bookbinder named Hyacinth Robinson, the illegitimate son of a woman who has murdered her aristocratic seducer. He stands as a provincial in social though not geographic terms and joins an anarchist cell whose leader charges him to commit a political crime. It's unlikely material for James, however brilliantly handled, and yet despite the advantages of his own upbringing, he too had once been such a young man himself. America might have given him an excellent preparation for culture, but it was a preparation only; and like Hyacinth, he soon found himself in thrall to the glitter and charm of his new world.

It's not my purpose here to chronicle James's progress through London life. He later claimed he could barely remember how he "came to know people, to dine out. . . it came rather of itself." He knew some Americans in London and had letters of introduction from others, Henry Adams included. He paid a call and it led to a dinner, and then one meal began to roll into another. His manners were impeccable, but he still seemed a breath of fresh American air; he was the new thing and yet not a juvenile lead, a man who had come upon the city full-grown. The *Atlantic* had many English readers, and James also had a backlist of stories and novels that had never appeared in Britain. He published two books in London in 1878, both of them with Macmillan, who became his regular publisher, and the next year he brought out six more. His name was suddenly everywhere, and once *Daisy Miller* made him famous, the invitations arrived from people he didn't even know; during the winter of 1878–79 he dined out 107 times. Those invitations all came from what he would call the "better sort," but that category is a loose one, and what strikes us today is their heterogeneity. Some of them were literary, but he also sat down with generals and lawyers and bankers. One evening found him "conversing affably" with the former—and future—prime minister, William Ewart Gladstone, a flinty mutton-chopped Liberal whose political life still left him the energy to write about Homer and theology alike. And James made a specialty of old ladies with long memories. His favorite was the great actress Fanny Kemble. She had starred at Covent Garden fifty years before and, after marrying and divorcing an American slaveholder, had become a voice of Abolition; she gave him the plots of several stories, *Washington Square* among them.

In his "American Journal" of 1882–82, James described his new home as neither "agreeable, or cheerful, or easy. . . . It is only magnificent." He drew up a list of the reasons why London should seem awful, beginning with the fog and the smoke and moving on to the city's brutal inhuman size. He felt all the ways in which it was both "vulgar at heart and tiresome in form," all the ways in which it was so entirely unlike Paris, but still it seemed to him "the most possible form of life"; most possibly precisely because of what made it so difficult, because there was simply more of it. He never lost his sense of excited fascination with his adopted city, and one of the last books he planned, though he didn't get beyond a few notes, was a volume called "London Town." Every corner appeared to have its bit of story, and to walk in London was to walk through time, to sense the arresting hand of the past on one's sleeve. So in an 1888 essay he remembered moving down Fleet Street with some lines of Thackeray in his head and his eyes full of scenes almost two centuries gone, as though the time of Queen Anne had come alive and he himself were part of it.

James especially liked to evoke the city of Dickens, the city only then just gone, and in time his successors would recall the London of Henry

James, a city on the brink of modernity, with the men in black and the women as if dressed by Sargent. We can see that London in some of the frontispieces to the New York Edition. The one to *The Golden Bowl* shows a hansom cab, in sharp-edged silhouette, wheeling through the fog along an almost empty Portland Place, the street wide and the buildings grand, and with an automobile shadowy in the distance. But James did not live in a disembodied Jamesian world; look closely and you'll see that the street is muddy and spotted with manure.

"You can do low life," wrote Robert Louis Stevenson, with some surprise, as *The Princess Casamassima* began its *Atlantic* serialization; the novel opens in Millbank Prison, where the young Hyacinth Robinson has gone to see his mother. Stevenson admired the book's sense of grime, and James had visited the prison himself to work up its details. Nor should this surprise us. Grime was unavoidable, and James walked with his eyes open to a city in which many of the poor bore on their face "the traces . . . of alchoholic action." If he did not penetrate to the worst of its slums, he was entirely familiar with its miles of dreariness. He knew how much of London had to be left out by anyone who wanted to draw a genial picture; knew that the stark glare of a corner gin shop could make the city seem even more brutal than darkness itself. He could describe the smell of close-packed bodies, and an article in *The Nation* allowed him to play sportswriter in a report on the annual Oxford-Cambridge boat race, standing on a bridge over the Thames amid "the dingy, British mob, with coal-smoke ground into its pores," and waiting for the eights to flash by.

James learned his London by writing about it, and throughout the spring and summer of 1877 he sent a string of travel articles back to America, making copy out of a walk through Green Park or a visit to Westminster Abbey. He turned some of his first country visits into pieces for popular magazines, bringing his readers into a house built upon the ruins of an abbey, a place with a ghost where a Gothic past and "modern conversation . . . have melted together." The English didn't notice such apparent anomalies, but James could not yet take them for granted, and in this he was more like Henrietta Stackpole than we usually recognize. In fact, he showed in those early years what now appears a surprising journalistic range. Books and travel, pictures and theater: that much is familiar to us, and yet James also wrote about the stinginess of the British taxpayer and even about the imperial politics that in the later 1870s brought the country into brief though bloody wars in Afghanistan and southern Africa. In *Henry James at Work*, Theodora Bosanquet noted that the world of "cabinets and parties and politics . . . remained outside the pale of his sensibility." But that absence of interest had to be learned, and in writing to Quincy Street this new Londoner was often astute in his reading of the world's headlines. In that sense, at least, his success would prove narrowing.

P erhaps that process had begun by the time James set to work on *The Portrait of a Lady*, for his letters make no reference to that spring's general election, a Liberal victory that put Gladstone back in Downing Street. He had six weeks of steady work in the wet Florentine spring, yet he still found himself asking Howells to put off the start of the novel's *Atlantic* run. The first installment was scheduled for August, yet now James wanted to bump it back to October. Italy had been "insidious, perfidious, fertile in pretexts" for doing anything but work. What he didn't say was that his visit to Zhukovsky had made him fall behind. But James was as expert as ever in rationalizing the delay. *Washington Square* would now complete most of its own serialization before the new book began to appear; he wouldn't be competing with himself. Moreover it would give him the chance "to get forward a good deal," a running start that would allow him to give this big novel the care he thought it would need.

He got back to England at the beginning of June and had at once to prepare for a visit from his brother William. Harvard's assistant professor of physiology planned to divide his summer between England and the Alps, and had left his wife and infant son in Cambridge as soon as his classes were over. James put him in the flat beneath his own, and immediately wrote to Quincy Street with a report on his health, noting that William still took "himself . . . too hard and too consciously." It was the first time they had seen each other since Henry's emigration five years before, and William's reaction to his brother's life provides a measure of just how far the novelist had come. The two of them often breakfasted together, and sometimes dined at the Reform Club in a comfort that William described as a "tremendous material bribe." Most of their days they spent apart, with the younger of them at work and the older mixing tourism with a series of professional calls. So William took himself to the National Gallery, where he found the Turners baffling, and dined with the Adamses, at whose table the talk was of *Daisy Miller* and another guest at first mistook him for Henry. He met Robert Browning at a reception, but couldn't get the poet to talk to him; Henry had no such difficulty.

William found England expensive and thought that if Henry weren't covering his lodging he would have had to run off to somewhere cheaper. In time his own books would pay him handsomely, but the profitable *Principles of Psychology* was still a decade off, and for now Henry's earnings far outstripped his brother's salary. Indeed, William's letters to Cambridge suggest a mixture of surprise and pique at his "inscrutable" sibling's worldly success. The younger man seemed utterly at home, and his very ease made William realize that his expatriation would be permanent. Yet the philosopher was also surprised by how busy he kept himself with "dinners and parties . . . especially as he was all the time cursing them for so frustrating his work." It was his old criticism once more, but envy gave it a new edge. Henry was superficial, preferring a glancing contact with many things to a "deeper one at a few points," and William thought it would only get worse with age.

About one thing William was right. Henry did complain about the pressures of social life, and especially about all the "transitory Americans" who insisted upon seeing him. Distant cousins, the friends of friends—they all left their cards and hoped for an attention that he had "neither time nor means to show them." All he cared about was the book on his desk. He resented anything that pulled him away from it, and that included Quincy Street itself. On 20 July he wrote to his parents that he would have to put off the visit to America on which they had begun to count. He *wanted* to go home, he told them—have no doubt about that. But he wouldn't sail with the *Portrait* only half-done and could not envision working in Cambridge under the schedule to which serialization would keep him. That same day he sent the book's first pages to Howells and apologized for the lateness of his copy. He sometimes suffered from crippling headaches when he had to deal with family questions, and he had just spent three days in bed, unable to hold a pen.

The 48 pages he mailed to Boston included the novel's opening serial installment and much of the second, and James promised the rest of it and "the whole of the third" within a few days, chapters that would take Isabel up past Warburton's proposal. They had been put in type by his British publisher, Macmillan, who both serialized the novel in its eponymous magazine and published its three-volume version; in America the book appeared in a single volume from Houghton, Mifflin. Macmillan pulled two sets of proofs for James to correct, with the second one crossing the ocean to Howells. That initial installment was a long one—it contained the book's first five chapters—and James thought that the later pieces might be shorter. Yet when he sent the fourth part in September, he noted that every part would be long, and the novel he had originally planned in eight installments was starting to look as though it would run for twelve; in the end, it took fourteen. The book was growing. Isabel's "many developments" were taking their space and time, and though he knew how it all would end, the road to that ending did indeed have its unexpected dips and turns. In later years he sometimes found, and inevitably to his surprise, that a story he had projected at 5,000 words seemed barely finished in twelve.

All that summer and fall he worked in a way he described as "*tant bien que mal.*" He spent most of his time in town, though he did go to Brighton for a few days in August; he enjoyed the breeze after the stilled air of London, but then had to flee the glare of the sun. In early autumn he wrote to his sister that though he felt homesick "for a sniff of an American October," he was nevertheless happy to be alone in London. The city still seemed to him empty, he had few dinners to attend, and "unadulterated leisure to work." The phrasing is interesting—the work of writing was a form of luxury, but an evening out was simply work itself. One distraction he did allow himself was a visit at the end of November to the Bedfordshire house of Lord Rosebery, a future prime minister who had married a Rothschild but wore his millions "with such tact and bonhomie, that you almost forgive him." Though James was becoming blasé, or at least enjoyed pretending he was. His invitations may have been smarter than ever, but he told Quincy Street that the party included "no one very important"—just a former viceroy of India and the great House of Commons orator John Bright.

And each day the *Portrait* grew, grew "steadily, but very slowly." The opening chapters came out in the October issue of *Macmillan's Magazine*, published on the first of that month; two weeks later they appeared in the November *Atlantic*. He sent Howells the fifth installment on November 11, pages that would run that February; by that time he presumably had the sixth part ready to be set, and a seventh under way. He does not appear to have struggled with a single deadline, and wrote to Alice of his pleasure in the success that had made it possible for him to take his time, to work deliberately and without haste. James usually had—he needed to have— several pieces on his desk at once, writing stories and essays alongside his novels. But now he kept the magazines waiting. *The Nation* and the *Cornhill*, *Scribner's*, and the *North American Review*—they all had to do without him. During the year and more that he spent on *The Portrait of a Lady*, Henry James wrote nothing else except a single piece on the London theater, working throughout with a single-mindedness he had never known before and would never have again.

9.

THE ENVELOPE OF CIRCUMSTANCES

O VER 10,000 LETTERS by Henry James survive today in libraries and private collections. Thousands more have been lost. Some of those were bread-and-butter notes or two-line responses to invitations, but others were likely as playful and newsy and wise as any now extant, letters thrown away upon receipt, left behind in a hotel room, or even burned as the older James asked his friends to do. Only a fraction of the surviving ones have been published, and though a complete edition is now under way, it will be many years before the full record is in print. Still, one thing seems clear: in all those many thousands of pages James rarely says anything substantive about his work. He might discuss its financial details with his father, or warn a friend against reading something in a magazine, telling her to wait for the book instead. He eventually warned William against reading him at all, so little was the pragmatist in sympathy with his late style. To publishers he sometimes sketched out a proposed work, but most of his letters to them remained pure business. Nor did he seek a reading from other writers, however much they might want—and fear—one from him.

His exchange with Howells provides a partial exception to all this, and in December 1880 he wrote the editor that his "strictures on [the *Portrait*] seem . . . well-founded." Howells thought Isabel overanalyzed and Henrietta overdrawn, and while James believed that the journalist was less of a caricature than she appeared, he also admitted that most American readers wouldn't see it that way. The problem with Isabel was more complicated.

He had drawn her at full length before he had made her do anything, and now could only offer a note of reassurance, writing that after the opening chapters she wouldn't "turn herself inside out quite so much." That was a partial truth, and late in the novel Isabel would pull herself to pieces once more. Still, that lay months in the future, and much of the intervening drama is conducted in dialogue.

James could write Mozartean ensembles of three or more characters all talking together, voices that remain clear and distinct even as they step upon one another's lines. But most of this novel's crucial scenes are two-handers. Isabel goes up to London soon after she rejects Lord Warburton, taking rooms with Henrietta at a Picadilly hotel, while Ralph, their nominal protector, camps out at his father's unused London house. And on her last day in the capital, she is made to suffer through three chapters of strenuous talk, in which she doesn't turn herself inside out so much as watch other people do it for her. First comes Ralph, who knows about Warburton's proposal and wants to learn her reasons for refusing him. Not that he's sorry. Her marriage would have finished off the story, but now he can have the same thing that we do: the pleasure of the next installment, the "entertainment of seeing what a young lady does who won't marry Lord Warburton." Watching Isabel has become his compensation for a spectator's life, but Ralph also takes a curious satisfaction in characterizing the terms of her actions and tells her that she exacts a great deal from other people simply by seeming to ask so little of them. She withholds herself, she refuses to take what the world offers; and by this he means something more than just Warburton's hand. She worries too much about "whether this or that is good for you," but the truth is that she thinks nothing in the world too perfect for her, and the corollary is that this bird of paradox will refuse to take anything less.

That evening she hears a knock at her door, and the hotel's servant shows in the stern-jawed Caspar Goodwood. Isabel doesn't expect him—she hasn't even answered his letter, and his visit is made with Henrietta's connivance. He knows he displeases her, and yet upbraids her as a way of pleading his cause; his very presence seems a form of assault. Nevertheless, he remains a part of her past and the "stubbornest fact she knows," a fact that requires an answer. So Isabel puts into speech everything she has told herself in justifying her rejection of Warburton, and ends by saying, with self-conscious grandeur, that if he ever hears a rumor of her marriage, "remember what I have told you . . . and venture to doubt it." She is agitated, and exhilarated, and once alone she drops to her knees as if in prayer. For Isabel has a sense of victory. James writes in his opening pages that her love of liberty is as yet almost entirely theoretical, but she has now tested it twice by saying no, and the pleasure Isabel takes from it is every bit as important as the end it gains for her. "She had done what she preferred," and when Henrietta returns, the two of them quarrel.

"You are drifting to some great mistake," the reporter tells her, and many of the things Isabel's friends say in these chapters will echo throughout, an encircling web of voices, of partial views that overlap enough to make us question her own sense of herself. For Isabel is all too liable to trip over her own imagination, a young woman who has no sense of what her freedom might be *for*. She knows what she doesn't want, not what she does, and has no other plot with which to affront what still seems her inevitable destiny. What she does have, though, is both courage and a sense of adventure, and she replies to Henrietta's words about drift by defining her own idea of happiness: "a swift carriage, of a dark night, rattling with four horses over roads that one can't see." Risk and speed and an open road into the unknown: the picture is enticing, even if Henrietta thinks it better suited to "an immoral novel," and in fact it's a close paraphrase of a line from *Madame Bovary*. Yet though Isabel sees herself as making her own life, the image she chooses undercuts her desire. For her language suggests that she herself sits inside that coach—and somebody else holds the reins.

In the morning Ralph has news. His father's health has been precarious for years, and a new attack has put him beyond recovery. Daniel Touchett will linger for weeks, as the autumn defines itself in rain, but he will not get up again. Isabel will take her turn in the Gardencourt sickroom, and so of course does Ralph, who is watching there alone one day when the old man finds the energy to talk. Save your strength, the son says, but Mr. Touchett refuses; "I shall have a long rest. I want to talk about you." The banker wants his son to find a new interest, something to help keep him alive. He should marry—should marry Isabel. And Ralph does admit that "if certain things were different," he would indeed be in love with his cousin. But he is dissembling here, and his father catches him. They have "never prevaricated before," and a deathbed isn't the place to start.

Mr. Touchett will not die on this day, but these pages are the last in which we see him. James would write other memorable deathbed scenes, including one later in this novel, but this was his first. No reader forgets it, and yet our interest changes from one reading to the next. Its point of fascination alters as we do ourselves. These pages know heartbreak, but not that of Mr. Touchett's death per se. What spikes an older reader to his seat is the way that the banker continues to worry about his son. He stays a father still, and attempts to guide and protect his boy even as his own breath fades. He is conscious of all that his son cannot do, and Ralph calls him "Daddy" even yet. He has remained dependent, and says that if his father dies "I shall do nothing but miss you." That, however, is precisely what Mr. Touchett doesn't want, and the two of them reach here beyond the temporizing of ordinary life. They speak as if the barriers that divide one person from another were down, and anything, everything, can be said.

What makes that clarity possible is the Touchetts' focus on this world, and not some possible next one. There are many deathbeds in Victorian fiction, some full of prayer, and others concerned with the dying person's attempt to make the world still feel his weight. Many of them show us characters sunk in fear, and others hit a high note of hope. But I have read no such scene so entirely untroubled by the hereafter as this one; its originality lies in what James feels himself free to leave out. Neither Ralph nor his father speaks of God, and they do not call a clergyman at the last. Isabel learns that Mr. Touchett has died only when she sees the doctor stand in the doorway and slowly draw on his gloves. In his ghost stories James did entertain the sense of some otherworldly life, but the characters in his major novels all live in a secular world. They may go to church as a social duty, though Isabel herself doesn't seem to. (In this she is unlike Minny Temple, who took religious questions seriously and enjoyed listening to the day's popular preachers.) They may go as tourists, as Isabel later will in Rome. But they lack any kind of formal belief, and neither God nor the institution of a church is present here even as something to fight against. That isn't the only reason why the *Spectator* described this novel as marked by the "cloven foot" of agnosticism—but it will do as a start.

Nevertheless, these pages *are* about the future, about money and a will. "I take a great interest in my cousin," Ralph says, though not the kind his father wishes, and he now tells the dying man that he wants "to put a little wind in her sails." Isabel is not a dollar princess, not one of the American heiresses who in the decades after the Civil War went hunting for husbands among the often improvident members of Europe's various aristocracies. The best known is Consuelo Vanderbilt, whose parents in essence sold her to the Duke of Marlborough. James would create such characters in both *The Wings of the Dove* and *The Golden Bowl*, but Isabel's father has spent down his own relatively modest fortune, and she has almost no money of her own. Ralph has thought of a way to change that, however, and as he explains, a "veiled acuteness" steals into his father's face. It is the last business proposition to which he will ever listen. Cut my own inheritance in half, Ralph says. Call it your own idea, let the lawyers think we have argued, and make Isabel rich. Let that money make her free—free to explore the life around her, to reach the limits of her own imagination, free of the need "to marry for a support." The old man has questions; a banker still, he wants to know if it's a good investment. What about the fortune hunters? That is indeed a risk, Ralph answers, a risk small but appreciable, and one he is prepared to take. The reply satisfies his father; whether it satisfies us is a different question.

Still, Mr. Touchett is rock-ribbed enough to suspect that this whole procedure is "immoral"; even an Isabel shouldn't have everything made so easy. But what really makes us pause is another of his judgments. Ralph says that he wants to "see her going before the breeze," and his father answers that he speaks as though it were all for his own amusement. He speaks, in fact, as if he were a novelist himself; as if, in the words of James's preface, Isabel "hovered before him . . . interesting him and appealing to him" by the simple virtue of what and who she is. For Ralph sees his own job as that of creating possibilities for her, piecing together the situations that will show her to the best and most brilliant advantage. The more money in her purse, the more wind in her sails; the faster she will fly, the longer she will take to reach her narrative fulfillment. Hers—and his, and James's own, and ours. For we too want to see what she'll do in these new circumstances. James criticized his contemporaries for dropping fortunes upon their characters in a book's last chapters, as though money were the resolution and reward of action. For him it is action's very cause, and by thrusting fortune upon her in the middle, he has created a new set of conditions against which Isabel might prove herself.

Yet it's one thing for James to do that for us, and another for Ralph to do it to her. A novel may have many ends in mind, but surely entertainment is one of them. What Ralph does, in contrast, is to use Isabel as a means to fulfill his own desires. I put the case strongly, because we need to see the crooked timber of self-interest in the most altruistic of intentions and the most likable of human subjects. I also put it strongly so that I may qualify it. For Ralph doesn't envision any particular scene as developing from his gift. He wants—he says he wants—only to "to see what she does with herself", to intervene just once, and then watch without taking further action. His father has a last question: what good will Ralph himself get from it all? But Ralph's own good will be precisely the one he wants to give Isabel, that of a fully gratified imagination. He sinks his life in hers; his identification with his character, her character, is complete.

James worked on this scene with the most confident of hands, and barely touched its dialogue in his 1906 revision. Isabel will inherit £70,000. It's impossible to say with any certainty just how large an income that gives her, but James tells us that the money will remain in the affairs of the bank, and bank stock in that period often returned upward of 8 percent. Let's say, conservatively, that she can spend £5,000 a year. The decision the Touchetts make about her will shape her life far more profoundly than any choice she has yet made for herself, and what Isabel calls her liberty is increasingly defined by what, in Ralph's words to his mother, other people want to "do with her." The girl is left alone when they first return from London, and in searching through the house she hears an unexpected ripple of music from Gardencourt's vast drawing room. She recognizes Beethoven, though in the New York Edition James would change it to Schubert: to nineteenth-century ears a figure not of stormy passion but of the social arts, and a better choice for this particular pianist. She plays with unusual skill, and Isabel is immediately intrigued by the fact that this new guest, though an American, "should so strongly resemble a foreign woman." And in fact her name is foreign. "I am Madame Merle," she says, as though "referring to a person of tolerably distinct identity."

James himself provides the best account of this moment, writing in his preface of how, as she enters the drawing room, Isabel "deeply recognizes . . . in the presence there, among the gathering shades, of this personage . . . a turning point in her life." The two women spend the next weeks in each other's company, as the house prepares for Mr. Touchett's death, and Isabel's admiration of her new friend grows by the day. Madame Merle is tall and fair and widowed, and something over forty. She works elaborate morsels of embroidery, she plays and paints, and though Gardencourt is hushed by sickness, she stays on because Mrs. Touchett wants her to; a welcome guest who also knows just when to leave and where to go next. Isabel thinks her a "woman of ardent impulses, kept in admirable order," and soon recognizes that she's under the older woman's influence; that at moments, indeed, she wants to be like her.

If Madame Merle has a fault it's that she seems "too perfectly the social animal." Even her new protégé admits that she cannot conceive of this supple creature in isolation, cannot imagine her inner life, and Isabel is troubled by the fact that Ralph doesn't like her. He says that he was once in love with her; but he does not like her, and Madame Merle knows it. They do, however, agree about one thing, for she too has an interest in our heroine's future. Yet their interest takes a different form. Ralph's generosity may be stained by his own longings, but he nonetheless wants to see what Isabel does with herself, to see the kind of life she will fashion. Madame Merle says, in contrast, that she wants "to see what life makes" of Isabel, and emphasizes the shaping force of the world around her. The difference is crucial, and points to a talk the two woman have shortly before Mr. Touchett's death.

The older woman admits to being ambitious, but she calls her own unrealized dreams "preposterous." Isabel answers that she herself has known success already. She has seen a childhood fantasy come true, and then blushes at the accuracy with which her friend defines and discounts it. A young man on his knees? We have all had that, and if "yours was a paragon . . . why didn't you fly with him to his castle in the Apennines?" The location is nicely chosen. Hawthorne gave his readers such a mountain refuge in *The Marble Faun*, and Anne Radcliffe had earlier used that setting in her 1794 Gothic romance, *The Mysteries of Udolpho*. Madame Merle's words suggest that Isabel's dream is above all a literary one, and tired. They remind the girl of the plot she's rejected, and they also suggest her lingering naïveté, in a way that makes her prickly. He has no such castle, she says, and besides, "I don't care anything about his house."

Madame Merle finds that sentiment crude, and the conversation that follows stands as one of the most probing moments in all James's work. He gives us here an understated examination of the very nature of the self, of the American self in particular, and the passage needs to be quoted at length. "When you have lived as long as I," the older woman says,

> ". . . you will see that every human being has his shell, and that you must take the shell into account. By the shell I mean the whole envelope of circumstances. There is no such thing as an isolated man or woman; we are each of us made up of a cluster of appurtenances. What do you call one's self? Where does it begin? Where does it end? It overflows into everything that belongs to us—and then it flows back again. I know that a large part of myself is in the dresses I choose to wear. I have a great respect for *things!* One's self—for other people—is one's expression of one's self; and one's house, one's clothes, the book one reads, the company one keeps—these things are all expressive."

A great respect for *things*. The phrase links her to Balzac, in whose world sexual desire is but a shadow of the lust for material goods, and whose great hero, as James himself wrote, is the 20-franc piece. And Isabel replies:

> "I think just the other way. I don't know whether I succeed in expressing myself, but I know that nothing else expresses me. Nothing that belongs to me is any measure of me; on the contrary, it's a limit, a barrier, and a perfectly arbitrary one. Certainly the clothes which, as you say, I choose to wear, don't express me; and heaven forbid they should! . . . My clothes may express the dressmaker, but they don't express me."

For one thing, it's not her choice to wear them—though Madame Merle puts a stop to that line of reasoning by asking if she'd prefer to go naked.

Early in *Anna Karenina*, Tolstoy writes that his heroine's beauty lies in the way that she seems to stand apart from her clothes. "What she wore was never seen on her," and even the most luxurious dress becomes an unnoticeable frame for the self. So it is for Isabel—or rather that's how she wants it to be. This passage comes a few pages after Ralph's conversation with his father, and we read her words with a certain irony, knowing what she doesn't: that whether or not her clothes express her, she's soon going to have a lot more of them. Still, this argument looks like a fair fight. We can't easily reject either woman's position, and while the balance does finally tip, we're not happy about it. We'd prefer to side with Isabel—with youth—and her ideal remains necessary, the ideal of some unified and autonomous self, independent of and anterior to its social circumstances. Madame Merle, in contrast, suggests that the self is socially determined, and not entirely separable from the world around it. The things around us may express that self, but they also serve to shape it. Our possessions represent us—they provide the shell within which the self is bound and through which other people come to know it.

Madame Merle speaks for the kind of self that Isabel had rejected in rejecting Warburton: the self as defined by its appurtenances, by a trailing penumbra of houses and history; the self as both person and personage. She speaks for age, for the things our young lady will need another twenty years to learn, and she also speaks as a "lady"; speaks for the social category to which both women belong and whose shaping force is so completely naturalized that Isabel can't even see it. But above all she speaks for Europe. And Isabel is the voice of American exceptionalism, a woman who sings of herself, and only herself; who believes her possessions are arbitrary, a limit imposed on her freedom, and who cannot accept the idea of merging that self in some other identity, in a moat or a name or a cotton mill. She likes instead to see herself as a version of what the critic R. W. B. Lewis called the American Adam, heroine "of a new adventure, an individual emancipated from history, happily bereft of ancestry, untouched and undefiled by the usual inheritance of family and race." Isabel is an orphan, and even as her Aunt Touchett pays the bills, she speaks of the girl as being her own mistress; someone who wants, as James tells us, "to leave the past behind her." The paradox is that she finds her clean start in coming to Europe, to an Old World in which she appears newborn. Yet her very desire to discard the past tells us that she has one. No "lady" is without a social inheritance. No one with Caspar Goodwood behind her—no one with a sudden £70,000 of family money—is quite so pleasantly bereft.

James historicized such ambitions in his study of Hawthorne, writing that the idea of "the supremacy of the individual to himself . . . must have had a great charm for people" whose society seemed bare of other amusements. The words come from his account of Hawthorne's relations with New England's reforming class in general and Emerson in particular, and this moment in the novel is in fact often read in terms of Emerson. Many critics cite a line from "The Transcendentalist," in which he writes that "you think me the child of my circumstances. I make my circumstances," and suggests that the thought "which is called I" has the power to mold the world into the form of its own desire. In truth, there's nothing easier than to find Emersonian tags for Isabel's self-conception. We may pluck a line from "Self-Reliance," in which he describes the human soul as defined by a continuous process of *becoming*, "self-sufficing, and . . . self-relying," and goes on to treat one's possessions as a form of accident, scorning a world in which people measure each other by what one has rather than what one is. We may look at "History," in which Emerson tells us that the self is greater than all geography, that history matters only because it allows us to make metaphors for our souls. But we also need to remember that the *Portrait* itself is larger than Isabel's own consciousness. It knows from the start some things that she will only gradually discover, and we must remember too that James thought Emerson's own great weakness was his "ripe unconsciousness of evil."

Isabel believes in her own autonomy, her own enabling isolation: a belief, and a dream, that all her later experience will challenge, as she learns what the Old World has to teach; a folly at whose cost she will purchase wisdom. For in the words of John Adams, there is "no special providence for Americans, and their nature is the same with that of others." The same, except in ideology, in our fixed belief that we aren't; a belief that makes us the perpetual victims of our own born-again innocence, lost one year and renewed the next. James asks us here to define our relation to the world outside, to the life beyond our borders. Do we need it? Can we stand alone? The stakes in this delicate talk about clothes are enormous, and his characters' words address not only the nature and limits of the individual self, but also that of our own country's relation to other lands; the relation that James's own expatriation had put into question. And that account of the limits of self-sufficiency is what, above all, makes *The Portrait of a Lady* stand as a great American novel.

We cannot, however, take the full measure of those limits until the very end of the book, and there are other things to say about this moment. Look again at Madame Merle's claim that "one's self—for other people—is one's expression of one's self." The qualification is important. It allows for a distinction between public and private, between the self in its social definition and the self in itself. Isabel herself doesn't hear that distinction, but we should, and we can gloss it by looking at some words from William James's *Principles of Psychology* (1890). In his chapter on the self the older brother writes that "*a man's Me is the sum total of all that he* CAN *call his*, not only his body and his psychic powers, but his clothes and his house, his wife and children, his ancestors and friends, his reputation and works, his lands and horses, and yacht and bank-account." Henry wasn't the only member of his family to enjoy lists, and it's hard not to be swept away by the charm and force of this one; and hard as well to believe William didn't have his brother's novel in mind when he wrote it, so closely does it track Madame Merle's account of our defining "envelope of circumstances." Yet William's conception of the self isn't limited to that envelope. For he splits that self into two parts, into a "me" and an "I." *Me* is "the self as known": not only as known by other people, but also as perceived by what he calls *I*, "the self as knower." The *I* is fully aware of that *me*, of its expression through one's hat and shoes and tone of voice, its "empirical aggregate of things objectively known." That aggregate is what the *I* knows of itself, how it describes itself to itself. William adds, however, that "the *I* which knows them cannot itself be an aggregate." *I* is irreducible.

William James speaks to both of his brothers' characters here, the *Me* of Madame Merle and the *I* of Isabel Archer; the Isabel who insists that the self remains separate from the sum of what she can call hers. Except that she's wrong. "Whatever I may be thinking of," William writes, "I am always at the same time more or less aware of *myself*, of my *personal existence*," and over the course of the novel Isabel's growing self-awareness becomes inseparable from the increasing complexity of that existence. She would not come to perceive so much if the shell around her did not so press, if she weren't forced to think her way through the circumstances that wrap her tight. And the knowing instrument of her *I* will take some part of its shape from the things that do indeed belong to her, as she does to them. At this point, however, Isabel speaks for an identity of *I* and *Me*—for an *I* that subsumes its *Me*. She speaks as though she has had some existence prior to or separate from her circumstances, and perhaps in a sense she has.

"She stood there in perfect isolation," James wrote in his preface, recalling the way in which, at first, this slim shade of an untethered girl was all he had to build on. He had nothing else, not at the start, no plans or materials or tools. He had to find them. He had to learn what destiny she would affront; had to invent a clutch of possibilities for her, a story, other people.

That makes James's own creative dilemma as one with Isabel's situation, and that dilemma is what determines the structure of his plot. He needs to envision the appurtenances of which she wants no part; must imagine a way to bring her into some full contact with the world around her. As we will see in this book's next part, the business of *The Portrait of a Lady* lies in discovering a set of possible actions and relations for a character who begins by standing alone.

PART THREE

ITALIAN JOURNEYS

Rome, Outdoor Market in Piazza Navona.
By Giuseppe Ninci, ca. 1870s. Albumen print.

10.

BELLOSGUARDO HOURS

A T THE FOOT of the Ponte Vecchio, I paused and looked back, turning away from its narrow shop-lined path for a view of the buildings behind me. Faceless buildings, now, and with their ground floors given over to tourist shops: gelato and postcards and a couple of ATMs. But one of them had been the Hôtel de l'Arno—"well spoken of" in Baedeker's words—where James had sat in an upstairs window making Isabel walk onto her English lawn. Much had been rebuilt here, and I had no way to determine which window had been his, or to find the door he would have taken from the street. Shrug, and walk on. It was early still, with the bridge's jewelry stores unshuttering for the day, and I walked over its crabbed arch in the milky light of an April morning, and then up the via Guicciardini toward the Palazzo Pitti. Every step here took me through a different bit of history. There was the palace itself, its dun-colored walls an exercise in brooding symmetry. It had been the massy home of the Medici dukes and was already a museum in James's time; he found its collection more sumptuous than interesting, and the place had given William a headache. There was Machiavelli's house, and then the many-windowed front of the Brownings' Casa Guidi. There were the Boboli Gardens, with their fountains and terraces and lanes cut like tunnels through the greenery. My business was elsewhere, though, and I kept to the busy street until I had passed through the old Porta Romana.

Florence began to undergo a partial modernization in the 1860s, during its brief period as the Italian capital, with its town planners copying the precedent of Paris's Baron Haussmann, and slicing wide avenues through some quarters of the city. In James's time, however, the defensive walls on the south side of the Arno had remained in place. Today only the gates are left, and the Porta Romana itself was pierced by four lanes of traffic. Still, after a minute I was able to get away from the cars, leaving the main road and beginning to climb. Here the city's fabric loosened. There were spaces between the buildings now, though the high walls that lined my way were almost continuous, with small green lizards running along them at shoulder height. Through heavy gates I had an occasional view of a villa, of mustard-colored buildings set back in a garden of umbrella pines and olives, and as the hill grew steeper, the villas got larger and security more elaborate. Signs warned about dogs, barbed wire ran above the concealing walls, and the tops of the walls themselves were a bristle of broken glass.

"If you're an aching alien," James wrote, "half the talk is about villas. This one has a story; that one has another," and today many of those stories have an American twist. James Fenimore Cooper had lived behind these roadside walls for almost a year at the end of the 1820s, and in 1858, Hawthorne rented the battlemented Torre di Montauto on top of Bellosguardo, the hill I was now approaching. For $28 a month he got a place that he described as "big enough to quarter a regiment," and he later used it as a setting in *The Marble Faun*. The road leveled out and a man jogged toward me, in Italy an unusual sight. But as he approached, I saw he was carrying a copy of the *Herald Tribune*; a part of this hill has stayed American. My own destination was a place James had described as "a little grassy, empty, rural piazza," no more, really, than a swelling at the juncture of two roads, and bounded upon one side by a villa with a "long, rather blank-looking . . . front." The grass was gone now, though that didn't stop a boy from kicking a soccer ball against a gate. But the villa itself remained.

Like many such places it has carried several names. For much of its life it was called the Belvedere al Saracino, but in the twentieth century it became known as the Villa Mercedes, and did time as a finishing school for American girls. James knew it, however, as the Villa Castellani, and some family friends of his kept an apartment there. I say "family friends" advisedly. The novelist made his own way in London, but almost everyone he saw in Italy was someone with whom he could claim an American acquaintance. They had dined with his parents, or he had gone to school with their cousins; a world composed of the friends of one's friends. James had met the widowed Frank Boott and his daughter Elizabeth in Newport and Cambridge, but their real home was in Italy, where Boott had first gone at midcentury, soon after the death of his wife. There he lived on the profits of a Lowell textile mill and gave himself over to the education of his daughter. Lizzie Boott had also been a friend of the dead Minny Temple, and in his autobiography James remembered her as almost too civilized, a girl varnished to perfection. Yet her letters show a lively wit, and her colloquial French could match his own.

James wrote about the Villa Castellani in three different works: in *Roderick Hudson*, in an 1878 essay called "Italy Revisited," and finally in *The Portrait of a Lady* itself. In the first of those he moves his characters into a place he calls the Villa Pandolfini, a building whose low façade is "colored a dull, dark yellow, and pierced with windows of various sizes." Inside, its rooms seem cool and still, while the garden behind offers his characters a prospect of the river valley below. The essay describes the house as a place he couldn't help coveting, and he loved both the tall cypresses outside and the sense, within, of a life dedicated to art and beauty.

Today the building is still painted an ochre-yellow. Its façade is modest, almost anonymous, and it sits directly on the street—no broken glass. And on this spring morning the house was unprotected in another way: its high, brass-studded doors stood open in the sunlight, and the caretaker waved me in for a look. There was a well in one corner of its lichen-covered courtyard and a Vespa in another, while the pavement was set with the gravestones of pets—"Bubeli, 1913." I noted the names on the mailboxes of the dozen flats into which the building was divided: a German, a Scandinavian, and then a lot of Italians, including somebody called Corleone. There was also an English name, a place belonging to a "Lawrence of Florence." In one of his Italian essays James describes himself as "peeping up [the] stately staircases" of one historic house after another, and wishing he could climb up for a view of the life within. So I paused with my finger over Lawrence's button, wondering just who might appear. In the end, however, I had no more courage than James himself, and left that bell unrung.

Instead, I must rely on his own account of the interior, and of the garden that from the street I could see stretched out behind. The description comes a few chapters after Mr. Touchett's death, when *The Portrait of a Lady* jumps in both time and space. James throws the action six months forward and rather suddenly moves us to Italy, where almost all of its remaining scenes take place. Here the villa goes nameless, and the language he uses for it has a new figurative power. The building seems "incommunicative," and the irregular windows of its façade reveal not its face, but its "mask. . . . It had heavy lids, but no eyes." The house isn't what it seems—it doesn't really show itself. Its different apartments are occupied by the citizens of this nation or that, foreigners long resident in Italy, and in one of them James shows us a room in which daily life itself has become a fine art. There are bits of tapestry and cabinets of age-polished oak, a scatter of books and modern chairs to read them in, oddments of medieval brassware and a wall of early masters. In this apartment lives an American widower, a man of forty with a daughter in her teens named Pansy.

W e first hear of this man from Madame Merle, who at Gardencourt uses him to define the limitations of expatriate life. "We are a wretched set of people," she tells Isabel with a certain complacency: parasites who have left their roots in one continent and haven't managed to stick themselves into the soil of the other. Ralph is a good example, though his illness lends him a substitute for the occupation he otherwise lacks. Women have it easier, she claims, if only because they have "no natural place anywhere," and so one land is as good as another. Yet men need an identity. Mr. Touchett's bank has given him a rather weighty one, but as for the others she knows . . . well, the more cultivated they are, the more pitiful. The worst of them is one of the most delightful men she has ever met, someone whose charm seems inseparable from his irrelevance. "He is Gilbert Osmond—he lives in Italy; that is all one can say about him." At home he might have become distinguished, and yet in living abroad he has made for himself "no name, no position, no fortune . . . no anything." Osmond paints, albeit as an amateur only; the rest of him is indolence and taste.

No anything—words that for Isabel will eventually stand as a form of recommendation. The surface truth of Madame Merle's account does, however, stay with her during a brief Parisian interlude, after she learns of her inheritance, when in looking over Mrs. Touchett's collection of "American absentees" she says that their way of being "doesn't seem to lead to anything." It may be extremely pleasant, and yet there must, she thinks, be more to life than dinner at the Café Anglais. Her aunt's circle isn't so sure, but one of its members does at least try to give her an answer. Ned Rosier is a childhood friend, a polite young man with a fondness for old china, and what it all leads to, he tells her, is shopping. Where else but in Paris "can you get such things?" But to most people that isn't enough. John Singer Sargent's parents came abroad before his birth in 1856, for what they thought was their health. For the next thirty years, while the future painter's mother moved with the seasons from one place to the next, his father dreamed of returning to his Philadelphia medical practice and seized upon every American newspaper he could find. They neither went home nor struck deep into Europe, and until John entered a studio in Paris, they knew only people like themselves.

For Dr. Sargent they were years with no purpose; Daniel Touchett did better. The young Sargent did of course develop that purpose, and so, to a lesser degree, did the generation of half-forgotten artists who formed the first American expatriate community in Italy. Such figures as the sculptors Harriet Hosmer and William Wetmore Story had gone to Rome in search of the training they couldn't yet find in the States. They formed a link between Hawthorne's generation and James's own; indeed James would later write Story's biography. And Hawthorne stands as the shrewdest of commentators on the issue that Madame Merle defines. He spent sixteen months in Italy, from January 1858 until May of the following year, and

in his notebooks recorded a meeting in Florence with the sculptor Hiram
Powers, whose *Greek Slave* had become a totem of the Abolitionist cause.
Hawthorne told him that he hoped he would soon take up the place, and
the fame, that his work had earned him at home, and yet added that Powers seemed without any plans for a return. To the writer it looked like an
"unsatisfactory life, thus to spend all the bulk of it in exile; in such a case
we are always deferring the reality of life till a future moment, and, by and
by, we have deferred it till there are no future moments." The next day
he added that a shy, thoughtful man might find a home in a small city like
Siena, and discover there a "sombre kind of happiness . . . but it would be
terrible without an independent life in one's own mind."

James himself always had that independent life—which doesn't mean
that he plunged more deeply. Italy had been the goal of his first adult trip to
Europe in 1869, a country that for him, as later for Isabel, had long stood
as a promised land. He arrived in Florence on October 5, and the next day
bought a two-week membership at the Gabinetto Vieusseux in Piazza Santa
Trinità. It was the city's largest subscription library, and its reading room
was as a center of expatriate life; the names inscribed over the decades in its
register amount to a history of European culture, from Mikhail Bakunin to
Isadora Duncan. James went there both to read the newspapers and in the
hopes of finding a familiar face. He had been in Italy for six weeks already,
with brief stays in Venice and Bologna among others, but he hadn't yet
found anyone to talk to.

That would set a pattern, and in 1874 he wrote to Grace Norton that
though he had been in Italy for a year he had "hardly spoken to an Italian
creature save washerwomen and waiters." He was once more in Florence
and at work on a series of travel sketches that delighted in the city's sense
of an ever-visible past, but admitted that he sometimes found himself over-
whelmed by the gap between Italy itself and the touristic rhapsodies he felt
he had to provide. One evening he found himself gazing at a line of time-
battered and almost mudlike houses along the Arno. Today those buildings contain some of Florence's most expensively renovated flats, but James
knew that in his native New York they would have been little more than

a slum, and he could only explain his pleasure in them by supposing that Italy created its own standard of beauty. The simple fact that they weren't brownstones had allowed the moonlight to refine their poverty away. At other times, however, those picturesque fictions seemed to explode in his hands. One day he stood at the gate of a hill town, with the road into the plain below winding down through chestnuts and olives, and watched as a young man came up toward him, his coat slung over his shoulder and his hat at a rakish angle. He was singing as he came, and James told himself that such a figure in the middle distance "had been exactly what was wanted to set off the landscape." But when the man reached him and asked for a match, James quickly discovered that he was a brooding, angry young communist, "unhappy, underfed, [and] unemployed," and very far from the operatic presence for which the novelist had taken him.

James came to know what he didn't know, what the traveler's view doesn't usually allow one to see, and he turned those limitations of knowledge into the material of his work itself. Only in a few apprentice stories does he allow himself the kind of detachable set pieces on which Howells relied in his own Florentine novel, *Indian Summer*, with its touristic accounts of an artist's trattoria or of the drive up to Fiesole. He more often uses Italy as a way to explore his own overvaluation of Europe. In his early "Madonna of the Future" he describes an expatriate painter named Theobald, who lives in the hope of beating out Raphael, and has spent a lifetime in the Tuscan capital in preparing—in delaying and deferring—his one perfect painting. Yet in the process his model has aged out of recognition, his blackened canvas has become illegible, and in his dream of an earlier age he has entirely missed the crude but undeniable energy of the modern land around him. Theobald's Madonna belongs to the past. It is not a place on which an American art can take its stand.

Florence did not shape James's imagination as powerfully as either Rome or Venice. But it made him happy, "a rounded pearl of cities," and over the years he found that it was, above all, a good place to work. I have already mentioned his stay in the fall and winter of 1873–74, when he spent much of his time with William, and in the spring he remained in the city after his brother had left. He took an apartment on the corner of Piazza Santa Maria Novella, where he settled into the opening chapters of *Roderick Hudson*, and years later he wrote that the book's first pages always recalled to him not the New England town of their setting but the Italian city of their composition. In his memory he could hear "the clatter of horse-pails" from a nearby cabstand and stood once more looking out at the dusty square through the slits of his shutters. That stay made the city seem a kind of refuge, and later James would sometimes go there as a way to avoid the invitations of London.

So it was in 1880, when he wanted a few uninterrupted weeks in which to begin *The Portrait of a Lady*. Not that he played hermit. He was happy to see the Bootts, and at another gathering met the Crown-Princess of Prussia—daughter of Queen Victoria, mother of Wilhelm II—and wrote home that she was "easy, friendly, intelligent." Still, he complained to his sister that "one is liable to tea-parties," and noted that he was expected to call on an American writer who had been chasing him across the Continent with a letter of introduction.

Contance Fenimore Woolson's life had been nearly as peripatetic as James's own. Born in 1840, she was the great-niece of James Fenimore Cooper, but though her family origins lay in New Hampshire and New York, she had spent much of her childhood in Ohio and on the Great Lakes at a time when they were still seen as the "West." In the 1870s she traveled through the South with her widowed mother, visiting battlefields and cemeteries and eventually settling in St. Augustine. She was, in the words of her biographer, Lyndall Gordon, both vulnerable and stubborn, someone who insisted upon "an unconventional course of action . . . it was odd to be a Northern woman living by choice in the ruined South," and it was even odder for such a woman to explore the alligator swamps of the Florida wilderness, alone.

Most of her fiction and travel sketches appeared in the New York–based and heavily illustrated *Harper's*; James preferred the more austere *Atlantic*.

Still, her work was in some ways the other side of his coin. If he wrote about Europe for what was at first an East Coast audience, then she wrote about the varied regions of America for that same audience; specializing in the "local color" stories that, in bringing the news of faraway places, paradoxically underlined her readers' sense of their own cultural centrality. Such tales usually depicted provincial life through the eyes of a city-bred protagonist; the classic examples are Sarah Orne Jewett's stories of coastal Maine. The self-conscious cosmopolitanism of James's work carried a greater prestige. It gave his readers something to which they might aspire. But the local-color writers often had more readers. Woolson's stories are both gimlet-eyed and affecting, and the best of them can stand comparison with Jewett's. The most widely known is the 1877 "Rodman the Keeper," which she based on a visit to the military graveyard at the Andersonville prison camp in Georgia. Soon afterward, however, her work changed, and changed in two ways. In 1879 she sailed for Europe, encouraged to do so by Howells among others, and she also began a series of tales about the lives of women artists.

In each of these things Henry James was very much on her mind. She had already written about him for the *Atlantic* and later claimed that in his work she had found "my true country, my real home." But he had begun to show up in her fiction even before they met, in a story called "Miss Grief" that is narrated by a parody version of James himself, an American writer in Rome. One evening he gets a visit from what can only be called a distressed gentlewoman, a shabbily-dressed figure named Aaronna Crief who has read his every word and wants him to look at her own work in turn. He tries to get rid of her, fails, reads, and finds to his surprise that her pages have force; later she tells him she would have killed herself "if your sentence had been against me." Yet no editor will take her, and "Miss Grief" soon sickens and dies, killed not by her poverty so much as by the neglect of the literary world itself.

The story seems almost naked in its sense of need; and in later years James might well have wondered if he should have read it as a warning. Still, in material terms Woolson had nothing like her character's struggle.

Her family connections had eased her way into print, and by 1880 her career was both settled and prosperous. She carried a letter of introduction from one of James's relatives and had been in Florence for some ten days when he arrived. There's no record of their initial meeting, but James first mentioned her in a letter to his sister Alice on April 25. He found her "amiable, but deaf," and full of questions about his books to which she couldn't quite hear his replies. A week later he wrote to his Aunt Kate that he had gone driving with an American "authoress," but added that he didn't know her work. Still, her manners were perfect, and though he found her "intense," he liked her. Woolson's own letters of the period describe James himself as a form of paradox. He was attentive and charming, and yet his self-presentation was both quiet and cold; a man who had driven all expression from his light gray eyes.

James often called for her in the morning, retreating to his desk as the afternoon grew hot. One day they strolled in the Cascine, the large park at the city's western edge; on another he took her to the vast empty Duomo and, as she wrote in a letter, tried to make her admire it. They went to Santa Croce, in whose sober Gothic majesty Florence's most illustrious citizens are buried, and where Woolson thought the Giottos beyond her; then to San Lorenzo, where she couldn't get herself to like nude statues. At times she thought James might need a break from her "horrible ignorance," and yet there's no doubt he enjoyed the company of this intelligent reader, a woman who admired his work in the same way that his friend Zhukovsky admired Wagner's. After his visit to Naples he may have needed that salve, that perceptive but largely uncritical appreciation. James took very few colleagues into his confidence, but to Woolson he spoke about his books with an openness that at this time he extended only to Howells. One mark of their friendship can be found in the story she wrote about those months, "A Florentine Experiment," which appeared in the *Atlantic* that October, a month before the *Portrait* started its own run. It's a tale of expatriate life in which Woolson describes the places they had visited together, and it ends with Trafford Morgan, a man who "likes to be listened to," confessing his love to Margaret Stowe. The wish embodied here needs no comment, and what matters isn't simply the fact that Woolson wrote such a story, but that James didn't object to it. A decade later the English writer Vernon Lee based one of her own characters upon him—and he broke with her.

At first James saw Woolson with the same sense of fond amusement with which Isabel regards Henrietta's intrepid naïveté. Later there was more, as he came to understand the shape of her loneliness and the place he had within it. Yet their friendship was not public. Two middle-aged writers might visit an Italian church without exciting speculation, but James had already needed to quell too many rumors of his own impending marriage, and when Woolson moved to England in 1883, he kept her apart from the main current of his life. Sometimes they went to the theater together, and in Florence she became increasingly close to Frank and Lizzie Boott, but to most of James's friends she remained hidden, as hidden, in a way, as Zhukovsky, and for much the same reason. People might have talked about their anomalous friendship, and talked all the more because there was in fact nothing to say.

Leon Edel writes that "the two destroyed each other's letters by mutual agreement," but four of hers do survive, two each from 1882 and 1883, years he spent partly in America and where he left some papers behind. They are extraordinary documents. They are extraordinary in her acute reading of his reputation and of the change in it that was made by *The Portrait of a Lady* itself; a reading to which I'll return in a later chapter. They are extraordinary too in possessing a voice, richer and more flexible than that of her fiction, that claims all while appearing to claim so little. In their aggressive modesty, their seeming denial of desire, these letters recall such great novelistic characters as Dickens's Esther Summerson from *Bleak House*, or the first-person narrator of Charlotte Brontë's sublime *Villette*, the emotionally famished Lucy Snowe. At one point Woolson imagines building a cottage in Cooperstown, New York, and then suggests that James must come and stay with her there, bringing along "that sweet young American wife I want you to have—whom you *must* have. . . ." And these letters have an anecdotal value as well. They are the richest portrait we have of James in the confidence, indeed the swagger, of his first mastery.

One example must do. From Leipzig she writes that she has been making a clean copy of her new novel. Her whole arm now ached, and the pain made her remember a morning in Florence when they sat on a bench, and

> . . . you said, in answer to a remark of mine, "Oh, *I* never copy." And upon a mute gesture from me, you added, "Do you think, then, that my work has the air of having been copied, and perhaps more than once?" I think I made no direct reply, then. But I will now. The gesture was despair,—despair, that, added to your other perfections, was the gift of writing as you do, at the first draft!

But *sprezzatura* is almost always a pose. James covered his proof sheets with corrections, and whatever his usual practice, with *The Portrait of a Lady* he did "copy," he did revise. Nothing came on the first draft, and in reading Woolson's letter I cannot help wondering just why he seemed so interested in impressing her, and perhaps so willing to deceive her as well.

11.

MR. OSMOND

I N A V I L L A on top of an olive-shrouded hill sits a man with a thin, sharp face. The ends of his mustache are twisted up, his grizzled beard has been shaped to a point, and he seems unmarked by any national origin; a man who might "pass for anything," or nothing. The open door lets in the Tuscan spring; he flicks his eyes toward the young girl standing across the room, and then his hooded gaze drifts back to the two nuns who sit facing him. They have brought the girl home for the summer from her convent school in Rome, but though Pansy is now fifteen, her father still sees her as a child: an obedient child, fluent in three languages, and so timid that she wonders if she dares do anything so grown-up as to make a pot of tea.

It will be some pages before James tells us the man's name, and perhaps only the most attentive of the serialized novel's first readers would have thought back a month, and remembered Madame Merle's account of her friend Gilbert Osmond, a figure without the solidity of either Caspar Goodwood or Lord Warburton, a man who has nothing to declare but his own cultivation. His income is small, he knows that he lacks genius or even talent, and he thinks of himself as someone who has renounced ambition. He does admit to envying the pope, "for the consideration he enjoys," but he has made up his mind to live quietly and "not to strive nor struggle." He will do nothing to risk failure. In Florence he almost never comes down from the top of Bellosguardo—he wants the rest of the expatriate world to know both that he's there and that he doesn't want to see them. Osmond pays just two visits a year to the Palazzo Crescentini, Mrs. Touchett's house in the city below, and dislikes Ralph, who returns the favor.

Madame Merle had spoken of Osmond in England, when Isabel was poor, and she speaks of him again now that the girl is rich and has come to Florence with her aunt. It is early May in 1872. Mr. Touchett has been dead for six months, and later that year, in America, Ulysses S. Grant will be elected to a second term in the White House. None of James's characters will notice, or care. His expatriates are not the kind who hang upon the news. They have more immediate concerns, and right now Madame Merle is occupied by the question of Isabel's future. One shouldn't live in Italy, the older woman tells her, without meeting Gilbert Osmond, who knows more about the peninsula than anyone but a few German professors. To Osmond himself she says something else—she tells him that Miss Archer has £70,000. Madame Merle arrives at the villa while the nuns are still there, and at the news of Osmond's visitors she hesitates, as if there were some risk in entering. But though she seems shawled in caution she's also an old family friend, someone who has visited Pansy in Rome, who has met these nuns before and can charm them. Osmond's own manners are offhand. He recognizes that her visit means something, that Madame Merle wants something, and once the sisters have gone, his voice acquires a touch of vinegar. She in turn appears on edge, and James explains their shared but apparently unmotivated temper by noting that they usually "approached each other obliquely, as it were, and addressed each other by implication." Yet that only begs a further question, and one that the author leaves hanging.

At first Osmond rejects the woman's suggestion that he should meet her new friend. Effort is such a bore, and "I know plenty of dingy people." Even the news of Isabel's wealth and beauty hardly appears to interest him, though he sharpens his ears at the sum. But he finally agrees to call at the Palazzo Crescentini, and when he does, Isabel listens to him talk with Madame Merle and thinks herself dull by comparison. The young woman remains quiet, even subdued, and yet does so precisely because something about Osmond arrests her, and makes "it seem more important that she should get an impression of him than that she should produce one herself."

He speaks simply about complicated matters and appears delicate even as he invites Isabel to come up and visit his garden. On this second meeting her impression deepens, even though the villa itself scares her a bit; its blank façade makes it seem "as if, once you were in, it would not be easy to get out." But she is delighted with Pansy, and she even enjoys Osmond's sister, the Countess Gemini, a prattling scandalous creature of fashion, unhappily married to a local nobleman. Moreover, Osmond himself seems genuinely beguiling, as he speaks of Italy's fusion of beauty and lassitude, of spending his life in a country that most other Americans only pass through.

And as Isabel looks at him with his arm around Pansy's waist, as she walks through his rooms and watches him take down a picture to bring it into the light, she begins to think that the man himself is far more interesting than his possessions. He resembles no one she knows—he has the air of being someone in particular. Most of her friends, she now realizes, belong "to types which were already present in her mind"; Ralph does, and Henrietta, and even Madame Merle. Osmond is different. She can think of no class or category to which he belongs, and he seems all the more original for not being in any way an eccentric. She finds herself attracted by his slender fingers and his overdrawn face; she admires his fastidiousness and even what she suspects will prove his irritability. He is shy and self-critical, and yet he treats her kindly, so kindly that Isabel wonders at his attention, and, as the afternoon proceeds, she becomes careful in her enthusiasms, lest she admire the wrong thing.

James's heroine carries a story away from that hill, a story about a sensitive widower, who holds his daughter by the hand as they pace across his moss-covered terrace. She sees his "studious life in a lovely land" as one that involves a choice between the shallow and the serious; a choice she imagines he has not hesitated to make, even while knowing that the latter path must lead to loneliness and sorrow. She sees him, that is, as he would like to be seen. Her eyes give him back a version of his own best self, in which his love of beauty is inseparable from his "half-anxious, half-helpless fatherhood." But James has already let his readers see enough to tell a different story. When the nuns deliver Pansy home to Bellosguardo,

Osmond's eyes drop with amusement at their claim to have made her a good Christian. Nevertheless, he uses their terms to cultivate Isabel's favor, and when she praises the girl, he says, as though his father's heart were full, that "she is a little saint of heaven!" Though he is not so bad as Madame Merle, who affects astonishment when Mrs. Touchett asks her if "that man is making love to my niece."

T his is the man Isabel will marry. She will make him wait, but a dozen chapters later she will marry him, and no one we like will be happy about it, not Ralph, or Henrietta, or even Mrs. Touchett, who thinks Osmond both a gentleman and a negative sum. James's foreshadowing has been heavy enough to make us suspect that Isabel won't be entirely happy in any marriage, but still everyone who reads this book thinks her acceptance of Osmond needs to be justified. With Warburton or Goodwood, in contrast, it was her refusal that required justification. But let us stop anticipating. James will offer an explanation in its place, and so let us, in Madame Merle's words, distinguish instead.

In the New York Edition, James didn't precisely soften his characterization of Osmond, but he did cut a long passage in which he tells us how to see him. It may, he had written, seem a "coarse imputation," and yet still it must be said: Osmond is "not untainted by selfishness." Even in the first edition, however, James backs away from that judgment as soon he makes it. For the word doesn't cover Osmond in his entirety. Isabel has some cause for the picture she draws for herself, and we had better start by admitting it. Osmond's literary tastes mix the expected—Machiavelli—with the recherché, and while few of us can share his enthusiasm for the rococo cream-puffs of the eighteenth-century librettist Metastasio, his interest in the sixteenth-century poet Vittoria Colonna is today worth taking seriously. His Tuscan primitives, bought cheap, are already worth something more, and though he speaks too much about his "willful renunciation" of chances he never had, even Ralph sometimes finds him good company. He may disapprove of Osmond's courtship, but in these early days he recognizes that the man's "good humour was imperturbable, his knowledge universal, his manners were the gentlest in the world." Osmond's pose works because it isn't only a pose; Isabel's view is partial, but not entirely misplaced.

Yet there's another and more interesting reason for Isabel's attraction, and one best approached by considering a few words of Madame Merle's. Your rooms, she tells him, "are perfect. . . . You understand this sort of thing as no one else does." Osmond would have liked to own the walls of the Uffizi itself, but even with modest means he has worked a great effect, and his apartment sounds attractive, mixing its modern furniture with elaborately carved wooden chests and pieces of antique pottery. "This sort of thing" is an art of its own, and we have to take it seriously before we can take it lightly. One of the Venetian essays in *Italian Hours*, James's 1909 gathering of his travel pieces, is a graceful obituary for his friend Katharine De Kay Bronson, at whose small house on the Grand Canal the novelist often stayed. In it he recalls her love of the decorative arts, and suggests that she would have surrendered a Tintoretto "for a cabinet of tiny gilded glasses or a dinner-service of the right old silver." Such pieces may be what Osmond has had to settle for, and yet a Tintoretto would overmaster almost any owner. You might envy the luck of the acquisition, but its possession points to little beyond a bank account. Yet to select just the right little goblets, to have no vulgar things—the ambition may be small but it isn't in itself unworthy. One may not be a personage, but one can still belong to an aristocracy of taste.

Isabel will come to think that there was nothing terribly refined about inheriting such a fortune, and sees good taste as a note of distinction in a society that has no other way to mark it besides money. It's not quite an alternative to money, but it does serve to justify her wealth—it will be what her money is *for*. James shared that prejudice, as his account of Mrs. Bronson suggests, and also saw through it. He enjoyed racketing around in curiosity shops, he delighted in things old and obscure, and in his fiction often allowed an appreciation of them to stand as a sign of intelligence. He bought little, however, and he never made the decoration of houses into an interest of his own. He knew how unsustaining good taste alone might prove, and had little sympathy with a younger generation's belief in art for art's sake, or indeed with Walter Pater's idea that our finest moments come to us through the sensory pulses of aesthetic appreciation. Osmond of course shares that idea—or seems to.

Still, if he were indeed the man he wants Isabel to take him for, he might prove genuinely attractive: someone who has accepted his limits and decided to cultivate his own garden. That would make him rather like Frank Boott, the Bostonian in whose apartment James placed him. None of the records suggests that Boott had as keen an eye for a painting as Gilbert Osmond. Instead, he wrote music, and though his songs were best suited to the amateur tradition of *Hausmusik*, he did occasionally find a professional performance. He was more sociable than Osmond, a good host, and a more devoted father; his daughter Lizzie had tutors in Florence rather than being sent away to school. Nothing about the Bootts suggests the isolation that Osmond seems determined to cultivate; indeed the reverse, for Lizzie grew up in a lively set of expatriate children, a community split between Florence and Rome and that even included some cousins. Nor did their life abroad preclude an occasional stay in America, and after meeting them in Newport the young James quickly grew fond of the daughter. Her father, however, he thought childish and didn't hesitate to describe him that way; even as he got to work on *The Portrait of a Lady*, James wrote to Quincy Street that the simplicity of Boott's "mental constitution only increases with age."

No one would use such terms for Osmond, and this brief sketch should be enough to caution anyone who might want to claim that the character was based upon Frank Boott. The difference between them is in fact so great that it could make one question the usefulness of tracing such "originals," or indeed the literary tourism of my own walks up Bellosguardo. And yet the reason for doing so seems to me simple enough. Searching for some putative original allows us to see what was in fact created; the difference between the fictional page and the gravel of documentary truth can stand as a guide to artistic practice. Matching the description of the villa in *The Portrait of a Lady* up against the similar account in James's "Italy Revisited," and then comparing both of them to an actual walk up the hill suggests the degree to which his Italian settings are traceable to a particular place. The people he puts in those settings are a different matter.

Isabel herself is a special case, but few of James's important characters have a source in a specific person. Or rather his characters' characters—their moral being, their personalities—don't usually have that source. What he does instead is to take not a person but a set of circumstances from the life around him. In the Villa Castellani he had an "Italianate bereft American," a widower and an aesthete, who had devoted his life to the education of his daughter; who had raised an American girl on a European model, protected and cosseted and formidably polished. Their situation planted itself in his brain, and waited there until it proved exactly what his work required. "I *had* it there," he wrote in his autobiography and had it all the more because Frank Boott "had no single note of character or temper . . . in common with my Gilbert Osmond." What James got from his family friends—what they suggested, what he used—was the drama of their position, not that of their particular individual beings. Gilbert Osmond is an interesting creation precisely because he differs from the man in whose house James put him. If we're looking for originals, we might do better to consider the twice-married collector James Jackson Jarves, who impoverished himself in buying the same kind of once-disregarded paintings that Osmond does; there's a version of his story in Edith Wharton's *False Dawn*, and most of the paintings are now at Yale. But Jarves was also less saturnine than Osmond, and perhaps the character owes his sense of unappreciated merit to James's good friend Henry Adams, who never got over his discovery that there was more to politics than intelligence and a family name.

Osmond's own paintings form a part of his "traditionary" pose: the work of a man who likes one to think that he could have been an artist if only he weren't a gentleman. And his watercolors are not in themselves bad, even if to Madame Merle they seem inadequate "as the only thing you do." One of the most puzzling things about this part of the novel is the tone that these two old friends take with one another. They speak bluntly, and yet their talk so brims with allusion that it amounts to innuendo, in a way that makes them seem creatures of another century—before, after, anything but Victorian. The more caustic they are, the more appears to go unsaid. Madame Merle tells Osmond that she wants to put Isabel in his way, and her phrasing is not disinterested. But we don't yet see what she herself might get from it all, and therefore read with a sharp sense of the unspoken. Even Isabel herself will wonder at her friend's eagerness, and at this point the novel's plot starts to hang upon a plot in another sense of the word, to depend upon the hidden and unknown. The motivations and desires of the book's other characters begin to exercise a shaping force upon both Isabel's experience and our own; motivations unsuspected by her and unclear to us. One mark of that change is the growing freedom with which James starts to handle point of view. Up to this point he has stayed so close to his heroine as virtually to exclude his other characters' sense of things, but now he begins to dip, however briefly, into their very different inner lives. So Isabel talks with Madame Merle about Osmond's family history, and in the space of a single long paragraph James allows himself to slide from one mind to another, from Isabel's perceptions of what the older woman has said to the latter's impression of the girl's response to Osmond's sister. For Serena Merle worries about the Countess Gemini, worries about what that particular piece of flightiness might say.

When Madame Merle first comes to Osmond's villa, her host tells her that she is "looking very well." She has got an idea. On her that's always becoming, and soon enough it begins to bear fruit. Osmond finds that "the girl is not disagreeable," indeed that she's charming. But she does have one fault. Isabel too has ideas, a lot of ideas—though fortunately, Osmond says, they are all very bad ones. Fortunately, for they must be "sacrificed." Not because they are bad, but because they are hers.

12.

STRANIERI

I N 1786 A German poet traveling alone and under an assumed name boarded a coach in the spa town of Carlsbad and set off for the south on a holiday from the growing burden of his own fame. He ate his first figs in Munich, and once he had crossed the Brenner Pass and begun his descent into Italy, he exulted in a basket of peaches and pears. Venice seduced him but what he really wanted was Rome, and when he left the Adriatic behind, he pushed on so quickly for the papal city that he passed through Florence itself in a single night. Rome was the goal, for Goethe no less than for any other northerner on the Grand Tour, Rome and its remains, Rome and his hopes that the city might enlarge his very soul. So it will prove for Isabel Archer. She enjoys her weeks in Florence, but she too wants something more, and she will eventually make her home in the ancient capital.

Still, her first visit is a short one—just ten days at the end of May. She travels down from Florence with Ralph and Henrietta and they take rooms at the Hôtel de Paris. James himself usually stayed at the much larger Roma, in the Corso, which was especially recommended for "passing travellers or bachelors." But he put his characters exactly where one would have found their real-life equivalents, just a few steps away from the Piazza di Spagna, in the center of what was called the city's "strangers' quarter." The Baedeker for 1879 lists an Albergo di Parigi in the via San Sebastianello, a steep and narrow little street that runs parallel to the Spanish Steps, climbing up toward the Pincio, the hanging gardens where Daisy Miller had scandalized her world by strolling unchaperoned with an Italian. Keats had died just around the corner, in a house near the foot of the Steps, and Dorothea Brooke in *Middlemarch* had spent her unhappy honeymoon close by in the via Sistina, which runs from their top down to Piazza Barberini. And today it remains a district of *stranieri* still, as anyone who has had to sidle around the crowds on those stairs will know.

In James's day as in ours, the neighborhood was crowded with hotels, most of them with similarly generic names—the Russia, the Europa, the Inghilterra. Among them the only thing that distinguishes Isabel's is the fact that it billed itself as suitable for families; an unostentatious choice for someone still getting used to her money. A few years later the Hôtel de Paris appears to have moved, while staying well within the quarter. My 1886 Baedeker gives an address on via San Nicola di Tolentino, a street in which many foreign artists kept their studios; advertisements note that it had one of the city's first elevators. In that later spot it faced the Palazzo Barberini, where the sculptor William Wetmore Story rented an apartment of some fifty rooms, an apartment that functioned as the unofficial capital of the American colony in Rome and in which James himself spent many evenings.

In Florence, Osmond had told Isabel that he would like to see her in Rome, to watch her take it in, and soon enough he will follow her down. She will have another encounter before he does, however, and one that says more about the Anglo-American experience of the city. One afternoon she goes to the Forum, and when Ralph strolls off with a guide, she sits down on a fallen column. Scenery in this novel is never inert, never just a block of description. James always uses it to serve some dramatic purpose, to tell us something about his characters' perceptions or desires. He has already suggested that though Isabel does feel the burden of Rome's past, she also finds the city full of "the fresh, cool breath of the future." Even the tumbled walls of the Forum make her think of nothing so much as her own prospects, and she's so lost in her thoughts of the life to come that she doesn't hear an approaching footstep, looking up only when a shadow falls across her line of vision.

The shadow belongs to Lord Warburton, and their meeting is accidental. He himself has been in Turkey and has stopped off in Rome on his way back home. In reading one certainly feels that the novelist is busily plotting; this way of bringing an old suitor onto the stage looks, at first, like coincidence on a Dickensian scale. Yet we shouldn't allow it to strain our credulity. In an 1860 letter Henry Adams writes of going to the Vatican and running into "a young lady whom I used to know at Dresden," while the letters his wife Clover sent from Italy are full of her chance encounters with other Bostonians. Warburton tells Isabel that he is merely passing through, but that doesn't mean he'll treat it "as if it were Clapham Junction. To pass through Rome is to stop for a week or two." Clapham Junction was and is a South London railroad station, and even now remains the busiest commuter interchange in Britain. For people in Isabel's world, however, Rome itself was a kind of Clapham Junction. It provided a major switching point on the routes of Victorian tourism, and in 1873 James wrote in a letter that "I have first or last seen in a cab in the Corso every one I ever saw anywhere before."

Warburton's entrance will have its effect on the plot, but it also has an effect on the reader today that's summed up by a line in the journals of John Cheever. The Forum now looks, Cheever wrote, as if it were "a double ruin: a ruin of antiquity and a monument to the tender sentiments of eighteenth- and nineteenth-century travelers, for we see not only the ghosts of the Romans here but the shades of ladies with parasols and . . . little children rolling hoops." Any experience of Rome is a layered one, with cars honking outside a church built atop a temple, but such things now also lie under a topsoil of Anglo-American perception, and all of Italy comes to us as filtered through our awareness of earlier travelers. We remember what James said, or Twain; we register the difference between their version of the Caesars and ours, and pat ourselves on the back for knowing more than Hawthorne, who described the church of San Luigi dei Francesi without noticing the Caravaggios. Tastes shift, and desires as well, and the chronicle of touristic appreciation stands itself as a part of the city's meaning and a measure too of America's ever-changing relations with Europe. We join our own perceptions up with our predecessors', and so place ourselves in history. We assert a sense of continuity; we give ourselves a past.

James delighted in what he called the "palpable imaginable *visitable past*—in the nearer distances" of a recently departed era. Such a period seemed close enough to reach, as by the long stretch of a mental arm, and for Cheever—for me—one face of that past now belongs to James himself. But the ghosts he usually saw were those of people still present, and in Rome he reserved a special fascination for the earlier lives of his expatriated elders, the lives they had led just before his own arrival. They were the relicts of the city he called old Rome: a quiet town, and underpopulated, a place in which the pope was both the secular and the spiritual ruler, and where all modern opinion was censored. James had known that city for just a few months at the end of 1869, on his own first excited visit, and could never quite shed his sense of it. But the next year the Papal States were annexed by the new kingdom of Italy, and by the time he returned, in the winter of 1872–73, the city seemed to him to have lost a part of its color and style. The pope's carriage no longer passed in the street; old Rome had vanished just when he got there, a fact that only increased his own sense of belatedness. America was a young nation, but even among other Americans he had come too late.

In 1903, James published one of his most curious books, a two-volume biography, in the accepted life-and-letters mode, called *William Wetmore Story and His Friends*. Its subject was the Salem-born son of a Supreme Court justice, and a bit of a prodigy; a man who in his twenties had produced treatises on contracts and personal property. But the law bored him. Story liked poetry more, and was also interested in the visual arts, an interest confirmed by his first visit to Italy in 1847. A decade later he took his family abroad for good. Money went far in Rome, and Story had plenty of it; his place in the Barberini seemed cheap. It was on an upper floor of a sprawling seventeenth-century palace, a building that made James meditate on "what the grand style for the few involved in the way of a small style for the many." The owners had kept the best rooms for themselves, including the one with the Cortona ceiling that celebrated Urban VII, the family's pope, and James sometimes caught a glimpse of history as he climbed the stairs to his American friends: the sight of the old Cardinal Barberini himself playing cards with his priests, whose resigned smiles announced that they had, once more, managed to let His Eminence win.

Story's smoothly classicizing sculpture has little interest for us now, but it was famous in its time; a fame helped by his friendship with Hawthorne, who described some of it in *The Marble Faun*. By the time James knew him, however, the sculptor's best work all lay in the past. He had settled into life as a host, and though the novelist admitted in an 1873 letter that the man's "cleverness" was great, he added that "the world's good nature to him is greater." James liked some of Story's travel sketches, but he thought the rest of it—the poetry and the marbles alike—nothing more than the work of a charming amateur. So he hesitated when, after his 1895 death, Story's family asked him to do the biography; accepting only because he needed the advance to furnish Lamb House. Still, James kept putting it off, believing that the materials were too thin, that neither the man's life nor his work contained enough to fill the project out. The money had been spent, though, and when he finally began, he discovered that he did have the makings of a book: not a biography per se, but a portrait of Story's generation, in which the narrative is carried by the letters the sculptor had written to and received from larger figures.

In that excursion into the visitable past Story appears as one of James's own "precursors": those Americans who went to Europe when the going was not yet easy. Writing in an age when America had become one of the world's Great Powers, James found himself fascinated by his nation's early but ever-growing "consciousness of the complicated world it was so persistently to annex." He himself belonged to a generation that had gone well supplied with guidebooks and photographs and letters of introduction. His elders had had no such luxuries, and especially the artists among them. They had had no one to tell them what and where and how to study, and James recognized that his own easy cosmopolitanism depended on the fact that his predecessors had cut the road before him. He knew that Story's or even Hawthorne's understanding of Europe appeared quaint in comparison to that of his own era; the era as well of Sargent and Whistler, no longer the Old World's students, but counted among its masters. Nevertheless, he saw them with a filial piety, for those precursors included not only Story, or his parents, but also his own earliest characters. They had made his world, his fiction—had made *him*—possible.

In Italy the Americans and the English often formed a single community, and James couldn't resist noting that during the fall of 1849 Elizabeth Barrett Browning read *Jane Eyre* in a copy she had borrowed from the Storys. But such homespun details should make us pause. The picture James's fiction gives us of expatriate life has become so emblematic a part of our culture that we need to ask just how many people lived and moved in the world he described. Or rather how few. The 1872 Murray's *Handbook of Rome* notes that in 1870 there were just 457 permanently resident Protestants in a city where the total population approached 250,000; given Italy's own religious homogeneity, the term functions as a proxy for "foreign." The Italian census for 1871 offers a rather different figure, however, and puts the number of Protestants at 3,798. The historian John Pemble explains the discrepancy as reflecting, first, a sharp increase in the scale of both business and diplomacy after Rome became the capital of the united Italy; and second, the possible inclusion in that figure of the temporary population in hotels and lodgings. The latter suggestion seems confirmed by the travel writer Bayard Taylor, who wrote in March 1868 that there were then 1,200 Americans in the city; most of them left immediately after Easter. Such transients were Rome's equivalent of summer—that is, winter—people, those who came for the "season," as James himself did in 1872–73. But the fixed population remained small. An 1894 survey of "Americans Abroad" in *Lippincott's* notes that while Rome then received 30,000 of James's countrymen as visitors each year, there were still just 200 permanent American inhabitants. Paris had 2,500.

That number would, however, have included many people who did *not* figure in James's world. The young seminarians from the Vatican's new American College were not likely to appear at the Storys' Sunday evening at-homes. Nor were the city's English tradesmen, to whom Murray and

Baedeker provide something like a gazetteer. A Mr. Shea arranged the lease of furnished apartments from his office in the Piazza di Spagna, and was also recommended as a trustworthy agent for those wishing to ship luggage or artwork to England and America. A "depot of London saddlery" could be found at Barfoot's in the via del Babuino, and G. Baker owned a pharmacy. There were no English booksellers as such, but the German-run Spithöver's stocked English publications and got the newspapers too. An erstwhile drawing master named Arthur Strutt had become a noted distributor of Italian wines, and the eponymous Ice Company made its wares from "Trevi water." A Miss Black is listed in Murray's as a "daily governess," an American dentist practiced in the via Nazionale, and a man called Jarrett kept a livery stable in the Piazza del Popolo. Thomas Cook had its office in the Piazza di Spagna, and an English company ran the city's gasworks from a plant at the Circus Maximus.

These businesses allowed visitors, or indeed the city's resident Anglophones, to arrange their lives without the need to know Italian or even any Italians. And certainly those tourists were needed to fill the Church of England Chapel, which seated 800; the American Episcopal church was even bigger. But the Storys' tea-parties would in any case have drawn upon a different population. Murray recommended three English doctors and one American. There were several English bankers, though James himself used the Italian house of Spada, Flamini. There were the embassies, and above all there were artists. The 1872 edition of Murray's lists 36 studios run by American or English sculptors and painters, while noting that the roster includes only established figures—not students, not beginners. Few of them have a reputation today. The real talent had begun to go instead to Paris, where one could study the painting of modern life, and of the permanent residents the most interesting was the sculptor Harriet Hosmer, a friend of Hawthorne's whom James described as looking like a "remarkably ugly little grey-haired boy." Her work has more tactile play than Story's; and she had also helped import a pack of hounds for the newly established Roman hunt.

The smaller Roman world-within-a-world in which James moved and of which he wrote contained just a few hundred people. I count some fifty names in the letters he sent to Cambridge in the winter and spring of 1873, and many of them belong to fellow transients. The Bootts fell into this category, down for the winter from Florence. So did a new friend, Sara Butler Wister, from Philadelphia. She was the daughter of the English actress Fanny Kemble, at whose London fireside James would later sit, and the mother of Owen Wister, the future author of *The Virginian* (1902). James admired her beautiful hair, but insisted to Quincy Street that he didn't "at all regret that I'm not Dr. Wister." He had other meetings with old friends and acquaintances who were, like Lord Warburton, simply passing through. Early in March he met up with a rather feeble Ralph Waldo Emerson; a few weeks later he saw the newly married Mr. and Mrs. Henry Adams on their way back from an Egyptian honeymoon. But such encounters were just hometown gossip, and James wrote to William that though he supposed Rome was full of interesting people, "I doubt that there is any very edifying society."

Nevertheless, he decided in these months to surrender himself to the entanglements of expatriate life. He complained about it, but he put his work on hold in order to absorb the sights and sounds of this rarefied milieu. He went to three weekly receptions, he lunched and dined and called, and in the floating world of the Roman spring this spare man soon found himself "in the position of a creature with *five* women *offering* to ride with him." His companions on horseback included both Mrs. Wister and Alice Mason, the divorced wife of the Massachusetts politican Charles Sumner; but his favorite companion remained Lizzie Boott. With such a routine it is perhaps no wonder that the emphasis of his Italian fiction would soon begin to change. Most nineteenth-century American novels about Italy—*The Marble Faun*, James's own *Roderick Hudson*, to some degree Howells's *Indian Summer*—devoted themselves to the lives of artists, providing a sanitized version of *la vie bohème* in which the pursuit of culture is entirely compatible with bourgeois propriety. As such, they offered a conventional account of what their authors believed their countrymen wanted from the Old World. One of the things that separates *The Portrait of a Lady* from those books is its indifference to the world of the studios. Its representative American in Rome is Madame Merle, who keeps a smart third-floor pied-à-terre, not Hawthorne's Puritan painter Hilda, with her home in an airy tower. James wrote to his brother that he hoped his winter of relentless socializing had given him "more impressions" than it seemed, and one of the things he got, which now makes *Roderick Hudson* look dated, was the sense that America's Italy was no longer what it had been in his precursors' age. It was no longer the site of artistic devotion, but had instead become a fashionable playground, a stopping point for an international society that moved from place to place and crossed the oceans with the seasons. If Gilbert Osmond were real, he would in his younger days have known such American artists as Story or Hiram Powers; he would have shared his side of the Arno with the Brownings. But not a trace of that appears in Isabel's world, a world that contains nobody remotely like James himself.

James wrote to Quincy Street in January that the American society he found in Rome seemed "without relations with the place, or much serious appreciation of it." To say that, however, is to beg the question of James's own relations with the place, and indeed with Europe itself. After he read the Story biography, Henry Adams told him that the book had exposed the ignorance of the world from which they both came, making him "curl up, like a trodden-on worm. Improvised Europeans, we were, and—Lord God!—How thin." Adams took some consolation in the thought that almost nobody would recognize the truth, but James's own characters had said similar things. The historian's phrases, however pungent, are simply a version of the standard complaint about "cosmopolites"—the usual thing said about them, said even or especially by themselves. As Ellen Olenska in Wharton's *Age of Innocence* would later argue, "It seems stupid to have discovered America only to make it into a copy of another country."

Of course, Adams's claim also points to a great paradox. His generation had gone to Europe in search of what they couldn't find at home, and yet in doing so they were also making a past, a heritage, for us; and at the turn of the twentieth century the intellectual life of Boston and Cambridge, which improvised upon that European legacy, was richer than that of Rome itself. As James himself knew. He knew that America would control the future by annexing the past. It would make its culture by exploiting its freedom to choose, to draw upon the heritage of different lands and centuries, taking a painting here and a philosophy there. Such, at any rate, is the burden of his last great novel, *The Golden Bowl,* which among other things explores the classical motif of the *translatio studii et imperii,* the movement of learning and power from one civilization to another.

Still, the Europe that draws that novel's ironically named art collector, Adam Verver, isn't that of the present day. He buys old things, not new; that was what America wanted, what it both lacked and desired. James recognized that his countrymen's fascination with the past made them ignore Italy's own preoccupation "with its economical and political future," and yet he too resisted seeing it as a modern state. Some English expatriates, like the Brownings, had identified themselves with the Risorgimento. Most Americans abroad did not, and modernity was precisely what they had come to escape. James came to speak good Italian and to read it with some ease, but he had few Italian friends, and though he had once thought of settling in Italy, his season in Rome persuaded him otherwise. Those months taught him that it was hard to write about a picturesque subject in a picturesque country. The city gave too much. The most intelligent conversation seemed unable to compete with the spectacle of its streets, and James wondered if even so limited an artist as Story might have worked with a "finer rage" in the unfriendlier air of Boston or London. He himself would write better of Italy—would have deeper imaginative relations to it—for not being there, and the most interesting question raised by his January letter to Quincy Street isn't about any particular place, about Rome or even all of Italy. It is instead the question of the place in his work of place itself.

During her first days in Rome, Isabel finds that the city seems to speak of her own future, and she will later see it as embodying her own psychic state: a place in which people have suffered, and in which "the ruins of her happiness seemed a less unnatural catastrophe." Such passages should make us ask if Europe ever stands for James as something more or other than a backdrop against which the dramas of his American characters might play. In what way is it integral, and in what mere scenery? One of the things that fascinated him about Hawthorne was what he called the "imported" nature of his sense of sin. Hawthorne certainly knew the world of his Puritan ancestors, but to James he didn't appear haunted by it. His relation to its almost mystical darkness was an intellectual rather than a moral one, and to James he seemed but to play with its shadows. On this reading, sin becomes an aspect of the picturesque, and indeed James's language takes on a geographic tinge; he speaks of the "rugged prominence of moral responsibility." Sin is atmosphere, it is contour and relief. It intensifies the drama, just as Isabel's sense of her own sadness gains from her awareness of the ever-present Roman past.

Let's say, then, that James uses Europe in the way he thinks Hawthorne does sin—as color or background, a way to ratchet up the stakes, but not as a part of his work's deepest being. Yet that claim in itself begs a central question about America's relation to the rest of the world. In many ways Europe provides as fresh a start for James's characters as it did for their creator. It lets them appear as though cut off from their pasts. Madame Merle's native Brooklyn no longer appears to matter, nor Osmond's Baltimore, and even Isabel's more significant antecedents dwindle by the page. But in stepping out of America she doesn't quite step into Europe either, and the bubble life of the expatriate becomes as one with her belief in her own exceptional fate. Her very disconnection from the world around her reinforces her claim that "nothing that belongs to me is any measure of me," and the American girl's Europe becomes a place in which one can explore the limits of the self in itself, unbound by the fetters of national origin. It stands as a paradox, offering liberty and history at once; a place in which one's exemption from history seems to provide a warrant for that liberty. But James's own Europe is very different from that of his characters, and never more central than when it seems mere background, than when it fosters the illusion of freedom on which Isabel depends.

James drew on his Roman winter for years to come; it gave him both

Roderick Hudson and the later chapters of the *Portrait* along with a number of short stories. Its most immediate results, however, were the two travel essays he published in the summer of 1873. "A Roman Holiday" purports to offer an account of the annual pre-Lenten Carnival, an event that provides a set piece in almost all touristic descriptions of the city. It is there in Goethe, in Dickens, in Hawthorne—and what's also there in each of them is an almost ritual sense of disappointment. *This* sorry show is the Carnival, this tired display of masks and confetti and forced hilarity? The festival began that year on the fifteenth of February. It was a Saturday, and James was at his desk in the Hôtel de Rome when a sudden intensification of noise pulled him to his window. He had formed his own idea of Carnival from a children's book that featured an elegant masked lady on a balcony, but the ladies on the balconies now were all shoveling lime and flour down on to the heads of the pedestrians below, and when he went out himself, James immediately got a pailful dumped upon him. Nothing in this "dingy drollery" could match his childhood fantasies, but once he had shaken the flour from his ears, he had a vision of just how empty the rest of the city must be. So he took a holiday from the holiday, wandering away from the festival's compulsory pleasures and out to the Forum and Santa Maria Maggiore—familiar places, but made fresh by his own sense of escape.

The essay's most suggestive passage describes a church James doesn't even name, though he offers precise directions as to how to find it. A little road cuts up the Palatine, running like a country lane between high walls, and then rounds a bend to a pocket-sized, barrel-vaulted church; any good map will give its name as San Bonaventura. Just five minutes' walk—but it's still enough, even now, for the city's bustle to fade out. The church remains so untouristed as to seem forgotten, and on the day I visited, there was only one other person inside, a man sitting in prayer before the high altar. I circled around behind him, walking as softly as I could and trying to make out the paintings on the walls—Caravaggio knockoffs, but so darkened by candle smoke that I couldn't really see them. On the day James discovered it, he too had found just a solitary worshiper. A young priest was visiting each of the church's seven altars in turn, and the novelist thought he could hear in the silence the distant bustle of the Carnival itself. The young man's pale face looked like a judgment on that merriment, and yet his piety came with privations so great that to the writer it appeared "a terrible game—a gaining one only if your zeal never falters; a hard fight when it does." The language James uses here is so charged with both the sense of his own vocation and a knowledge of its price that it makes the priest seem a kind of stand-in, a figure on whom he can place the burden of his own choice. "I made no vows," Wordsworth writes in *The Prelude* as he remembers the moment of his dedication to poetry, "but vows were then made for me," and James here makes an altar of words before which to renew his own pledge.

A few weeks later he hired one of Mr. Jarrett's horses in the hope that riding would give him some much-needed exercise, and wrote to Quincy Street of his pleasure in keeping a "close seat." He would leave the city from the Porta del Popolo, heading out across the Campagna, and though he usually rode in company, he depicts himself in "Roman Rides" as traveling alone. The essay stands as his most deliberate attempt to create a picturesque landscape. The remnants of the Claudian Aqueduct along which he rode spoke more of Claude Lorrain than they did of the emperor who built it, and its ruins felt to him as though they were themselves "the very source of the solitude in which they stand . . . [looming] with the same insubstantial vastness as if they rose out of Egyptian sands." Such an image belongs to the mind as much as it does to the ground itself, the mind that produces the scenes it expects to find. James did indeed see the Campagna as landscape, not land, looking for the accustomed bits of broken column or a shepherd in the foreground, and his readers will once again think of the Romantics. Only not Wordsworth this time, but rather the Coleridge of "Kubla Khan" and the Shelley of "Ozymandias."

In Rome every moment chimes against the past, every moment has its echo, and in riding over the countryside, James knew that he was riding through history as well, as though space and time could be plotted with the same coordinates. Every step spoke of an "unbroken continuity," and he found a paradoxical freedom in the humbling fact that everything he saw had already "suited some one else." He couldn't flatter himself that he had discovered it. Goethe had found in Rome a sense of the everlasting. The city outfaced any change of fashion, and the poet used it to underwrite his own claim to permanence. And what James took from the Eternal City was a national variation on that truth. Rome taught him that freedom depends upon accepting the bonds of history. These places have all been named before. As an American, he may be a new man but he isn't an Adam, and what Europe offered was the chance to decline the burdens of the American condition. It allowed him to declare himself free of the need to make all things new, to strive and struggle in pursuit of some manifest destiny. "Roman Rides" attempts to define the relation between the modern self and the past, the American mind and the past. It is a more profound piece of writing than any of its author's early fiction.

13.

AN UNCERTAIN TERRAIN

IN FLORENCE, ISABEL and Osmond had talked about his joining her party in Rome; that is, he had proposed the idea while making it seem like hers. He gives her a few days' start and then comes on, tracking her down at Sunday vespers at St. Peter's, and James lets his readers know that Osmond is now as tense with desire as he has ever been for a painting. Isabel tells him, as they stand in the church's incense-thickened air, that her other friends are somewhere in the crowd, but his answer is explicit: "I didn't come for the others." Those words make her color. They're too close to what Warburton had said in beginning his own proposal, almost 200 pages earlier, and she blushes at both the burden of Osmond's statement and at the fact that Warburton himself is standing nearby. He may even have heard, for a moment later the Englishman will walk away with Ralph and ask just who—and what—Osmond is. The reply isn't comforting, and when Warburton asks if Osmond is a "good fellow," Ralph pauses for as long as he can before answering: "No, he's not."

James must have thought that answer too definitive. He retouched this moment in the New York Edition, and his changes shift its emphasis away from Osmond himself and onto the dramatic situation as a whole:

"Does she like him?"
"She's trying to find out."
"And will she?"

"Find out—?" Ralph asked.

"Will she like him?"

"Do you mean will she accept him?"

And that, Warburton admits after a moment, is indeed what he "horribly" means. To understand this moment we need to look not only at what James says about Isabel, but also at what he has now, in revision, decided *not* to say about Osmond. In the novel's 1881 version Ralph admits the man can sometimes seem delightful but that doesn't shake his confident appraisal. Osmond's not a good fellow, and if he makes a favorable impression, that's merely a sign of his artfulness. The later version offers something more probingly tentative. Faulkner sometimes explained the discrepancies between the linked novels of his Yoknapatawpha cycle by claiming he had simply learned more about his characters since writing the first one, as if they had a continuing life outside his pages. James's own revisions offer something similar. Reading the two versions of the *Portrait* alongside one another suggests that the gap between them has allowed him to see things he didn't at first, to explore the possibilities latent within his initial conception. Backing away from Ralph's earlier judgment lets him emphasize, not Osmond's nature, but the drama of the young woman's choice. The change underlines questions that any actual Isabel would have asked herself, and to Ralph she now looks like someone trying to crack the puzzle of her own emotions. Osmond is someone whom she cannot yet place, an unknown quantity, a figure she can't sum up. And while we might have made up our own minds about him, the passage leaves us hanging as well; we may suspect the answer she'll reach, but we can still hope she won't act upon it. The paradox is that in withholding Ralph's explicit judgment, these revisions make Osmond seem more dangerous than ever.

Osmond quickly realizes that Warburton is a rejected suitor—which only increases his interest in Isabel. By turning down an English peer, this American girl has "qualified herself to figure in his collection of choice objects," and a few evenings later he appears in her sitting room at the Hôtel de Paris. He knows she plans to travel, and claims to wonder if she'll ever return to Italy. Isabel in turn thinks he's laughing at her ignorance, at the blundering way she goes about as if the globe itself belonged to her. But Osmond is gentle and reminds her that in Florence he had told her that "one ought to make one's life a work of art." Those words had seemed to shock her, and yet he thinks that's exactly what she's now doing. Go everywhere, he says, be happy and triumphant too, and then some day when she feels tired—well, that will be the moment to come back to Italy. And perhaps, he adds, perhaps he should wait until then for something he wishes to say.

Of course, he doesn't wait, but what's more important, and more determinative, is what he doesn't say. He tells her "that I find I am in love with you," but he doesn't ask her to marry him. He speaks as though he expects nothing from the act. He speaks as if for his own relief only, and though Isabel asks him to keep those words for when she is tired indeed, her plea lacks the air of crisp decision with which she had refused both Warburton and Caspar Goodwood. For she has nothing here to refuse—a declaration has been made, but nothing has yet been asked of her. Maybe that's why she remains willing to listen; why, in fact, she will accept him some months later. Yet though Isabel hears an "immense sweetness" in his words, she still retreats before him. Osmond would say more if she offered the barest shred of encouragement, but Isabel dreads the moment of decision. She knows here once more the kind of fear she had felt on her visit to Lockleigh, and that fear seems all the greater because she now knows what is in her heart.

For Isabel remains in terror of surrendering herself to the very passion that "ought to have banished all dread," the passion that stands as the greatest of threats to her sense of self-sufficiency. Once again James's revisions are crucial. They provide both a retrospective gloss on her hopes and fears, and a suggestion of how much his own world had changed. The issues of his own affective life had been settled, for better or worse, for good or nil. The tacit censorship of the publishing world had loosened, the three novels of his "major phase"—*The Wings of the Dove*, *The Ambassadors*, and *The Golden Bowl*—had all turned on the question of sex outside marriage, and the older writer often employed an imagery of which the younger one was largely innocent. In both versions Osmond's words produce a "pang" in which pleasure and pain have an equal part. In the New York Edition, however, James likens "the sharpness of the pang . . . [to] the slipping of a fine bolt, backward, forward, she couldn't have said which." The erotic charge is too obvious to miss, and yet let's take that simile at face value. The crucial word has been a part of this book from the start. Isabel has always refused to keep her imagination "behind bolts," as if in a locked room; the phrase appears in an early chapter of the 1881 edition and stands unrevised in the later one. Here, however, it's not clear if that slipping bolt will open a door or close one, free her or bind her, protect or confine her.

James borrowed the image from Matthew Arnold, who in his 1852 poem "The Buried Life" describes a world in which emotion must struggle for expression, struggle until the sound of a loved one's voice makes us feel that "a bolt is shot back somewhere in our breast,/And a lost pulse of feeling stirs again." For Isabel is indeed stirred by Osmond's words, and knows that something has happened here that didn't happen with the other men, even if she doesn't yet know what she should do about it. Two things Osmond says before he goes are worth lingering on; they will help us understand both her eventual decision and the later course of her married life. He tells her that he likes the idea of her doing "everything that's proper; I go in for that," but when she asks if he is conventional, he denies it. "I am convention itself." He hasn't simply accepted convention. He has actively chosen it, and we will learn that the most important of those accustomed practices are the ones he's defined for himself. The other thing Osmond does is to ask her to call on his daughter in Florence. Pansy has remained with a servant at the villa, where she seems something close to a prisoner, allowed to enter the garden but no more. She stands as the most expertly played of Osmond's cards, a low trump that still allows him to make his bid—and Isabel's visit with the girl will remind us that she too had lost her mother young.

After Osmond leaves, Isabel finds herself in the emotional equivalent of an oxymoron, suffering from an "agitation" that is nevertheless "very still, very deep." The man's words aren't entirely unexpected, but they nevertheless bring her imagination to a halt, as if she stood on the uncrossable brink of a "dusky, uncertain tract which looked ambiguous, and even slightly treacherous." James's phrasing recalls his evocation of the Campagna's broken ground in "Roman Rides," and it might also remind us of the murky borders of the Kantian sublime, with its sense of threat and loss, the loss of self-posssession. That indeed is what Isabel fears, that surrender to the buried life within. It makes her stop as at the edge of an undiscovered country. But it will not stay undiscovered for long.

*T*he *Portrait of a Lady* contains two significant gaps in time: ellipses in its narrative, holes in our knowledge, moments of undescribed action that nevertheless determine the shape of both Isabel's life and that of the work itself. She stands on the rim of that uncertain terrain called marriage, her foot is raised, but her creator does not show her in the act of putting it down. When she visits Pansy in Florence, Isabel listens to the child speak of her father with an interest that it torments her to conceal, but she then leaves Italy with her aunt and travels north with the seasons. It is just a page, and yet almost a full year before we see her again, standing at the window of Mrs. Touchett's Florentine palace: a year that begins with Osmond's declaration and ends with Isabel's reappearance as his fiancée. The second and even more significant rupture comes five chapters on. James skips not only his heroine's wedding but also the next three years, and our first view of the Osmonds' marriage will make it look damaged from the start.

It's as though the need to make Isabel cross that boundary has engendered a form of disturbance, a pair of cracks in the book's sequence that stand as a version of James's own figure in the carpet—absent causes, in Tzvetan Todorov's phrase, unwritten moments of decision. For the novelist's own imagination has been brought to a halt here as well. He too needs to cover that territory, and will do so without entirely meeting its difficulties. Isabel stands waiting for a visitor, and James tell us that she's newly returned from another stay in Rome. What he doesn't tell us is that she has come back engaged; that's something we won't learn until she herself announces it. She seems to have leaped over that terrain, and to have carried her author with her. Or maybe he's the one who has jumped. He can show us Isabel in the act of refusal, but what he cannot or will not do is to show her in the moment of choice; the moment in which she accepts a role in a plot she had once rejected.

James wrote in his autobiography that he had known since childhood that life consisted of "scenes." But he also tells us that Isabel isn't fond of them, and the *Portrait* suggests that there are a few he doesn't much like either, scenes he would just as soon avoid doing. A novelist's "individual technique," in Graham Greene's words, "is more than anything else a means of evading the personally impossible, of disguising a deficiency." Lesser writers never recognize their limitations. Many great ones stumble over something a hack might do with ease. James has a preference for finished states and an unwillingness to dramatize the process of decision. Nevertheless, he needs to marry off his heroine and he needs to do it not at the end of the book but now. He needs to do it in the novel's broad middle because he is not, paradoxically, all that interested in courtship. He needs to do it because he wants to give us the portrait of a lady, not a girl, and he has to do it now because he wants to avoid the teleology of the marriage plot, in which Isabel's progress would be defined by the choice of a husband alone. And yet James also knows, again paradoxically, that marriage remains one of the most complicated destinies a woman might face. Some of his best early stories—tales like "Madame de Mauves" or "The Last of the Valerii"—depict the drama within marriage, the drama of those who are already locked together. But James was also known for his reluctance to end his books with a wedding, and his imagination is persistently drawn to the moment of refusal, to events that don't happen. In his later work he would write about passion with a depth and precision that he could not as a young novelist command, but he would never be comfortable in showing us the drama of acceptance. Tolstoy could do that, and Trollope. Not James, and we don't need a biographical explanation to see its effect on his work. Grant that he does not depict the moments in which Isabel persuades herself to discard her fears. What does he do instead—and what might he gain by *not* showing it to us?

When the novel returns to Florence, we don't at first know how Isabel has spent her year. We don't know for whom she's waiting, or if she's been in contact with Osmond; and James will delay telling us for as long as he can. Still, he recognizes that we do need to be told something, and filling us in on her year of frenetic travel will both satisfy that desire and allow him an extra pause. So he tells us that she has gone to Switzerland and Paris with her sister Lily, who's come over from New York; and then with Madame Merle to Italy, Egypt, and Greece. Isabel travels so restlessly because she has seen what she wants even if she can't yet make herself take it; a literal displacement of desire. Yet the movement hardly satisfies her, and perhaps nothing on her itinerary proves so entirely rewarding as a November walk across London.

She has just put her sister on a train for Liverpool and home, and turns away from the station into the brown fog of the city streets. It's evening and the gaslight seems dim as she walks back from Euston to her Piccadilly hotel, delighting in the shops and stalls, in "the dark, shining dampness of everything," delighting above all in the fact that nobody in the world knows where she is. The sidewalks are crowded and the streets full of fast-moving cabs, but she walks through the town as if she owns it, walks alone in a way that was then rare for women of her class, without a servant or a male protector, and loses her way in order to magnify her experience. She walks in the belief that she has taken possession of London itself, but what she's really done is to take possession of her own life, and at this moment she truly thinks that "the world lay before her—she could do whatever she chose." But so too "the world was all before" Adam and Eve on their expulsion from Paradise; James's Miltonic echo is deliberate, and in this fallen world not even Isabel can have that freedom entire.

On our first encounter with the novel we read about Isabel's travels in the belief that James is simply preparing us for the next stage of her adventures. We read of London and Cairo without realizing that there's been a gap of anything more than time. But Isabel has already taken her next step; taken it without our knowledge, without the knowledge of anyone but Osmond himself. Or no: she has told one other person. She has written a letter to Caspar Goodwood in America. He's the one she is waiting for at the Palazzo Crescentini, and we first hear of her engagement when he says that "I would rather think of you as dead than as married to another man." The words are like a slap—a slap not to her but to us—and even then James will make us wait for another page before he allows Goodwood to produce Osmond's name, a page on which we ready ourselves for a second blow. For the news fills us with the same sense of surprise and dismay as it does the book's other characters. It makes us feel that Isabel had better explain herself.

James's sleight-of-hand forces us to realize that we don't know his heroine as well as we thought. "I had no idea . . . you were choosing," Ralph will say a few pages on, "and your silence put me off my guard." We know she finds Osmond attractive, even without the slipping bolt of those late revisions, but the moment has crept up on us, and James's masterly delay makes it look as though she's been hiding things. She seems more elusive now than ever, as if he had decided to smudge the carefully drawn lines of her face. Yet though he doesn't dramatize the process of choice, James does allow her to justify her decision. To Goodwood, it's true, she will refuse an explanation; the poor man crosses the ocean to protest for ten minutes, and returns to America at once. Ralph is different, however, and we can best understand Isabel by listening in on her conversation with him.

"You are going to be put in a cage," he says. Ralph arrives in Florence from a winter on Corfu, more helplessly ill than ever, and though Isabel believes that his mother has told him the news, he at first gives no sign of knowledge. But when she finally makes him speak, he speaks bluntly indeed. He had thought she would choose a man of "more importance." Those words make her angry. The man, she says, is important enough to her, and her position seems credible to the precise degree that their conversation makes her realize that Ralph isn't as disinterested as she had always thought. It will be many chapters yet before she learns what he's done for her, but James does let him confess here that he has loved to think of her as "soaring . . . sailing in the bright light" above, that he has taken his pleasure in planning out her destiny. His shocked response to her choice doesn't simply mark his belief that she's making a mistake, but also the fact that the story she's about to write for herself doesn't match the one he had sketched out; it's as though his character had gotten away from him.

Ralph's dismay prompts one of the novel's great moments. His reaction forces Isabel to tell him what she sees in Osmond, to define what she wants in a husband, and her words echo her earlier conversation with Madame Merle about clothes: a definition of individual autonomy in which liberty itself is now couched in negative terms. Osmond isn't important, no, he is instead "a man to whom importance is supremely indifferent," a man who makes his own standards. She has already told Goodwood that the collector is a nonentity, and the industrialist has caught the sense of peculiar pride that makes such nothingness stand as a positive attraction. Osmond is what other men are not. He has refused the indignity of effort; at first, we remember, he did not even ask her to marry him. He hasn't "scrambled nor struggled—he has cared for no worldly prize," and to Ralph she even praises the dignity with which he carries his relative poverty, as though it were an infirmity about which he had had no choice. He is, she claims, a man with "no property, no title, no honours, no houses, nor lands, nor position, nor reputation, nor brilliant belongings of any sort," and many readers have noted the resemblance of that list to *Hawthorne's* catalogue of American absences. Defined by his residence abroad, by his loss of the distinguishing marks of origin, Osmond is nevertheless cast in an American mold. Isabel will say that he's not a proprietor, but what she really means is that he isn't a personage like Warburton. He is simply a private citizen, a privacy reinforced by his expatriate's distance from any surrounding social fabric. He is Gilbert Osmond. He lives in Italy; he has chosen, she thinks, to rely upon himself alone.

In the days before her marriage Isabel spends her mornings with Osmond in the Cascine, and as she walks through that Medici park, two things seem perfectly clear. First, she is deeply in love. And second, in choosing a husband she has picked out an idealized version of the unconfined self she wants to be, a self that appears to transcend its envelope of worldly circumstances. To Ralph, of course, she seems to love the man for "his very poverties dressed as honors," and when he criticizes Osmond's exacting taste, Isabel replies that "I hope it may never be my fortune to fail to gratify my husband's." Those words make him flinch. They sound like Osmond's, not hers, as though she had begun to live at some remove from her own voice. And in fact she now feels "disjoined" from every previous tie—she believes that marriage itself must lead to some break with all her earlier friends. What she doesn't yet know is that marrying this particular man will also entail a separation from herself, that her very aspirations will require her own negation. Osmond says that he wants a wife with a mind like a plate that he can heap with fruits of his own sensibility. Only they are his fruits, not hers, and Isabel will have to learn to hide her every independent thought away. The curious thing is that if she weren't in love she would already have seen enough of Osmond to share Ralph's judgment. She may claim that he cares for no earthly prize, but in Rome he describes Warburton as "detestably fortunate," and Isabel teases him for the way he seems "to be always envying someone." She may joke. Osmond never does, ironist though he is. He means what he says, and we can already see the barred shadow of his cage upon her face.

14.

A VENETIAN INTERLUDE

JAMES WROTE OF England in Italy and of Italy in England, and then, in the winter of 1881, he took himself south once more. The weather that year was hard, a season of blizzard that on January 18 covered southern England in snow. Drifts of 10 feet mounded themselves over Gloucestershire, and though London itself was not so heavily hit, James wrote a week later that the snow remained high and "the temperature ferocious." His work had gone smoothly, with the dark, short days given over to his account of Isabel's first Italian spring. But he had also paid a too steady round of country visits, most recently to Lord Rosebery's place at Epsom Downs, where he admired the Gainsboroughs and walked over the racecourse. James liked boasting about such invitations to Quincy Street and yet also felt impatient with the interruptions of his London life. He wanted the space and freedom in which to "quietly bring my novel to a close," and on February 9 he left for the Continent; the weather reports for the day suggest he had a rough time in the Channel.

Later in his career James would need both his secretary and her typewriter, but in these years he could write anywhere he found a table, and all his holidays were working ones. He was bent on Italy but traveled slowly from place to place, resting here and extending a stay there; everything about his journey was leisurely except the motion of his pen. He made his first stop in Paris, where he enjoyed three long talks with a gout-ridden Turgenev even as he found himself increasingly impatient with the city's "Frenchified"

American residents, whose cultural horizons were defined by the conservative newspaper *Le Figaro*. Then he moved down through France, pausing at both Avignon and Marseilles, and reporting from the latter that he eaten the "obligatory . . . mess of *bouillabaisse*, a formidable dish, demanding a French digestion." Next, he settled for three weeks at San Remo on the Italian Riviera. He had used the place as one of Ralph Touchett's winter refuges and now enjoyed a series of morning walks through the "dusky light" of the olive groves And it was from San Remo that on March 8 he sent the June and July installments of the *Portrait* to the *Atlantic*, where Howells had now been succeeded as editor by Thomas Bailey Aldrich; chapters that take Isabel through her engagement and into her marriage.

He stopped at Genoa and then again at Milan, still unsure, after six weeks on the road, whether Venice or Rome would be his final destination. Venetian winters could be cold, and the Adriatic's clammy fog made him think of choosing Rome's sunshine. He worried, however, that the latter city would be too full of people he knew, and couldn't stomach the idea of exchanging the English social season for an Italian one; the only thing he really liked about Milan was not having any calls to pay. In the end, he chose the surety of quiet, and left for Venice on March 25. He had been there twice before, but each stay had been brief; he knew the city only as a tourist and had already let his heroine pass through it in a phrase. Now he would stay until the end of June, working until *The Portrait of a Lady* was "virtually finished." But there would be other consequences as well.

The Venice of 1881 had reached a tipping point. It had joined the new nation of Italy in 1866, after fifty years of Austrian rule, and both its trade and its population had begun to increase. Neither of them approached the levels of 1797, however, when Napoleon put an end to the city's thousand years of independence, and the Baedeker for 1879 notes that fully one-fourth of its 128,000 inhabitants were paupers. James was acutely aware of the city's poverty, of the "painfully large" percentage of its citizens who appeared never to have enough to eat. It bothered him in a way that the poor did not in Florence or even Rome, and he was conscious too that the city's buildings seemed all out of scale with present needs, buildings that

could no longer "be lived in as they were intended to be." Nor was he the
only one to see the place as fundamentally at odds with modernity. There
were even Venetians who wanted to fill in the canals as a way to bring the
city up to date, and a few of them indeed were; the Strada Nuova got its
name for a reason.

A more realistic threat came from the introduction, in the year of
James's own visit, of the "awful" vaporetto. He thought the churning
screws of those steam launches would both undermine the city's foundations and threaten the livelihood of the gondoliers, who in fact went on
strike at the boats' first appearance. Yet the city's greatest challenge came
from precisely those forces that were to preserve it. James's stay led to an
essay, called simply "Venice," that remains as interesting for its account of
tourism as for its picture of the city itself. Venice had had more annual visitors than inhabitants since the 1840s, and by James's day the place seemed to
belong to them, to the tourists who wanted above all to confirm the impressions they had already formed from prints and paintings and now photographs, the mechanical reproductions that made this "battered peep show
and bazaar" seem familiar even to those who hadn't been there. The city
had become a place about which it was impossible to say anything new; a
decade later James added that it was now but "the most beautiful of tombs,"
a monument to its own lost importance.

He quickly became an expert at knowing when the masses of other foreigners would empty out of the galleries for lunch; still, the pressure of
people he already knew was slight in comparison to Florence or Rome, and
the expatriate colonies were small. An attempt, at the end of the decade, to
raise monies for an Anglican church numbered the English population at
just 50. He found lodgings on the Riva degli Schiavoni, the esplanade that
runs east of the Piazza San Marco, where the Grand Canal spreads into what
is called the Basin. The Riva is wide and in some ways uncharacteristic of
the city as a whole, for it offers a long straight view and a sense of space
and open water. Even now it seems in the early morning to provide that
breadth; at midday, however, the crowds make it a gauntlet run between a
line of *vaporetto* stops on the one hand and hotels on the other. The grandest

of those hotels, the Danieli, was already in business then; its rooms went for four shillings a night. But the building where James himself stayed is today one of the more modest, a place called the Pensione Wildner. He took a room on the fourth floor, with a view across the water to the pink-walled church of San Giorgio Maggiore; a view he described as *"una bellezza; the far shining lagoon . . . the movements of the quay, the gondolas in profile."*

In London, James wrote in the mornings and went out into the city only after finishing his hours at the desk. In Italy he reversed that order. He took his morning coffee at Florian's, in the Piazza, a café whose small, elegant rooms are even today defined by their rococo moldings and crimson uphol-stery, by bright gold leaf and slightly darkened mirrors. James described going there as one of life's "simpler pleasure[s];" a phrase that will stun anyone who has ever picked up one of its checks. Afterward, he crossed the Grand Canal for a daily bath at the Stabilimento Chitarin, where salt water was piped in from the Lagoon and heated. He walked, he looked at pictures and churches, and returned to the Piazza for lunch at its other historic café, the Quadri. Then he strolled the few minutes home for an afternoon of work. If he quit early, he would float out in a gondola before dinner; they were still cheap, cheaper even than his bath or a London cab. In the eve-ning he often went back to Florian's, sitting outside and listening to the orchestra, and sometimes he took himself to the house of his old Newport friend Katharine de Kay Bronson, leaning on her balcony with a cigarette and watching the lamplight gleam upon the water below. Such hours were a kind of witchery, and the city itself possessed him so completely that he began to imagine a future of annual returns; he even went so far as to look for a pied à terre. At the same time, he knew that this spring was "one of those things that don't repeat themselves." Nevertheless, Venice did now begin to supplant Florence and Rome in both his affections and his imagina-tion alike. There might be nothing left there to discover, but the rhythm of its life was a lotos and the city itself seemed "sentient."

James would have no need for a Venetian bolt-hole of his own. Mrs. Bronson's small house on the Grand Canal would always have room for him, and so did the Boston-born Daniel Curtis and his English wife, Ariana, at their much grander Palazzo Barbaro, near the foot of the Accademia Bridge. Expatriate society in Venice had no intellectual pretensions to anything more than a gentlemanly good taste. That conventionality had irritated him in Paris. His expectations of an Italian holiday were different, however, and in Venice his mind was sustained by his eyes. The Curtises had a decided sense of their own social importance, but they also collected artists and writers, and by the time James returned in 1887, both the *Portrait* and *Daisy Miller* had made him into one of the most celebrated of his day; favored guests would later be given "his" room. Their other prizes included Robert Browning and John Singer Sargent, and they are now best remembered as the subjects of the painter's masterful 1898 group portrait, *An Interior in Venice*.

Sargent makes the Barbaro's salon seem as shadowy as a Rembrandt, its walls a rusty black in which one can just pick out the faint gleam of a picture frame. The Curtises sit in the foreground, aged and serene, and the gray of their clothing seems almost bright in contrast to their surroundings. But the real color lies off to one side, in the splashes of white that define their son and daughter-in-law, more elegantly dressed than the parents and with the son half-sitting on the edge of a table. Sargent's brushwork is looser here than in his portraits of single figures, and the Curtises did not like it. They found the picture entirely too casual, almost deprecatory in the posing of its figures and its seemingly unfinished surface alike, and declined its offer as a gift. James thought them foolish; he had seen few of the painter's works that he "craved more to possess." Yet perhaps Mrs. Curtis's eye was better than James knew, and she had seen an implicit criticism in Sargent's rendering of the richly furnished chamber, a suggestion that their lives were not as large as their rooms.

James's account of this period in his American journal swells with detail, an invaluable record of dates and addresses and names. What seems more interesting in retrospect, however, are the names of the friends he *didn't* make. John Addington Symonds was in Venice during these months, taken up with both his work on the history of the Renaissance and his affair with the gondolier Angelo Fusato. James had met him in England, and we have

seen in an earlier chapter the interest the novelist took in him: the eagerness with which he questioned their mutual friend Edmund Gosse about
Symonds's domestic situation, and the fascination with which he read his
books on homosexuality. More suggestive are the accidents of timing that
kept James and the young Sargent from meeting one another. The painter
came to the city in the fall of 1880 and spent six months there, leaving more
or less as James arrived. The writer would certainly have noticed a young
American with a sketchbook and a studio on the Grand Canal, an American
who was already a fixture in the Paris Salon; while Sargent himself read
everything and would surely have known the older man's work. By this
time they had spent the better part of a decade just missing one another in
both France and Italy. They finally met in Paris during the winter of 1884,
and James was then instrumental in persuading Sargent to base his career in
London. In Britain they became friends though not intimates, something of
which Sargent had even fewer than James himself; there is, in fact, just one
extant letter between them, a brief 1915 note from the novelist.

The two have so often been spoken of as artistic counterparts that it's
easy to forget the differences between them. The painter kept into his last
years a sense of ease and immediacy that James did not, especially when
working in watercolor; and within their privileged world he depicted a
wider range of social types, industrialists and politicians among them. Yet
few of his subjects can be described as caught in the act of thinking, as
James's are, and we still say that his pictures serve as an illustration of the
writer's world, and not the other way around. Sargent is a great painter, but
his work isn't an event in the history of his medium; he concludes a period
but doesn't begin the next one. James does. In other ways, though, they do
seem similar, and not only in crude biographical terms as expatriate bachelors from monied families. Each had an acute sense of the artistic past on
which he drew. Each was conscious that he both depicted and appealed to a
rarefied audience, and in consequence longed for a large popular or public
success; while in chasing that success each of them spent years on mistakes.
James's 1890s fascination with the theater finds its match in the dead end of
the painter's religious murals for the Boston Public Library, a grandly inert

attempt to revive the spirit if not the technique of Renaissance fresco. More-over, in Venice these two reticent artists liked the same things, so much so that one wants to imagine an early meeting between them, when they were each alone and working in a city they both loved. They saw the same place, saw the city in the same terms, and James's impressionistic 1882 account of its hidden interior, of a young girl crossing over a bridge arched "like a camel's back, with an old shawl on her head" finds a precise equivalent in Sargent's Venetian pictures of the period, with their bead-stringers and water carriers and narrow closed-in streets.

In his preface to the *Portrait* James wrote that he seemed always drawn to the window, "in the fruitless fidget of composition, as if to see whether, out in the blue channel, the ship of some right suggestion, of some better phrase . . . mightn't come into sight." The pen drops and leaves perhaps a smeared drop of ink on an almost illegible line; the bearded man in shirt-sleeves walks to the window that stretches from his knees to the ceiling and looks out, his arms grasping its frame. Maybe he wishes for a room on the floor below, with its little balcony; here he has only a window box. Though the view is distraction enough, and he raises an opera glass to look across half a mile of water at the campanile of San Giorgio, and then sweeps right to the low long line of the Giudecca, the sleepy, narrow island that from here seems like the city's southern boundary. He is, he knows, on the verge of losing his concentration and remembers with thanks that his first month had been wild with rain. It had been easy then to sit down to his work, but in this city "even the brightest page of MS. looks dull beside the brilliancy of your milieu," and now half an hour passes before he knows it. Boats jostle at the landing below, and voices drift up from the quay. Sunset hits the water and the lagoon begins to shimmer, as if streaked by a giant's finger; and some pages in his novel will always make him see again the city's bridges and hear once more the distinctive Venetian footstep of heels striking upon a hollow pavement.

Indeed, James must have had Isabel in mind when, in his 1882 "Venice," he adopted one of the standard tropes of touristic description and presented the city in gendered terms: "The creature varies like a nervous woman,

whom you know only when you know all the aspects of her beauty. She
has high spirits or low, she is pale or red . . . fresh or wan, according to the
weather or the hour. She is always interesting and almost always sad." The
novel's later chapters will indeed give us a heroine whose sensibility appears
stretched and taut, and the sadness and the fascination belong to her as well.
She too remains as difficult to know as this Adriatic city itself. Yet if his
window over the lagoon showed him an ever-changing and elusive beauty,
James's lodgings presented him with a woman who seemed all too easy to
understand. What, he coyly asked in his essay, was the exact connection
"between the niece of the landlady and the occupancy of the fourth floor?"
She was a dancer at La Fenice, the city's famed opera house, and seemed
always to be loitering nearby, dressed in velvet and her face heavy with
powder. Byron had come to Venice sixty years before, where among other
things he began to write *Don Juan*. He would have known what to do with
the opportunity put so transparently in his way. But James was not that kind
of *straniero*, and perhaps his landlady found him a less remunerative tenant
than she hoped.

In Italy, James was always conscious that he himself came from a new
nation, but he was even more aware of it in Venice than elsewhere, where
the city's very obsolescence gave some special point to his own sense of
novelty. Rome, in contrast, wanted so much to be modern itself, but James
thought it would "be a sad day indeed when there should be something
new to say" about La Serenissima. Such newness would mean the place
was no longer the city of one's dreams, and James's sense of his own belatedness makes his essays about it seem densely allusive, in a way that can't
be entirely explained by his belief that his readers already knew it. None
of his other travel pieces relies so heavily on the second person, putting
the reader into the scene and then showering him with a Baedeker's worth
of names. The darkness of Venetian churches means that "you renounce
all hope . . . of approaching the magnificent Cima da Conegliano in San
Giovanni in Bragora," and as for his beloved Tintoretto, you may admire
and adore him, "but in the great majority of cases your eyes fail to deal with
him." Paintings, churches, palaces—James describes none of them in detail

but instead evokes them with a phrase, compares them, reminds us of what we've already seen, plumps the mental furniture that he suggests we have always had. Or should have had, for James's own love of Venice had come late, long after he had taken possession of Florence and Rome, and perhaps he had a sense of lost time. Perhaps too the author of *The Portrait of a Lady* could afford simply to gesture in a way the young writer could not. Nevertheless, the casual familiarity with which he presents it all appears hard-won; the learning is real but the names look to be dropped.

When James left Venice, his work on the *Portrait* was very nearly finished. He reached his London home on July 12, 1881, and the next day sent Aldrich the copy for the *Atlantic's* October issue, working as always with *Macmillan's* proof sheets. November's penultimate installment followed on August 8, and by that time he was already waiting for the concluding chapters of Isabel's story to come back from the typesetter. Those dates suggest that the book did get its final polish in England, but James's letters give no hint as to where he first drafted its last pages, and so maybe we have warrant enough to imagine him as trying, for a few more hours, to ignore that view from his fourth-floor room. No part of *The Portrait of a Lady* is set in Venice, and yet something of the city's color and space—of its amplitude— did enter the novel as he worked. And so maybe did the city's reputation for treachery, as Isabel Archer's life turns grim; some whiff of its closed-in streets, in which one can seem lost without hope of escape.

15.

FENIMORE

JAMES WAS RIGHT in believing that his Venetian spring of 1881 would not repeat itself, with its doubled sense of discovery, its fusion of the great book and the great city. But he could and did return to Venice itself. He revisited it six times between 1887 and 1907, and its splendid decay would determine two of his greatest works of fiction, *The Aspern Papers* and *The Wings of the Dove*. To understand the full importance that the city would have for him, however, we not only need to look ahead a few years, but must also go back to Florence and to Constance Fenimore Woolson, whom James had first met there in the spring of 1880.

Woolson's travels after those opening weeks of their friendship appear to echo James's own earlier experience. She moved up to Venice, and then to Switzerland for the summer and fall; the winter of 1880–81 brought her back to Italy, where she settled into an apartment in Rome. Her biographer Lyndall Gordon suggests she might have been among the crowd of acquaintances that James hoped to avoid in choosing Venice over Rome that year. Yet James craved both solitude *and* society, and at the end of April he broke his stay in Venice for a visit to the capital. One afternoon he went to tea in what Woolson called the "sky-parlor" of her fourth-floor apartment, and she remembered their conversation in a letter she wrote him the next year. The chapters describing Isabel's first visit to Rome had just appeared in *Macmillan's*, and James was uneasy about his handling of both Madame Merle and Gilbert Osmond. The one was developed all out of proportion, he thought, and the other wasn't clearly enough depicted. Writing with the whole novel before her, Woolson felt sure his judgment had been mistaken, and her readings of those characters are as penetrating as any in the criticism of the period. About Isabel she was less firmly analytical: "Poor Isabel! Poor idealizing imaginative girls the world over—sure, absolutely sure to be terribly unhappy."

In a second letter of 1882, Woolson wrote that she had had no fixed home since the death of her father in 1869, even though "I suppose there never was a woman so ill fitted to do without a home as I am." She always tried to create a sense of domesticity in the temporary spaces of hotels and pensions, and professed to dream of a lakeside house at Cooperstown. But she never tried to buy or build one and, once in Europe, made no attempt to rejoin the American family she claimed to miss. Instead, she saw herself as cut off from the life she craved, a woman who had to do without the things she wanted. And chief among them was Henry James. It is too simple to see her desire in sexual terms alone. She also craved his imaginative freedom. James had the liberty to go anywhere and to think anything; a woman did not, and in consequence, she wrote, "a woman . . . can never be a complete artist." She wanted him, but she also wanted his independence and his life: the independence that she was just conventional enough to believe her sex denied her; the life behind those works in which she thought she had found her true home. She knew he wouldn't marry, and knew as well that the demands on his time were ever-increasing. Her books sold well and she had friends enough if only she would draw on them; she was deaf in one ear but her loss of hearing was not in itself responsible for her sense of isolation. Her commitment to James, or to her idea of James, seems rather to have defined in her some prior space of loneliness. She settled for the limited attention he might give her, a suspended life in which, with the years, she seemed always to be searching for some place to be.

At first that place was London, where in 1883 she took an apartment in Sloane Street. They knew few people in common and, as I have already noted, James did not introduce her to his London world, where their friendship could not have passed without comment. One who did know about it

was Lizzie Boott, in Florence; in writing to Bellosguardo, James referred to
Woolson as the "Costanza" and spoke in amused though affectionate terms
of her "immense power of devotion (to H.J.!)." Woolson in turn noted an
excursion to Stonehenge in 1884; she had taken lodgings in Salisbury, and
James came down on a day so blustery she "thought the carriage would be
overturned." Soon, however, she found herself pulled to Italy once more,
and here James worked to cement her relations with the Bootts, who in the
fall of 1886 found her an apartment in the Villa Castellani. Her lease ran for
just a few months, but Florence suited her and she almost immediately took
a house of her own just a hundred yards down the hill. It was called the Villa
Brichieri-Colombi, and it provided the setting for one of the most curious
episodes in James's life.

He too went to Italy that fall, arriving in Florence on December 8.
He planned to stay a month, but in fact he did not return to England until
the following July. That year James had seen both *The Bostonians* and *The
Princess Casamassima* through the press. He felt exhausted and wanted to
"hide" for a time; and he meant that literally, writing to the Bootts that
they shouldn't mention his arrival to anyone. He planned to see only them
and the woman he now called "Fenimore," and his lodgings would make
that easy enough. For Woolson had taken the Brichieri a month before she
needed it and now offered it to him, complete with a cook and a maid; on
Christmas Eve, James wrote to their mutual friend, John Hay, that the two
of them often dined together. At the beginning of the year he took a hotel
room in the city's center, where he was caught by the same "promiscuous
polyglot" society that he claimed he wished to avoid, and in February he
went on to Venice for six weeks. But James came back to Tuscany in April
1887—and moved into the Brichieri once more, occupying a ground-floor
apartment while Woolson herself had one on the *piano nobile* above. It is the
closest he ever came to living with someone who was neither a servant nor
a member of his immediate family. During that second visit James wrote
to Edmund Gosse that he felt as though he were "making love to Italy"
and inhabiting a house all "supercelestial, whence the most beautiful view
on earth hangs before me wherever I lift my head." Yet no letter from this

period refers to the woman upstairs, and no biographer has learned very much about their lives together.

What we can know is the house itself. The Brichieri is walled and gated, with a curving walkway that runs uphill from the gate to the house, a building with a classical pediment and with a main floor that opens onto a balcony. I visited it one winter afternoon when the mist obscured my view, but even on fine days it is just high enough, and just far enough, for the air to soften the lines and color of the city below. My hostess buzzed me in to the grounds, but at first I couldn't find the stairs that led to her—to "Fenimore's"—apartment. Instead, I stumbled into a wide ground-floor hallway, cool and comfortable and with a file of rooms running back on each side. This space had been James's own, but now it belonged to somebody else and I was expected for tea; the stairs I wanted were outside and around a corner. James sometimes wrote of not wanting to betray hospitality with a description, but in truth there is little enough to say. My hostess was an elderly descendent of the Florentine-American world that James had described, and while the walls were hung with abstractions from the 1950s, the rest of the apartment spoke to an earlier generation. I remember heavy draperies and tables covered with photographs in small silver frames, and a conversation sprinkled with the kinds of names I know only from the labels on bottles of Chianti. When I left, she gave me some oil pressed from the fruit of her own trees.

Biographers are properly wary of imagining a time for which we have few records. Presumably, James and Woolson shared the servants, but we don't know how often they also shared a table, and in May he wrote to his brother William that most evenings he went down into the city for dinner. Was that a blind, a touch of cover for a position he recognized as equivocal? We know they took pains to mask the details of their arrangement, and know too that James enjoyed the Brichieri's few acres of garden, a foretaste of the pleasure he later took in his bit of ground in Rye. The weather was cold on the day I visited, and we didn't step out onto the balcony. Yet let us imagine that step. Let us walk with Fenimore onto her terrace and look down at Henry James as he sits with his morning coffee; each of them wondering, for the brief time that these walls concealed them, if they might have somehow been different.

James had already written an essay about Woolson's work for *Harper's*; he admired her ability to evoke a "local tone," but the compliments all carry a sting. And the piece he now wrote is sometimes taken as a peculiar reflection on their weeks together. He had heard a curious story in Florence that winter, a bit of gossip about a woman named Claire Clairmont, the last survivor of the circle around Byron and Shelley. She had been Mary Shelley's stepsister and Byron's mistress, the mother of his daughter Allegra, and she survived into old age, dying at eighty in 1879. In her last years she lived with a niece in Florence; rather poor, but guarding a trove of letters and other memorabilia. Then an American appeared, a sea captain from Boston named Silsbee. He asked to rent a few rooms in her house, but he really wanted the papers and hoped, in James's words, "that the old lady in view of her great age and failing condition would die while he was there, so that he might then put his hand upon the documents, which she hugged close in life." She did die, though Silsbee failed to get his treasure, and James used the anecdote to seed one of his most perfect tales, *The Aspern Papers*.

In writing he switched the scene from Florence to Venice. The change hid the story's origins in the chitchat of a small expatriate community, and Venice did have more associations with Byron in particular. There were other reasons as well. James had already described Venice as the most splendid of tombs—a relic, as indeed is his character Juliana Bordereau, the aged mistress of the long-dead poet Jeffrey Aspern. The Florence of the 1880s was, however, the very reverse of a relic. It had briefly been the capital of the united Italy, and had since become a builder's site, a place of newfangled trams and boulevards; subject to a process of modernization that exposed and made legible the mysteries of its crooked medieval streets. Moreover, James himself saw the city as though from Bellosguardo—an image of human felicity nestled in its splendid bowl of hills. Venice, in contrast, was a place for secrets, a city in which it was easy to get lost, and maybe even to lose yourself. So he put his Juliana there, a woman living "in obscurity, on very small means, unvisited, unapproachable, in a dilapidated old palace."

Jame's syntax here twists and turns, a prose that serves, with all its commas and pauses, its addition of one nugget of information to another, to evoke the experience of Venice itself. One walks on, trying to find one's way in a world of dead ends, to penetrate the city's hidden spaces; and yet its secrets persist. In Venice it remains hard to find answers, and its very stones may seem the creatures of duplicity.

James wrote the story in the first person and made his narrator both a collector, like Silsbee, and an editor too, a "publishing scoundrel" obsessed with Aspern's poetry and life. We never learn his name—neither his real name nor the false one he uses with Miss Bordereau. Yet it would be too easy to describe that narrator as unreliable. He's instead someone who believes he has scruples, a man given to elaborate justifications of his own desires. He persuades the old woman to rent him the ground floor of her house on "an out-of-the-way canal," while Juliana lives on the *piano nobile* with her middle-aged niece, Tita, who is fiftyish, unworldly, and plain. At first he's not even sure that Aspern's papers survive, but once he knows that they do, he realizes that the quickest way to get them will be to "make love" to the niece. Yet Tita herself goes further, and proposes to him; the papers for his hand. The narrator is looking at a miniature of Aspern as she does so, and imagines that the portrait itself tells him to "get out of it as you can;" and some versions of the anecdote on which James relied suggest that Claire Clairmont's niece did indeed make such a proposal. Only a naïve critic would insist on an autobiographical reading of this scene, would see a clear connection between the story's narrator and its author. But it seems equally naïve to find no connection at all; each of them a tenant in a large old Italian house, and each an object of fascination to the spinster on the floor above.

Few of James's friends knew about the house on Bellosguardo. Even fewer knew of his meeting with Fenimore the next year in Geneva. They made their holiday plans in secret, and their choice of a rendezvous in the fall of 1888 was designed to keep them so. Geneva was both an intermediate point between London and Florence and a place without much of an Anglo-American colony; neither of them had friends there, neither of them was known. He told people that he planned on a month in Paris, though the Bootts knew the details, and his sister Alice knew enough to tell William that "Henry is somewhere on the continent flirting with Constance." That secrecy shouldn't be taken as an indication that he and Woolson had anything to hide—not by our standards, anyway. But for discretion's sake they stayed in hotels a mile apart, and joined one another for dinner when each day's work was done. Probably they said very little that could not have passed at anyone's table, and yet the intensity of their conversation would have drawn notice: its discussion of their shared profession, its exclusivity, its essential privacy. The social mores of their day didn't allow for such friendships between men and women, and their age made little difference; in James's late novel *The Ambassadors*, the fiftyish Lambert Strether sees himself as doing something almost indecent in dining alone with Maria Gostrey in a restaurant. Theater people could do that and excite little notice. They were expected to break the rules of social observance. James wasn't, and didn't allow himself to; the rules he broke were never those of the drawing room.

We know that they spent their days at their desks. Woolson had her deadlines to make on *Jupiter Lights*, a love story set in the American South, while James struggled with his long novel of artistic vocation, *The Tragic Muse*. But we know almost nothing else about those three weeks. One of its few records survives in a copy of *The Aspern Papers* that James gave to her there on October 16, adding the place and the date to his signature. It was, however, to be their last long period together, and the next year Woolson began a new course of restlessness, one that took her to Athens and Cairo before it dropped her down again in England. She settled briefly in Cheltenham, and then Oxford; she spoke of going back to America, but also of sending for the silver and linen she had left there a decade before. Each winter brought depression, a term to which she gave the meaning it has today; most people in her period called it neurasthenia instead. Yet she cherished her isolation and complained about the invitations that threatened

it. She complained unless they were from James himself. He saw her with
some regularity in England, but the letters that mention her are careful to
place her at some rhetorical distance, as though hiding from both his correspondents and himself just how important Woolson had become to him. He
clearly found something in her that he didn't in his friendships with other
women—and yet she never filled as large a space in his life as he did in hers.

What do we owe our friends? Each writer's biographers have suggested
that she moved to England to be near him. Was he then bound to repay that
decision with the same attention he had showed in Florence and Geneva? I
fall back upon rhetorical questions because there are no absolutes here, and
there is so little that we can know for sure. Some writers finish a book with
a sense of exhilaration; Woolson always ended her own in a state of nervous
collapse. In the spring of 1893 she pushed through a draft of her fourth
novel, *Horace Chase*, and then forced herself to make one last move, to Venice. She knew it was a sacrifice; as she wrote to a nephew, it meant "giving
up being near my kind friend Mr. James." But she added that the novelist
had promised to come to Italy each year. At first she found rooms in a house
with some other American women, and then in the fall she gained a sense of
privacy and space by taking the top floors of the Casa Semitecolo, near what
is now the Guggenheim Collection. The house backs onto the Grand Canal
but nevertheless faces away from it, looking onto one of the smaller and
darker of the city's interior streets or *calle*. She hired a gondolier, and curiously enough the man recommended to her was Angelo Fusato, the lover of
the now-dead John Addington Symonds.

Each month she grew ever more expectant of the visit James had promised for that fall—even as he himself made no firm plans for the journey.
James's sales had crashed at the end of the 1880s, for reasons I'll describe
in a later chapter, and he had now spent four years in trying to turn himself
into a playwright, dreaming of a popular success he had rarely known in fiction. He was exasperated by the theater's world of meetings and rehearsals
and provincial tryouts, by the days of discussion with agents and managers
that seemed never to have a result. But he was absorbed by it too, and all that
fall the stage seemed to hold him tight. Perhaps he might manage a trip in

the winter—though he also wrote to Ariana Curtis at the Palazzo Barbaro that he was afraid he had clumsily suggested "to Miss Woolson . . . that I was coming [to Venice] to 'live.'"

He did not come. With whatever excuses or justifications, that was still the end of it. He did not come, and as winter set in, the city itself seemed to empty, with many of Woolson's acquaintances running from its raw damp air. On her first visit to Venice ten years before, she had wondered "whether the end of the riddle of my existence may not be, after all, to live here, and die here. . . . This prospect doesn't make me sad at all." In the middle of January she fell sick, and her days became a routine of vomiting and fevers, doctors and laudanum. Woolson wasn't alone—she had a nurse and a secretary, but no one for whose services she had not paid. She got worse, and then better. She gathered herself and found one final bit of strength. Soon after midnight on January 24 her nurse discovered that her bed was empty and the window open. Angelo Fusato found her body on the pavement below.

James got the news in a telegram, learning the fact of her death but not its manner, and prepared to go to Rome for the funeral, where she had asked to be buried in the city's Protestant Cemetery. Then he received a newspaper clipping that referred to the death as a suicide and canceled his plans. He had thought she was merely "alone and unfriended at the last," but now a more dreadful image seemed to hang in his eyes, and he felt himself collapse at its horror; the very power of his emotions made him see the journey as impossible. He wrote to John Hay that Woolson's enduring melancholy meant that half one's fondness for her took the form of anxiety, though he also believed that she hid her depression so successfully that only those who knew her well could have perceived her suffering. To Frank Boott he claimed that nothing short of a "sudden *dementia*" could explain her action, and yet he also began to think that she had never been entirely sane.

We need here to parse both James's reactions and the different interpretations that have been put upon Woolson's death. Her family wanted to believe that in the delirium of fever she had simply fallen from the window. But the "sills overlooking the *calle*," in Gordon's words, "are not low." One would have to climb over them, not simply topple out. A more common reading of her death is James's own. Her action was the result of some frenzy or fit; suicide, yes, but not planned, not consciously willed or chosen. The most convincing interpretation, however, belongs to Gordon herself. Her careful examination of the surviving evidence, including a precisely cir- cumstantial account by Woolson's secretary, suggests a deliberate purpose, and suggests too that she was entirely lucid in the days immediately before her death. I would part from Gordon, though, in her reading of James's own actions. She is troubled by his decision not to travel to the funeral, and views his hypotheses as self-exculpatory: if Woolson was both the victim of "sudden *dementia*" and also already disturbed, then no visit of his own could have prevented her action. Yet I think we must allow that even Henry James could feel so confused, so uncomprehending and distraught, that he would need to grope for an explanation. Even he could know grief's alter- nating moments of incapacity and anger.

Suicide imposes a teleology. "*After* such an event," as James wrote to Frank Boott, "one sees symptoms, indications in the past." One of Wool- son's doctors was the New York–born and Florence-based William Bald- win, who at different times had also treated both James and his siblings. James wrote to him soon after learning of Woolson's death that two years earlier he had finally made up his mind as to the depths of her mental illness. The reasons for that judgment were "too many and too private" to put in a letter, and he suggested they might talk it through at their next meeting. Two years before would have been around the time she moved to Oxford, and his sense of her troubles might have made him both reluctant to join in her Venetian experiment, and hesitant about saying so. Delay seemed the soft option; but he could not have imagined the end.

Over the next few months, however, he would imagine it again and again. In April, James went to Venice, where he met Woolson's sister and niece, and joined them in breaking the seal that the city authorities had placed on her apartment. What happened then is less easy to justify than his earlier reluctance to go either to Venice in the fall or to the funeral in Rome. Woolson carried her life wherever she went, accompanied always by the heavy trunks that contained her possessions—her clothes and mementoes and above all her papers. Her relatives had come to see the place where she died, and to take charge of those trunks. James stayed with them for weeks, helping them to sort and to sift until, as her niece wrote, "all her precious things were packed and boxed and sent to America." Those things did not, however, include any of the letters James wrote to her, and the supposition has always been that in Venice he burned them.

Yet what was there to hide? Gordon writes that it was during the years of his friendship with Woolson that the idea of secrecy became central to James's art. Todorov makes no reference to the author of "Miss Grief," but he too defines this period as that in which an absent cause, an unnamed referent, came to stand as James's own figure in the carpet. We may picture him before the fireplace, dropping one sheet after another into the flames, and yet can presume nothing about the contents of those letters from the simple fact that he burned them. Years later, at Lamb House, he made a pyre of the ones he himself had received, Woolson's presumably among them. He asked his friends to destroy the letters they'd gotten from him and hoped he would have no biographer. It's unlikely that the papers he destroyed in Venice contained any particular confession or scandal. To believe that they did, we would have to believe that their friendship had become an affair. Or we would need to believe he had told Woolson of his own hidden figure, offering some fuller explanation for his own refusal to marry, perhaps in response to a pointed question of her own. This too seems unlikely. Certainly her expectation that he would travel down to Italy each year does not suggest that she knew, while her pained realization that he wouldn't come that winter speaks of some final defeat of hope. Perhaps those letters referred to uncertainties he hadn't yet surmounted; perhaps he let the veil of familial piety drop and wrote more frankly to her than to others about his parents or siblings. The content of the secret matters less than the fact that there was one. They had met without telling others, and with all the limitations I have described above, she had still meant more to him than anyone knew.

Woolson's relatives asked one last service of him. They wanted his help in disposing of her dresses, and rather than ask such friends as Katharine Bronson—she would have known the right charities for such things—James decided to drown them in the Lagoon. He hired a gondola one day toward dusk, and told the boatman to row far, far out, where the water was deep and they might presumably remain alone and unwatched. He took each piece of her clothing up from the deck and threw it into the water, but the sleeves puffed up from the trapped air inside, and the wide skirts spread out over the waves. The dresses would not sink, "and they came up like balloons all around him . . . horrible black balloons" that he tried again and again to beat down into the sea, only to find them swimming up to the surface and surrounding him. The scene has long provided one of the set pieces of Jamesian biography: a transparent image of psychic trauma, of the haunting return of the figure whose love he had denied. Both horrible and comic at once, the anecdote seems almost too good to be true, but the story did figure in the expatriate gossip of the period, a tear in the careful fabric of privacy that the two writers had tried to maintain. And perhaps it figured all the more because it recalls one of James's own early ghost stories, "The Romance of Certain Old Clothes." In that tale a woman opens a trunk containing the dresses and jewels of her dead sister, whose life she had destroyed—and is strangled by what lies inside.

The duplicitous narrator of *The Aspern Papers* writes that he had "never failed to acquit" his subject, that he was always able to justify anything that looked like "shabby behaviour." James's own chroniclers stand warned. Woolson's death left him with questions that, in Fred Kaplan's words, can be summed up like this: "If her depression had external coordinates, might he have been one of them?" She might have lived if he had come to Venice. She might have lived if he had been able to give more of himself; if, that is, he had been someone entirely different. Or, indeed, if she had. Her illness began early, long before their first meeting, and James's presence in her life may well have helped more than his absence hurt. And finally, any reckoning must consider his own sexuality and the limits it placed upon their relationship; not just the physical ones, but those of knowledge too. I do not think we can blame him for what his century would not allow him to say, or her to recognize. When Woolson killed herself, she had known thirteen years of his defensive charm. In another age she would have known other things too, he would have spoken, she would have understood. That would not have made things simple, but it would have made them easier.

Not all of James's readers will acquit him here. What matters more is that he did not acquit himself. The letters he sent immediately after Woolson's death do, admittedly, try to push the thought of his own responsibility away. But the tales he now began to write seem to offer a different answer. In the fall of 1894, James started to work on a long and extraordinary series of ghost stories, *nouvelles* in which the protagonist finds himself haunted by a sense of missed opportunities. "The Altar of the Dead," "The Beast in the Jungle," "The Jolly Corner"—they are among his most perfect works, but there are other crucial stories from this time as well, like "The Friends of the Friends," in which a man falls in love with the ghost of a woman he never met. None of them tracks his biographical situation directly, and yet we cannot minimize the effect of Woolson's suicide on these pieces about love and responsibility, mourning and forgiveness. For these tales don't use their ghosts to convey the experience of evil, as James does in *The Turn of the Screw*, which also belongs to this period. What they offer instead is the troubling sense of an alternate life. A solitary man, a sympathetic woman: it's as though James were shaking the dice of character, and rolling them again and again; different combinations of the same two pieces, chronicles of could-haves and should-haves and even second chances.

"The Beast in the Jungle" remains the best-known, the 1902 story of a man who thinks himself marked for an extraordinary fate. Something is going to happen to John Marcher, probably something awful. So he believes, and he holds himself in readiness for it, aloof and separate from life's ordinary run. He confesses that belief to but one other person, the sympathetic May Bertram, who tells him that she will share his ordeal, will wait with him, and watch for it. In time, Marcher's conviction of his own special destiny becomes a form of vocation, and May herself never figures, to him, as anything more than a friend. So they live through the years, with evenings at the theater and quiet dinners in which they discuss his case. Then May sickens and on her deathbed tells him that he need wait no longer. What *was* to happen has, though he himself doesn't understand it until later, when he visits her grave and sees a man standing at a nearby tomb, his face ravaged by loss. Then Marcher knows that the fate for which he has waited was simply her love. But he has kept himself off, he has missed the great event of his life, and now a more powerful beast waits to spring: the knowledge that he is the one man of his time "to whom nothing on earth was to have happened."

In recent years Marcher's sense of a hidden self or fate has often been read in terms of sexual identity. It is "The Beast in the Closet," as Eve Kosofsky Sedgwick puts it, and the story has become a central text in queer readings of James's work. Still, we should be wary of any interpretation that merely substitutes one secret for another, that sees either Marcher's tale, or James's work in writing it, in terms of a key that might unlock its door. Maybe only a gay man could have written "The Beast in the Jungle," but though it's now impossible to read this tale in terms of its heterosexual content alone, we must also recognize that it is not, or not only, about being gay as such. It is about both things at once, and like the other pieces with which I've grouped it, "The Beast in the Jungle" insists upon and yet disclaims an autobiographical reading: a parable of loss and regret whose uncanny power depends on an ever-unspoken dialectic between its two versions of the unlived life.

With time, Constance Fenimore Woolson became one face of all James knew he had missed. He returned to Venice repeatedly, a city whose decrepitude served but to intensify its style; returned with pleasure but with an increasing sense that the place was a tomb indeed. The city appeared to linger on after its own end, and that coincidence of death and beauty made him chose a Venetian setting for *The Wings of the Dove*, his late novel about the relation of treachery and desire. Today, Venice seems more a tomb than ever, its population less than half of what it was in James's day, and yet with more tourists each year. One morning there I went out looking for Woolson, hoping to find the house where she had died. James had stayed always in the open light of the Grand Canal, and as one steams by on a vaporetto, the Palazzo Barbaro looks today as ageless and fine as in the photographs from his own era. Its Gothic windows seem almost natural, a rock formation sculpted by the very water around it. But the Casa Semitecolo had looked away from such splendor. The streets on my way were narrow and close, and every turn a dead end, as though the city had curled in upon itself. There was an extraordinary force in the metaphoric relation of her spaces to James's own, and in the end I could not find her, could not say for sure which had been the house or the window.

I had better luck the next week in Rome, where Woolson lies, as she wished, in the city's Protestant Cemetery. James visited her each time he returned to the capital, and perhaps in doing so he recognized that she rests near the spot where he had put his own Daisy Miller; Daisy, who would "have appreciated one's esteem." Keats is buried in the older and relatively open part of the graveyard, where the tombs are widely spaced, and the city's cats can spread themselves on the warm rocks in the sun. Woolson can be found in the newer and more crowded section, its walkways laid out as precisely as a grid of city streets. But her company looks good. Shelley is close by—someone had left a spray of red roses on his monument—and her stone is but two steps away from that of John Addington Symonds, whose life had so curiously crossed both James's and her own. William Wetmore Story lies near as well, and then many other names of the kind that provide the footnotes of nineteenth-century culture. Woolson's grave consists of a marble coping with a Celtic cross inside. It was planted with ivy, and well-tended. I found a pebble to lay on it, and then made my way home.

Part Four

SEX AND SERIALS, THE
CONTINENT AND THE CRITICS

Paris, La Rue de Rivoli. Anonymous, undated. Albumen print.

16.

MAUPASSANT AND THE MONKEY

S HE LIES ON her side in a sparse patch of clover, her head pillowed
upon a shawl, and stretched out from the loose curls of her light red hair
to the flash of crimson at her shoe. She's all red, in fact—the hair matches
the lips matches the dress, a russety thing with a black collar and cuffs that
speaks of a New England autumn. Her lips are pursed and her eyes intent on
the book she holds before her, the book that occupies the space where her
breasts should be. *The New Novel* is one of the many watercolors of young
women that Winslow Homer made in the 1870s. Some of them show girls
sewing or standing at a blackboard, and one is even called *Portrait of a Lady*,
a painting of a white-robed woman in a garden. *The New Novel* differs from
these other pictures both in its horizontality—the sheet is twice as wide as
it is high—and in the degree to which it mixes sensuality with innocence.
Homer has positioned his subject on a green-gray field, with a sheltering
wall of rock rising behind her. And she herself lies in the middle, one long
slash of red, a girl so entirely focused upon her book that she would not,
one imagines, even hear an approaching footstep; as though her reading has
made her vulnerable.

James was no great admirer of Homer's. He acknowledged the painter's skill, but in an 1875 review he claimed that Homer's subject matter was
banal to the point of ugliness, "suggestive of a dish of rural doughnuts and
pie." He was living in New York then, his last attempt at an American life,
and couldn't quite forgive Homer's success in making a world of "calico

sun-bonnets" seem as picturesque as Capri or Tangier. *The New Novel* was painted after James had settled in England. He probably never saw it, but he would have recognized the problem it defines. The dangerously absorbing pull of fiction was itself one of the novel's great themes; a subject at least as old as Cervantes, who warned his readers against placing their trust in other people's books. In the nineteenth century those warnings were usually couched in terms of the particular perils that novels presented for young women. Jane Austen had gotten a comedy out of her heroine's visit to the eponymous country house of *Northanger Abbey*, allowing the girl to imagine it in terms of the Gothic romances she loves to read; and Flaubert made something brutal from the same essential idea in *Madame Bovary*, whose heroine can't accept the fact that her own life isn't closer to the world of Balzac or George Sand.

Novels gave one a false impression of the way the world works; that was a standard complaint against them. But they might also reveal things that young people like Homer's Yankee maiden shouldn't yet know, and their dangers were the subject of an active debate. Some Victorian commentators even believed that reading could have physiological consequences, that too many thrilling books could damage a girl's physical health. For our purposes those fears matter because they affected what novelists felt themselves free to write. James thought that they had made the whole of English fiction into something diffident and shy, committed to caution on the questions of sexual life. The best-known example of those fears is Dickens's satiric account, in *Our Mutual Friend*, of a character called Podsnap, who objects to anything that might "bring a blush into the cheek of [a] young person." Such persons were inevitably female; what a son might be allowed to read was an entirely different question. The fact of that blush suggests, however, that by the time such a book got into the house it was already too late; one can't blush at what one doesn't know.

Nor was Podsnap pure fiction. New novels were almost ruinously expensive to buy. A standard three-volume first edition cost 31s. 6d., a figure frequently cited as equivalent to the weekly wages of a skilled artisan. It was steep even for James, over half of what he paid each week for his Bolton

Street flat. Most readers who didn't want to wait for a book's 6s. cheap edition got them from commercial lending libraries instead; James himself had joined the largest of them, Mudie's, during his first days in London. Founded in 1842, Mudie's had branches all over England and was as important to the success of a new novel as Amazon is today; it sometimes took a full third of a book's first edition. I'll look more closely at the firm's relation to the structure of the British book trade in a later chapter, but for now it's enough to say that its owner, Charles Edward Mudie, firmly believed in the Podsnap principle. He was reluctant to stock any novel that couldn't be read aloud in the family, and his power in the marketplace meant that his own standards usually prevailed, an unofficial censorship that kept both novelists and publishers away from certain subjects. One who slipped through was the Irish writer George Moore, who in 1883 published an unusually frank novel about the art world called *A Modern Lover*. Yet though Moore found a publisher, he did not find a market, for Mudie almost immediately told him that he would not carry it. "Two ladies from the country" had objected to the book on moral grounds, and despite its strong reviews, he felt bound to respect the wishes of his customers.

Still, many readers kicked against those restrictions. James Fitzjames Stephen was a Cambridge-educated lawyer who supplemented his earnings with journalism, and in 1857 he took on a review of *Madame Bovary*. No English translation of the novel would appear until 1886, but Stephen's French was good and the book was already notorious, in part because Flaubert and his publishers had been indicted for obscenity; a rap they beat after a one-day trial. Stephen found the novel repellent, yet while it had some passages that "no English author of reputation" would have published, he wasn't troubled by the presence of sexual issues as such. What he objected to instead was the absence of any suggestion that Emma's adultery was wrong in itself, and not simply because of its consequences. Nevertheless, he thought this French writer offered a lesson for his British peers. The English fiction of the day contained nothing "which a modest man might not, with satisfaction to himself, read aloud to a young lady." But that in itself was the problem. Was it really desirable that the only fiction available should be that "fit for young ladies to read?" Stephen admitted that there were passages in *Othello* that he himself couldn't read aloud to a woman. Still, that restriction would have blotted many of Shakespeare's best lines, and he suggested, with an eye on London's streets, that such prudery had done nothing to improve English conduct.

Fitzjames Stephen's brother Leslie would become the father of Virginia Woolf, who praised him for giving her unfettered access to his library. Few fathers let their daughters browse so freely, and there were even some novelists who agreed with Podsnap. The prolific and fiercely Christian Margaret Oliphant is now little read, but she was said to be Queen Victoria's favorite novelist and was a formidable critic for the Scottish monthly *Blackwood's*. In an 1867 essay there she worried about the corrupting spread of French ideas about fiction, and claimed that the special pride of the English novel lay in a "cleanliness" that made it "free to all classes and feared by none." English writers had agreed to relegate certain issues to their appropriate place in a scholarly or scientific literature, and in consequence the nation's children could pick up any novel that came into the house. Nothing was locked away; the "domestic Index Expurgatorius" had been abolished. Which only begs Stephen's question—should all fiction be written as if for the young?

Evidently not in France, where, in Oliphant's words, a girl often found "the novels of her own language . . . rigorously tabooed," *Madame Bovary* very much included. In fact, the prosecutor at Flaubert's trial spoke of his fear that the book could fall "into the hands of young women, sometimes of married women," to whom it might give ideas. Most of the young Emma's own early reading is illicit, romantic tales smuggled into her convent school by a seamstress. In contrast, the young woman in Homer's painting reads outdoors, unsupervised, and alone. Her position may present dangers, but it's also a natural place in which to find her. Yet such readers were more free, as Oliphant's argument suggests, only insofar as the novelist was less. Restrictions on content were in inverse proportion to restrictions on access, and James himself didn't think that bargain a good one.

He took up the issue repeatedly, most famously in "The Art of Fiction."

Both the English and the American novel were, he argued, far too scrupulous in observing the distinction "between that which people know, and that which they agree to admit that they know . . . between what they talk of in conversation and what they talk of in print." Such reticence kept the work from anything like a full engagement with its material, and maybe he would have agreed with the popular writer Eliza Lynn Linton, who in an 1890 symposium on "Candour in Fiction" suggested that English literature would be all the better if parents did put a lock on the bookcase. For almost no one thought that adolescents should simply be allowed to read everything. One possible exception was Thomas Hardy, who in his own contribution to that symposium wrote that whether young people "should read unvarnished fiction . . . [is] a different question from whether the novel ought to be exclusively addressed" to them. He claimed to take on that second question only, but added that most of society's ideas about "budding womanhood" were false; the young could use some more accurate information.

Still, English fiction was a good bit more open than these accounts suggest, albeit in a peculiar way. Its surface remained varnished indeed, but so long as one already knew what to look for, the truth was there to see. Or at least a part of it. Today many first-time readers of George Eliot's *Adam Bede* are startled to learn of the unmarried Hetty Sorrel's pregnancy; the first definite word of it comes with her arrest for the murder of her newborn child. Few adult Victorians were so surprised. They knew what would come of her secret meetings with the young squire. Stories of illegitimacy were common, and so were novels about bigamy, which allowed a heroine to have a sex life that was both within and thrillingly outside of marriage at once. But "there is a terrible coercion in our deeds," as George Eliot herself wrote, and for Hetty, as for the title characters of Gaskell's *Ruth* or Hardy's *Tess of the D'Urbervilles*, every sexual act—no, her every act of any kind— will have its consequences. Flaubert gives us the endlessly rocking carriage in which Emma and Léon bounce around Rouen and winkingly invites us to imagine what's going on inside. George Eliot, in contrast, doesn't show us what happens when the girl meets the boy, not merely because of English silence but because she's more interested in the consequences of that meeting than she is in the moment itself. There is no event in an English novel but that leads to something, and in Victorian fiction it seems that no unmarried heroine can lose her virginity without getting pregnant. Usually the very first time—a biological law that doesn't operate in France.

James too had ways of defining the things his characters were "rather shy" of admitting. Pansy Osmond has read little except Walter Scott, that model of innocuous virtue, but even Isabel's more extensive reading hasn't prepared her as well as it might. Just before her marriage she receives a visit from Osmond's sister, the Countess Gemini, who wants to gossip about Florentine indiscretions, her own included. But first the Countess decides to send Pansy out of the room. Isabel is twenty-three and on the verge of marriage, but still she exclaims that "I would rather hear nothing that Pansy may not." Those words imply that she knows full well what she's about to hear. They speak less to innocence than to a knowledge she would rather not have; they suggest the fears with which this particular young person will enter her future life.

G uy de Maupassant wrote hundreds of short stories, many of them so frank in their account of sexual life that few young persons in England would have been allowed to read them. But there were some stories that even he couldn't publish, stories he had to tell instead, and one of the best was about the drunken Englishman who tried to go for a swim off the Norman fishing village of Étretat. Maupassant was still a student then, an oarsman known more for his athleticism than for his brains, and he dove in for a rescue. By the time he reached the drowning man, a lifeboat had already hauled him out, but the Englishman was grateful for the boy's effort, and invited him to lunch. The drunk lived with another fellow named Powell, who was said to be an English lord, and they kept a large monkey, who moved freely around the dining room. And every so often Powell would reach out and try to masturbate the animal—the French verb is *branler*. The monkey didn't like it, but whenever he managed to escape, he would in turn rub up against the back of Maupassant's neck. Afterward, his host offered a spontaneous translation of his own verses, and gave the French youth a liqueur that almost knocked him out. Only on a second, and final, visit did he notice an inscription from the Marquis de Sade over the cottage door.

Maupassant loved to tell this story of his 1868 encounter with Algernon Charles Swinburne, a poet whose reputation still owes more to his alleged taste for the whip than to his innovations with meter and rhyme. He had been only eighteen, and "Boule de Suif," the tale of a Norman prostitute that would make his reputation, was still a dozen years in the future. But he did have a family friend with whom to talk about writing. His mother had known Flaubert since childhood, and in Paris, Maupassant soon became a regular at the Sunday afternoon gatherings of Flaubert's *cenacle* in the rue du Fauborg Saint-Honoré, the circle of writers that included Turgenev and Zola among others. "Le petit Maupassant" told his story on the 28th of February 1875 to a group that included Edmond de Goncourt, who set it down in his diary. At some point during the next winter he told it again, to a gathering that now included Henry James, who kept no diary but remembered everything. And over thirty years later James pulled the anecdote up in a pair of letters to Edmund Gosse and noted with bemusement just how little of the "right mental preparation" he could have had for it.

As we have seen, James had come to Paris in November 1875, determined to settle in Europe at last. He found a two-bedroom flat in the rue de Luxembourg, a residential street in the center of the Right Bank's opulent charms, with the Tuileries to one side and the Madeleine to the other. (Now renamed the rue Cambon, it's best known as the site of Coco Chanel's first boutique; her house there is today a museum.) The Opéra, the Louvre, the Palais Royal and the Comédie Française—all of them were within a short walk, a world whose splendor seemed to increase by the week. The Franco-Prussian War of 1870–71 lay but a few years in the past. The civil conflict of the Paris Commune was even more recent, when in the aftermath of that war a popular uprising had been viciously suppressed, with thousands put before the firing squads. Yet to James the city appeared to have recovered so quickly that it looked "as if her sky had never known a cloud." The shops offered anything one might desire, and the confectionery seemed as delicate as the work of a Renaissance goldsmith. In the *Portrait of a Lady*, James would send Isabel to Paris during the winter of 1872, just a few months after the Commune was put down; but really the majestic city of her visit belongs to the year of his own residence.

He soon began a second major novel, *The American*, and gave it a Parisian setting, but much of his effort during his early months in the city went into his series of biweekly letters for the *New York Tribune*. He wrote about theater and art and the reactionary impulses of the American colony, who wanted another emperor or king, anything but a republican government. He wrote about Chartres and the death of George Sand. Yet James barely touched on what was to become the most important consequence of his time in France, even more important than his friendship with Paul Zhukovsky: his meetings with French writers and his sustained encounter with French fiction. He had called upon Turgenev soon after his arrival, and in mid-December he went, at the Russian's invitation, to Flaubert's. Writing to Quincy Street, he was almost blasé about the meeting. The French writer seemed much kinder than his books had made James expect, and "rather embarrassed at having a stranger presented to him." Two other visitors also looked worth noting. Edmond de Goncourt had begun his career by collaborating on everything, fiction and diary alike, with his now-dead brother Jules; for a while they even shared a mistress. Only a few of their novels are now much read, but the many volumes of their pungent journal remain an inexhaustible mine of gossip and bile. As for Émile Zola, who in books like *Nana* and *Germinal* would have an incalculable effect on the future of the novel . . . well, at that point James thought him a bit common.

In the room that day were five men who either were or would become great writers; Maupassant makes a sixth, and Alphonse Daudet brings the number to seven. Peter Brooks has given us our richest account of what the American learned in France, writing in *Henry James Goes to Paris* of the lessons that finishing school taught him: lessons that on the one hand stressed the importance of formal rigor and conscious design, and on the other showed how unflinching a novelist might be in dealing with sexual passion. James would not fully draw upon that education until the early years of the twentieth century, in books like *The Golden Bowl* and *The Ambassadors*, novels about adultery that offer as well a minute account of consciousness itself, of how one knows what one knows. That knowledge, in his late fiction, always turns on the question of sex, but in the 1870s he simply didn't have the right background. Not even his long stays in Italy, let alone his years in Cambridge, had gotten him ready for something like Maupassant's little tale.

Still, he was at least prepared to register the great difference between his own world and the one he was now entering. One might hear anything at Flaubert's, and James enjoyed setting down just enough of it to shock one of his correspondents back home. Writing to Howells in February 1876, he told him of a subject for a novel that, as "editor of the austere *Atlantic*," he would never have to consider. Goncourt was at work on a book called *La Fille Elisa* and had "got upon an episode that greatly interested him, and into which he was going very far. *Flaubert*: "What is it?" *E. de G*: "A whore-house *de province*." Nor was James the only one there with open ears. Goncourt later claimed that Zola had stolen his research, and in "La Maison Tellier," Maupassant would write one of his greatest tales on precisely that subject. Howells, meanwhile, replied that he thanked God he wasn't a Frenchman. He would have been even more appalled by the bits of conversation James *didn't* record. For Goncourt's account of the day skips over his own work-in-progress in order to concentrate on Daudet's minute description of his venereal symptoms.

Their host spent much of the year at his family home in Normandy, in the old house along the Seine in which he had grown up. Paris was Flaubert's winter retreat, and his apartment there was a modest one, up five full flights of stairs. On Sundays his one servant was out; he opened the door himself, and James remembered the flat as sparsely furnished. The American was shy and had as yet published little of importance; he never became an integral part of the *cenacle*, and some of its regulars never quite caught his name. But a few times he managed to be the first to arrive, and then he had Flaubert to himself for an hour; once he called on a weekday, and the older man recited from memory some poems by his dead friend Théophile

Gautier. At larger gatherings the room was always clouded with smoke and much of the conversation turned on questions of artistic form. By English standards the apartment was full of aesthetic radicals, men who all denied that a book had any business in trying to teach a lesson. Art to them had no more to do with morality than it did "with astronomy or embryology," and any attempt to bring them together was the mark of a primitive mind. "The only duty of a novel was to be well-written," as James wrote in an 1884 essay on the death of Turgenev, and a few years later Oscar Wilde would echo those words in his preface to *The Picture of Dorian Gray*.

Flaubert's own books, with their obsessive search for the right word, the right rhythm, might seem to stress formal concerns above all. Yet in bracketing off moral issues, his aesthetic allowed a space for other kinds of freedom, and one his disciples were quick to explore. No subject matter could be excluded, every aspect of human life had a legitimate place upon the page, and for James the test of those principles lay in the work of Zola. In the spring of 1876 the French writer's first unequivocal masterpiece, *L'Assommoir*, had just started its serialization in a popular left-wing newspaper. James had some sympathy with the idea that art and morality were fundamentally different things, and that the problems of art were above all those of execution. But he never doubted that fiction should depict the moral life of its characters, their awareness of the complexities of the world around them and of the choices they make about living in it. Zola did—he questioned the very idea of the moral life itself. His characters are the creatures of heredity and environment, and their individual efforts have virtually nothing to do with their fates. They are instead the victims or beneficiaries of the impersonal forces around them, a vision of the world that goes by the name of "naturalism." But the term means something more than that, and Zola also provided an unflinching account of his characters lives. He reproduced their speech exactly, he recorded their enslavement to drink and to sex, and he described their work in precise and often painful detail. *L'Assommoir* is the story of the washerwoman Gervaise Coupeau, who lives with her family near the Gare du Nord. The title refers to the ever-bubbling still in the local pub, the source of the family's downfall, and at the end of the book Gervaise's young daughter is already on the streets, a girl who will return as the courtesan title-figure of *Nana*. Zola hoped that the book would make his fortune and was at first devastated by the news that *Le Bien Public* would stop running it after just six weekly installments. The French reading public may not have had Mudie's to guard it, but many of the newspaper's readers had still complained, criticizing both the story's indecency and its unsparing portrait of the working class.

The news was all anyone talked about at Flaubert's one Sunday that May, when "the subscriber, as a type of human imbecility, received a wonderful dressing." James himself had just been asked to stretch *The American* from nine monthly installments to twelve, and when he met Zola on the stairs, there was a certain irony in the American's greeting. In the end, however, the suspension of the serial did Zola a favor. Another newspaper picked it up, the whiff of censorship sparked the public interest, and the novel became the bestseller he had hoped for. Writing in 1903, a year after the French writer's death, James suggested that no one had ever created a "more totally *represented* world." Zola's method and mind and, above all, his material may have been utterly different than James's own, but the American nevertheless thought that *Germinal* had the full scope of an epic, a book that "never shrinks nor flows thin . . . nothing for an instant drops, dips, or catches." None of his contemporaries ever received higher praise.

Still, he always wondered why Zola's imagination was so frequently drawn to scenes of "misery, vice, and uncleanness," and if the older writer admired *L'Assommoir* almost beyond measure, the young one had found it "prodigiously disagreeable." Art and morality might have nothing to do with one another, and James did recognize the realist's need to take in all aspects of human life. Yet surely the picture should not be so unrelieved? James learned enough in the rue du Faubourg Saint-Honoré to attempt to disguise his prejudices, but he still had an Anglo-American suspicion of French subject matter. In his criticism he granted each writer what he called his *donnée*, his choice of material and his view of the world. He criticized only the execution—or so he claimed, for his aesthetic objections often took an ethical twist. So in his review of *Nana*, written just before he began work on *The Portrait of a Lady*, he protested against a view of "nature . . . as a combination of the cesspoool and the house of prostitution," a view that made nature itself seem in need of washing. In 1902 he even criticized Flaubert's conception of Emma Bovary, whose "poverty of . . . consciousness" made her less fully "illustrational" than she might have been. Her world may not have offered her much, but to James she herself did not have so very much to give.

James disliked the bitter partisanship of French intellectual life; at home in Quincy Street he had enjoyed many books that members of the *cenacle* felt themselves obliged to hate. Nevertheless, he valued the clarity with which his Parisian world thought about the purpose and the capabilities of fiction. Zola might be excessive, but English taste was too often insipid. Such masters as Dickens might have worked with their eyes on the young, but as James wrote in his piece on *Nana*, there was some justice in the French belief that no serious book could be written under such restrictions; the "English system was good for virgins and boys, and a bad thing for the novel itself." Each year made his Parisian experience seem more valuable, and after an 1884 reunion with Goncourt and Zola among others, he wrote to Howells that nothing more interested him now "than the effort & experiment of this little group. . . . They do the only kind of work, today, that I respect; & in spite of their ferocious pessimism & their handling of unclean things, they are at least serious and honest." James thought, in fact, that Howells had the chance to become an American Zola, though he doubted that his friend would ever go far enough. And indeed by that time Howells himself had so conquered his own Francophobia as to read everything of Zola's that he could find; only "I have to hide the books from the children!"

That appreciation lay still in the future. Early in *Nana* there appears a sentence that no English writer of its time would have allowed him or herself to write. The girl is appearing on stage in a revue called "Blonde Venus," wearing nothing but a veil of gauze. Zola describes her hips and thighs and even the rosy tips of her nipples, and then writes that "when Nana raised her arms, the golden hairs in her arm-pits could be seen in the glare of the footlights." Statues have breasts, but those little hairs make us realize that Nana has a body, as none of her contemporaries across the Channel ever really do. Of course, James didn't notice that detail in his review. He writes of the book's "foulness," but says almost nothing about what it actually contains. He doesn't tell his readers that *Nana* is about a teenaged actress who drains the purses of her lovers, sleeping her way from success to success in an ever-unsatisfied frenzy; who seems happy only in a lesbian affair, and who late in the novel is startled to find herself pregnant, having so used "her sexual parts . . . for other purposes" that she has forgotten they can still make babies. James writes about none of that. Even as a critic he can't help but observe the distinction between that which he knows and that which he can admit that he knows.

F rench novels circulated freely in England—in French. Translations were a different matter, and James must have been dismayed to find his words about *Nana* used in an 1884 ad for a translation of the novel by the publisher Henry Viztelly. The listing quoted James's statement about "virgins and boys" and suggested that Zola was instead the real thing, strong stuff for an audience of adult males. Viztelly's translations were lightly expurgated and published in cheap editions—they started at 2s.—in order to circumvent the circulating libraries. Even so, they got him convicted of obscenity in both 1888 and 1889, and the second time he spent three months in jail. Reading Zola in French was, for an Englishman, a mark of an educated taste; reading him in English showed only a taste for the gutter. For Viztelly the risk must have been worth it; in France, after all, *Nana* had sold 45,000 copies on the day of its publication. And the publisher himself, as we will later see, would have an important role in changing the terms of the Victorian book business.

Still, the fact of a book's availability doesn't answer the question of who should be allowed to read it. One of Nana's lovers is the middle-aged Comte Muffat de Beauville, a man with a sixteen-year-old daughter whom Zola describes as being of "l'âge ingrat." The idiom is not easy to translate, but its many possible versions all refer to puberty, to the difficult years when one is neither a child nor yet fully grown, and the phrase gave James the title for the oddly intriguing novel, written almost entirely in dialogue, that he published at the very end of the century. At eighteen the deliberately named Nanda Brookenham has just reached what can be called *The Awkward Age* (1899.) She has begun to take her place in the adult world, and yet her mother isn't sure that the girl belongs in the drawing room. For she herself is part of a very fast crowd, whose every conversation carries an allusion to one love affair or another. Might there be a danger for the girl in being exposed to such "'good' talk?"

What lifts the novel to its climax is the discovery by one of Nanda's suitors that the girl has read a book that he himself has left lying around, an untranslated and famously indecent French novel. That troubles him. The kind of knowledge contained in French novels is exactly the kind that the young man doesn't want his bride to have, and he stops himself before making a declaration; though in fact the printed page has told Nanda nothing that she hasn't heard people speak of already. She knows everything, and it doesn't appear as if the news has surprised her. But that knowledge has left her untouched. She is innocent, except in the eyes of others, and that makes *The Awkward Age* itself into a kind of paradox. For though the book isn't nearly as explicit as Zola, it's still about someone who would not, in theory, be allowed to read it herself. Such concerns had been a part of James's work from the start. This apparently lifelong celibate was more entirely fascinated than any other English-language writer of his time by the question of sexual education. What can one know, and when? Under what conditions is that knowledge admissible? On what terms can be it be represented and made the subject of fiction? James never grew tired of these questions, and given the nature of his own life and period, it's perhaps no surprise that he usually approached them in terms of a young woman on the cusp, not only in *The Awkward Age*, but also in the much earlier tale that had first made him famous.

Daisy Miller is among other things about a fissure in the American language. The title character thinks of Europe as a jumble of "old castles," while Frederick Winterbourne, the young man through whose eyes we see

her, views it as a repository of "ancient monuments." Her speech is colloquial and direct; his more formal diction is saved from stiffness only by an
irony that Daisy herself doesn't always catch. They meet at a hotel on Lake
Geneva, and she flirts with him there as she has learned to do at home in
Schenectady. Girls should flirt, she thinks, while married women shouldn't,
and she speaks proudly of having always had "a great deal of gentlemen's
society." But Winterbourne has made his own superstitious valuation of
Europe. He has lost his ear for American speech, American manners, and
though he flirts himself, in proposing an excursion to the Castle of Chil-
lon, he's rather shocked when Daisy accepts. He doesn't know how to read
her, and when they meet again in Rome, he decides that she is nothing but
a "clever little reprobate." She goes around with a well-dressed Italian, a
small-time lawyer named Giovanelli, and her willingness to appear in public, unchaperoned, has set every *straniero* in town to talking. For "when in
Rome"; and Giovanelli would never have suggested to an Italian *signorina*
that they might stroll about the streets together. One woman does attempt
to warn Daisy of her risk, a Mrs. Walker, who tells the girl that she is "old
enough . . . to be talked about." The young woman is at first incredulous—
but a second later says that "I don't think I want to know what you mean . . .
I don't think I should like it."

She knows and she doesn't; and her face hints at a blush. A few years
later, as we have seen, James would make Isabel claim that she doesn't want
to hear anything that Pansy might not; wants instead to remain in the awkward age, not yet forced to confront the world of adult knowledge. Nor
can *Daisy Miller* itself confront it, not if the story is to remain available to
the young girl in the Winslow Homer watercolor, lying on the grass with
her novel. One evening Daisy asks Giovanelli to take her for a moonlight
walk in the Colosseum. Winterbourne sees her there, and at that moment
thinks he knows the worst. Then the girl sickens, and dies. She has caught
the Roman fever, the *mala aria* that people then believed came from the
city's nighttime miasmas. Hawthorne's daughter Una had gotten the same
disease on a sketching expedition to the Colosseum, and the city's Protestant Cemetery is full of tourists who had not built up the native's immunity;

the mosquito's role in communicating malaria wouldn't be understood until the end of the century. But in reading it's hard not to think that James has killed Daisy off in order to avoid answering questions. He kills her so that he won't have to give a name to just what Mrs. Walker means, kills her just before he needs to say if Winterbourne's suspicions of her "actual or potential *inconduite*" are justified. He kills her so that his characters won't have to admit what they know. Or rather what they believe, for once she is safely dead, the story allows Giovanelli to tell Winterbourne that she was the most innocent of girls, that the whole American community has been so naïve as to mistake appearances for reality.

Some readers might wonder—I certainly did, at eighteen—just why a nighttime walk in the Colosseum was so much worse than a walk anywhere else. For the story itself refuses to explain. It preserves both its young readers' modesty and its own; and as for the Colosseum, that was just one of the things that adults were supposed to know about. It would take Edith Wharton to make it all explicit, in her great story "Roman Fever" (1934), a story about a different kind of heat than that from which Daisy suffers. On a visit to Rome two American women, old friends and rivals, watch their daughters chat up some Italian aviators. As the day passes, the women remember their own early visits to the city, at the turn of the twentieth century, and even those of their mothers, in Daisy's day; young women of the 1870s who had in their turn to be carefully protected from the city's dangers by *their* mothers. So Wharton evokes four generations of American women in Europe, the generations whose history both James and she herself had chronicled. Then she ends with a kill shot, a few sentences in which one woman tells the other the truth about the past, sentences that provide the best gloss of all on *Daisy Miller* in showing us just what, with all those massive arches to hide behind, the Colosseum was so famously for.

That wasn't the only time Wharton used her work to comment on that of her predecessor and friend. After all, the hero of her greatest novel, *The Age of Innocence*, is named Newland Archer, a lawyer who seems the very "portrait of a gentleman," as if he were indeed related to that girl from Albany. Wharton set the novel in New York during the early 1870s, in the world of the Knickerbocker cousinage that Isabel has left behind her, and the book opens at the city's old Academy of Music on 14th Street, not far from James's own birthplace off Washington Square. The performance that night is of *Faust*, and as Newland watches his fiancée, May Welland, he fondly allows himself to believe that she hasn't a clue as to what the opera's seduction scene is about. Though in fact she does, and just before their wedding she tells him that he "mustn't think that a girl knows as little as her parents imagine." On every page the novel reminds us of the gap between its 1920 publication and the date of its setting, showing us a New York in which telephones are the latest thing and the trains from the south don't yet cross the Hudson. And among the historical changes it tracks are those in fiction itself, registering all that the novels of Isabel's day were not allowed to say, and that Wharton now can. Everyone here knows and talks about a corrupt financier and his mistress, and some of them worry that their children will marry his "bastards"; while late in the novel May will lie about her own pregnancy as a way to keep her husband faithful. The gap between what people know and what they've agreed to admit they know has gotten a bit smaller, as James foresaw that it would. But such moments aren't the only echoes Wharton offers of the *Portrait*. For Newland also remembers having spent a few weeks "at Florence with a band of queer Europeanized Americans," with rakes and dandies and strange deracinated women who insist on telling him about their love affairs. One imagines a fling with the Countess Gemini; and one imagines as well just how Newland Archer's own innocence would have been caught and pinned by Gilbert Osmond's cold and ancient eyes.

17.

THE MAGAZINES

*M*IDSUMMER, *1881*. HENRY James has had his Venetian spring and brought *The Portrait of a Lady* to within a shout of its close. But an Italian July is another matter, and at the start of the month he left the peninsula's "stifling *calidarium*," and went north. James never traveled quickly, but on this journey he paused for only a week, at the Swiss resort of Engelberg near Lucerne. He crossed the Channel on July 12 and, as soon as he was back in Bolton Street, sat down to an awkward bit of correspondence.

He had another part of his serial ready, as he wrote to Houghton, Mifflin, and would send it to Aldrich at the *Atlantic* the next day. But his publishers expected that afterward there would be just a single installment left and so, he wrote, "I am afraid you will be a little alarmed to learn that I have had to ask from Messrs Macmillan *one additional month* of their magazine, and I shall have therefore to beg the same favour of you." James had no doubt they would grant his request. Nevertheless, he apologized for stretching out what was already a long novel and, as if in compensation, noted that the last three installments would be short; each filled about twenty of the magazine's pages, while the usual ones took twenty-five or more. Still, he would need that extra month, and what two years before he had described, in writing to Howells, as a serial of "*probably* not less than six, & more than eight" months' duration would instead take fourteen.

Most of the Victorian novels we read today were serialized in one form or another. The important exceptions are the Brontës in England and

Hawthorne and Melville in America, all of whom worked before the age of the great monthly magazines like the *Cornhill* or the *Century* or indeed the *Atlantic* itself. James often told friends to wait for the finished volume, but serialization was an unavoidable fact of almost every writer's economic life. Nor was there anything odd in the book's beginning its run before he had completed it. Nearly everyone did that, and Dickens in particular sometimes had to fight his way to a deadline. But serialization took several forms, and the kind of story a novelist told depended in part on the medium in which the work initially appeared. James's request opens a window on the publishing practices of his day. We need to consider it carefully, and can start by looking at the magazines in which the *Portrait* first came out.

The two were surprisingly alike. They had begun publication within a few years of each other, the *Atlantic* in 1857 and *Macmillan's* in 1859, and they shared the same politics. The American journal spoke for a progressive humanism, and the British one for what was called Christian socialism, a movement that played a role in the early history of Britain's Labour Party. Each was pro-Darwin, and in their early years each took an antislavery line; the latter was taken for granted in Abolitionist Boston, but not in a Britain whose textile industry relied on American cotton. Neither had pictures, and instead used double-columned pages of unbroken type. That would later hurt the *Atlantic*'s circulation figures in particular, and despite the magazine's influence, its sales never threatened those of the lavishly illustrated and New York–based *Harper's*. In 1880–81 it sold just 12,000 copies a month, while *Harper's* topped 100,000. Both magazines suggested that culture was serious business and served as high-toned apostles to an aspiring middle-class; James himself made fun of the *Atlantic*'s sobriety. Even their prices were virtually identical. *Macmillan's* cost a shilling and the American magazine 25¢ at a time when the pound fetched a bit under $5. Though the Americans got more for their money—an issue usually ran 144 pages, as opposed to *Macmillan's* 80.

James wasn't the only writer to put the same piece in both journals. Harriet Beecher Stowe had done it with an 1869 article that provided the first hint of Byron's incest with his half-sister Augusta, but nothing so scandalous appeared in either magazine during the year of the *Portrait*'s run. The novel began in the October *Macmillan's*, an issue that also included a piece on the ancient town of Glastonbury, then as now associated with King Arthur. Over the next months the readers got an essay by Matthew Arnold and a poem by George Meredith alongside Isabel's story, and articles on public libraries, the prevention of floods, and "Political Somnambulism" by J. R. Seeley, the historian who later argued that the British Empire had been acquired "in a fit of absence of mind." In the *Atlantic* the first installment came out in November along with a piece on weather forecasting. Early the next year there was an essay by the naturalist John Burroughs, and James's own father offered his recollections of the recently deceased Thomas Carlyle. Nothing in these issues looks so frivolous or, the *Portrait* aside, so purely pleasurable as a piece *Harper's* ran at the same time about going "Down the Thames in a Birch-Bark Canoe." Later in 1881 the *Atlantic* published stories by Sarah Orne Jewett and an anonymous review of Twain's *Prince and the Pauper;* while one continuing feature was the back-of-the-book "Contributors' Club," a section of unsigned pieces on books or manners or travel. Often these brief notices responded to those of an earlier month, producing the sense of an ongoing conversation; "club" is indeed the right word.

There were some differences. The *Atlantic* was hospitable to women writers; *Macmillan's* went further and pushed women's issues, education in particular. In terms of daily operations, however, their biggest difference lay in the relations of owner and editor. The American magazine had been started by a clutch of Boston intellectuals, the poets James Russell Lowell and Oliver Wendell Holmes, Sr., among them, and changed hands several times before it was bought, in 1874, by the printer H. O. Houghton. The new owner would build the greatest of Boston publishing houses; he kept a strict eye on expenses but didn't often interfere with editorial questions. The *Atlantic*'s editors became public figures in themselves, and while Houghton, Mifflin often took a book from its pages, the *Portrait* among them, the monthly never functioned as a house organ. *Macmillan's* was very different. It bore the name of its publisher, and no matter who edited it, the magazine was controlled by Alexander Macmillan, a Scotsman who began his career with a London bookshop in 1843. In 1880 the editor was George Grove, whose own monument is his eponymous *Dictionary of Music and Musicians*. Grove himself had reservations about James's work, but almost all the novelist's dealings were with the firm's junior partner, Alexander Macmillan's nephew Frederick. The novelist approached him soon after settling in London, and they quickly became friends. Over the years he placed work with several other firms as well, but Macmillan's was his most important English publisher, handling virtually all of his books up through *The Tragic Muse* and later holding the British rights for the New York Edition. Or to put it another way, James was a Macmillan author who, with the exception of the *Portrait* itself, did not often publish in *Macmillan's*. He was an *Atlantic* writer who did little business with Houghton, Mifflin as such. In Britain he made his deal for the *Portrait* with the publishing house; in America with the magazine.

James discussed the book with Frederick Macmillan in the spring of 1878, but though he noted his plans in letters to both Howells and Quincy Street, his surviving correspondence with the publisher doesn't mention it again until the next year. Clearly they had been talking about it, however, for in July 1879, James wrote to canvass the possible dates for starting. Nevertheless, there were difficulties. The Macmillans had him committed to a serial, and yet James had also agreed to write something for Howells and told his Boston editor that he wanted to make the "next *long* story I write . . . *really* a long one." Doing that would mean pushing the *Macmillan's* piece back beyond a point that they were willing to accept. James found a solution by flexing the biceps that the popular success of *Daisy Miller* had given him. The *Atlantic* usually objected to simultaneous publication in England. It wanted to be the exclusive home of the things it ran and didn't want to look, even with James, as if it were in the business of importing culture. But the competition at *Harper's* made no such objection, and James reminded Howells that if he lost the chance to "double my profits . . . I shall have, to a certain extent, to remember this." The editor recognized the threat, and by late August, James had arranged to publish the same novel in both magazines at once. On Macmillan's part there was no difficulty; the firm offered £250 for the serial, and half the profits on its book form. Howells grumbled, but he wanted a similar arrangement for his own novels, and once he accepted the deal in principle James worked him hard on the price, asking for $250 each month; he had gotten only $150 for each piece of *The American*. Still, the *Portrait*'s installments were to be longer, and the page rate came to about $10, the *Atlantic*'s standard payment to established writers; the success of the *Portrait* would drive James's fee to fifteen.

The novel's serialization also involved a second balancing act. Until 1891 there was no reciprocal copyright agreement between Britain and the United States, and publishers on either side of the Atlantic often pirated the other nation's books, paying little or nothing to the writers themselves. English copyright depended on the book having first appeared in Britain, but American citizens could assert their copyright in the United States by registering the work with the Library of Congress, whether they were in the country or not. There was, however, some danger that a pirated edition might appear before that registration took place, as indeed happened with *Daisy Miller* after its appearance in the English *Cornhill*. British writers could not file for copyright in Washington from abroad, and could only tap the U.S. market by selling advance sheets to an American publisher, giving the chosen house a chance to get ahead of any competition. That is what George Eliot did with *Middlemarch*, but because it could only delay and not prevent privacy, her American earnings were small in comparison to her English ones.

James got two copies of his proof sheets from *Macmillan's* and, after correcting them, sent one to each publisher; the *Atlantic* then reset the text to fit its slightly larger page. The arrangement depended on a fast and regular mail service—letters took ten or twelve days to make the crossing—and yet that service could also be too fast. *Macmillan's* published on the first of each month, and the opening installment of the *Portrait* appeared in England at the start of October; the same chapters came out in the *Atlantic*'s November issue, released on October 15. The two week gap seems nicely calculated both to ensure James's English copyright and to keep off the pirates at home. But *Macmillan's* had many subscribers in the States, and at Christmas, James wrote Frederick Macmillan a plaintive note. The mails were too fast, the presses too slow, and he had heard that the *Portrait* was "devoured in the American papers before [it] appears in the *Atlantic*." Couldn't Macmillan find some way to stop this? James had already put out a dozen books; but then no author, however experienced, can quite believe that his publisher has done everything possible.

With most writers Howells didn't hesitate to offer suggestions, and in his early stories James took a number of them. But we have no record of any editorial work on the *Portrait*; the only revisions appear to have been James's own. Still, Howells was surprised by the scale on which his friend had begun to build. He knew from the start that the book's install-ments would be longer than those of either *Roderick Hudson* or *The Ameri-can*, but he also remembered James's first proposal, and almost as soon as the serial began, he announced that it would end in the spring of 1881. Which in turn startled James himself. Whatever his initial plans, he now saw that the *Portrait* would cover a "stretch of months or years" in its characters' lives, and he thought he had "been explicit as to its longitude—twelve months." It would live and breathe through its sense of duration, and in doing so would strain his own ambition to the limits; a novel that would justify and fulfill his many years of preparation. Still, he did acknowledge that he had been "strangely vague" about its length. To *Macmillan's* he had first sug-gested a run of eight or nine months, but by December his projected twelve were already becoming thirteen. At the start of the year he sat down to block out the remainder of the book's plot and noted that "after Isabel's marriage there are *five* more instalments." The italics suggest a moment of revision, as if he were underlining an additional change in the book's longitude. The wedding scene is itself unwritten—it takes place in the gap between the novel's eighth and ninth installments. But the novel continued to grow. Those five became six, thirteen stretched itself to fourteen, and in July of 1881, James asked for that extra month.

He was not, however, asking for more time in which to work. There's no suggestion that he hadn't been able to cover his pages, that he would need that month just to finish off. Nor is it simply a plea for more space. Printing the book's last chapters in just two parts would, admittedly, have made for long installments. But it could have been done, and at roughly 30 pages they would have been only a few columns longer than those for several earlier months. Nor, finally, can James be accused of wanting that month for the sake of an extra month's check. His fees were important to him and we know he could be a shrewd negotiator. But in terms of pace and balance the book's nine concluding chapters do indeed work better in three pieces rather than two, and each of these late installments forms a discrete dramatic unit.

That's especially true of the book's final part, three extraordinary chapters that begin by moving Isabel back from Italy to England, back to Ralph and the novel's opening scenes at Gardencourt. I suspect that what made James ask for the extra month was the discovery, as he worked in Venice's brilliant light, that he needed to prepare that conclusion more fully. In roughing out the novel's later stages he admitted to himself that its early portion was "too exclusively psychological," but he thought the installments after Isabel's marriage could make up for that. They would be crowded, perhaps too crowded, with incident. Yet though he knew what those incidents would be, he wasn't yet sure how to handle them all, and wrote that certain issues of motive and crucial moments of revelation were "to be settled later." It's easy to imagine how that might have made the book grow, especially because James characteristically found a way to cover all the possibilities he had sketched.

Of course, he was hardly the first novelist to ask for more time. Margaret Oliphant was a regular contributor to *Macmillan's*, and one of her own serials there makes James looks like a model of exactitude; *A Son of the Soil* (1866) was projected at four parts, and came in at seventeen. Other writers were told after a few months to tie things off as quickly as they could, and even Elizabeth Gaskell, in working for the popular *Household Words*, was made to shorten up the concluding parts of *North and South* (1855). In extending the *Portrait*'s run, James presumed on his status as both Howells's friend and one of the *Atlantic*'s most valued contributors. He also knew that the pages of a monthly magazine were within certain limits fungible. Articles, poems, and even the start of a new novel could be delayed from month to month; short pieces and long ones could be switched around as needed to make an issue fit its appointed size. But that wasn't true of all kinds of serial publication, and especially not of the particular form that had given the nineteenth century its taste for long-running novels.

Serials had a particular job of cultural work to do in the ever-expanding Victorian world; a world in which all things seemed to grow, and literacy among them. Such works, as the critics Linda K. Hughes and Michael Lund have argued, fostered a belief in "process and progress," a sense of "steady development in installments over time, seeds planted in spring leading to harvest in distant autumn." They required, from both their readers and their writers, an ability to hold disparate things together, to make a mental link between the first month and the last, and yet they weren't really exercises in delayed gratification. Instead, one lived in the moment while also anticipating the future. Pleasure and peril in the present, and fulfillment in the months to come—that was what they offered, and no one more regularly satisfied that desire than Dickens. Books like *David Copperfield* and *Bleak House* were first published in monthly parts that sold for a shilling and contained exactly two illustrations and 32 pages of text. There was no other editorial material, though the pamphlet did include many pages of advertisements, some for books but others for laxatives, opera glasses, and the "London General Mourning Warehouse." The finished novel took up twenty such parts, each containing three or four chapters, though the last two installments appeared together in a single booklet, producing a sense of acceleration at the end.

Thackeray, among others, often worked in this form as well, and the writer who chose it needed to keep two structures in mind—that of the book as a whole and that of each separate month, which readers expected to end with a satisfying climax. In consequence, the novelist often set three or four different plots going at once; plots that at first might appear loosely connected but which are far more tightly linked than they seem. Dickens usually managed to touch on most of his different story lines in every install-ment, building up and tamping down his readers' expectations that one of them might resolve itself. At the same time, he had to ensure that some piece of his narrative was ready each month to produce a moment of crisis or change. So he ends a chapter of *Bleak House* with the news that its heroine has been blinded by smallpox, and then finishes the installment by turning to other material, another climax, making us wait until the last pages of the fol-lowing month before we learn that she can see once more. But that example is too easy. Dickens's greatest long novels can seem terribly episodic—and yet try to unpick them! Try to dispense with any single character or point in the narrative, and the whole begins to unravel at once.

Publication in monthly parts created the multiplot novel that is often taken as the Victorian norm. Only by keeping several story lines going at once could the writer develop enough plausible moments of climax to give his readers a reason to buy the next issue. The weekly serials of Dickens's later years—books like *Great Expectations* or *A Tale of Two Cities*—required something different. Their installments were shorter, and that relative brev-ity necessitated a tighter focus. A good comparison is that between the first-person narratives of *David Copperfield* and *Great Expectations*. The former appears to meander, and David himself often seems a mere witness to other people's stories. The short weekly installments of the latter may twist and turn, but they never mark time. Nor do we ever doubt its central concern—our eyes are always upon its narrator, Pip. Neither book could have been successfully serialized in the other one's form.

The period's most complicated case of serial publication is that of *Mid-dlemarch*. George Eliot didn't like working ahead of herself in the way serial-ization required, and she released both *Adam Bede* and *The Mill on the Floss* as three-volume novels, without the benefit of any prior magazine appear-ance. In *Middlemarch*, however, she wanted to write on a very large scale, and eventually decided to publish in a bimonthly series of eight short books, each about the size of three of Dickens's monthly parts. They had soft green covers, sold for 5s., and fit comfortably in a coat pocket. The volumes vary slightly in length—that flexibility was part of the form's attraction—and their scope allowed for a more complicated interplay of the novel's different plot lines than do even Dickens's monthly installments. George Eliot begins with the story of Dorothea Brooke, and at first holds it apart from the rest of the novel's concerns; we stay with Dorothea for 80 pages, but when George Eliot switches focus, she is banished for another 80. Then slowly, gradually, symphonically, the novel's different sets of characters begin to entwine themselves with one another. The multiple plots start to merge; and by the end of the book they are all one. Yet even this form reflected the material realities of the novelist's working life. For *Middlemarch* is a fusion of what George Eliot had originally imagined as two separate stories, and we owe its long initial account of Dorothea to the fact that she had already written it before she began to splice.

Weekly serials allowed a bit of room for the writer's improvisation and uncertainty, a week or two to swell or shrink. Freestanding volumes or pamphlets had none. There could not be more of them, or less; with Dickens, indeed, the very page count was fixed. They couldn't stretch out their time, as James did, and for all their seeming looseness, they required that the narrative be defined in advance; a model made, and stuck to. There is a paradox here. The *Portrait* seems to discover its final shape as it grows, as though it were unplanned; but its action appears as a taut and single motion. Dickens looks rough in comparison, and yet his books were rigorously planned, their outlines carefully developed before he began to write. James never worked in such monthly parts. The form had begun to die by the time his career began, supplanted by the journals for which he himself worked. Those magazines offered a different set of possibilities, however, and reading a serial there was a fundamentally different activity from reading one in separate parts.

The Portrait of a Lady was the main attraction in both *Macmillan's* and the *Atlantic*, but it was still just one attraction among many, and not even the only novel. Most of a magazine's readers were regular subscribers. No one story had much power to make the monthly circulation rise or fall, and readers came to the journal for many reasons; an *Atlantic* reader who didn't like James wouldn't necessarily stop receiving it, not so long as he enjoyed the "Contributors' Club" or the poetry. An installment of *Bleak House*, however slender, could seem to become the world. That illusion wasn't possible for a reader who held a monthly magazine in his hands, and might open to a different piece each time. In consequence, the expectations for an *Atlantic* serial were different than those for a novel published in monthly parts; and different again than they would be in a more popular periodical. And in some ways those expectations were less.

Unlike Dickens, James did not have to keep the customers coming back. He didn't have the same need for a regular monthly crisis and often chose to avoid the obvious high notes, to end an installment off the beat. Warburton's proposal falls in the middle of a part; Mr. Touchett's death at the start of one. Osmond's declaration does indeed conclude a month, but then so does Isabel's statement that she would "rather hear nothing that Pansy may not." That's the last thing we hear her say before her marriage, and her words don't signal a change so much as they serve to reinforce our impression of her fears. It is a curiously understated ending and suggests that James had a very different sense than Dickens or even George Eliot of what constitutes a turning point in a narrative. It suggests that though *The Portrait of a Lady* may have been serialized, it is not, when seen against its Victorian predecessors, a serial novel.

A generation later Joseph Conrad was at work, and desperate, upon one of his greatest books, the story of Russian guilt and terrorism that he called *Under Western Eyes*, and a part of that desperation came from his fear that "no magazine will touch it." For though one finally did—the *English Review*, with a circulation of just 1,000—the kinds of books Conrad wrote were increasingly difficult to publish in parts, and his ambitions were at odds with the progressive thrust of serial form. Dickens's world had possessed something close to a pure linearity. The story unspooled month by month or week by week, and the order of events in his characters' lives was virtually identical with the order of their narration. In contrast, Conrad's books were full of flashbacks, of great looping motions in time and sudden shifts in point of view; they would skip into the future and then back up to plug the chronological hole. But then many narratives of the *fin de siècle* were at odds with what Hughes and Lund describe as the serial's emphasis on "slow, sure growth and development." Instead, they offered a world of disorder and even chaos, a world best contained in the "autonomous whole" of a single volume.

James played his part in that change. Nevertheless, serialization remained a financial necessity even for those, like Conrad, whose work was unsuited to it. Most nineteenth-century novelists made their money from magazine publication rather than the sale of finished books. Advances against royalties were not yet common, and in England those royalties might amount to nothing at all. Macmillan issued just 750 copies of the *Portrait*'s first, three-volume edition, and many of those went at a discount to Mudie's or its competitors. James's income from books in 1881 was under $1,000, a figure that includes both American and British sales; though to be fair, he got more than that the next year in the States alone, as the *Portrait* went into a series of reprintings. At the same time, he received a bit over $5,000 for the novel's serial rights. His earnings fluctuated over the course of his career, and with time his income from books increased. But in the first twenty-five years of his European residence, he often made four or five times more from magazine sales than from books.

Five thousand dollars was indeed a substantial figure; Henry Sr. had supported a large family in comfort on an income that never exceeded $10,000. Five thousand dollars was what Howells got for editing the *Atlantic*, a job he left only when he felt he could make as much from his fiction. It did not, however, put James among the top earners of his period. Anthony Trollope kept scrupulous records and listed his takings at the end of his autobiography, at great cost to his reputation. Other writers, James among them, resented the way that the older man's balance sheet made him seem like a tradesman rather than an artist, though James himself maintained a comparable but private ledger. Trollope made £3,200 from *Phineas Finn*, over $15,000. George Eliot did even better; by the time *Middlemarch* was finished, she had earned over £4,000 from its serial sales alone.

Middlemarch's commercial success owed a great deal to the idiosyncracies of its first edition; those eight little volumes were an encouragement to buy, not borrow. Moreover, George Eliot watched the response to the novel's opening installment and used it in shaping the later ones. For serials were often reviewed, and several of *Middlemarch*'s separate parts got full write-ups in both the *Spectator* and the *Athenaeum*. Those first reviews were so entirely engaged by Dorothea that at the last minute her creator swapped a few chapters from one volume to another in order to bring her back more quickly. The *Portrait* didn't receive such extensive coverage, and most of it came in the roundups of periodicals that many newspapers and magazines then featured. The *Atlanta Constitution* reviewed most issues of the *Atlantic*, and so did the *Detroit Free Press*; but neither paper much liked the story. The *Spectator* gave it an occasional line in its monthly "Some Papers from the Magazines," writing of the first installment that "nothing can be more delicate," and after that took the serial's quality for granted. In America the richest commentary came in *The Nation*, where James had been a contributor since its 1865 founding. In March 1881 the magazine thought the book "considerably the most important" he had yet written; in August it foresaw some coming catastrophe to the characters, but was agreeably unable to predict its shape. But its most interesting account of the novel came early, in response to the second installment, when the paper's anonymous critic spotted what even now remains, for some people, a source of James's appeal. His every sentence is so nuanced and full that "the reader feels irresistibly flattered at the homage paid to his perceptive powers."

In Britain the novel received its most regular coverage in the *Examiner*, a weekly that ceased publication in the late winter of 1881. Its critic usually concentrated on James's introduction of new characters; Henrietta Stackpole was "quite too lifelike," and Madame Merle exquisite. One comment, however, looked directly at the question of serial form, and suggested that James presumed just a bit too much. None of the magazines he wrote for offered a way to fill one in on the story thus far, and the *Examiner* thought that "the author evidently counts on the strong interest of his readers when he commences a monthly instalment with 'He took a resolve after this not to misinterpret her words.'" That's the opening line of the novel's third part, and any reader coming to it cold can be forgiven for wondering about the antecedents of those pronouns; for the record, they refer to Ralph and Henrietta. James did count on that interest. Or rather that sentence shows why he usually told his friends to wait for the finished book. In that form there's no difficulty in simply turning the page and moving from chapter to chapter. We know where we are and what's going on, we know to whom those pronouns refer, and the transition is seamless. Serialization may have been necessary, and yet James often did his best to ignore its requirements. He wrote instead with his eyes on the book—on the novel's permanent form.

He did, however, begin one installment in a way that even the most old-fashioned of readers would have found unexceptionable. He sent his letter asking for more space in July 1881, and in that month's *Atlantic* the serial's ninth part started with this sentence: "One afternoon, toward dusk, in the autumn of 1876, a young man of pleasing appearance rang at the door of a small apartment on the third floor of an old Roman house." It is the only date James ever gives us, and it signals a change: a shift in point of view, and a disruption of chronology. Isabel has gotten married—in the space between the lines, one might say—and we have moved forward by more than three years. That's long enough for the marriage to have grown unhappy, as we are almost immediately told, and we will at first see "Mrs. Osmond" from outside, from that young man's point of view. But James will eventually take us within, and the way he tells us about those missing months will make a revolution in the history of fiction itself.

18.

THE ROCCANERA

T HE DOOR BELONGS to Madame Merle, and the young man with his finger on the bell is named Edward Rosier. James writes that we "will perhaps not have forgotten" him, but we have met this character just once before and readers of the *Atlantic* would have had four months in which to lose track of him. He is a childhood friend of Isabel's, with an inherited income of £1,600 a year, and so thoroughly Frenchified that he sometimes has to hunt for the right English word. He hunts, and fails to find it; referring to Isabel, for example, not as Pansy's stepmother, but as her *belle-mère*. For that is how he sees her now, as the stepmother of the perfect young girl he has met that summer in Switzerland. Ned Rosier has never in his life done anything indiscreet, but he does follow the Osmonds down to Rome, where they have lived since their marriage, and after a month he has learned two things. He knows that Osmond doesn't think he's rich enough, and that Madame Merle has some unexplained pull with Pansy's family. So he rings, and hopes she'll help him.

This is the second of the novel's great ellipses. The first, as we have seen, came just before Isabel's marriage, when James skipped over the year that ended with Osmond's successful proposal, and presented us with a *fait accompli*. We didn't even know she was engaged until the novelist made Caspar Goodwood cross the ocean simply to express his outrage. Now he has jumped again, a gap in time that corresponds to a gap in our knowledge of his heroine, and new readers inevitably find it disorienting; they may even feel cheated. We have not been to Isabel's wedding; we have not witnessed the start of her life in marriage; all we know is that she has settled in Rome and that her stepdaughter has met a boy. We don't even know how much time has passed, and then James knocks the wind out of us. Madame Merle tells Rosier that Isabel will probably favor his suit "if her husband does not." Nothing more, not yet, but it's enough to show us that the marriage has broken down even before we have seen it begin. We may not have trusted Osmond, but we knew that Isabel did and hoped that Ralph was wrong about him. Instead, we have gone from promise to ruin in the space of three pages, and it is as if our hopes have been drowned.

Three pages, and three years. We can work out the time from something else Madame Merle tells us. Isabel has had a son, "who died two years ago, six months after his birth." Those details allow us to date the novel's every scene. We will be told that her wedding was in June, and Rosier appears at the door at the start of December 1876. So we can place the marriage in 1873, and can even say that she conceived later that summer. But the child is dead, and in truth it's hard to make very much of him. James does not connect that death to whatever has blighted the Osmonds' marriage, and when Isabel later thinks back over its failure she will not spare the infant a thought. James gives her a child because it's both the most efficient and least explicit way he has of telling us that the marriage has been consummated, and yet motherhood itself has no part in his conception of Isabel's future. She believes that in marrying Osmond she has acted freely, and at the end of the novel she will need that liberty once more. She will need to choose with a freedom that she would not have in a child's presence.

That baby aside, James refuses here to give us any direct knowledge of the inner life of Isabel's marriage, and as a reader I'm split between my frustration at his refusal to take us over the brink and my admiration at the skill with which he switches his lens and approaches her through a hitherto-forgotten character. Still, that change does signal a larger change in mood, and perhaps a loss of *brio*. No scene after Isabel's marriage offers the expansive delight of the book's early chapters, the feeling of enchanted discovery with which she enters her European life. She no longer has decisions to make but must learn to live with the one she did, and the book shifts to a minor key, less exhilarating but with a new gravity and indeed nobility, whose force increases with each chapter.

At first, however, James's decision to present Isabel indirectly can seem bewildering. He shows her through Rosier's eyes and Rosier's story, shows us only her social self, and it will take him sixty pages to open the closed door of her private life. We need something to do while we wait, however, and he uses the question of Pansy's suitors and possible marriage to delay and distract us. Another American girl will have to choose. Madame Merle promises to help Rosier as much she can, and then she immediately tells Osmond. The news is disturbing—so disturbing, in fact, that Osmond signals his disapproval by offering the young man his *left* hand at the next of Isabel's regular Thursday evening receptions. Rosier has no choice. He has to take it, but he turns away as soon as he can, and then finds himself face-to-face with Isabel once more.

She stands framed in a doorway, as at Gardencourt, and again she is dressed in black. The repetition is unobtrusive, but James means us to notice it and it serves to mark a difference; almost as if her story were starting over. She no longer wears the traveling dress of a girl in mourning, but is gowned in black velvet instead, and we don't need to imagine the clinging stuff of Sargent's scandalous and contemporaneous *Madame X* to see her as bare-armed and décolleté. At Gardencourt she had stood in the door of an ivy-covered house, gazing onto a green lawn, and then stepped out into the world before her. Here, however, the door that encloses her is smothered in gold leaf, and she looks only from one interior space to another, a receding vista of rooms enfilade. Isabel waits for others to approach, a hostess who appears to Rosier as the very picture of a lady, a woman whom the "years had touched . . . only to enrich." But Rosier has never been to Gardencourt, and the reader will see a greater change. This portrait allows for a fourth dimension.

. . .

W
e need to pause over that doorway, over the setting that James has provided for her. Money went far in Rome. Servants and food, horses and houses—all of them were cheaper in Italy than in London, and with the painted ceilings thrown in for free. Isabel lives with a magnificence that even her substantial fortune would not have allowed in Britain, and as he walks through her rooms, Rosier finds himself admitting that "these people were very strong in *bibelots*," in the beautiful decorative objects that he himself most covets. But the sensibility behind it all belongs to Osmond alone. Isabel has had nothing to do with furnishing their house and claims to have no taste of her own; her husband, in contrast, has what she calls a "genius for upholstery." The place is his, an assertion of his will, of the self he wants to project. It is an old "high house in the very heart of Rome; a dark and massive structure overlooking a sunny *piazzetta* in the neighbour-hood of the Farnese Palace." Rome may be bright, but the building itself is called the Palazzo Roccanera, the Black Rock, and to Rosier its darkness matters. For it seems to him as if Pansy's home is a kind of fortress, a place in which she might easily be locked up.

James describes it as marked with a "stern old Roman name, which smelt . . . of crime and craft and violence," a place mentioned in guide-books and visited by tourists. It has been most reliably identified with the Palazzo Antici-Mattei, a complex of sixteenth- and seventeenth-century buildings whose austere façade was built to designs by Carlo Maderno, and where the rooms on the *piano nobile* have ceilings by Domenichino and Pietro da Cortona among others. James masked the original just a bit by giving it some frescoes by Caravaggio instead. That makes one start. The Victorians did not admire the painter we call by that name, and he gets just two one-line references in *Italian Hours*; nor is he known to have worked in fresco. Still, the Mattei family did own a few of his canvases. They had made their fortune buying up real estate after the city was sacked in 1527, and quickly became one of the most powerful clans in Rome; three centu-ries later they were still turning out cardinals. The building now houses the

Centro Studi Americani, and many visiting lecturers have found themselves in the rooms that were in some sense once Isabel's. Nevertheless, the palazzo remains forbidding indeed, darkened by age and with barred windows on the ground floor. Inside, the courtyard walls are encrusted with fragments of ancient statuary, and the loggia overlooking it is lined with "a row of mutilated statues and dusty urns," just as James described it. But there are many palaces in Rome, and I suspect that what drew him to this one wasn't just its architecture or its atmospheric history, but rather its particular location in the city itself.

It lies indeed in the heart of the town, and not that far from the Palazzo Farnese. It is closer, however, to both the church of the Gesù and the Capitol, and closer still to the Palazzo Cenci, itself associated with crime and craft and violence. Every literate Victorian knew Shelley's play about Beatrice Cenci, who at the end of the sixteenth century was executed for killing the father who had raped her. It is closest of all to the Ghetto, whose walls lay just a few paces off and which was abolished only with the final unification of Italy in 1870. The quarter is ancient and aristocratic, and was in Osmond's period decayed; a neighborhood beyond all question of fashion, a place of squalid streets and private interior splendor. Which makes it a very good address indeed—a good *Roman* address, and about as far as possible from the American colony that gathered around the Spanish Steps. That's where Madame Merle lives, but Osmond detests the modern city of hotels and English bankers. Not everyone is invited to their Thursday evenings, and even those who are might discover that the house isn't easy to find, buried as it is in the narrow twisting streets of history itself. Its location stands as both a sign of his originality and a mark of his "tradionary" pose. This part of Rome may lie on level ground, but so far as the *stranieri* are concerned, the Roccanera is a Roman equivalent of Osmond's Tuscan hilltop.

One unexpected caller does, however, find his way to them, an Englishman whom Osmond doesn't at first recognize. Lord Warburton has come south with Ralph, whose consumption has grown worse each year and who now thinks of wintering in Sicily. But the journey has worn him out. He cannot move from their hotel, and one reason for Warburton's visit is simply to announce their arrival. For Isabel has had no advance word, and to us that's the truly startling thing: the cousins have fallen so far apart that they're no longer in regular touch. James writes that the "reflective reader" shouldn't find this surprising, given Ralph's view of Isabel's marriage, and we are told something similar about each of her old friends. Mrs. Touchett has faded from her life, and even Madame Merle has grown distant. Until this winter she has preferred England to Rome, and she now tells Isabel, a bit too often, that she doesn't want to presume on the fact that she's known Osmond for so long. Marriage often does attenuate old friendships, and yet the novel insists that we notice it, reminding us of it each time that the author brings back an old name.

James has a difficult task here. The chapters after Isabel's marriage do not introduce a single new character, and he needs instead, as the novel starts over again, to catch us up on all his old ones after a gap in years if not in pages. He keeps both Henrietta Stackpole and Caspar Goodwood alive in our minds by bringing them down to Rome, and there is a special brilliance in his retrospective account of Ralph in particular. Ralph has come to Rome only once since Isabel's marriage and quickly realized that his very presence made Osmond so unaccountably nervous that he in turn made it uncomfortable for his wife. Now he has returned, close to death and yet kept alive by his belief that his cousin's story isn't yet over, and James dives down into the character's memory and then swims up to breast the novel's present. It fuses these years into a single image of Ralph's estrangement from her, a verbal equivalent of a medieval miniature in which several incidents share the same space. But let me put it a different way. There is a prismatic quality to these chapters. James doesn't let us look at the white light of Isabel's being directly, but instead refracts it through the differently shaded impressions of his other characters. Once he has done that, however, once he has reintroduced his cast, James needs to move forward into the new relations created by her marriage, and at this point the novel becomes thick with plot in every sense of the word.

The most important element in that plotting concerns Warburton's surprising interest in Pansy. He finds her charming, at once polished and ingenuous, and comes repeatedly to sit with her at the Roccanera, even as he worries that Isabel won't be pleased by his interest. For of course, as he tells Ralph, "there's the difference in our ages." It's the most round-about way to suggest that he's thinking of marriage, and the idea so startles the invalid that it makes him risk Warburton's anger. "I hope," Ralph says, "you are sure that among Miss Osmond's merits her being a—so near her stepmother isn't a leading one?" Nor is Ralph the only one who has noticed Warburton's attentions. Rosier has, and grown jealous. And Osmond has seen it too, and seen deep. He has seen what Ralph fears, and decided he can use it.

Isabel herself has seen something else. James hasn't yet defined the precise contours of her marital troubles, but one day she returns home from a drive and stops short at the entrance to the drawing room. For she has, James writes, "received an impression," and must pause to take it in. She has found Madame Merle standing while Osmond remains sunk in his chair, two old friends caught in a moment of ruminant silence. There's nothing particularly unusual in that silence, but the image does offer her a flicker of perception, albeit one that's gone before she can read it. What catches her is their physical posture—the gentleman sitting while the lady, his guest, stands. In fact, Madame Merle herself recognizes its oddity, and after Osmond leaves the room, explains that she herself was just about to go away. Now she stays to talk, however, to muse over Rosier's jealousy and the odd fact that Warburton seems to have fallen in love with Pansy. Isabel too has spotted the Englishman's interest but hasn't discussed it with her husband, and the subject makes her impatient. So their conversation grows snappish, and becomes only more so when Madame Merle alludes to something that Isabel has never told her. For the older woman knows of Warburton's proposal at Gardencourt, and hopes that she will now "make him the reparation of helping him to marry some one else."

Indeed, Isabel wants to—wants anyway to try. She believes that to give her husband this personage as a son-in-law would be to "play the part of a good wife. She wanted to be that; she wanted to be able to believe, sincerely, that she had been that." Still, she finds Warburton's attachment strange. Pansy seems to her so small, so limited, but she does try to talk herself into it; then she remembers Rosier and admits that the girl prefers the young American. That night Isabel is sitting by herself in the drawing room when her husband comes in. It's the first time James has shown them together and alone since their marriage, and Osmond now tells her that he wants their visitor to declare his intentions. That admission costs him something. He's so used to acting as if none of the world's prizes are ever worth an effort, and his words make Isabel recognize how intensely he wants to see his daughter at Lockleigh. Still, the girl can't make it happen on her own; any proposal will depend upon Isabel's willingness to use the influence he knows she still has. "The moment you really wish it, you can bring him to the point," he says, and his words mean exactly what Ralph had earlier suggested. Osmond may speak of loving his daughter, but he knows that her chief merit in Warburton's eyes can only be her nearness to her stepmother.

"It lies in your hands," he tells her, and then walks out, while Isabel remains by the fire. What she sees as she sits there will produce a moment of reverie that lasts the full length of a night, a chapter that stands as one of James's greatest achievements and a turning point in the history of the novel.

Isabel will sit long that night, until the oil lamps have burned out and the candles have guttered down to their sockets. She will sit and think, motionless, while her mind moves over the whole history of her married life. Nothing happens in the *Portrait*'s famous forty-second chapter, and yet her meditation "has all the vivacity of incident," as James put it in the novel's preface, a reverie that throws the novel's action forward by returning her to her past. And she begins by working through the situation that Osmond's words have put before her. Those words make her see that Warburton does indeed want to please her, and she wonders if he believes even now that she might be something more to him than a friend. Still, she cannot quite square the idea with the evident sincerity of his fondness for Pansy. That fondness may be a delusion, but she immediately acquits him of pretending to be in love with the girl as a way of pursuing her instead. In fact, Warburton himself has been genuinely startled by Ralph's earlier suggestion; a few chapters on he will look at it squarely and take himself back to England. But to acquit Warburton is not to acquit Osmond, and with each minute the "service her husband had asked of her" seems more and more repugnant. He wants her to flirt—but that puts it too mildly. He wants her to use what sexual hold she has over Warburton as a means to her stepdaughter's marriage; as though she were bait. He's pimping her, and she knows it. So her recognition of the Englishman's innocence brings her no peace, and as she sits through the night, she finds herself "haunted with terrors," among them the curious sensation of seeing her friend and her husband together.

On this night Isabel will think, more than ever before, about just why she married, and what made it go wrong. She—we—will feel the continued power of Osmond's charm, and we will understand just how her distrust of her husband has grown. Neither of them is the partner the other one expected, though at first he had believed "he could change her, and she had done her best to be what he would like." We will get the explanation that James refused us when the novel resumed after Isabel's marriage and at the end of these dozen pages will know almost everything of importance about the early years of their union. That ellipsis will be closed. James's work here offers a new way of presenting the interior life, a new kind of fiction, and yet the chapter gives us more than an early example of what William James would soon name the "stream of consciousness." It will of course give us that, and in a moment we will see how. But it also has a structural task to perform in the novel as a whole.

James either could not or chose not to dramatize the week-by-week dissolution of trust that is the Osmond's marriage. He offers us Isabel's retrospective understanding of its failure but doesn't depict the process of that failure itself, and I do not think it possible to define with any precision the complex of psychological and technical reasons that made him refuse such scenes. So let's presume instead that such a depiction was never his purpose, that his interest lies elsewhere, in Isabel's understanding of the consequences of her marital choice. Still, we do need to know why it's the wrong choice, and at this point George Eliot can help us. Though not in the obvious way. She writes brilliantly about marriages going wrong in both *Middlemarch* and *Daniel Deronda*, and that of Gwendolen Harleth and Henleigh Grand-court in the latter novel is in some ways a model for Isabel's own. Another aspect of *Daniel Deronda* seems to me equally important, however, and far less often remarked upon.

We're now accustomed to novels marked by narrative disjunctions, books predicated on flashbacks or memory that seem to glide back and forth in time; books in which the order of events and the order of their telling are at odds. We have read Conrad and Faulkner, Proust and Woolf, and know how to piece a chronology out of a story's discontinuous shards. But the readers of James's day were not nearly so used to such structures. Most novels of the period relied on a linear narrative, and though they might allow themselves brief moments of retrospection, the story thrust always forward. *Daniel Deronda* is different. George Eliot liked the opportunities that the massive serial parts of *Middlemarch* had given her, and she returned to that form in the later book, once more dividing it in to eight parts of about 100 pages each. This time, however, she did something more than use that architecture as a way to ease her movement from plot to plot. She also used those large blocks of narrative to disrupt chronology in a way that a more conventional serial novelist like Dickens could not. The epigraph to her first chapter suggests that any such opening is but the "make-believe of a beginning"; all starting points are arbitrary, and "no retrospect" ever takes us back to the true origin of things. Narrative form isn't given by the calendar, but must instead be made, and so, after a dramatic opening scene at a German casino, George Eliot falls back in time for 200 pages in order to show how her characters got there. The opening chapters hold us—an English girl losing at roulette. We want to know why she plays with such abandon. And what about the man who returns the necklace she pawns?

Of course, George Eliot wasn't the first to begin in the middle; her structure has one of the grandest of all pedigrees in the *Odyssey* and the *Aeneid*. Very few Victorian novels used that gambit, however, and none so successfully. Nevertheless, such breaks in sequence would have an incalculable effect on later fiction, beginning with *The Portrait of a Lady* itself. Not that James appears, at first, to disrupt chronology as such. The jump that puts young Rosier at Madame Merle's door is not in itself a violation of narrative order. But it does create a gap. It puts us into a situation we don't fully understand, and here James found an elective affinity with his predecessor's experiment in time. George Eliot presents her own retrospective in an omniscient third person that's indistinguishable from that in the rest of her narrative, fully dramatizing each stage in the process that has brought her main characters to the casino. James's narratological problem is more complicated. In the preface to *The Golden Bowl* he described his own inveterate preference for an "oblique view of my presented action"—not an impersonal God-like account of the affair, but rather one "of somebody's impression of it." And so it is at this crucial moment in the *Portrait*. The middle of Isabel's marriage lies itself in the middle of the novel, and James needs to fill us in, not as George Eliot does on what happens before the book "begins," but instead on the events of its unwritten center. He closes the gap by breaking chronology, allowing Isabel's memory to stitch over the tear in the novel that is the moment of her marriage itself: a chapter of interior monologue in which there is no physical action beyond the burning of a candle.

Still, a full understanding of just how this chapter covers—or perhaps recovers—the past will require a closer look, and before proceeding we had better get the taste of it in our mouths:

> He had told her that he loved the conventional; but there was a sense in which this seemed a noble declaration. In that sense, the love of harmony, and order, and decency, and all the stately offices of life, she went with him freely, and his warning had contained nothing ominous. But when, as the months elapsed, she followed him further and he led her into the mansion of his own habitation, then, then she had seen where she really was. She could live it over again, the incredulous terror with which she had taken the measure of her dwelling. Between those four walls she had lived ever since; they were to surround her for the rest of her life. It was the house of darkness, the house of dumbness, the house of suffocation.

Osmond's beautiful mind gave neither light nor air; Osmond's beautiful mind, indeed, seemed to peep down from a small high window and mock at her. Of course it was not physical suffering; for physical suffering there might have been a remedy. She could come and go; she had her liberty; her husband was perfectly polite. He took himself so seriously; it was something appalling.

In some ways there's nothing particularly difficult about this passage, and its first readers had few problems in comprehending it. It provides an example of the free indirect discourse that most of James's contemporaries used in depicting their characters' inner lives. He allows Isabel's own particular idiom—her vocabulary and biases and ways of understanding—to percolate through his own narration, and the language provides a series of tip-offs that tells us we've been put inside the character's mind: the verb "seemed" in the first sentence, the reiterated "then, then" with which James suggests Isabel's incredulity, the afterthoughts represented by all those semicolons. We come particularly close to her in the passage's last words—"something appalling"—which offer a colloquial summation of Osmond's character. Yet though Isabel's notes do infiltrate James's voice, they don't undermine it. His own tones are muffled, but they remain very much in place, and he maintains the distinction between author and character. So we see through her eyes, and at the same time look at those eyes; we have just enough distance on her to mix our sympathy with judgment.

All this is conventional enough, and yet there is indeed something different about the way Isabel's mind works here. Her language is intensely visual, and while the imagery in this passage runs to the domestic, in other places it refers to the garden or the seashore or the vista of a "dark, narrow alley." Those images are, however, all metaphors; the four walls that surround her are not precisely those of the Palazzo Roccanera. Osmond may seem as if he had "deliberately, almost malignantly . . . put the lights out one by one," and yet the shadow in which she now lives belongs to a moral and not a physical climate. Very little in this chapter points to a particular moment in Isabel's married life, to the individual events of those missing three years: an account, say, of her first dinner with Osmond after the death of their child; or an argument over his belief that even the best of women all eventually take lovers. That's not the kind of thing she remembers. Instead, she allows her mind to slip from one generalized moment of perception to another, collapsing those years into a sense of the "everlasting weight upon her heart." But that sense, like the rest of the chapter's richly imagistic language, remains untethered to an account of any one incident, and even as James fills the gap in his narrative, the actual events of her life go undramatized.

In this, his account of Isabel's reverie differs markedly from his predecessors' accounts of their own characters' inner lives. One example must serve for many. Near the end of *Middlemarch*, Dorothea Brooke sobs herself to sleep on the floor, believing that her hopes of happiness are now forever gone. When she wakes, however, she forces herself to relive the shattering events of the previous day and to weigh the role of other people in the scene that has so broken her. She thinks consecutively, she asks herself questions and answers them, she comes to a final understanding and determines to act upon it. It takes about a page, and similar moments could be found in Austen or Trollope, Thackeray or Howells. Isabel's night before the fire occupies a much greater space in the novel, a much longer time in the reader's experience, and part of its originality lies in the simple fact of duration. Her meditation is long enough to provide its own justification. It doesn't have to lead to any course of action, and it ends without her having reached a conclusion of any kind. Yet there is a greater originality in what the chapter *doesn't* do, in its refusal to fill those missing years with what James called "solidity of specification." For Isabel's mind, ordinarily so hampered by Osmond's mocking egotism, here seems to float free. She roams, she wanders, unconfined by reference to any particular moment, and it is no accident that her mind is most active when she sits most perfectly still, as though consciousness itself were briefly disembodied.

We can get a richer appreciation of James's work here by looking at something his brother wrote just a few years later. William James spent the 1880s at work on his own first book: a massive project, intended as a college text, which he turned in ten years late and that finally appeared as the *Principles of Psychology* in 1890. Early versions of some of its chapters did, however, come out along the way, and in 1884 he published an essay called "On Some Omissions of Introspective Psychology" in *Mind*, then as now one of the most important of all journals in the academic study of philosophy. There he coined a phrase that has, for better or worse, become central to our understanding of modern fiction. William James argued that what first strikes us about what he called the stream of consciousness is its absence of uniformity, "the different *pace* of its different portions." It pools and it flows, spreads wide and runs deep, but its activity never ceases and there is no part of our mental life that does not belong to it. In putting it that way he underlined his difference from earlier thinkers, who conceived of consciousness "like one who should say a river consists of nothing but pailsful, spoonsful, quartpotsful, barrelsful, and other moulded forms of water. [Yet] Even were the pails and the pots all actually standing in the stream, still between them the free water would continue to flow." That, in fact, is what George Eliot had done with Dorothea—she had drawn out a few buckets of interiority, and stood them in a row. But for William James consciousness wasn't a set of propositions or conclusions. It was a process, unbounded, and his essay provides an exceptionally rigorous account of how, in the years to come, the novel would describe that inner life. It is a kind of crib sheet for modernism itself.

Except that Henry had gotten there first. His 1906 preface to the *Portrait* is the product of memory, and maybe we should be skeptical when he depicts his younger self as saying that he wanted to focus upon "the young woman's own consiousness," that he would make the story one of "her relation to herself." But if any single chapter of the *Portrait* does embody those ambitions, it is this one, and it stands as an ever more central part of his *oeuvre*. He wrote to William in the spring of 1884 that the essay in *Mind* had "defeated" him, and yet some lines in that year's "Art of Fiction" do seem to echo it. For him consciousness isn't a stream but a "chamber," and our sensibilities are like a spider's web suspended within it, capturing everything that comes within reach of its filaments. Forty years later Virginia Woolf—he had known her from birth, he had dined with her parents—would describe that consciousness as a "luminous halo, a semi-transparent envelope." The metaphor changes but the phenomenon remains, and what James does in this chapter is much closer to Woolf's own achievement in *To the Lighthouse* than it is to Eliot's *Middlemarch*. Of course, Woolf's very sentences gave her contemporaries trouble, as at this period James's own did not. In some ways the *Portrait*'s might seem but to extend what other writers had already done, to differ from them only in degree. Yet in his avoidance of buckets, in the inconclusive and associative flow of Isabel's thoughts, and even in his sheer ability to sustain his account of those thoughts, James here goes so much further than his predecessors that it amounts to a difference in kind. No writer in English had yet offered so full an account of the inner life, and in remembering this chapter for his preface he allowed himself, for once, to make an unqualified judgement—"It is obviously the best thing in the book."

Probably it is; but best or not, it is clearly the most important. Yet nothing in James's plans for the novel seemed to anticipate it. The notes in which he blocked out the book's last stages make no mention of Isabel's motionless vigil, and though he does write of needing to characterize her estrangement from Osmond, he gives himself no suggestions as to how he might do it. I suspect that the idea for this chapter came to him late. Only when he was at last upon it did he discover the technique that would allow him to handle her revulsion. Only then did James find a method, at once expansive and abbreviated, with which to define Isabel's marriage. Whatever the history of its composition, however, there is no doubt that this chapter marks a turning point. James's earlier work had often substituted a character's impression of an event for the event itself. These pages do more—they change our very sense of what counts as an event in fiction. Sitting still counts; thinking, doing nothing, not moving. Emotions count, and the activity of perception as well. James would write many kinds of fiction over the next twenty-five years, but from this point on the central events of his characters' lives increasingly take place, not in the social world, but within; interior acts of interpretation or understanding. Chapter 42 marks the point at which James stopped being just an important American writer with a special knowledge of Europe on the one hand and the predicament of young women on the other. It marks the point at which his own work became Jamesian: the point at which he began to shape the future, a writer whose books made other books possible, a central figure in the history of the novel itself.

James closes the gap in his story only when it becomes dramatically necessary to do so. Osmond has left the Warburton business in Isabel's hands, and at this point we can't fully understand either that request or her reaction to it without some fuller understanding of their marriage. So the requirements of the present produce a return to the past, a break in sequence in which both Isabel's mind and the novel itself rove back in time, working to fill the hole in our knowledge. Later writers would take this further, would violate chronology with a recklessness that James himself could not imagine. Conrad would make a career out of retrospection; Faulkner would seem to freeze time itself in its place. In some ways James remained a Victorian, and when in *The Golden Bowl* Maggie Verver brings Isabel's kind of freely moving intelligence to bear on her own marriage, she directs it toward the present and not the past. She thinks her way through a situation that she wants not simply to understand but to shape. By that time James was willing and able to write about the inner life of a marriage, indeed about passion itself. And perhaps both the *Portrait*'s great ellipsis and the idea of consciousness that he developed to deal with it did indeed allow him to evade a difficulty.

That indirection is inseparable from the fact that he asks us to see the failure of that marriage in broadly sexual terms: to remember Isabel's earlier fears of surrendering her very self, and to think of them now as realized. Not in any crude or even precisely physical way. James made few substantive revisions to this chapter for the New York Edition, but one of them does suggest the nature and presence of Isabel's own desire. There may indeed be things she doesn't want to hear, forms of knowledge from which she wants to protect herself, but where in 1881 she had merely "loved" Osmond, in the later version she "anxiously and yet ardently" gave herself to him. That shift clarifies; it lets us know that what's gone wrong isn't some insurmountable reticence or dysfunction. James also tells us—and in the first edition—that Isabel "was not a daughter of the Puritans" and writes too that Osmond has committed no crime, no moment of violence or cruelty. What's gone wrong isn't a question of some particular action, and perhaps it isn't even sex itself but rather some aspect of Osmond's being for which James finds a sexual language. For we cannot miss the charge with which he writes that at a certain point the man's "personality, touched as it never had been, stepped forth and stood erect." It stands up, makes itself visible, its presence felt. The image is there in 1881 and unchanged in the later edition, and though the metaphor could if necessary be disowned, it does define Osmond's threat, the force with which he assaults her very sense of self. Her "real offence . . . was her having a mind of her own at all," and he wants to knock it out of her. He wants to treat her mind as an annex of his, and furnished only with his tastes and opinions. He has not counted on her resistance, however, and at every obstacle his hatred grows.

Isabel resists both because she must and because she finds Osmond's own beliefs so entirely repugnant; above all, his claim that life is a matter of prescribed forms and not freedoms. We will learn much more as she thinks through the night, will learn everything we need to know. She will meditate on Osmond's contempt for everyone in the world except the handful of people he envies instead, and of his desire to extract from the world some acknowledgment of his own superiority. She will contemplate his claim that it's somehow "indecent" for her to visit Ralph at his hotel. And in thinking about Ralph's invalid life Isabel will at last understand his attempt to warn her off this marriage. She will recognize that his generosity is in itself a form of intelligence and one her husband lacks. So she sits quietly on as the candles burn down, her mind a cauldron of activity. But at last she rises, and then stops, her memory caught, in the chapter's last words, by that afternoon's impression of "her husband and Madame Merle, grouped unconsciously and familiarly."

19.

THE ART OF FICTION

M ACMILLAN RELEASED THE first book edition of *The Portrait of a Lady* at the start of November 1881, immediately after it finished its serial run. Houghton, Mifflin followed two weeks later with the first American issue, and anyone looking at them together will find it hard to resist an obvious joke: their difference says volumes about the differences between the British and the American book trade. The English edition appeared as a standard triple-decker, albeit one whose 750 pages were more closely printed than the norm. In America it came out as a single volume, and its 520 pages were even more tightly packed. Macmillan observed the standard pricing as well—retail customers paid 31s.6d. or 10s.6d a volume. The Boston firm sold the book for $2, or just a bit more than the 6s. the English one-volume cheap edition would fetch the next year. And that difference in price forecasts a difference in sales as well. The first English edition of 750 copies did sell out, and Macmillan ordered a small second printing in the new year, before releasing their cheap edition that summer. But Houghton, Mifflin ran through six printings by August 1882, after an initial impression of 1,500 copies, for total sales of just over 6,000. These figures are small in comparison to those of Twain or even Howells, and yet for James it was a major success; indeed, the *Portrait* would prove both the most popular and the most lucrative of his full-length novels.

That difference in sales is worth noting, and can't be explained by assuming that even an expatriated American would inevitably sell better at home. Most novels published in London had even smaller runs, and what matters here is the structure of the industry itself. English publishers could produce cheap books. They chose not to. Prices remained what they were in the days of Walter Scott, and ignored the technological developments in both printing and papermaking that had brought the real costs of publishing down. What kept those prices artificially high was the existence of such commercial libraries as Mudie's; Macmillan's ads for the *Portrait* announced not that the book was in the shops, but rather that it was "now ready, at all the Libraries." I've already described how such businesses worked from a customer's point of view. An annual fee—Mudie's standard was a guinea, or 21s.—allowed subscribers to take out the first volume of as many works as they chose, with subsequent volumes costing a shilling a throw. That wasn't cheap; a subscriber's ticket was itself a mark of middle-class respectability. But it *was* economical, and the system accustomed the public to borrowing instead of buying. The libraries needed the three-volume novel to make their money, and because they invariably took a large percentage of any first edition, albeit at a steeply discounted price, the publishers gave them what they wanted. That collusion ensured both that the libraries remained lucrative and publishing had few risks, but its consequence was to keep the retail price of new books so high as to discourage purchase. American libraries didn't exercise the same power in the marketplace; for one thing, they tended to be free. Prices therefore remained closer to the actual cost of manufacture, reflecting what a buying public was willing to pay, and there was no incentive to spread a book over several volumes.

Both editions used British spelling. The type was set by the firm of Clay & Taylor, Macmillan's regular compositors, and two sets of stereotyped plates were made from it, one for Boston and one for the cheap impression the English firm assumed it would eventually need. Then the set type was leaded out for the three-volume edition: adjusted, that is, so that there was more space between the lines and fewer lines per page, though the type itself remained small. James read proof in the summer and early fall of 1881, but he made few significant changes from the serial version. For the one-volume edition he numbered the *Portrait*'s chapters consecutively, and the novel appeared without any other internal divisions; the first English edition, in contrast, starts a new sequence with each volume. Yet while the first of them does end with the death of Mr. Touchett, the second concludes without any such turning point. That separation serves no consistent dramatic purpose, and in that the *Portrait* differs from many other Victorian novels, such as Charlotte Bronte's *Villette*, where each volume defines a different stage in the heroine's progress. All later editions number the *Portrait*'s chapters consecutively throughout, including the two books of the New York Edition, in which the break merely reflects the novel's midpoint. These volume markers mean less than they seem, confirming the sense that James wanted his readers to see the work as a single and continuous whole.

That, in fact, was the argument of one of the novel's first reviewers. A generation later W. C. Brownell would become Edith Wharton's editor at Scribner, but in the early 1880s he was one of *The Nation*'s leading critics, and wrote there that the novel "gains in its complete presentation . . . the whole is equal to no fewer than all of its parts," and one that wasn't entirely apparent in serial form. Not that Brownell was entirely smitten. He missed some quality of "fervor" in the book's second half and thought its pleasures were too purely intellectual. James wasn't for everyone. Howells had said that from the start, and the *Portrait*'s reviewers, faced with what Brownell admitted was a masterpiece, struggled with the meaning of that restricted appeal. Dickens *had* been for everyone, famously so, and there was a lingering belief that a great novelist ought to be. Even George Eliot had drawn a wide, if not universal, audience. Some American newspapers connected the polish of James's art to the rarefied world of his characters. The *New York Sun* thought the distinguishing marks of "good society" were so precise that in writing about it James could only use "pencils of the finest point"; the *Californian* of San Francisco admired the book's finish but thought its material barren. Even the *Atlantic*'s critic, Horace Scudder, argued that James's imagination seemed cold, while in *Blackwood's*, Margaret Oliphant claimed the book's dazzle could fatigue. Everyone admired James's workmanship, and yet most of the book's critics felt some impatience as well. Ought novels to be so finely made?

Oliphant had a more particular charge. Many of James's readers at home found him insufficiently patriotic, but she saw him instead as the voice of American triumphalism, a writer who depicted the Old World as though it were arranged for his pleasure. Some of her animus was, admittedly, directed not at James so much as his countrymen as a whole, who loved nothing more than to "inspect our antiquities . . . [and] patronize our institutions." But though her tone was priggish, her eye was deadly, and in his last books James would indeed depict his homeland, however ironically, as what she called the "heir of time." Oliphant offered other objections as well, in which she was joined by the equally conservative critic of the *Spectator*, R. H. Hutton. James may have provided portraits of his secondary characters, but the "one thing which the book is not, is what it calls itself." Isabel herself lacked definition, and Hutton added that her character remained "nothing but haze, a laborious riddle." Both of them were troubled by the book's open ending, by the fact that James finished without letting his readers know his heroine's fate. The last chapter seemed to imply a catastrophe that it wouldn't allow itself to dramatize, and Hutton was troubled by the absence of anything like a religious sense; it was an "agnostic" book, and its conclusion a "sign-post into the abyss."

A book's initial reception often sets the terms of later discussion, fingering the issues that will continue to matter; this is no exception. My own account of that open ending will have to wait until we get there, and for now it's enough to say that it puzzled most readers at the time and still puzzles some of them now; *Lippincott's* claimed that James couldn't "bring himself to the vulgarity of a regular *dénouement*." Still, his best critics were already used to that, and Scudder argued that it was now time to accept James's method. He used his own review to distinguish the novelist's approach from that of such predecessors as Thackeray or George Eliot. Those writers had often stopped the flow of their narratives to generalize about "all sorts and conditions of men." James limited himself to his own characters, at whose motives he worried and tugged, as though he were pulling his own people apart. Such a minute dissection had a name. It was called the "analytical" method of characterization, and though the term isn't used now, it figured heavily in the criticism of the next few decades. Most English critics didn't like it and thought that approach an American peculiarity; but Conrad later described Proust in those terms, and they apply to his own work as well.

The shrewdest early appraisal of the *Portrait* belongs to Constance Fenimore Woolson, who in an 1882 letter offered James a perceptive reading of individual scenes and characters, and singled out Isabel's vigil by the fire; none of the book's reviewers had especially marked it. The crux of her letter lies, however, in her account of the difference the book would make to his reputation. She thought the critics had now taken a new and probably permanent tone about him. They had enjoyed anticipating his future— had thought "your talent, your style, your this and that . . . marvelous *in* a young fellow." But he had gone by them and they knew it; he was no longer the coming man, and other writers were prepared to be jealous. Woolson thought the *Portrait*'s reviews remarkably bad-tempered for all their praise; praise that was almost always hedged, even in recognizing it as an advance on his earlier work. For with the *Portrait*, the future had "become the present. They see it and cannot deny it. They don't like it." *The Portrait of a Lady* got the kind of mixed reviews that are only given to a writer who matters. Henry James had become inescapable, and to be ambivalent about him was, from this point on, to be ambivalent about the direction of fiction itself.

Woolson believed the attack would come from other Americans. Instead it found its origins in what should have been a moment of triumph. The *Century* was the glossiest New York monthly of its period, its circulation high and its slick pages sprinkled with illustrations. The issue for November 1882 included a story by Frank Stockton whose title— "The Lady, or the Tiger?"—survives though the tale itself does not, and an obituary essay on Victor Hugo by Alphonse Daudet. But James led the magazine with "Venice," one of his best travel sketches, and the piece was followed by both his engraved portrait and a tribute from Howells called simply, "Henry James, Jr."

This amounted to the period's equivalent of a media blitz, but Howells's essay wasn't a puff piece. Or at least it doesn't seem so now. He touched on *Daisy Miller* and a number of other international tales, but he always circled back to the *Portrait*, and assumed a knowing audience; he wrote as if even minor characters needed no introduction. His tone was measured, but the claims he made were still large enough to cause trouble. He thought that only George Eliot could match James's analytic bent and suggested that they had created the two noblest heroines in contemporary fiction. Howells also argued, however, that Isabel was more subtly depicted than *Middlemarch*'s Dorothea and thought that James himself stood at the head of a "new school" in the writing of fiction. That school avoided the often sensational plots of the past, the catastrophes and coincidences, on which even George Eliot had sometimes depended. Instead it found its material in the everyday world, and in a way that—the depiction of sexual life aside—one might even be tempted to call French. Howells wasn't sure that readers would be content with "an analytic study rather than a story," with books in which nothing much might seem to happen and the narrative shoelaces were left untied. But about one thing he was certain. The art of fiction had in these latter days become a much finer one "than it was with Dickens and Thackeray."

Fighting words, red flags to John Bull. By "fine" Howells meant "refined," but the evaluative note was inescapable, and the British reaction against what critics called the American school was both immediate and fierce. By January, Oliphant had a piece in *Blackwood's* that depicted American literature as engaged in a hostile takeover of the English language. Howell's own novels had just come out in London, and she admitted to begrudging the praise a British audience had given him. Yet why should that audience defer to America on any question of taste whatsoever? It wasn't so long ago, as she reminded her readers, that American culture had been defined by the spittoon. Still, she preached tolerance—the tolerance of parents who are inclined both to applaud and to laugh "at the exploits of the little one." In the *Quarterly Review*, L. J. Jennings took on the *Portrait* along with Henry Adams's anonymously published *Democracy* and books by both Howells and George Washington Cable: all of them written on the oddly modish "principle that the best novelist is he who has no story to tell." Jennings admitted that James himself occasionally betrayed his own aesthetic and produced something that looked like a plot. Howells never did, and as for the *Portrait*, its many hundreds of pages of small type followed that principle so relentlessly as to make it the most tedious book of the year.

Howells's argument was fatally easy to caricature. British critics saw him as claiming that not only the methods but also the pleasures of Dickens and Thackeray were obsolete, that there was something wrong about liking a story that was a story, densely plotted and thrilling, and with a last chapter that told us what happened to everyone when it was over. "The indictment is rubbish," James wrote in a letter, but it stuck, and a few months later he added that articles about the two of them were still "as thick as blackberries—we are daily immolated on the altar" of the English classics. The most interesting of those articles came out simultaneously with Howells's own, however, and it anticipated rather than responded to the argument. Robert Louis Stevenson's "A Gossip on Romance" suggested that though it might be clever to write a book without a story, that cleverness remained at odds with what drew us to fiction in the first place. He had just finished writing *Treasure Island*, and the essay is the most sophisticated defense of simple delight imaginable. Stevenson believed that no books are so passionately read and loved as those we discover in the "bright, troubled period" of childhood. At that age we read for "incident" above all, pulled on by our need to know what happens, and he wasn't embarrassed to admit that he still felt a primeval pleasure in turning the pages. Such pleasures weren't everything, he acknowledged, and yet the novelist who forgot them in concentrating on the "slips and hesitations of the conscience" was also apt to forget whole sides of the human experience.

Together, Stevenson and Howells inaugurated a period of competing manifestoes of a kind more familiar in France than in Britain. But the energy of that debate depended on the fact that the English novel had reached a moment of generational change. Both George Eliot and Trollope had just died, the last great novelists of the century's middle years. Their chairs were empty, while the newcomer Thomas Hardy was still on the cusp of his own major work. The English critics wrote in fear that the best things lay behind them, while the Americans were bouncingly confident, in everything from what Jennings called the "Boston Mutual Admiration Society" to the vigorous regionalism of Bret Harte. "Henry James, Jr" stood as a tribute both to its subject and to Howells himself. He had been James's editor, he had a stake in his success, and the essay played a major role in his own career as a maker of taste, marking the start of what have been called the "Realism Wars" of the 1880s. The *Atlantic* had made Howells a powerful figure in American culture. But he became even more influential in the second half of the decade, when he used a new column in *Harper's* to map the connections between fiction and the social realities of a sprawling, diverse, and increasingly urban nation; a debate that would shape the work and reception of Theodore Dreiser and Stephen Crane among others.

James kept his distance from those wars; or rather he entered them through his interest in such French writers of the period as Zola and Maupassant. Still, he did respond to the furor Howells's essay had created, and did so in the one piece from the battle that continues to be read on its own merits. In April 1884 the journeyman novelist Walter Besant gave a lecture called "The Art of Fiction" in which he argued that fiction was indeed a fine art, something comparable to and as worthy of respect as music or poetry or sculpture. The claim is uncontroversial now and even at the time was less remarkable than most writers pretended; though Trollope, it's true, had compared the novelist to a shoemaker, a skilled craftsman, and nothing more. Besant offered younger writers some advice of the kind that's still given about keeping a notebook and writing from experience, and the piece as a whole is both inoffensive and dull. It would be entirely forgotten if James hadn't taken it as the occasion for the playfully magisterial essay he published under the same title later that year. I've drawn on his own "Art of Fiction" throughout this book, using it for the light it casts on his career as a whole. But we also need to consider it as the product of a particular moment in that career.

James begins with disarming modesty. He wants merely "to edge in a few words under cover" of Besant's "encouraging" work, encouraging because until recently he had had no idea that the English novel was

. . . what the French call *discutable*. It had no air of having a theory, a conviction, a consciousness of itself behind it—of being the expression of an artistic faith, the result of choice and comparison. I do not say it was necessarily the worse for that: it would take much more courage than I possess to intimate that the form of the novel as Dickens and Thackeray (for instance) saw it had any taint of incompleteness. It was, however, *naif* (if I may help myself out with another French word); and . . . . there was a comfortable, good-humoured feeling abroad that a novel is a novel, as a pudding is a pudding, and that our only business with it could be to swallow it. But within a year or two, for some reason or other, there have been signs of returning animation—the era of discussion would appear to have been to a certain extent opened.

James never mentions Howells, but he chooses his examples deliberately, his use of French looks mischievous, and he knows but does not allude to the reasons for that "returning animation." What he *does* say is that the discussion looks worth having. British criticism will be better for having to define and defend its tastes, for having to say what the pudding is made of. James admits that nothing will ever take the place of "liking" a book, though he still wonders why so many of them have to end with the fictional equivalent of a "course of dessert and ices," a doling out of the appropriate rewards and punishments. He acknowledges that readers like a good ending, and yet argues that in some cases the truer course might "render any ending at all impossible." And as for those books in which nothing seems to happen—well, doesn't a "psychological" motivation stand as an adventure in itself?

At point after point James offers a tacit reply both to Howells's critics and his own, and it's possible to read the piece as an elaborate series of coded references, in-jokes accessible only to those who sit at a groaning board of the period's magazines. The essay offers far more than that, however, and what has made it last is its sense of joy. James's prose here is as buoyant as a Mozart serenade, sly and generous and, above all, confident, the voice of a writer who knows the worth of his own achievement. If he writes for those dining off the magazines, he also writes with a zest and a clarity that endures

today, and one that doesn't need the benefit of footnotes. What he offers—
what "The Art of Fiction" gave me as a student and what it gives still—is
a sense of the exhilarating complexity of form itself. Usually we talk about
books in pieces: plot and character, language and theme. We pull them apart
because it's easier that way, and if we're lucky, we manage to put them back
together again. James won't let us do that. He insists that we take it whole.
The critics of his day usually distinguished between a work's "subject" and its
"treatment," but to him a novel was "a living thing, all one and continuous . . .
and in proportion as it lives will it be found, I think, that in each of the parts
there is something of each of the other parts."

One aspect of that claim seems worth an extra degree of consideration,
and worth it precisely because it points to the limits of James's own assumptions. He praises *Treasure Island*, but he also has Stevenson's essay on his
mind, and as I noted in an earlier chapter, he rejects the period's customary
distinction between the novel of character and the novel of incident. The
only distinction he recognizes is that between good novels and bad. For
"What is character but the determination of incident? What is incident but
the illustration of character?" It's an incident, James writes, for a woman to
give you a particular look. At the same time, the way in which she looks will
also provide a glimpse of her character. Plot and character in this economy
are interchangeable and transitive, an equation that will forever balance.
A closer examination suggests, however, that for James character always
takes precedence. Character creates incident; incident merely illustrates
some already-existing way of being. Events reveal character, but they do
not make or mold it, and the force of circumstance alone is never determinative. Most of the novelists James admired would have agreed with him,
Turgenev in particular. Start with a character—with a girl in a doorway—
and then look for the incidents that will best display her essence. Yet James
claims too much. This method may work for his own kind of fiction, but
he won't allow that there might be other kinds, that under certain circumstances one could begin and begin better with incident instead.

Stevenson offered what he called "A Humble Remonstrance" to James's
argument, but he would lose the debate, and forty years later E. M. For-

ster started his *Aspects of the Novel* by worrying over the fact that the novel tells a story. "That is the highest factor common to all novels, and I wish that it was not so, that it could be something different—melody, or perception of the truth, not this low atavastic form." The modernist suspicion of story itself—Woolf had it too—dates to James, and to "The Art of Fiction" in particular. His aesthetic is predicated on the belief that we have the freedom to act and to choose, that character in the nonliterary sense makes fate. Other writers would develop a different model of the relation between character and incident; Hardy's people, for example, often seem pursued by some external fate, by circumstances against which they are helpless. James did, however, recognize one particular challenge to his own ideas. He ended "The Art of Fiction" with the briefest of bows toward France in general and Zola in particular. James could not quite get himself to walk in the naturalist's path, and thought that his peer's great effort suffered from its overriding pessimism. He nevertheless preferred it to the "shallow optimism" of the English, and in the winter of 1884 he found in Paris what he told Howells was the only kind of new work he could respect.

That February, James gave himself a working vacation, crossing over to the French capital "on the principle that anything is quieter than London," and taking a room for the month at the Hôtel de Hollande near the Palais Royal. It was the easiest of strolls to both the Louvre and his beloved Comédie Française, but on this trip he was concerned above all with his memories. Turgenev had died at the end of the previous summer, and Flaubert in 1880; James couldn't walk the city's streets without remembering them, and without recalling as well that earlier self who had come there almost a decade before. The young man had stayed on the edge of Flaubert's group, listening more than talking, but he now decided to renew his acquaintance with its survivors. He had just written for the *Century* about Alphonse Daudet, the Provençal author of *Lettres de mon Moulin*, and he now asked a mutual friend, a journalist named Theodore Child, to arrange a meeting. Daudet invited the two of them for tea at his apartment overlooking the Luxembourg Gardens and asked Zola and Edmond de Goncourt among others to meet the now-famous American. Child wrote about the meeting for the *Atlantic*'s Contributors' Club, referring to James as "Mr X," and in the telling describes these remnants of Flaubert's *cenacle* as surprised to discover just who their guest was. "'Why, I have known you a hundred and fifty years!' exclaimed Daudet." But while the French writers all remembered his face from those long-ago Sundays, they had none of them connected the face and the name.

Even in 1884, James's books remained little-known in France. Few of his colleagues there read English, and though *The American* came out in French in 1880 and *Daisy Miller* in 1883, James later discouraged the translation of his work. He thought the process would make his very style "evaporate," and in fact the *Portrait* would not have a French edition until 1933. But it was of style that he spoke with Daudet and the others, of the toil and torment with which they fought their way to the one right word. They thought everything that could be said in French had been said already, and Daudet talked enviously of Turgenev, working in a language that "had as yet so few foot-prints." James thought they looked exhausted by it all, like "galley-slaves"; though Daudet's own beautifully wasted face was also the product of syphilis. He himself had never struggled for a word—his difficulty lay in choosing from among the many that so readily came to him. Still, he respected their effort. They too saw the act of writing as one guided by conscious intention, and he admired the passion they brought to their job; most English fiction was a vomit of "tepid soap and water" in comparison.

That intelligence must have seemed especially appealing in the months after his immolation in the British magazines. None of the French writers believed that books should be as edible as puddings, and James drew on their sense of vocation in writing "The Art of Fiction" later that year. What he got from French fiction is a quality that Mario Vargas Llosa has defined as the double legacy of *Madame Bovary*. The Peruvian novelist argues that two distinct schools of fiction trace their descent from Flaubert. One finds its inspiration in such things as Flaubert's account of the little drops of sweat on Emma Bovary's shoulders. It dedicates itself to an almost photographic realism, trying always to extend the range of material with which the novel can deal. Zola worked in this spirit, and Maupassant in his stories of prostitutes, and most writers about war: an unflinching look at the represented subject. The other limb of Flaubert's tree takes on his obsession with form, his hostility to cliché, and his awareness of the sounds and the colors of the language itself. Vargas Llosa links that to Proust and then to the *nouveau roman*, and also indeed to James. But I am not so sure, and for the American the two appear almost as inseparable as they were for Flaubert himself. Certainly, James saw the naturalists as engaged by questions of form; and certainly he too worried over the question of what could and could not be represented on the page. "The Art of Fiction" may speak of the novel as a finely balanced and organic whole; but it also bemoans the reticence of English fiction, its substitution of a moral qualm for a "moral passion."

James told Howells that he saw him as "the great American naturalist." The words must have made Howells shudder, and yet his 1882 *A Modern Instance* had offered a vision of marital dissolution that, physical questions aside, was very nearly as bleak as that of his Gallic contemporaries. Of course, James added, he still had "a tendency to fictitious glosses; but you are in the right path." Howells would always pull himself up short, and two years later, in writing about Dostoevsky, he tried to say why. He admired *Crime and Punishment*, which he read in French translation, but thought it would be a mistake to imitate its relentlessness. Any novelist who wanted to give a true picture of American society would have to acknowledge what he called "the more smiling aspects of life." Realism itself required him to register the possibility of happiness, and while Howells did recognize the Dostoevskian tragedy of American slavery, he also believed that in the 1880s his countrymen could hardly draw upon it in fiction. Someday they might; but in the Gilded Age the troubles most readily available to the American writer seemed to him those of private life, not public wrong.

Nor would James himself go far enough, albeit for different reasons. In 1876 he had thought Zola a writer of "brutal indecency," but in 1903 he wrote that the battle scenes in *La Débâcle*, Zola's 1892 novel about the

Franco-Prussian War, were fully as rich as Tolstoy's, and suggested that
L'Assommoir in particular would have been destroyed by any shred of
"timidity." Its greatness depended on Zola's willingness to soak himself in
a world gone rank. He did, however, have one final reservation about the
French fiction of his age. He was willing to grant Zola and Maupassant their
subjects, and knew that the day of "hard and fast rules, *a priori* restrictions"
was over. But he also thought that their concentration on the "carnal side of
man" had limited their sense of human possibility. They saw all life in terms
of lust, a matter of compulsion and desire, a struggle for existence in which
people were at the mercy of forces they could neither resist nor control.
That determinism was entirely at odds with his belief in the shaping force of
character, in the freedom of conscious choice. He remained skeptical of the
young Isabel Archer's faith in Emersonian self-fashioning, but he was too
much of an American not to feel the seductions of that faith himself. Those
other Victorians named Freud and Nietzsche would tell us that Zola was
the more nearly right of the two, but James always maintained that there
was both a drama and a liberty in resisting desire, and that other things
mattered as well.

James was right that the age of a priori restrictions was over. In an earlier chapter I touched on the challenge to Mudie's de facto censorship of
British fiction that was presented by cheap one-volume editions of the novels the library refused to handle. Those novels included books by the Irish
writer George Moore along with English translations of Zola. Both writers
were published by the firm of Henry Viztelly, but other companies soon saw
the advantage of a 6s. price, and the single-volume format also suited the
wildly popular and relatively short adventure novels by writers like Stevenson or H. Rider Haggard that began to appear in the 1880s. The lag time
between a novel's first edition and its cheap reprint began to dwindle, the
number of public libraries grew, and Mudie's profits shrank. In 1894 the
firm announced it would pay no more than 4s. for any volume of fiction,
no matter its length, and that decision changed the whole structure of British publishing. It killed the triple-decker. At that price the three-volume
novel, with its wide margins and heavy paper, could no longer turn a profit,

and soon everything came out in a single inexpensive volume instead. Book sales boomed, and though Mudie's lasted for decades more, it had in effect destroyed its own power. Zola's challenge was not in itself sufficient to change that system. But it was necessary. In England the contents of his work required a change in the physical form of the novel itself, and that change made further experiments possible. The pornographic bookshop in which Conrad's *Secret Agent* begins could not have been written about in Mudie's era; nor could Lawrence's *Sons and Lovers*.

The first British editions of James's late novels appeared in a single volume. And he continued to think about the issues his reading of French had presented, above all in an 1899 essay called "The Future of the Novel." English fiction had long insisted upon innocence and avoided any but the most cautious treatment of what he called, elliptically, "the constant world-renewal." But the young were older than they used to be, and that omission could no longer stand. James imagined, however, that Anglo-American fiction would deal with sexual questions in a different way than the French had. Great changes were taking place in the condition of women, and though the New Woman of the nineties was not yet a suffragette, James still saw things shifting "deeply in the quiet." Such women didn't want to be protected from knowledge, and he thought they would use their own elbows to smash the windows of discretion. He suggested, moreover, that in doing so they wouldn't show much consideration for the modesty of their erstwhile protectors. A generation later Virginia Woolf would echo that sentiment in her "Professions for Women," noting that one of her difficulties in writing honestly about her own physical experience was the fact that men would be shocked; she felt "impeded by the extreme conventionality of the other sex." James was not shocked. He was reticent, and he believed that an emphasis on passion alone would "falsify the total show." But he looked forward to a fiction that might say the unsayable, a novel in which the truth could be told.

PART FIVE

PUTTING OUT THE LIGHTS

Henry James. By Katherine McClellan. 1905.

20.

THE ALTAR OF THE DEAD

O N THE LAST day of 1882, Henry James went out to the Cambridge Cemetery, along the Charles at the city's western edge, and stood over a freshly filled grave. The air on that New Year's Eve morning was sharp and clear, a sky of bright winter sunshine, and the novelist stayed there for a long time, muffled against the cold and holding a letter in his hands. The letter was dated from Bolton Street, but he had not written it. It was in his brother William's hand instead, and James had carried it with him from London on a final voyage of filial duty. Now he opened it and began to read his brother's sentences aloud, each phrase forming a puff of vapor in the empty space above a modest headstone, and then vanishing. "Darling old father," he began, and as he read, it seemed as though the two sons were united in the communion of words, and united as well with the parent whose last illness had brought them no true sense of shock. Henry Sr. was old enough, and had written enough; he would not be forgotten. Death in such circumstances could not be "inharmonious." There was another reason why their father's death now seemed fitting, however, and it wasn't the first time that James had stood in the graveyard that year.

As I have already noted, James left England a few days before the *Portrait* had concluded its serial run, and arrived in Boston on the first of November 1881. He had delayed his homecoming by a full year, having first planned to cross the Atlantic the summer before, only to decide that he could not travel with his novel half-done. Or at least he couldn't go to

America; Venice was another matter, but then he didn't have a family there. Once finished, though, he could indeed return, and return as one who has known success. Still, the Quincy Street to which he came back was a very different place than the one he had left in the fall of 1875. William had married and had taken his wife and son to live on Beacon Hill, but James had shown him around London the year before. His sister Alice had visited him in England just that summer. Yet he had not seen his parents in six years, and no matter how many letters had gone over the ocean, he wasn't prepared for the changes he now found in his mother. Mary James seemed "worn and shrunken," and in time he would recognize the depth of her weariness.

He planned an American stay of five months, and wrote that he felt glad to have come, glad to have seen his family, though not simply for the pleasure of it. Renewing his relations with them was also a form of measurement. It allowed him to define both who he was, and who he had become, and one of the things that measurement immediately showed him was that he could not stay in Quincy Street. His hours and habits were different now, he was too used to an independent life; he could not simply turn himself into a son again. After just a few days he moved across the river to Boston, and took a room at the Brunswick Hotel on the corner of Clarendon and Boylston streets. The city's Back Bay was still in the course of development, with trainloads of gravel arriving by the hour, but many of the finest buildings in this suddenly opulent neighborhood were already up. Henry and Clover Adams had a house nearby on the narrow, elegant Marlborough Street, and at his hotel James had for a neighbor the city's most majestic temple, H. H. Richardson's newly finished and neo-Romanesque Trinity Church.

One morning he sat in his hotel room over a notebook that he had bought at a stationer's in Piccadilly and began to compose the résumé of his European life that is paradoxically known as the "American Journal" of 1881–82, the journal on which I've drawn throughout this book. The notebook offers a roster of the country houses he had visited and the clubs that had welcomed him, and it describes his books in terms of the places in which they were written: Paris, Florence, Venice, and above all the Bolton Street apartment that "ought to be sacred to me" as the place in which he had thought and learned and above all produced. James wrote in that hotel room with a quick and unerring fluency—the manuscript is without the scratchings of revision—and his pages are elegiac and anticipatory at once. They mark the beginning of the self-mythologizing that so colors the autobiographical writing of his later years; pages that define a narrative about the shape and nature of his own career, and in which his new sense of triumph reaches back a "hand to its younger brother, desire."

James had kept occasional notes before, but this journal signals the beginning of a regular practice, not a diary but a cache of anecdotes on which his fiction would draw in the years to come. He was at the end of his thirties and told himself that he had no time to waste, or rather no impressions to waste; it was too late for him *not* to turn his every perception into usable material. Among those impressions, however, was the sense that, his family connections aside, the trip had not been necessary. Nothing he had yet seen in America had surprised him, and after a just a few weeks he already missed his London life. For he had long ago made his choice of the "old world—my choice, my need, my life. . . . My work lies there." It lay there precisely because he *was* an American. James believed, at the very moment when the Gilded Age was beginning to assert its own self-sufficient power, that no American who wanted to take the earth's full measure could avoid the burden of coming to terms with Europe. He wouldn't have put it this way, but his country needed to know the world it was about to swallow.

But James's notebook contains something more than a meditation on his own career. At the New Year he moved south, to Washington, where he spent much of his time with the Adamses. He met and liked the new president, Chester A. Arthur, who had succeeded to the office after the assassination of the Civil War hero James Garfield, and he also liked the city itself, a place where social life and conversation alike seemed more varied than in either Boston or New York. And he was in Washington when he got the news that sent him scrambling for the first train to the north. At the end of January his mother fell ill with a bronchial infection, and on the 29th he wrote her a tender note in which he described her as someone who had always hovered around other people's sickbeds. It was hard for him to imagine her as sick herself, and he hoped that by the time she received his letter she would "have ceased to suffer as you must have been doing." Indeed she had, though she never read those lines. Mary James seemed to rally, and then sank. She died that very day, and while a telegram had already gotten her favorite son en route to Boston, he arrived too late to see her.

Only once before had James known such a deep sense of personal loss— almost a dozen years earlier, when Minny Temple had died. Then his words had confirmed an absence; Minny was dead, and all he could do was write about it. His mother's death said something else, and when he returned to his journal on February 9 it was to evoke everything he thought he had lost. He believed it impossible to describe "all that has gone down into the grave with her. She was our life, she was the house, she was the keystone of the arch. She held us together, and without her we are scattered reeds. She was patience, she was wisdom, she was exquisite maternity." Yet in that loss he also felt himself possessed by a memory so powerful that it amounted to a sense of her presence, and he could not believe that death alone might bring an end to her love. Her being was immanent still. Henry James had nothing like an orthodox religious faith; no child of his father did, or could. But as William would write about the belief in an unseen world in his *Varieties of Religious Experience* and test the claims of psychics in a way that grew steadily less skeptical, so with the years the novelist defined his own sense of the numinous in a series of extraordinary ghost stories. The dead may exist only in the psychology of the living; that doesn't make them any less real.

We could tell a different story about Mary James. The novelist felt in retrospect that he had been blind to her "sweetness and beneficence" in the few short weeks he had spent in Boston; those few weeks after an absence of six years. Leon Edel writes, however, that James could only create that image of maternal solicitude in memory; in his fiction the mothers are "neither ideal nor ethereal." Often they seem as dry and forbidding as the *Portrait*'s Mrs. Touchett, and Edel's own bent makes him take that fiction as an always more faithful record of the writer's emotions than either his letters or his journals. This seems a simplistic version of the relation between the life and the work. Yet many of her contemporaries did think of Mary James as stiff and conventional, an unlikely mother to such brilliant children, and the younger ones were indeed crushed by the internal contradictions of their family life.

She was buried in the Cambridge Cemetery, in what then became the family plot; today the novelist lies there as well, as does his sister and William's family too. Her funeral on February 1 was the last time that her children were all in the same place together. The ground was frozen and the snow high; they laid her in a temporary vault until spring. Wilky arrived from Milwaukee just a few hours before the service, crippled by both arthritis and his wounds; he died the next year of heart failure. Bob's wife had enough money to allow him a peripatetic life, and the novelist once returned from abroad to find him staying, uninvited, in Bolton Street. He lived until 1910—waspishly funny, alchoholic, and unfaithful—having found in the end some satisfaction as a painter. And Alice has a story of her own, one of undiagnosable illness and long bedridden years spent trying, as she put it, to get herself dead. She passed her whole adult life as though waiting for the cancer that a decade later would kill her, and when she knew that it was coming at last, she wrote that death appeared to her as "the most supremely interesting moment in life, the only one in fact, when living seems life."

None of the James children escaped the irrationalities of their immediate milieu, and yet it's mistaken to attribute their problems, in Edel's words, to the "tensions and emotions generated by the mother which played against the easy compliance of the father." It's much more likely to have been the other way around. Mary James certainly aided and abetted the oddities of her husband. She was a pliant wife, and acceded far too easily to his peculiar ways of educating their children. But she probably gave her children whatever stability they knew, and their emotional turbulence can be more readily laid at their father's door: the father with his sudden changes of direction and his own susceptibility to depression, to those moods in which, in his own best phrase, the "obscene bird of night" stood gibbering at his side.

. . .

Two weeks after his mother's death James wrote to Isabella Stewart Gardner that losing her had produced a sense of suffering utterly unlike anything he had ever experienced; he felt thankful that it could only happen but once. He added that he wished for the time to stay near his father, and told his other friends that he would probably remain in America for the rest of that year. He took rooms on Beacon Hill, and after working through the day he often crossed the Charles for dinner in Quincy Street. The February air felt solemn and still, and he always kept the memory of walking back in the starlight on the cold and empty roads. James had expected that his sister and father would need his care, but they now appeared to live in a "beneficent hush," and as the weeks went by, they each seemed to grow in tranquility, convinced that there was some meaning in even the greatest loss. Alice looked stronger than she had in years; running her father's house had given her some long-needed sense of purpose. And as for that father— well, he had "a way of his own in taking the sorrows of life." He was physically feeble but at peace, and the novelist soon knew that he could count on returning to England that May.

Henry Sr. did indeed have a way of his own. In early December the word came to Bolton Street that he was dying. William was on sabbatical in Paris that fall and, at the news, came over to England, where the brothers decided that Henry would be the one to go, carrying with him William's note of farewell. He sailed from Southampton on December 12, his second voyage home in little more than a year, but the boat took nine days and as he stepped onto the dock in New York, he was given a letter from his sister. Henry Sr. had died three days before; William had already seen the news in the London papers, a notice sent through the transatlantic cable. Once again James had missed a parent's deathbed, and this time he wouldn't even make the funeral, which was scheduled for that very morning. Henry Sr. had asked that the entire ceremony consist of these words: "Here lies a man who has thought all his life, that the ceremonies attending birth, marriage and death were all damned nonsense." The family could find no clergyman willing to pronounce them, and Alice arranged for a Unitarian service instead.

James learned on his arrival that his father's death was not due to any medical crisis as such, even though his doctors talked of a "softening of the brain." Or perhaps a hardening, a hardening of purpose. One speaks of losing the will to live, but the old man willed himself to die, through what James described as a form of self-starvation. He simply refused to eat, and yet never appeared to suffer. Instead he held court at his sickbed, welcoming his friends, talking even as his strength faded, explaining that he was about to enter into a spiritual existence and did not wish to maintain the "mere form" of bodily life. James wrote to William that to many people this would all seem strange, and yet "taking father as he was—almost natural." Years before, in one of her deepest depressions, Alice had asked her father whether the desire to kill herself was sinful. He had told her it wasn't, and knowing that it was not forbidden had robbed the idea of its attraction, and calmed her. Now he himself had chosen death, and though none of his children called it suicide, the novelist recognized that Henry Sr. had indeed prayed and wished for that death. He prayed for it because he did not recognize it as an ending—because he believed he was traveling to a reunion with his wife, whom he claimed with his last words to see.

Once in Boston the novelist collapsed and spent the next week in bed with what was probably a migraine. But on the year's last day he was finally able to go out to the Cambridge Cemetery, stand by his parents' graves, and read William's letter aloud in the cold of the dying year. He stood there for a long time, remaining on after his voice had fallen into silence, and he later told William that he was sure their father had "heard somewhere" that message of farewell. And yet just where is somewhere? William himself had written to the dying man about the afterlife with a mix of hope and open doubt, while to Henry standing there in Cambridge it was "difficult not to believe that [their parents] were not united again in some consciousness of my belief." But that sentence claims less than it seems. Even leaving its double negative aside, it suggests that it is only his own mind that calls his parents' departed selves into being.

. . .

Their father's death left his children, in William's words, "feeling some-what unprotected, old as we are." Not that they all reacted in the same way, and perhaps that statement best describes William himself, the son who had stayed near home. At Harvard he had taught physiology, psychology, and philosophy in succession without being able to choose between them or—as yet—to combine them. His achievement lay still in the future, while his younger brother was publishing two books a year. That brother, meanwhile, quickly moved to drop the last vestige of parental protection. Out of habit he still sometimes signed his letters as "Henry James, Jr." but that spring he asked his publishers to remove the "Jr." from the title page of any new books, and he never published under that name again. Each of the James children inherited a capital of around $19,000, more than they had expected and most of it invested in real estate that they continued to hold in common. The novelist made his share over to Alice; only after she died did he receive an independent income, one that eventually amounted to about £600 a year.

His parents' deaths had bookended the year, and though it didn't leave him feeling so vulnerable as William, it did make him see himself as a solitary figure. Nothing James wrote about his parents is so effusive as the letters he sent home in 1870 when he learned of Minny Temple's death. Indeed, he did not write about them at all, his letters and journal aside, until he himself was old: *A Small Boy and Others*, the first volume of his autobiography, appeared only in 1913, the year he turned seventy. Once their funerals were over, he did not mourn in public. But over the next few years he did often write about the deaths of others, working his way through a series of extraordinary obituary essays about his literary forebears. Flaubert had died in 1880, as I noted in the last chapter; he went in May, when James was still at work upon the *Portrait*'s first chapters. George Eliot died that December, then Emerson in April 1882 and Trollope just a few weeks before Henry Sr.; and finally Turgenev in September 1883, the first great writer whom he had been able to count as a friend. James had known them all, and he wrote about them all in the years immediately following Henry

Sr.'s death. Some of these pieces may have begun with an editor's request, and their sheer number doubtless owes something to the accidents of death itself. Still, James usually chose his own subjects, and what he chose, at this moment, was to mark the passing of his parents' generation.

Over the years he became an expert undertaker, fixing the terms and sealing the vault of one reputation after another. Later essays looked at both Zola and Robert Browning, and one of his later stories even begins with the writing of an obituary. In "Greville Fane" a journalist assigned to come up with a bit on the death of a popular novelist finds it hard to fulfill his editor's charge that he "let her off easy, but not too easy." That's exactly what James himself did in his 1883 essay on Trollope; he got many things wrong about the most prolific of the great Victorians, but in praising his "complete appreciation of the usual," he nevertheless set the terms of debate for the next century. James wrote the piece that spring in Boston, in the house to which Alice and Henry Sr. had moved after his mother's death; wrote it, indeed, while living in his father's own room. So too was his study of Emerson, one that found its occasion in an edition of the Transcendentalist's correspondence with Thomas Carlyle. In writing, James suggested that their letters belonged not only to a vanished generation, but also to a vanished world. The people and things that concerned them had faded into "a past which is already remote," and those two difficult minds were now for the ages. Which meant, in a way, that they weren't for his, and James thought that Emerson's optimism in particular was unsustainable, the voice of an earlier America, unmarked by civil war.

The most interesting of these essays is that on Turgenev. Written immediately after his death, it appeared in the January 1884 issue of the *Atlantic*, and begins on a rhetorical note that even for James seems high: "When the mortal remains of Ivan Turgenieff . . ." The piece differs from James's other obituaries in saying almost nothing about the writer's work. Its details are instead personal, and evoke such things as the look of Turgenev's green sitting room in the rue de Douai, or his physical appearance, tall and broad-shouldered but with "an air of neglected strength." James recalls fragments of conversation, the raciness of Turgenev's spoken French, and their Sunday afternoons at Flaubert's; and he remembers too that the Russian had a reservoir of experience into which neither a young American nor their French colleagues could enter. The article is fond, but it's something more as well, and ends with his memory of their last meeting, in November 1882, when they shared a ride into Paris from the countryside. The older man was wracked by gout, and yet despite his suffering his talk kept up its accustomed flow of brilliance. The coach dropped James on an outer boulevard, and he could hear the sounds of a Punch and Judy show nearby. Then "I bade him good-bye at the carriage window, and never saw him again." At that moment the essay becomes filial.

A dozen years later James published a tale called "The Altar of the Dead," in which the main character, Stransom, remains ever full of the memory of his long-dead fiancée, "ruled by a pale ghost . . . ordered by a sovereign presence." Stransom isn't a believing Christian, but he still arranges to take charge of a chapel in an out-of-the-way church, and makes its altar into a burning forest of candles, tapers that in his mind are numbered and named for each of his lost friends, "a silent roll-call of his Dead." The tale is usually counted among James's ghost stories, but it differs from such pieces as "The Friends of the Friends" or "The Real Right Thing" in that there's never any question of an apparition. Its ghosts are those of memory alone. James had suffered two more great losses by then: his sister Alice in 1892 and Constance Fenimore Woolson in 1894. He was fifty-two, he was beginning to think of himself as old, and had already begun to build an altar of his own. Only he built it in words, and with time he came to speak of his own dead in increasingly hallowed terms. He conjured the presence of those he had lost with a retrospective tenderness that became in itself a part of the myth he made about his own life. Indeed that summoning of the past would dominate the final years of his career, whether in the prefaces to the New York Edition or in the memories that he at last set down as he himself prepared to cross the bar.

To the younger James, however, those dead writers, his predecessors, might well have suggested something else. That on Turgenev aside, his obituary essays don't speak with any special reverence. Even his 1885 piece on George Eliot offers a sharp account of her limitations, and, taken as a group, his articles of the 1880s depict an era that in its passing has left him not so much unprotected as alone. The deaths of such figures as Trollope and Flaubert meant that there was no longer a great and still-present older generation to whom he could compare himself, and against whom he might be judged. He himself now set the standard, and the English critics who thought the claims of the American school presumptuous could only point to the past by way of contrast; they had no living alternative whom they might praise instead.

James was still a young writer when he began the *Portrait*, a book intended to be his masterpiece in the old sense of the term, an announcement that he had arrived and was open for business. Then suddenly the competition was gone. He had some space, he could swing his arm freely, and one result of that was the voice of confident mastery in every sentence of his 1884 "Art of Fiction." Years before, he had used his expatriation to rescue himself. He had broken away, and the deaths of his different elders in the early 1880s now underlined that sense of independence. Hard work made him feel happy and strong, and in his "American Journal" he wrote that he now expected himself to "do something great." He already had. But not even *The Portrait of a Lady* was an achievement on which he would choose to rest.

21.

"I WAS PERFECTLY FREE"

S OMETHING GREAT. ISABEL'S vigil by the fireplace had ended with
her memory of the moment she had interrupted, of the tableau in which
"her husband and Madame Merle . . . [are] grouped unconsciously and
familiarly." But she cannot yet puzzle it out, and having left both her and us
with that constituted scene, James then does something surprising. He puts
the image behind him. He doesn't allow Isabel to think about it for some
80 pages, as though it were all forgotten, and masks that omission by making the novel itself grow busy with the exits and entrances of its different
characters, walking both Henrietta and Caspar Goodwood on and off the
stage, and sending Warburton back to an English future and, eventually, an
English bride.

In all this, the novel seems to pause, as though waiting for its narrative
yeast to work, and the chapters that follow Isabel's night before the fire paradoxically contain some of the finest comic writing of James's entire career.
A lot of the laughter depends on Osmond's sister, the Countess Gemini,
who is said to have had fifteen lovers and to have given her heart away "in
small pieces, like a wedding cake." Bored in Florence, she is delighted when
Osmond invites her down to the Palazzo Roccanera. She knows she's not
as intellectual as Isabel but still believes she has mind "enough to do justice
to Rome—not the ruins and the catacombs, not even perhaps the church-
ceremonies and the scenery; but certainly to all the rest." That semicolon
is beautifully timed, and James's use of the Countess recalls the appearance

of the drunken porter in *Macbeth*, just after the murder of the king. The sharp lowering of tone makes us realize how tense everything around her has become. Still, Amy Osmond's presence isn't as trivial as it seems. Nor is the whole business of Pansy's prospective marriage simply a detour. On a first reading it may look as inconsequential as the girl herself, and yet it's precisely what James will use to bring us back to that riddling tableau.

For while the comedy may divert and distract us, we can't help but remember that it stands upon the fact of Isabel's sadness, the sadness this "visibly happy" woman so tries to keep her friends from seeing. Isabel knows that Osmond wants to put out the lights of her mind, but she has not yet begun to act in "direct opposition" to his wishes. Before her marriage this principled girl from Albany had thought she could give herself entirely; it's a part of what James calls her great good faith. Even now she cannot forget what she calls the "traditionary decencies and sanctities of marriage," sanctities that include the injunction not only to love and honor her husband, but also to obey him. She shrinks from any rupture, telling herself that to break with Osmond on even a single question would be to break with him forever. "I can't publish my mistake," she says to Henrietta, for doing so would amount to a repudiation of her life's most serious act. Isabel believes that she should accept the consequences of her deeds, of anything she has freely chosen to do, and it is therefore with a sense of shame and dread that she begins to see that she might one day "have to take back something that she had solemnly given." She might have to take back her word and her promise; she might have to reclaim her very self.

But she hasn't yet reached for that remedy, and in the meantime the only thing that makes her trouble bearable is the city of Rome itself. One of the novel's richest passages describes Isabel's habit of driving through the city, descending from her carriage to visit the emptiest of old churches or to seat herself upon blocks of stone "that had once had a use." She grows especially fond of a spot from which she can look across the Campagna, where emptiness itself has both shape and substance, and each field seems the ghost of a vanished world. James writes that Isabel has taken "old Rome into her confidence, for in a world of ruins the ruin of her happiness seemed a less unnatural catastrophe." She can confess to it, can admit her misery— the place has seen everything and doesn't expect one always to smile. It has been crumbling for centuries and yet so much of it remains upright; its very age makes her realize the smallness of her own troubles, so small in the city's long record that at times she can almost laugh at them. What she finds there is a sense, at once haunting and exhilarating, of the continuity of human experience; what she finds is what James found there himself.

Nothing in the whole of the *Portrait* brings Isabel closer to her creator— nothing makes the identity between character and author more complete— than this evocation of the help she gets from the stones of the ancient city. Rome may stand in her mind as a "place where people had suffered," but that in itself works to normalize her own trouble in a way that a setting in New York's bustling modernity would not. It gives her a language with which to understand her experience, a set of images that nothing in her own past can match; it suggests that her condition isn't some odd individual exception, but the ordinary lot of human kind. The young James had often used a European setting to intensify his characters' situation, but he had grown beyond that by the time he wrote this novel, and here that setting works to subsume his people instead. So in a passage that recalls the "Roman Rides" of the previous decade, Isabel looks "through the veil of her personal sadness at the splendid sadness of the scene—at the dense, warm light, the far gradations and soft confusions of colour, the motionless shepherds in lonely attitudes." It's scenery, true, and psychology as well, the warm confused mind of the character herself. But it is also a passage of history, and one that throws Isabel's American newness into the shade. She inserts herself, as James did, into the long corridors of the past. She asserts a sense of continuity as a way to survive, to endure, in the present.

"I was perfectly free." So Isabel says to Henrietta, and so she believes. Nobody made her marry Osmond; she elected her own fate. That faith in the individual's freedom to shape the terms of his or her own life stands as one of the founding principles of nineteenth-century fiction, of a form that presents its people, in Iris Murdoch's terms, as being at once "free and separate and related to a rich and complicated" social world. Murdoch's phrase is one I'm always tempted to misread—I imagine her as having written "free and separate *but* related," as though those qualities were in some necessary opposition. Yet she doesn't present them as contradictory. George Eliot's Dorothea has the freedom, and even the free will, that she needs to make her own choices; so does Tolstoy's Levin in *Anna Karenina*. Yet neither those characters nor their authors would have denied that their freedom has limits, that they remain connected to and shaped by the life of their time and place.

Isabel claims something more radical. As a young woman, she had insisted on her right to choose which rules she might follow and had refused to believe that she could be measured by anything that belonged to her, by such possessions as a house or clothes. She was separate from all that, liberated from her enveloping circumstances, and her belief in that freedom speaks, as I have said, to an Emersonian conception of individual identity. It is autonomous, self-made, self-reliant; in a word, American. Nevertheless, she has decided to surrender that freedom, as marriage itself requires; she has chosen to form a part of something larger than she is alone, and thinks that she must bind herself to the very degree that her earlier state was free. But now her faith in that earlier and perfect liberty begins itself to erode; an erosion that stands as a direct consequence of Osmond's hopes for Pansy's marriage. James will not go so far as Zola. He won't suggest that Isabel's environment determines her fate and character, though he recognizes the challenge that naturalism provides, not only to Emerson's ideal, but also to the more traditional sense of the self on which books like *Middlemarch* depend. He does, however, confront her with a set of facts that will force her to revise her peculiarly American understanding of her own past, of the degree to which she has made her own life.

James defines Isabel's response to the Roman sadness as habitual, her customary way of thinking about the place, but he also offers his account of it in terms of a particular moment. She drives out one day determined *not* to think of a conversation she has just had with Madame Merle, and at this point James returns us to the tableau with which her midnight reverie had ended. For the older woman has seemed unreasonably disappointed to learn that Warburton has gone back to England instead of proposing to Pansy. She had so wanted that marriage, she says, and excuses her show of interest by adding that "when one is such an old friend, one can't help having something at stake." But what? Then her questions bubble up, and as she probes and pushes, as she tries to discover just what Isabel thinks of it all, one thing becomes clear. She believes, with Osmond, that Isabel has sent Warburton away, and not out of charity, not because she knows that Pansy loves Ned Rosier instead. No, Madame Merle suspects that Isabel wants to keep the Englishman for herself. Which makes her somehow desperate beneath her smiles, until she finally—commandingly, beggingly—asks the younger woman to "Let him off—let us have him."

The pronoun startles—"us"—and makes one wonder just why this family friend feels free to use it. Nor can we miss the note of ravening hunger with which she speaks. But Isabel has already begun to hear a "mocking voice" in her head, telling her that "this bright, strong, definite, worldly woman . . . was a powerful agent in her destiny." So indeed her aunt has always claimed, insisting that Madame Merle had arranged Isabel's marriage, introducing her oldest friend to the young woman's fortune. Isabel has never believed it: Madame Merle had perhaps made Gilbert Osmond's marriage by prodding him out of his lassitude, but the older woman has had nothing to do with her own. That was a matter of her own free choice. Now, however, she has a chill on her soul, and at that "us" she grows pale. "Who are you," she asks, "what are you . . . What do you have to do with my husband. . . . What do you have to do with me?" And her friend, whose eyes seem to radiate darkness, answers in just a word. "Everything."

Which makes Isabel realize that her aunt was right. Madame Merle has indeed made her marriage; which means that Madame Merle has made her. She has never been free, and was in some ways least free when she imagined herself most, when her new fortune allowed her to indulge her imagination, to believe she could do what she liked. Isabel remembers here that her friend had become especially affectionate after learning of her inheritance, and though she has long recognized that her husband's ascetism is but a mask for his worldliness, she also realizes, now, that "the man in the world whom she had supposed to be the least sordid, had married her for her money. Strange to say, it had never before occurred to her." He has measured her by the things that belong to her, and married her, in Madame Merle's words, for the shell of her appurtenances.

Perhaps, she thinks, perhaps he might be willing to take that money and let her go, to swap her freedom for her fortune. This is as close as Isabel gets to the question of divorce, which Italian law, like that of the rest of Catholic Europe, did not then allow; even in England it remained extraordinarily difficult. For that she would probably have had to return to America, where in some western states it was relatively easy; easy enough, at any rate, to figure in the books of James contemporaries, Howells's *Modern Instance* among them. Still, such novels almost always depict divorced women as morally "light," and Isabel doesn't appear to consider that journey. Her thoughts refer instead to a legal separation, in which she might pay Osmond to go away, using the investments otherwise secured to her by her marriage settlements. An English lawyer would find that easy enough to arrange, and yet even so it would make public what she sees as the shame of her failure. But Madame Merle's words also prompt another thought. Isabel has always said to herself "that the worst was still to come," and now she thinks it has. Being married for her money is the "worst [thing] she could think of," and yet James chooses that phrase to make us remember what his heroine has forgotten. He wants us to recall Edgar's claim in *King Lear* that "So long as we can say 'This is the worst,'" we have still greater troubles before us.

Isabel's talk with Madame Merle is but the first of the series of inter-views—let me use the Victorian word—that James uses to move the novel toward its end. It makes her wonder if the older woman is someone to whom she might apply "the great historical epithet of *wicked*," a term she knows only from books and of which she has always believed she had no personal knowledge. Any full account of James's conception of evil will have to wait until the novel's conclusion, however, and for now it's best approached through his handling of plot, in every sense of the word; not only his own narrative plan, but also the designs his characters have upon each other, the secrets they hold, the metaphoric daggers in their sleeves. Osmond, for example—Osmond decides to put a bit more pressure on his daughter, to give the screw another turn. Warburton's interest has suggested that Pansy can "aim high," and he's disappointed that she's still fond of Ned Rosier, still has some remaining shred of an independent life. In Florence he had spoken proudly of bringing her up "in the old way," but what he does now is the old way indeed. He sends her back to her convent, he demonstrates his power by locking her up. It is, he says, just a brief retreat, "a chance for a little seclusion." She will soon be out again; once she has learned the right way to think.

Then a telegram arrives from Gardencourt. Ralph has been back in England for some weeks, but his life is now counted in days, and Isabel knows at once she must see him; whatever came between them has now lost its force. Except it hasn't—or rather *he* hasn't, Osmond hasn't. When Isabel goes to tell him of her plans, she finds him preparing a watercolor copy of a print of an antique coin. Critics have always had fun with James's description here, for it perfectly captures both Osmond's values and limits. He is a copy of a copy; even his money comes to him thirdhand. But he has a bitter sting, and nowhere more so than in this scene, the last in which he appears. He sees no need for the trip, and tells Isabel that her relations with the visiting invalid had kept him on tenterhooks all winter, albeit for reasons he will not specify. He thinks her desire to go is simply an act of marital revenge, and his words are worth quoting at length:

> "It's dishonourable; it's indelicate; it's indecent. Your cousin is nothing whatever to me. . . . Your cousin is nothing to you; he is nothing to us. You smile most expressively when I talk about *us*; but I assure you that *we, we*, is all that I know. . . . You are nearer to me than any human creature, and I am nearer to you. . . . You don't like to be reminded of that, I know; but I am perfectly willing, because—because. . . . Because I think we should accept the consequences of our actions, and what I value most in life is the honour of a thing!"

Ralph is nothing to him, and can therefore be nothing to her. The pronoun he uses—"your cousin"—may undermine his argument, but Osmond speaks here as if a wife finds her being both in and through her husband alone. His *we* is really *I*, and the dishonor of which he speaks lies in his eyes only, the product of his own indelicate imagination. Still, we can't simply dismiss his statement. Isabel herself has said much the same thing to Henrietta, in explaining why she cannot leave him, and Osmond's words, at once calculated and strangely sincere, will have a terrible effect. She may think that his very soul is "malignant," but she cannot act against this conception of matrimony. So she finds herself in check, unable for the moment to move, unwilling to take a step, not against her husband, but against the idea of marriage itself. To see Ralph before he dies, she is going to need some help.

That help comes in the form of Osmond's sister, the Countess Gemini. James wrote in his preface to *The Tragic Muse* that the art of fiction was in large part the art of preparations, and what he does now with Amy Osmond justifies her entire scatterbrained existence, her intrigues and love affairs and cries of enthusiasm over ruins that she never leaves the carriage to see. He makes her do what she was invented to do—to tell Isabel something that only a sister can. James's heroine passes her in the hallway, her misery beyond words, and an hour later the woman comes to her in a despair of her own over Isabel's terribly "pure mind," and offers her a bit of old family history, a piece of gossip that the Countess thinks she should have guessed long ago. The news is simply that her "first sister-in-law had no children." And that little fact will give an extra and awful meaning to Madame Merle's "Everything."

Pansy is indeed Osmond's daughter—but also, the Countess says, the daughter of "some one else's wife. Ah, my good Isabel, with you one must dot one's *i*'s!" Then the story tumbles out. Some readers will not be surprised to learn that Osmond and Madame Merle were once lovers, and that they had a daughter a year after the death of Osmond's first wife. That was in Naples. Osmond then moved north, telling people his wife had died in childbirth, and was believed; and yet the story did require the actual mother to renounce "all visible property" in the girl. Soon enough Madame Merle's own husband died, but Osmond was poor and the widow wanted a fortune; besides, the Countess adds, by that time he had tired of her. Nevertheless, they plotted to help one another, and Isabel herself is the result of their pact. "I have watched them for years," Amy says, and "I know everything—everything." She even knows that to Isabel her brother has been faithful, as he was not to his first wife. Or faithful at least in the usual sense; he is "no longer the lover of another woman. . . . But the whole past was between them," and with Pansy so visible a reminder of it that Madame Merle dreads being seen next to her, lest people spot a resemblance. The Countess believes that the mother has never given herself away, but Isabel knows better. The mother has indeed betrayed herself—"Let us have him"—even if she had not then recognized it.

Which is, of course, the crucial question. Why hasn't she? And though it's not quite the same question, why haven't we? To the Countess, Isabel's innocence is really a great bore. She hasn't known because she remains willfully naïve; as she said before her marriage, she doesn't want to hear anything that Pansy may not. In *Daniel Deronda*, George Eliot allows her heroine, Gwendolen Harleth, to marry despite knowing that her husband supports a mistress and their children. She makes her drama out of the character's knowledge; James, out of her ignorance. Isabel hasn't known because she didn't want to, because she trusted: because she had such an extraordinary conception of what marriage to Osmond would be like, because her imagination so looks for the good, the ideal, that it amounts to a failure of imagination itself. The more interesting question is why *we* haven't known—not just why James hasn't told us but why the book doesn't allow itself to know the truth until Isabel does. The novelist himself had of course planned it all from the start; his working notes are uncertain only about how best to manage the revelation. And some readers do figure it out. They know enough about the conventions of fiction to spot the twists in James's plot; they manage to interpret instead of just noticing the burden of the unspoken in that opening conversation on Bellosguardo. Some readers stay on their guard because life has made them do so, and others because James has; because they know that in his work the profession of fine motives is so often a mask. Yet even the most skilled and suspicious members of his audience have not been told the truth in what are literally so many words, and more first-time readers than not are surprised by the Countess's tale.

To me James's refusal to acknowledge the truth in advance stands as one of the greatest things about this book; and it functions in a number of ways quite aside from giving us a melodramatic thrill. Let me suggest two of them, one concerned with the drama of Isabel's situation and the other with the drama of our own reading. The precise nature of Osmond's secret matters. He hasn't stolen his Italian primitives; he hasn't robbed a church or forged a will or stabbed someone in a brawl. His sin is a sexual one, and it requires Isabel to recognize the kind of knowledge that both she and the English novel itself most firmly resist. Daisy Miller had refused to know what she was suspected of, and James had finessed the issue by killing her off. But Isabel is a married woman. The fabric of her ignorance must be rent, and so must that of any fiction that claims to address itself to grown-ups. The book must have its own *i*'s dotted, and in this the novel and its protagonist stand as one; they reach maturity together. But there's another reason why James has kept his secret until we are near the end, a reason that has to do with our own relation to Isabel's dream of freedom. He may at times present her ironically, in his opening chapters in particular, but he does not want us to believe as we read that she is simply a dupe. He wants us to share her illusions and therefore to experience their loss, and so we can't know, not at first, the precise nature of the cage into which she's been put. There will be time enough for that on our second reading, in the pity with which we then watch the bars close round.

What we learn with Isabel here goes beyond the simple fact that other people have shaped her fate, that she hasn't had the freedom she thought. The critic Arnold Kettle once called the *Portrait* a nineteenth-century version of *Paradise Lost*, a book about the end of a dream, about the loss of faith in the idea of individual autonomy; and the novel's last pages will give that comparison some point. But many, indeed most, of the great nineteenth-century novels are concerned with the limits of that autonomy. They work to fix the border between social order and tradition on the one hand, and individual desire on the other; it is the great question of the age even in those countries, like Russia, where the *ancien régime* has not yet died. Isabel has something else at stake and maybe something more, something that makes the novel into a peculiarly American version of that shattered dream. For what she now learns is simply what the Old World has always had to teach us. She learns that her own life has been determined by things that happened before she was thought of, by a past of which she was ignorant and that she only understands when it's already too late. What Isabel learns in talking with Amy Osmond is nothing less than the fact that America itself has had no separate or special creation. No fresh start, no city on a hill, no truly new world; no exception to or exemption from history itself. She learns what Hawthorne had realized already, and what almost fifty years later Fitzgerald would understand too, dreaming of a green light whose promise he knows is illusory; learns a truth so at odds with the American imaginary that it must be repeated again and again, an innocence lost in each generation.

This is the real drama of *The Portrait of Lady;* this, and not the mere decay of Isabel's marriage. And in that drama one lesson still remains for her, one last fact that may prove the worst of all. The Countess's tale breaks her impasse. There is a train for the north that evening, and Isabel will be on it, for her new knowledge makes her see that her marriage bonds can have no force. Or rather they have only the force that she herself might give them. She does, however, have a promise to keep before she goes, and late that afternoon she rings the bell at "a high door in a narrow street in the quarter of the Piazza Navona." The convent's portress shows her in, but as she waits to be taken to Pansy's room, she discovers that there is another visitor just leaving: the friend of whose mendacity she has been thinking all day, her mind aflood with the woman's lies, and yet kind enough still to think of her as suffering too. The meeting makes Isabel feel so faint that she can hardly speak as the older woman fills the air with this excuse and that scruple, with praise of the nuns and of Pansy's clothing alike. Then Madame Merle sees. She sees that Isabel has learned something new, and her voice fractures as she recognizes the change in the younger woman's attitude. For the briefest of moments Isabel enjoys the power of her knowledge, enjoys the fact that Madame Merle has recognized it, and then her whole being swells with bitterness at the thought that she has been this woman's "dull un-reverenced tool." She can taste the bile on her lips, and wants to use her anger like a whip, to find the words that can sting and lash and wound. Then the hiss in her mind dies away, and her only revenge is to remain silent; to leave Madame Merle searching for something to say.

Isabel's conversation with Pansy need not detain us, though it is one of the most affecting scenes in the novel. She gives the child the chance to leave the convent at once, to come away with her to England, yet what little spirit Pansy ever possessed has been crushed. The girl does, however, exact a promise, and with her last words Isabel pledges herself to come back. But when she goes to leave, she finds that Madame Merle has waited and now has something to say. The woman has guessed something with which she can punish Isabel for her new knowledge, a punishment that lies in telling the young woman the one fact she doesn't yet know about her own past and position. "Your cousin once did you a great service," she says. "He made you a rich woman." It was his idea to give her the one thing "required to make you a brilliant match," and Isabel should thank him; without that money Osmond would not have thought of her twice. Madame Merle speaks in a blandly feigned innocence, as if imparting good news; speaks with a sense of triumph that reminds me of Oscar Wilde's claim that a gentleman never hurts another person unintentionally. Isabel herself may hesitate to use what weapons she has, but this lady knows just where her knives will do their deepest and yet least visible harm.

22.

WORKING IN THE DARK

HENRY JAMES WAS just thirty-eight when *The Portrait of a Lady* appeared. He had written something permanent, but he had a long career ahead of him, and now had to ask himself just what to do next. It wasn't an easy question, and though he would know many kinds of success in the *Portrait*'s aftermath, James's story in the remaining years of the nineteenth century is in some ways one of failure. He failed to exceed its achievement on the one hand or to extend his audience on the other, and yet that failure grew from his persistent attempts to expand the range of things he could do. Some writers go dead when they finish a book; Joseph Conrad collapsed whenever he completed an important novel, and might take months to recover. James was not one of them. Nor did the deaths of his parents appear to slow his pen, even if his father's did make him spend nine unexpected months in America. He wrote tales and essays, he put out a book of French travels; the pages came as quickly as ever. Nevertheless, he sometimes accused himself of sloth, and resisted the temptation to begin another long serial, "despite the constant solicitation that presses upon me, both from within and from without." For James was now bored with his stock-in-trade, with the kinds of things he already knew how to write. He had vowed in his journal to do something great, but the *Portrait* had said everything he then wanted to say about the international theme, and in consequence he seemed to himself to pause, to tap his foot as though waiting for what might happen.

He was in search of a second act—and in the spring of 1883 he looked for a moment to have found one. James spent that season in the small brick house on Boston's Mount Vernon Street to which his sister and their father had moved the year before. It was in a quiet neighborhood just to the west of Charles Street, where Beacon Hill flattens out toward Back Bay, and James kept house there with Alice in the months after their father's death. Only a year earlier he had told himself that his work lay in the Old World, the world he had chosen and to which he longed to return. Now he seemed to go back on those words, and in his first sketch of the brilliant, abrasive, and finally unsatisfying *Bostonians* (1886), he wrote that he wanted to try himself on a novel as "local . . . as possible . . . an attempt to show that I *can* write an American story." Those italics suggest a reply to his critics, but James's way of meeting that criticism must to many readers have looked odd. For his attempt to do America depended upon examining the intense "friendships between women which are so common in New England," friendships for which he had a model in his own family, in Alice's connection with a woman from the Boston's North Shore named Katherine Loring.

I don't intend here to pace out each step of James's career, or to trace his every relation with the same sense of detail as a full biography. Alice James has her own chroniclers, and they have persuasively shown that her "case" is every bit as interesting as the ones Freud would describe just a few years later: her periods of hysteria and nervous collapse, the inexplicable paralysis of her legs, the diary she began in her last years and in which she recorded, among other things, her memories of the summer in which William was married and she seemed to herself to go "down to the deep sea, its dark waters closed over me and I knew neither hope nor peace." Only in illness could Alice suffice unto herself; only in illness could she make her world take full note of her presence. For my purposes, however, it is enough to chart the ways in which she affected her brother's work. Without those months together on Mount Vernon Street, he would not have written *The Bostonians*; without those months, his *oeuvre* in the rest of the decade would not have taken the shape that it did.

Katherine Loring came from an old and monied family with interests in shipping and the law. She had a rigorous mind and a talent for organization, and wore pince-nez that suggest the dean or college president that in a later generation she would have become; indeed, she worked with other women from similar backgrounds in starting what was then called the Harvard Annex, and later known as Radcliffe. She and Alice became close friends in the late 1870s, and when Henry Sr. died, Alice fled for a few weeks to the Lorings' estate on the ocean in Pride's Crossing. They would make their lives together, living in the kind of relationship that came to be called a "Boston marriage," a term used to describe the shared households and often tacit lesbian partnerships of two educated women. None of Alice's brothers were happy with this arrangement, and William's wife, herself named Alice, was open in her dislike and fear of it. But James himself accepted its necessity.

In writing *The Bostonians* he could not, however, approach the question of sexual identity directly; no more, perhaps, than he could approach the question of his own. Instead he defined the friendship between his two female protagonists in terms of the struggle for women's rights, the right not just to vote, but also to a full place in public life. In consequence the book seems to quiver with the unspoken, and though James was at least as hard on his male lead as he is on his women, the effect was to make the whole of New England's hallowed reforming impulse seem a type of quackery. Attacks on the novel began with the appearance of its first installments in the *Century* at the start of 1885. Its readers skirted the question of sexuality even more widely than had James himself, but Boston wasn't prepared to be laughed at, and the book's American reviews were among the worst of his career. They implied, as though still prickly over *Hawthorne*, that the expatriate had lost his right to criticize; that like one of his own characters he had become "dishabituated to the American tone."

James never again wrote a purely American novel, and yet *The Bostonians* did set the pattern for the very different books he wrote after it. He placed *The Princess Casamassima* in a working-class district of London, just a few steps up from a slum, and moved out from there into an account of the period's revolutionary movements. *The Tragic Muse* (1890) has not a single American character, and James splits its action between the world of Parliament and that of the theater. Yet like *The Bostonians*, they each study the effects of milieu upon character, of the way in whch ideology and environment intersect to shape one's choices. None of these books allows the reader to entertain Isabel's illusion of perfect freedom. Not one of their characters believes in that freedom. All of them know that choice is always constrained and individual liberty something for which they must fight, and together these novels stand as James's answer to the naturalism of Zola; works designed to test the determinative force of ideas or environment or even heredity. Yet among the things he tests is the explanatory power of naturalism itself, of a method he continues to doubt, and that's why these books, though more intellectually provocative than Zola's, are never so entirely absorbing.

What James tried to do with *The Bostonians* and its successors was to show both his readers and himself that work wasn't limited to the international theme. He wrote a long American novel, and then two English ones. He set himself a challenge, abandoning his accustomed mid-Atlantic pose, and in some ways he met it. Certainly no other writer of his time could have managed both settings with an equal authority, and yet even the most partial reader must admit that they lack the *Portrait*'s sense of equipoise. In my Prologue I quoted from an 1888 letter to his brother William, in which James wrote that he wanted to make it impossible for his readers to know "whether I am, at a given moment, an American writing about England, or an Englishman writing about America." He saw the two countries as melting together in a common culture, though he also complained about the awkward straddle of trying to stand in both places at the same time. The truth is, however, that both his hold on the public and his work in itself was most secure when he did stand that way, when he didn't seem to be either English or American, but rather each of them at once.

In the middle years of the twentieth century, *The Bostonians* and *The Princess Casamassima* found an audience among those interested in the relations between politics and the private life, and *The Bostonians* remains essential for anyone interested in the problems of gender in nineteenth-century

America. At the time, however, neither book seemed to have any appeal at all, and in January 1888, James wrote to Howells that he felt staggered by the "inexplicable injury wrought . . . upon my situation by my last two novels. . . . They have reduced the desire, and the demand, for my productions to zero." James put things too strongly; within a few months he would publish a string of great stories, *The Aspern Papers* among them. Nevertheless, his income fluctuated wildly, and in 1887 he made less—only $1,320— than at any time since his apprentice days. The sales of his books remained small, and the advance of £250 that Macmillan reluctantly offered for *The Tragic Muse* did not earn out. Fortunately there was still the *Atlantic*, where he got more for the novel's serial version than he had for the *Portrait* itself. But editors had whims, and now even that magazine had begun to reject some of his stories: to reject him at a time when he was almost entirely dependent on periodical publication; at a time when he thought, more than ever, that he needed to worry about money.

Constance Fenimore Woolson had been right about the change that the *Portrait* would make in the way people looked at him. He was no longer the coming man; he had arrived, and at once became worth taking down. At the same time, however, he had become a kind of celebrity, someone other people wanted to see, someone to boast about knowing. Woolson was certainly prejudiced on his behalf, but there's some truth to her claim in an 1887 letter to John Hay, that she had never known "anyone to be so run-after" as James was that winter in Florence. Indeed, the attacks only served to increase his fame. He was talked about all the more for being disapproved of, whether as an example of the "American school" or as someone whose recent books lacked the old charm of *Daisy Miller*. But celebrity itself brought neither the large readership he craved nor what he thought was an adequate financial reward. James was always more secure than he believed. Nevertheless, we need to look at his bank balance if we are to understand the decisions he made at the end of the 1880s; we need to consider his fear that he had not held the place his great book had won for him.

James had always written stories about the lives of artists, but in his earlier days he usually gave a starring role to the work itself, like the scandalous novel of "The Author of 'Beltraffio.'" Now his emphasis changed, and his new sense of the precariousness of his own position made him concentrate instead on a series of tales about the difficulties of establishing and maintaining a literary career. "The Lesson of the Master" issued an injunction against the money pit of marriage, "The Death of the Lion" imagined a famous novelist whom everybody knows but nobody reads, and "The Next Time" depicts a writer who keeps on trying to produce bestsellers, only to find that he's written a series of unremunerative masterpieces. These fables of the creative life seem at once ironic and transparent in defining the perplexities of his own situation, and the most suggestive of them is "The Middle Years," in which the protagonist Dencombe suffers from an artistic failure detected by nobody but himself. I mentioned the piece in this book's Prologue, but it's worth recalling its central situation. At fifty, and ill, Dencombe lives with the thoughts of his own "shrinking opportunity." He has achieved much but doesn't believe he has yet done anything great, and only in his latest book has he finally glimpsed his own potential. He now hopes that he might hold off death for just long enough to achieve the splendid "last manner" of which he knows himself capable. But Dencombe will have no "second chance," and on his deathbed he recognizes that the very dream of one has been a delusion. Even the most conscious of artists must struggle blindly. "We work in the dark—we do what we can—we give what we have. Our doubt is our passion and our passion is our task. The rest is the madness of art."

We do what we can, and one of the things James himself did in his own middle years was to settle more deeply into his London life. So long as his parents were alive, his native land had had a claim on him; a place that might somehow compel his presence. Now that string was cut and, unmoored by any sense of home, he had no sooner returned to Britain from his stay on Beacon Hill than he began to see his furnished rooms in Bolton Street as dingily provisional. He found something more permanent in a tall white block of flats just south of Kensington Gardens, and today a blue plaque by the door of 34 De Vere Gardens commemorates his residence there. His own apartment was on the fourth floor, and "flooded with light like a photographer's studio." He took it on a twenty-one-year lease, he bought furniture and hired servants; he even got a dog, the first in a series of dachshunds. In middle age he joined fewer house parties, and his letters became less heavily studded with the names of peers and cabinet ministers. His new friends were often other writers or artists. He loved talking with Robert Louis Stevenson and also loved his work; James suffered keenly from the loss of a rare and growing friendship between equals when the tubercular Scotsman moved for his health to Samoa. Edmund Gosse became ever more a confidant, and he spent many Sundays in Hampstead with the illustrator George Du Maurier, who sometimes gave him the germ of a tale.

One of them was an anecdote about a genteel but impoverished couple that he turned into "The Real Thing," his finest account of the nature of artistic illusion. And in his stories of the 1880s and 1890s, James became a great chronicler of London's smoky metropolitan life, a life that in his fiction includes the servants and the shopgirls along with the drawing rooms and gentlemen's clubs. Tales like "The Altar of the Dead" or "The Real Thing" itself offer a picture of the city's hidden pulse as vivid as anything in a volume of Sherlock Holmes. James may have feared for the future, but he never doubted his own ability, and the stories of these years have an assurance that the novels of the same period do not. Individual editors might be capricious, but nothing kept him from his work, and in 1887, when his takings fell to their lowest point, he still mailed off what he described to William as eight or nine stories "of about the length of 'Daisy Miller.'" He got paid for them the next year—and banked over $8,000. The dollars mattered. They mattered greatly. Yet James also knew that that year was a bubble, and as he moved through his forties, he was nagged by the thought that he had topped out too soon. His second act had not pushed his plot along.

The strongly built and heavily mustachioed Edward Compton was what the Victorians called an actor-manager. He chose the scripts and hired the cast and ordered the sets for a company that bore his own name, doing what are now the jobs of director and producer alike, and he usually kept the play's starring role for himself. Most of the great English actors had run their own theaters, going back to David Garrick the century before; in James's day the most famous of them was Henry Irving. The Compton Comedy Company was minor by comparison. It had made its reputation with a ten-years' tour of the provinces, but Compton now wanted to set himself up in London, and thought that a play—a first play—by an important novelist would provide an attention-grabbing start. Early in 1889 he made an offer. Would James consider adapting his 1877 novel *The American* for the stage?

James had always loved the theater, the French theater in particular; loved its tight, vivid, overdrawn gestures, its sense of the word embodied in performance. He wrote that the "dramatic form seems to me the most beautiful thing possible," and yet he was attracted to it by something other than beauty alone. The professional in him also loved its financial opportunities; on a successful play the author's share of the house far outran anything he could have gotten for a novel. In 1889 the foundered hulks of *The Bostonians* and *The Princess Casamassima* still whispered to him of failure, and his negotiations over *The Tragic Muse* had been so difficult that he now spoke of giving up on novels as such and of writing nothing but tales instead. Compton's invitation came at the right moment, the precisely wrong moment. James had already made one bid for the footlights, an unproduced 1882 version of "Daisy Miller," and had been so willing to compromise with the demands of the box office as to give it a happy ending. Now that dream revived, and though he hadn't yet met Compton in person, he imagined that the theater itself had called to him. The stage had sought him out, it would let him escape the difficulties of his recent past, and he saw himself writing "half a dozen—a dozen, five dozen plays for the sake of my pocket, my material future."

A London run, as he wrote to his sister, might earn him as much as £350 a month, and any play so popular in the capital would immediately spawn touring companies as well. James's decision to commit himself to the theater mystified many of his contemporaries and in many respects it puzzles us still, this belief that he could find the popular success in a new medium that he hadn't found in an old one. It suggests a mixture of ambition and desperation; it suggests too a peculiar naïveté about the nature, and the limits, of his own talent. The English theater of his day was a popular art for a mass audience, and it relied on popular genres, on love stories and melodrama and often broadly adapted versions of Shakespeare. Actors played to the crowd, and the scenery was as heavily illusionistic as possible. Star vehicles were as common then as they are in the movies today, and successful novels were often translated onto the stage; Dickens was still an inevitable hit. No great play had been written in England for a century, however, and the only theatrical works of the 1880s that still receive a regular production are those of Gilbert and Sullivan.

There were rumors of a new theater in Scandinavia, of Strindberg and Ibsen and the tragedy of modern life; and a few years later the British stage itself would be revived by the Irish spark of Oscar Wilde and George Bernard Shaw. But James did not believe that a real art was possible on the English boards of his day. The solitary worker hated the idea that the script was a notion and not a finished form, he detested the freedom with which managers made cuts or demanded revision, and he never got over his disgust at the sweaty compromised world of life behind the curtain. In some ways he knew exactly what the stage required, and wrote in his notebook that this new version of *The American* must be "pure situation and pure point combined with pure brevity." His next sentence betrays a contempt for the medium itself: "Oh how it must not be too good and how very bad it must be." Fifty years later a new generation of American novelists would take the same attitude to Hollywood.

Compton's production of *The American* had its premiere in Liverpool in January 1891, and his company mounted the piece once or twice a week as it toured the country that spring. In September the play opened in London, and though the reviews were mixed and the box office slow, it held the stage through the fall; success enough to make James go on with the experiment. "The Middle Years" lay still in the future, but he thought he had seized his second chance at last and had three more plays planned out within a month. Yet none of them found a platform, and by May 1893, James was longing once more to "dip my pen into the *other* ink—the sacred fluid of fiction." Its ghost still hovered, and waited for him; a refuge, a promise entirely under his own control. His fantasy of success began to flicker, and his hopes eventually came to rest on the fate of one script, the story of a would-be Catholic priest. Its production was to be the single most dramatic incident of his entire career.

A costume drama set in the eighteenth century, *Guy Domville*'s protagonist stands ready to leave Britain for a seminary on the Continent when the news comes that his only male relative has died. He is now the final representative of a fabled name, and his friends persuade him that he has a duty to perpetuate it. He renounces his vocation—and then, at the end of the third act, he revokes that renunciation, spurning the woman who loves him and sailing off at last for the cloister. James offered the play to Compton, but the actor refused it, believing that English audiences wanted happy endings, and that a happy ending meant marriage. Another company proved more hospitable. George Alexander had just made a hit out of Arthur Wing Pinero's *Second Mrs. Tanqueray*, a drama about a woman with a scandalous past that ends in suicide. Audiences loved it, and Alexander thought that the crowd at his St. James's Theatre might accept another such unconventional evening. Or at least they would accept it from him. For Alexander was popular, he had fans, and boasted that he could fill a room for a month with anything in which he chose to appear. But if this actor-manager chose *Guy Domville*, it wasn't for either its ending or its author. He liked it, in Leon Edel's words, for "the quantity of tailoring that would be necessary." Everybody would wear wigs and he himself could show off his legs in tight-fitting breeches. Rehearsals began in December 1894, with the opening scheduled for January 5.

The story of that night has been told many times, but the richest version is in *The Treacherous Years*, the fourth volume of Edel's life of the novelist; an account whose 30 pages stand as the finest piece of narrative in that entire work. The stalls were peppered with James's friends, Sargent and Gosse among them, an urbane crowd that arrived expecting to applaud. The upper galleries, where a spot went for as little as a shilling, looked to be filled with Alexander's own following, an audience that simply hoped for an evening's entertainment. All the established theater critics were there, working for all the best London papers. So were three younger reviewers, writers who though still largely unknown would soon be ranked among the country's most important: the novelists H. G. Wells and Arnold Bennett, and the future Nobel laureate Shaw, whose play about prostitution, *Mrs. Warren's Profession*, had just been banned as indecent.

James himself was too nervous to watch the performance. He had spent the day answering letters from well-wishers and now took himself off to sit in the audience at the nearby Haymarket Theatre, where a performance of Wilde's *Ideal Husband* did not make him laugh. He had first met Wilde in 1882, when they were both briefly in Washington, and did not like him. The younger man had managed to snub him with an epigram, and James had described him then as "repulsive and fatuous." They both believed in the sanctity of art; but Wilde was irreverent about his own idols in a way that James could never be. Nor could he ever have allowed himself Wilde's knowing flamboyance of dress and manner, the flamboyance that announced everything that James determinedly kept hidden. That night at the Haymarket made him uneasy. He had no taste for the drawling hauteur with which Wilde made the outrageous appear obvious; no stomach for the balanced paradoxes of his dialogue. *An Ideal Husband* seemed "clumsy, feeble and vulgar," and yet the audience had swallowed it all down. So as he walked back to his own theater, Wilde's triumph made him stop dead with fright, as though paralyzed. For how, he wondered, how could his own work "do anything with a public with whom *that* is a success?"

Still, the first act went smoothly, enjoyed by both the stalls and the gallery above. Then the trouble started. An actress had problems with a hat; a bit of stage business turned sour. Feet began to shuffle, a few lines produced a skirl of unintended laughter, and when just before the end Guy proclaimed that he both was and would remain "the *last* . . . of the Domvilles," a voice from the gods replied that "It's a bloody good thing y'are." The curtain calls made it all worse. Any competent actor knows whether or not a performance has gone over, and the audience's restiveness had put Alexander on edge, tense with what Wells later described as the air of "audible defeat." James's friends, however, were not so sharply attuned to the mood of the house, and after the cast had taken the usual bows, they began to call for the author. He himself had returned too late to hear that moment of heckling and was willing enough to be led on stage. Then the upper galleries began to boo and jeer, only to find that their catcalls were answered from below by the ladies and gentlemen who redoubled their clapping. Nothing was thrown, but still the two audiences faced off, a confrontation in which questions of taste were also matters of social class. And all the while James stood before his audience, stood there for "an abominable quarter of an hour," humiliated, exposed, indeed naked. He seemed trapped by the footlights, pinned to his place by the hissing crowd, and the press reports of the evening all criticized the producer for having brought him out in the first place. Some members of the audience thought he looked scornful and cool; others remembered his gallantry in the face of assault. But one of the actors thought that the author of *The Portrait of a Lady* had simply turned green.

Guy Domville was a flop almost before it had begun, even though the St. James kept it up for a month and the later performances were without incident. What made it worse was the fact that the theater followed it with Wilde's own *Importance of Being Earnest*, a new property at which Alexander grabbed once it was clear that James's work had failed. Two things should be said about that failure. First, the disaster of the opening night wasn't entirely James's fault, and the theatrical press of the day reported that the boos had not at first been directed at the author himself. His appearance was rather their occasion; a claque was rumored to have been organized against Alexander, and some men in the galleries had been paid in drinks to shout the house down. But the second thing is that *Guy Domville* is a very bad play indeed. Its opening moments remain effective. James quickly defines Guy's situation, and there is some drama in the character's changes of heart. Only it's not one that works in the theater. At the very least, his decision demands soliloquy, though what it really requires is a carefully prepared chapter in which he might sit before the fire and review the course of his life. It needs a sense of interiority for which nothing in the Victorian theater allowed. Its failure was bitter and the jeers unjust, but *Guy Domville* did not deserve to succeed. The English stage would find its future instead in the self-conscious wit and entirely modern settings of Wilde and Shaw.

James walked home through the gaslit streets, through Piccadilly and on past Hyde Park Corner, two miles to Kensington in the rain. Five years of work—five years of hope—had vanished. He still believed, would always believe, that it was a good play, but his eyes were now open, and he knew he needed to find a future. He knew it with a certainty that he wouldn't have felt if *Guy Domville* had had the same kind of straggling success as *The American*. He wasn't crushed. Instead he was angry, and in the weeks after the opening he sent William a few letters of full-throated outrage. Yet in the privacy of his notebook he seemed simply to draw a line, telling himself that he "need say no more" about it. He was newly aware of everything his theatrical temptation had smothered, and was ready once more to take up his old form. He had been working in the dark for too long, but he now had more stories in mind than he could possibly write, and at 34 De Vere Gardens the future looked strangely open and full. James took hold of his pen and wrote two wildly optimistic sentences: "It is now indeed that I may do the work of my life. And I will."

23.

THE SECOND CHANCE

I F JAMES HAD died at fifty, like Dencombe of the "Middle Years," we would see him as a creature of fits and starts, of unfulfilled and even wasted potential; and we would wonder at the mixture of blindness and vanity that had led this once-brilliant novelist to scatter his time and talent on a series of unproduced plays. Instead he got his second chance, his chance at some final arc of achievement. Two months after the failure of *Guy Domville*, James told a friend that even if he had wanted to go on working for the stage, the truth was that he could no longer afford to. Five years had passed since he had stopped writing novels because he thought the theater might earn him more. Now he stopped making plays because he knew that while the market for his fiction was small, at least there was one.

Nevertheless, he felt the need to rescue something, anything, from his wasted years, anything that might give his loss a purpose. He found it in what he called the "*scenic* method," drawing on what his work in the theater had taught him about how to block a narrative. James had always been good at entrances, but now he began to extend that skill to the book as a whole. He began to write novels as though they were plays, and in saying that I mean something more than that he composed *The Awkard Age* almost entirely in dialogue. First, he started to plot his work out more carefully than ever before, to mock up an elaborate plan before he began to write. His notebooks contain only two pages on the *Portrait*, in which he outlines the later stages of a novel he had already half-finished. For *The Ambassadors* he produced a 20,000-word preparatory sketch. Second, he realized that the *"march of an action* is the thing for me to . . . *attach* myself to." There must be nothing incidental or extraneous; everything on every page must work to further that march. Even the *Portrait* has its trailing fringes and furbelows, but though the sentences of James's later books grow ever more complex, their dramatic situations are stripped as naked as a knife.

The scenic method did not, however, come easily, and James's first conscious attempts to push it out to the length of a novel were more rigid than rigorous. *The Spoils of Poynton* (1897), which he began almost immediately after his West End failure, describes a family quarrel over a collection of fabulous old furniture; furniture that in itself goes famously undescribed. Its protagonist has a mind too fine for the world in which she lives, but with the stage still at the front of his own brain James begins a new chapter whenever a character enters or exits, and that creaky machinery remains at odds with his heroine's darting inner life. I have already described the way that *The Awkward Age* explores the limits of what both young girls and English novels can be allowed to know about sex. But its interest outweighs its success, and whatever else James got from the theater, it didn't help him to write dialogue; a skill at which the author of the *Portrait* had once been a master. *The Awkard Age* would be miserably unplayable, with its characters all talking alike and its speeches reliant on an ever-receding line of antecedent pronouns.

James had to figure out how to drape and clothe those knobby narrative bones. He needed to learn—or to relearn—how to give his fiction the illusion of flexibility. Nevertheless, he did write one marvelous book in this period. The opening chapters of *What Maisie Knew* have a sustained brilliance of phrase unmatched in his work since *Washington Square*, though what one most feels in reading it today is its terrible contemporaneity. It is the first important English novel to take divorce as a starting point rather than as an almost unimaginable conclusion, the first predicated on a child-custody case; and certainly the first to see such things through the child's own limited comprehension. We never do find out exactly what Maisie knows. We're not even told how old she is, let alone what she understands about the peculiar family of which she is the motive force. What we *do* know is that in learning to hide her feelings she has also learned that she has an inner self. James builds the novel upon—or perhaps within—that self, and he uses Maisie's limited awareness to avoid having to specify the sweaty facts of adult life, of the lies and love affairs going on around her. In writing the *Portrait*, James had told himself to "place the centre of the subject" in Isabel's ever-developing understanding of her own situation. Now he was doing it again. He had found his way back, and in his late novels he would work almost exclusively as if from within the mind of one character or another, locating his material in their slow, fumbling movements toward knowledge. He took his seat before the low-burning fire of the Palazzo Roccanera; he learned to stage consciousness itself.

One more thing happened as he wrote *What Maisie Knew*. Thirty years of his ceaseless scrawl had had their effect, and by the summer of 1896 the physical act of writing had become a torture. The pain shot through his arm and hand, it put him on the edge of missed deadlines, and the printers "denounced" him for holding them up. He called it writer's cramp. We would describe it as a repetitive motion injury, but the result was the same, and his daily work became ever more debilitating. He hired a shorthand specialist and typist named William MacAlpine and began to dictate, employing him at first for letters only. However, at some point in the composition of *What Maisie Knew* he also began to use MacAlpine for his fiction, and the process exaggerated the development of his increasingly elaborate late style. A few of his friends even thought they could spot the chapter in which he had begun to speak the novel out. I wouldn't claim so much myself, but something does change just over halfway through, as the chapters lengthen and the dialogue begins to lose its speed. The novel quickens again at the finish, and yet in allowing James to reproduce the stretched cadences of his spoken voice, the typewriter was to mark him to the end.

There were other movements in James's life as he approached the new century. London had always satisfied and sustained him, it had always seemed to contain more of human complexity than anywhere else he had lived. But it exhausted him too. In his teens he had wandered Newport's beaches and coves, and in the summer of 1895 he had searched out the ocean once more, staying on into the fall in the resort town of Torquay, on the mild Devonshire coast, and learning to ride a bicycle while his London flat was wired for electricity. The next summer he went to the coast again, this time taking a Sussex cottage that overlooked the ancient port of Rye. That stay changed his life, and in the years after his theatrical failure the quiet cobblestoned town would fill what he described as his "long-unassuaged desire" for a refuge from the city's summer heat and social requirements alike. Rye might be sleepily unsophisticated, but in the season it was lively enough: not so small as to be wary of newcomers and yet sufficiently tight to have the air of an extended family. It was a place in which he might know and be known by everyone.

Before the summer was over James began to think about finding some-thing permanent in the area. It took a year, but then the news came that the owner of Rye's best house had died and his heirs wanted a tenant. James grabbed it at once, a long lease at £70 a year, scarcely more than half of what he had paid in Bolton Street, and began to furnish it in "not too-delusive Chippendale and Sheraton." Two years later he bought it outright. Rye sits on a hill and Lamb House sits at its top, on the outer corner of a right-angled street. A minute's walk in one direction took him to the town's high-towered church; a pew came with the house, by custom, though he hardly ever used it. On the other the pavement fell away, down to the shops of the High Street below. The house had a high Georgian doorway, a wide imposing hall, and a garden shut in by a wall that looked heavy with espal-iered fruit trees. There were two guest bedrooms and an upstairs study, and in that garden was the studio in which he would pace out the great work of his later career.

James did not abandon London. He kept his flat in De Vere Gardens for a while, and afterward had a bedroom at the Reform Club, a *pied-à-terre* that he took by the year. He spent most of the winter in the city, in fact, for in the rain and cold Rye often felt too far from a world of ready conversation. Nevertheless his move to Lamb House in the summer of 1898 did signal an enormous change in his habits. His travels had never before interrupted his work, but by now his fiction was dependent on MacAlpine and the sound of his heavy Remington typewriter. He couldn't really write in hotels anymore, or even while staying with friends, and it's no accident that his decision to make himself a home came after he had begun to dictate, after he had recognized that he couldn't wander as freely as before. The Continent had once been a retreat from the distracting pace of the capital, and James had often left the city to finish a book in quiet, as he had done with the *Portrait* in 1881. Now from the concentrated solitude of home he would instead retire to the excitement of London itself; the home without which his late books would not have been possible. MacAlpine found rooms in Rye, as did all of James's later typists, and the two men enjoyed bicycling together through the "wide, sheep-studded greenness" of the marshland that surrounded it. And James himself soon found a new vocation as a fussily benevolent host, welcoming guests and issuing elaborate instructions about the trains from Charing Cross.

Still, he did continue to cross the Channel, and it was on a trip to Rome in the spring of 1899 that Henry James was surprised by one change more. Hendrik Andersen had a long straight nose and shadowed, penetrating eyes. He had been born in Norway but grew up in Newport, blond and lean and hauntingly handsome, and had come to Italy to learn the sculptor's trade. Andersen dreamed of using his art to create a new "World-City" of peace and harmony, but the ambition he put into his monumental nudes would always outrun his talent. He was, however, good at attracting the interest of older male artists, and in Rome had found a sponsor in a Scottish aristocrat called Lord Ronald Gower, a fellow sculptor and friend of Oscar Wilde's.

He was twenty-seven when James met him, and the novelist felt such an immediate and unprecedented bolt of longing that it has to be called love. But his only way of acting upon it was to buy a piece of the young man's work, a portrait bust of an Italian boy for which he paid £50, some 70 percent of his annual rent for Lamb House. He put the statue on a sideboard in the dining room, where it still rests today; he could see it from the table, and looked forward to Andersen's promised visit. The sculptor stayed for only three days, however, and when James wrote to him that September, he sounded an atypically importunate note, asking him to "come back next summer and let me put you up for as long as you can possibly stay. There, mind you—it's an engagement."

James had just turned fifty-six when he found himself so suddenly vulnerable to emotion, so open in his need for another person. He was acutely aware of the thirty years between them, and had an increasing awareness of his own mortality, one spurred by the shock of his professional crises; he also had a new and ever-more-settled sense of domesticity, and perhaps too the belief that age had brought safety. He offered to help his protégé set up a studio in Rye, and so fondly remembered a bicycle ride together that he couldn't pass a particular corner "without thinking ever so tenderly of our charming spin homeward in the twilight and feeling again the strange perversity it made of that sort of thing being so soon *over*." Andersen did visit again, playing the role of a coddled nephew, but though James's heart rose at every prospect of seeing him, each stay was brief. He acknowledged the novelist's kindness, but he was even more self-absorbed than most artists and thought of the older man chiefly in terms of the boost their friendship might give his career. As for James himself, if he ever recognized that his life had begun to imitate his art, that he had now stepped into his own first novel and taken on the role of the ever-encouraging patron Rowland Mallet to Andersen's impetuous Roderick Hudson, he never admitted it. In time he lost his faith in the prospect of Andersen's achievement, and cared less each year for the way his statues flaunted "their bellies and bottoms." The "Beloved Boy!" of his early letters became simply "Dearest old Hendrik"; yet he kept his interest in the sculptor to the end.

There would be other young men in James's future, other crushes, other loves, and many letters written with a similarly eager tenderness. Some of those to whom he wrote did have an active sex life with other men. The journalist Morton Fullerton was one of them, and so were the minor novelists Howard Sturgis and Hugh Walpole. And in certain cautious and ambivalent ways James now began to admit both the presence and the nature of his own desire, though he always held himself apart from the world-within-a-world of London's homosexual life, with its secret addresses and all but open bits of code, like the green carnations that Wilde had made famous. Indeed, Wilde himself was much on James's mind, and he wrote to William that the "squalid violence" of his fall had given him "an interest (of misery) that he never had for me—in any degree—before." The arresting detail here is that interjected "in any degree." It suggests an allusion to something the letter itself can't say, as though Cambridge needed reassurance. Yet while James remained careful, he did increasingly allow a passionate if largely metaphoric physicality to enter the language with which he wrote to his male friends. When, for example, Fullerton told him of a troubled love affair in the fall of 1900, James offered to give him whatever help he needed, "absolutely *holding* out the assurance of it. Hold me then *you* with any squeeze; grip me with any grip; press me with any pressure; trust me with any trust."

With its faint echoes of John Donne, James's imagery attempts to conjure up being, to create an impossible presence through words alone. The novelist lards his other correspondence with effusive compliments on the recipient's bounty or beauty or benevolence or talent. In writing to Andersen and his successors, however, he did something that he hadn't done in any extant earlier letters. He gave physical expression to emotion in a moment of physical absence, and expressed an active wish for the other person's bodily presence. Not in bed. A bicycle ride will do, a squeeze of the hand, a seat across the dinner table, and he writes as often as not in the expectation that such things will be withheld. But he never wished for his brother's company in these terms, or for that of any of his female correspondents. He didn't write in these words to anyone of his own age, and if at times with these younger men he wore an avuncular mask, we need to remember that he was also an uncle in fact, and he did not sound this way with William's adult children. Whether James ever knew anything more than this must remain an open question. But there can be no doubt that from the moment he met Hendrik Andersen he felt himself free to describe the gasping force of desire itself.

. . .

The essayist and cartoonist Max Beerbohm is best remembered for the parodies he collected under the title of *A Christmas Garland* (1912), a book that snares every stylistic excess of such contemporaries as Conrad and Kipling, and above all those of James himself. In "The Mote in the Middle Distance" two children in their nursery look at the "pendulous" shapes hanging by the foot of their beds, and speculate about the treats Santa Claus has left "so blatantly suspended in the silhouettes of the two stockings." But Beerbohm also did several caricature sketches of the novelist, and the most interesting of them shows him on one knee, bent to examine two pairs of shoes outside a hotel room door. The door remains shut, and James can only—*we* can only—infer what's going on behind it from the simple presence of the shoes themselves, asking ourselves if they're where they should be, the right shoes in front of the right room and the right people in that room. We peer down at those boots, and wonder about the connection between the private self and the public life, the life that's left out in the hallway for everyone to see. We ask ourselves, indeed, if we can draw any conclusions at all, and Beerbohm's 1904 sketch has a special relevance to the three long novels that James wrote in the early years of the new century.

James had worked well in both *What Maisie Knew* and the short fiction of the *fin de siècle*, but these books amount to a break in scale as sharply dramatic as that which had led to *The Portrait of a Lady* itself. At once austere and grandiloquent, they are both modern and modernist in the pointillism with which they catch the human mind in the second-by-second act of perception, and modernist too in the symbolic force and weight of their language. Different readers will have their preferences among them. James himself thought *The Ambassadors* the most perfect of all, and to me *The Golden Bowl* captures the sublime terror of the inner life in a way that remains unmatched in American fiction. Still, the three are sufficiently alike to be dealt with as a group, and in each of them James returns to the international theme that, after finishing the *Portrait*, he had virtually surrendered as a novelistic subject. The books of his splendid last manner all hang on the question of Americans in Europe, and it's no coincidence that in doing so they also concentrate on the great drama of an expanding consciousness.

Each of them describes the encounter of innocence with a wider world, an access of understanding that proves punishing and liberating at once. But perhaps it is time to listen:

> It wasn't till many days had passed that the Princess began to accept the idea of having done, a little, something she was not always doing, or indeed that of having listened to any inward voice that spoke in a new tone. Yet these instinctive postponements of reflection were the fruit, positively, of recognitions and perceptions already active; of the sense above all that she had made at a particular hour, made by the mere touch of her hand, a difference in the situation so long present to her as practically unattackable. This situation had been occupying for months and months the very centre of the garden of her life, but it had reared itself there like some strange tall tower of ivory, or perhaps some wonderful beautiful but outlandish pagoda, a structure plated with hard bright porcelain, coloured and figured and adorned at the overhanging eaves with silver bells that tinkled ever so charmingly when stirred by chance airs.

The Princess is named Maggie Verver, the last of James's American girls, a dollar princess now married to an actual prince, an Italian whose family history fills whole rooms in the Vatican library. James will go on, in the rest of this long paragraph from the middle of *The Golden Bowl*, to describe Maggie's walk around that imaginary pagoda, a walk in which its "great decorated surface" remains impenetrable. Some readers will take that as a description of the novelist's own late style, and those of us who love it had better admit that. For it can look here as if James has given up on his audience. Or rather he's stopped worrying about it, stopped trying to please it. He writes now as if he wants only to please himself, and to the degree that he's concerned with his readers at all, it's to pay the fit and the few the compliment of assuming that they'll be able to follow. He is not, to my mind, as difficult as Joyce, not a creature of fragmentary allusions and broken syntax.

Nor is he as elliptical as Faulkner or Woolf, in whom time itself can fall through the floor. But his doubly compounded sentences are indeed hard, and it's worth taking a moment to ask why.

Look at the words that James's free indirect discourse assigns to the Princess: idea, something, postponement, recognition, situation. He doesn't define any of them, but lets them stand instead as her mental shorthand for the family problem that's developed in the book's earlier chapters. Whatever the Princess may have done, the nouns that define it remain abstract, without any "solidity of specification." Though "define" is the wrong word. *Un*defined, rather, and undefined not only because she herself knows to what those words refer, but also because she doesn't, because she isn't quite sure what she's done. Maggie too is groping, as we are, or indeed as James himself is, walking the length of his studio and hunting for the next phrase as his typist sits at the keys. The Princess wants a name to put to her experience, something more precise than "situation." She tries to take in a set of facts that she also wants to resist, and in staying close to her consciousness James must also stay close to the imprecision of her understanding. Paradoxically, however, he does so by becoming very precise indeed. He turns that situation into an extended architectural metaphor, in which Maggie scans that unreal pagoda's elevation for "apertures and outlooks," and looks for a door on which to knock. He uses such metaphors, both here and in all his late work, to give physical form to the disembodied perceptions of his characters' moral and intellectual lives; and in reading, it's sometimes hard to remember that Maggie's hand has in fact touched nothing. For James's reliance on such metaphors creates in turn a further abstraction, a further set of difficulties. His description isn't tethered to a particular moment, but evokes instead a habitual practice, with whole weeks of Maggie's inner life collapsed in a phrase. Yet no matter how often she walks around it, the pagoda still lacks a door, and like the novelist himself in Beerbohm's caricature, the Princess will need all her imagination to understand what's inside, to understand what lies behind the eyes of that stranger, her husband.

Many critics of an earlier generation found the late James to be the best of all, as some of their titles suggest—*The Major Phase, The Ordeal of Consciousness, The Expense of Vision.* I understand their claims, and yet rather than concentrate on James's depiction of consciousness as such, I want to look instead at just who in these books perceives what. The anecdotal germs of *The Golden Bowl* and *The Ambassadors* each concerned Americans in Europe, and as James worked over his idea for *The Wings of the Dove*, it too developed an international thrust. In *The Ambassadors* a man from Massachusetts tries to rescue a friend's son from an affair with a married woman in Paris. James had a sly awareness of cliché, and knew his countrymen's belief that "people's moral scheme *does* break down" in France, but rather than resist that convention he decided to play with it. Lambert Strether refuses at the start to admit that Chad Newsome's relation with Madame de Vionnet is above all a sexual one. He sees that she's charming and that the boy has grown up, and insists that their attachment is "virtuous"; but at the end his own moral scheme cracks, and he recognizes that Chad's affair has been both adulterous *and* virtuous. In *The Wings of the Dove*, sex becomes an instrument of power, the ground on which two of the book's main characters meet to seal a pact against the third. *The Golden Bowl* depends on Maggie's growing knowledge that her husband has betrayed her. At first the young woman recoils. Then she begins to understand just how much she needs and wants him, even as she realizes that in fighting to keep him the one thing she cannot do is to admit what she knows.

The Golden Bowl never uses the word "adultery," and yet it remains as central to that book's concerns as it does to *Madame Bovary* or *Anna Karenina.* But there is one crucial difference between them, as the cultural historian Barbara Leckie has argued. The European novels concern themselves with passion, the passion that starts an affair and sustains it, and whose waning brings despair. Their concern lies, that is, with the guilty. James gives his interest to the wronged spouse instead—to Isabel in the *Portrait*, and above all to Maggie. He's drawn not to the sex as such, but rather to the process of finding out about it, to a mental act of discovery and not a bodily one. He is interested, finally, in epistemology, in how his characters know what they come, in the end, to know. Or at least Isabel's knowledge comes at the end.

Maggie's in contrast arrives early, and James gives her many more pages in which to discover how to live with it, pages in which she learns not to shy away from what she has learned but rather to move toward it.

For these late novels don't simply depict a developing consciousness. They also take sex itself as the focal point of that development. Each of them catches its breath at its power and its mystery, catches it and then finds it again in a newly powerful understanding of the knowledge it brings of the world, the other, and above all of the self. In a way, that had always been James's subject, in *Daisy Miller* or *What Maisie Knew* or even in the *Portrait*. He had always been fascinated by the struggle to acknowledge the facts of sexual life, by characters who no more possess a language in which to admit what they know than did English fiction itself. But something had changed by the time he began to write *The Ambassadors*. Both Strether and Maggie can take in those facts in a way that neither Isabel nor Winterbourne can ever quite manage. They meet their difficulty, and are far from powerless in the face of it; Maggie in particular finds a personal force that she could never before have imagined. Probably some of that change came from the fact that 1901 wasn't 1881, that the intervening years had seen the work of Hardy and the translation of Zola; and they had seen too the waning power of the circulating libraries. James had always argued on behalf of a greater frankness, hoping to close the gap between what people might say in private and what they could say in print. There would be many battles to come over the question of candor in fiction; nevertheless the range of admissible knowledge had grown. Still, that change in what James's characters are capable of must also have had a source in the author's own life. Probably we can attribute it, in some unquantifiable and unspecified way, to what his own knee-trembling love for Hendrik Andersen had taught him.

So make a Venn diagram, with four circles called Europe, America, sex, and consciousness. *The Portrait of a Lady* lies at their overlap, so does *Daisy Miller*, and so do these late books; not all of James's great work, but enough of it, enough to call it his most characteristic terrain. It was a place to which he had returned after twenty years—returned when he found he had something new to say about it. For now the moral shading on the map has changed. In *The Ambassadors* the people who stay at home in New England see Europe as a trap. They know its inveigling ways, these culti-vated descendents of the Puritans, readers of the *Atlantic* and even perhaps of Henry James. They know its iniquitous sophistication—they know all about Madame Merle, an American who has, as it were, gone native. That's what Strether expects to find in Paris and yet doesn't, as his soul expands beyond his own earlier standards; grows even as he recognizes that his own liberation has come too late. But Maggie Verver will rewrite Isabel's his-tory. She learns of the past that her husband and her best friend have shared between them. She learns of it, and suffers from it, and she will survive it too, as she moves on with him into a new life. Europe may have done a job on her mind, but it has also made her grow up.

O nce before, James had marked his own sense of accomplishment with a voyage, sailing back to America on the eve of the *Portrait*'s 1881 publication. He had gone to see what he called *les miens*, and gone with full hands, believing that he had something to show for his time abroad. Now he heard that inner note of achievement once more. He knew as he worked upon *The Golden Bowl* that in these last years he had written at a pace and a pitch he had never before been able to sustain. He had a renewed conviction of his own force, and confessed in a letter that his native land had begun to look romantic in a way that England itself had "hugely and ingeniously ceased to be." Time and change and absence had made his old country seem exotic, and the trip now appeared as if it might be the one true adventure left to him. He was, admittedly, afraid that at sixty his habits had become too rigid for even a little "molehill" of a six-month visit. But he got rid of his fears, found a tenant for Lamb House, and sailed on August 24, 1904, for what he thought would be his last visit to America. It was twenty-one years, almost to the day, since he had seen his birthplace.

Everywhere he found himself surprised by the country's size: not only by the physical stretch of the land, but also by the changed scale of the things he had once known. The Washington Square of his childhood had spoken of a smaller and slower world, one now overpainted by a modernity that seemed interchangeable with energy itself. New York Harbor throbbed with whistles and explosions, it rushed and shrieked in an intricate dance, a "steel-souled machine-room of brandished arms and hammering fists and opening and closing jaws." The bridges looked like pistons, and the skyscrapers told him of a New York that never meant to be old. Such buildings were all "expensively provisional," and each individual one of them would survive only until the city's money had invented something bigger and better, more profitable and doubtless more temporary. Indeed, everything everywhere was bigger—hotels, and Harvard, and the summer houses of Newport, where the seacoast of his early manhood had been conquered by the whited sepulchres of the new American plutocracy, by the "distressful, inevitable waste" of a wealth so grand that it could dispense with history or taste.

In their imitation of European splendor those houses paradoxically reminded him of his own deliberate alienation. So did his visit to a Yiddish theater in New York. His brother William had warned that American speech and manners might shock him, but James was less startled than fascinated by his evening on the Lower East Side. The families he saw there had kept the customs of their origins in Danzig or Budapest. Yet if they spoke Yiddish, they also spoke a fluent New Yorkese, and their very ease and carriage owed less to "the moral identity of German or Slav" than it did to the spirit of 1776. James confessed himself puzzled here, and an earlier visit to Ellis Island had made him uncomfortable. Even in living abroad he had assumed that America was his, but he now had a haunting awareness of his own dispossession, a sense that the country belonged to somebody else. These immigrants had assimilated "our heritage and point of view" in a way that made him feel as though he himself were the foreigner, and he wondered what such new citizens might make of the older New York and New England from which he had come. Long before, he had written that it was a complex fate to be an American, but as he traveled throughout his old homeland, he began to see more whorls and layers in that complexity than the young man had ever dreamed of.

James had thought that his two countries might merge into one English-speaking culture; it had been the wager of his career. Now he began to under-stand that the ocean between them wasn't so much a girdle as a gap. The eleven months of his American tour showed him both that he had become more English than he knew, and that his birthplace had made a culture of its own, albeit one about which he would always be ambivalent. He visited William's summer house in the White Mountains, and saw old friends wher-ever he went; he traveled down through the south to Florida, and then as far west as San Diego. Yet each mile made him fear that the land's very spread and bounty might lead to the permanent "triumph of the superficial and the apotheosis of the raw," and it was out of that fear, that ambivalence, that he wrote *The American Scene*, a book that on its best pages is as brilliant as, if less systematic than, Alexis de Tocqueville's similarly uneasy journey.

His trip had other results, however, and among them was the depth of his new friendship with Edith Wharton, at whose house in the Berkshires he stayed in the fall of 1904. The two had met the year before in England, and James had already issued his famous command that she should *"Do New York!"* She should take him as a negative example and stick to an American subject, "the immediate, the real, the ours, the yours, the novelist's that it waits for," the opportunity that was uniquely hers. Wharton would accept that advice in *The House of Mirth* and its many successors, while doing much else besides, and their friendship—their letters and visits, their excursions in Wharton's chauffeur-driven Panhard—would be one of the great plea-sures of James's last years.

The other great consequence of his American journey took the form of a publisher's contract. James appeared under many imprints over the course of his career, but his relations with the long-established firm of Scribner were recent. Nevertheless the house had released both *The Wings of the Dove* and *The Golden Bowl*, and their books were as handsomely made as their Beaux-Arts office building on Fifth Avenue. As early as 1900 the com-pany had cabled James's agent, J. B. Pinker, to ask "Would You Care on any terms to arrange for Collected Edition Henry James," and negotiating such an edition was a secondary motive in his American voyage. James let the issue hang through the fall, but in the spring of 1905 he asked Pinker to come settle the terms of an agreement in person, and in July he himself wrote the publisher to describe his plans and desires. He had loved the elegance of their job on *The Golden Bowl* and hoped for something similar. He planned to sift out his lesser pieces and to revise his work where necessary "as to expression, turn of sentence, and the question of surface generally." He promised to write a preface for each book and suggested that the whole be called the "New York Edition" in honor of his "native city." James would spend the next four years at work on it. He had had his second act, he had found his late manner, and his long shelf of books now had the coherence and the sense of teleology that it lacked a decade before. The New York Edition would stand as the final glory of his long career, and perhaps its last disaster too.

24.

ENDGAME

THE OLD MAN in Rye drew his pen through a line and wrote two in its place; he gave a colloquial twist to a moment of dialogue and eliminated a demonstrative pronoun. He set aside a scribbled-over sheet for his typist and refined his sense of a character with a newly vivid image. James spent his mornings in that Edwardian spring of 1906 at work on *The American Scene*, recounting his impressions of such things as the "rushing hotels" of a Pullman train and the "hot-looking stars" of a Florida sky. He stopped for lunch at half past one, and then went out into the town's quiet streets; perhaps delivering an order to the butcher as he went or pausing on a corner to chat with another of its 3,900 inhabitants. Then in the late afternoon he returned to a desk spread with the pasted-up sheets of *The Portrait of a Lady*, each of them with a wide margin in which he could scrawl around the set type of the book's early self.

On that desk James hoped to build himself a monument. Other novelists had revised their published work; others had written introductions. No one had yet done so on this scale; no one has done so since. James wanted to smooth down his career's rough edges, and he used the New York Edition to suggest that his *oeuvre* had some overarching shape. He threw his emphasis upon the international theme, eliminating a few purely American works like *Washington Square*, and in doing so both underlined the power of his final manner and cast its retrospective majesty over his earlier work. He told his friends, moreover, that he was always astonished at how "filthily" he used to write, and his secretary, Theodora Bosanquet, noted that he believed his first books all needed to be redone before they were "fit for appearance in the company" of his later ones. That was true even of the *Portrait*, successful though it had been. Every page of the novel now had its changes, every page differed from the version his readers had known for a quarter of a century. Yet those revisions were meant to do something more than kick his early style into line. For he also wanted, in Bosanquet's words, to uncover the "values implicit in his early works, the retrieval of neglected opportunities," and her two statements point in effect to different things. Both suggest James's sense of the inadequacies of that work, but the one stresses its problems and the other its potentialities, the things he might do that his younger self could not.

Some of those problems would remain insoluble; he couldn't alter what he now saw as *The American*'s false and melodramatic conclusion. Other changes came at a cost, and many readers prefer the initial versions of his early tales, where his relatively lean narrative prose better suits the comic bubble of his dialogue. With the *Portrait*, however, his revisions speak to his sense of its potential. Its style was already rich enough to sustain the black brocade of his later manner; the novel's foundations were sound and its windows in all the right places. Many of his revisions seem inconsequential, substituting a proper name for a pronoun, or making a character "hint" instead of "intimate." Others are substantial, and James took an additional care in establishing his people. So his opening description of Madame Merle now gives her an eye "incapable of stupidity," adding an early note of danger to a character who was at first simply enigmatic.

But of course the largest changes occur in his account of Isabel, and they will have a special importance in the last pages of the novel's last chapter. For the moment, however, I'll simply look at one of them, unimportant in itself, as a way to illustrate their burden. It comes after Isabel has left Rome and Osmond to sit at Ralph Touchett's deathbed; after she has crossed the Channel to fall into Henrietta Stackpole's arms at Charing Cross; after she has gone down to Gardencourt, where Ralph's new servants don't recognize her and she has to wait while her name is brought up to her aunt. She waits a long time, in this place where her story began, and in the book's first version James had written that "she grew impatient at last; she grew nervous and even frightened." The words say enough, but by 1906 he wanted to say something more, and now Isabel grows "nervous and scared—as scared as if the objects about her had begun to show for conscious things, watching her trouble with grotesque grimaces."

Those grimaces recall the terrors that had crowded in at the start of her fireside vigil, and James's revision does two things. He shows us the shape of Isabel's fears in a way that takes us far more deeply into her mind, and he figures that interior plunge in physical terms. The very furniture of these "wide brown rooms" now glows with malicious life, as though the material world were responsive to the terms of her inner being; as if thought itself had all the flex and thrust of a body. In 1944 the Harvard critic F. O. Matthiessen noted, in the first systematic study of these revisions, that many of the changes stress the presence of Isabel's own consciousness as such, and indeed often substitute that word for others. When she first meets Osmond, for example, she's no longer merely "entertained," but has a "private thrill [in] the consciousness of a new relation." Few of these small changes will register upon even a careful reader as he or she moves from line to line. Nevertheless, they have great cumulative force, and that additional access of interiority does make the 1906 *Portrait* more closely resemble James's last books. It reminds us that the novel isn't finally about a young woman's choice of a husband, or even about Americans in Europe. It is instead a drama of the perceiving mind, and one that, like *The Ambassadors*, hangs upon the point of view of its protagonist.

That might suggest James has simply revised the book in the light of his own later interests. But there's something more complicated here, and we can best understand it by looking at the different ways in which his prefaces define the act of revision. Sometimes he saw his books in organic terms, as living things that were necessarily capable of growth and change. They were his children, and could be trained up into a presentable maturity. More often he accounted for them in pictorial terms, as if he were putting each story back up on the easel and asking himself what "time and the weather" had done to it. Some had faded, and no varnish could bring them back. Other seemed to contain "a few buried secrets," and as he went to work with his brush and his sponge, they began to flush into color. An expression could be heightened, a pose adjusted, but he saw himself as working on what was already implicitly present, allowing the "latent" aspects of an old work to vibrate into life. This is what Bosanquet meant in speaking of the New York Edition as a recovery of the chances he'd missed. By particularizing Isabel's fears at Gardencourt, by giving an expressive power to the room itself, James recalls not only her own midnight thoughts, but also the link she makes between her suffering and Rome's long record of misery. It tells us how much has happened to her since she first stepped onto that English lawn; tells us that even in returning to it she has not managed to escape her own life.

But James says other things about revision as well, and in his preface to *The Golden Bowl* suggests that in going back over his early books he has indeed tried to close the gap between "the march of my present attention . . . [and] the march of my original expression." To some readers that statement suggests he has done more than simply retouch his work, that the concerns of his later career are now dominant. I myself see the *Portrait*'s second version as a fulfillment of its first; as though the book, like a person, had grown up while remaining in essence the same. Others find the changes so great as to make Isabel a different character in each edition, and in an influential essay the critic Nina Baym has even suggested that we have in effect two novels. That of 1906 is the work I've described as an interior drama, a modernist look at the question of Isabel's "awareness." The novel of 1881 is in contrast concerned with her "independence," and written against the background of an ever-increasing discussion of women's rights and opportunities. It is the product of its historical moment, and explores the questions James had once asked about his cousin Minny Temple; questions about the kind of life available to a spirited and intelligent girl in a world where her fate still largely depends upon marriage. In this account of the 1881 version, "the inner life is only one aspect of character, which is defined by behavior in a social context."

That argument might hold if the novel had gone on as it had begun, if it had remained a book about a young woman's progress through that social world. It might hold if it were not for Isabel's night before the fire. But at the moment James set her there, in motionless activity, he discovered both the formal and the thematic preoccupations of his later career. His revisions to *The Portrait of a Lady* don't change the novel so much as they make its opening chapters fit the book that it had by its last chapters become.

One of the first things James makes Isabel say is that she wants to know the things she shouldn't do: not so she can do them, but so she may at least have the power to choose. And now the question of choice returns to the novel. Isabel doesn't believe that she consciously *chose* to return to England. Her need to see Ralph was instantaneous; the obstacles came later. At Gardencourt, however, she has both the time and the distance she needs for reflection, and if she weren't herself aware that she faces the forking paths of a decision, the book's other characters are determined to remind her of it. Henrietta bluntly tells her not to return to Rome, and though Ralph can barely talk, he will stammer out the question to which we all want an answer: "Are you going back to him?" But Isabel hardly knows. She has promised little Pansy that she will return, though she cannot now remember just why she made that pledge. She tells Ralph that "I don't think anything is over," and yet her statement doesn't lead us to any one conclusion. It suggests that if she does go back, Osmond will make her "a scene that will last always." It also points, however, to the moment of strange exhilaration she feels on the train across Europe, when she recognizes that "life would be her business for a long time to come" and understands that she will someday be happy once more.

The last serial installment of the *Portrait* was a short one, just three tightly packed chapters. James uses the first of them to take his heroine from the train to Gardencourt, raising the question of choice in a series of oddly comic conversations with Henrietta. Yet the mood changes once he gets Isabel off into the country, and the novel's penultimate chapter contains two of the most searching moments in all his work. The first of them comes in a conversation with Mrs. Touchett and is so brief that many readers might miss its importance. The old woman asks after Madame Merle, and Isabel admits they are no longer friends, that indeed she has done something "very bad." When Mrs. Touchett asks what it was, however, all Isabel says is that "she made a convenience of me." She has earlier recognized, during their meeting at the convent, that the woman has employed her as though she were a piece of hardware, an instrument or tool. She's been used. Her money—her means—have made Serena Merle see her *as* a means, and one whose only purpose is to serve Pansy's future. Isabel realizes that now, and recognizes that in treating her as a convenience her erstwhile friend has also treated her as something less than a person.

Scholars have often glossed this moment in terms of Kant's idea of the categorical imperative. The philosopher writes that we must act so "as to treat humanity, whether in thine own person or in that of any other, in every case as an end withal, never as a means only." Probably James himself didn't know those words. He had an unmatched grasp of fiction in both English and French, and read widely in poetry, drama, and the literature of travel; he had as well a special fondness for memoirs of court and military life in the Napoleonic period. He did not, however, often turn to works of politics or philosophy, and had little interest in any form of German culture. William James would have known Kant's 1785 argument, and so would George Eliot. Henry James didn't need to, for Kant's ethic is in many ways at one with the ethic of the realistic novel itself. Of course, James does employ some of his imaginary people in the service of others, using such figures as Henrietta to illuminate Isabel's story. But he also and always suggests that his secondary characters have a case and a claim of their own; they are valuable in themselves, and not for what one can get out of them. People are an ends, not a means, and the novel as a form explores the gap between that ideal state in which they are not to be used and a world in which they always are. James would have gotten some of that from George Eliot, but it also characterizes the less grounded work of Balzac, in whose books the sinners are those who eat up the lives of others, consuming first their money, then their hearts, and sometimes even their souls. That ethic is present in Dickens's anger against utilitarianism. It figures for Hawthorne in stories, like "The Birthmark," of those who force their own vision upon others, and in Turgenev it carries a political meaning. His insistence upon starting with an individual character was itself a blow against autocracy, and in briefly exiling him to his estate after the 1852 publication of *A Sportsman's Sketches* the Russian government showed that it knew it.

In James the great crime remains that of imposing your will upon another person, of using him or her to implement your own desires. The stern father of *Washington Square*, so determined to be right that he wrecks his daughter's faint chance for happiness; the revolutionary cell of *The Princess Casamassima*, for whom Hyacinth Robinson is but an instrument; the parents and stepparents of *What Maisie Knew*, who treat the girl as a shuttlecock: all these have broken Kant's law. Or look at *The Turn of the Screw*. If the ghosts in that famously problematic story are really there, then their wickedness lies in trying to control the fate of the tale's children; if they aren't, then its madwoman of a governess wants that same control. In either case the work carries the same weight. And finally there is "The Beast in the Jungle," in which John Marcher grows so used to thinking of May Bertram as the repository of his secret that he never recognizes either her love or her own autonomous being. James worked that theme for the whole of his career, and his insistence on showing how people consume one another has made his biographers especially sensitive to the ways in which he might have done so himself. This, certainly, is the argument of Lyndall Gordon's *Private Life of Henry James*, with its close examination of his relations with Minny Temple and Constance Fenimore Woolson alike.

Madame Merle is an easy case; Osmond too. Their desire comes unmixed with any pretense that what they want is for Isabel's benefit too, and for them we may use the word "evil." It is a quality that James thought his optimistic fellow-Americans had trouble recognizing. Isabel remains blind to it for years, and in her creator's eyes the Emerson who stands behind her self-conception never overcame his own obliviousness of its very existence. Yet insofar as Pansy's parents present us, for once, with something simple, they cannot hold the same disturbing interest as do James's more ambiguous pictures, and in the *Portrait* the most troubling of those images is that of Ralph Touchett himself. For how else can we understand his desire to make Isabel rich—his attempt to gratify his own imagination by watching what she'll do?

Ralph is generous indeed and yet he also wants to see his cousin going before the breeze. He thinks of himself as having bought a ticket for a show, and though he's right in warning her about Osmond, his objections grow in part from his hope that she will, for his sake, do something better and more. When Isabel arrives at Gardencourt, he is too weak to say anything, and she sits with him for hours in silence. Only on the third day does he find the strength to speak, and when Isabel encourages him to be quiet, he murmurs that he will soon "have all eternity to rest." Now is the moment for one final effort; and we recall that on his own deathbed, old Mr. Touchett had said much the same thing. At first, however, all that Isabel herself can do is cry, and yet in that wet face she finds a new resolution, finds that she has "lost all her shame, all wish to hide things." For she wants Ralph to know that she has finally learned what he did for her, and so she sobs out an apology. "I never thanked you," she moans, "I never spoke—I never was what I should be!"

Those words make Ralph turn away. He knows what he has done for her, what he has done to her. He has made her rich but "that was not happy," and when he turns to face her once more, he tells Isabel that he believes he "ruined" her. The verb is deliberately chosen. It's one most often attached to a seducer—a rake may ruin a girl for his pleasure—and by making him choose it James suggests Ralph's awareness of what he has done. He has made Isabel vulnerable, someone attractive enough to be a victim, and he understands the blight that has flowed from his good intentions. Few readers will find it hard to distinguish Ralph's use of Isabel from Osmond's, and yet his own generosity has made him commit a weak version of the same crime: by amusing himself with his thoughts of her future he has failed to recognize the complexity of her own individual being. He has failed to feel the whole weight of his relations to her. Yet nobody could accuse him more than he accuses himself, and Isabel wants now only to admit to her own weakness and vanity. So the walls between them fall, and they see each other fully. They recognize each other as "an end withal," and speak of ignorance and knowledge, of death and pain and the question of Isabel's future; and finally they also speak about love. For pain will pass but love remains, and Ralph believes that in her heart "I shall be nearer to you than I have ever been." On the last pages of his life the two of them can admit to each other what every reader has always known, and as they speak of what will last beyond his death, something odd seems to happen—something wonderful, uncanny, sublime. James no more invokes the idea of God or an afterlife than he did at Mr. Touchett's deathbed. Nevertheless, the two of them seem, in confessing all, to float for a second beyond their bodies, unbound by any sense of self and with their minds moving at the end as one. It is as if their souls stood naked to one another, a flash so powerful—so rare, so brief—that it makes all the suffering needed to produce it seem worthwhile.

I cannot read this scene without tears.

The New York Edition took almost four years of steady work. The two volumes containing the *Portrait* appeared early in 1908, and Scribner issued the rest of the set over the next year and half, finishing up with *The Golden Bowl* in the summer of 1909. As physical objects, they fulfilled James's hopes, substantial but not heavy in the hand, the paper deckle-edged and creamily thick, and the typeface of an elegant sobriety. Yet sticking to his publisher's schedule became first a slog and then a nightmare, and the work had a cost beyond the moment. It finished him as a novelist. James was sixty-six when the edition's final books came out, but though he continued to write stories, *The Golden Bowl* was the last long piece of fiction he managed to complete. The remainder of his writing life would be devoted to the retrospection that began with his biography of William Wetmore Story and continued with *The American Scene* and the edition's own prefaces.

Still, most readers would rather have those eighteen prefaces than another long novel. James left some work in fragments at his death, but neither *The Ivory Tower* nor *The Sense of the Past* would have added to his achievement. These essays do. Sly, demanding, rigorous, and playful, they give us both our most vivid sense of their author's mind at work and a newly rich vocabulary with which to think about the art of fiction. James's description of how to handle a protagonist, his instructions on the shaping of narrative endings or the management of point of view, his strictures on the inadequacies of the first-person: all of it remains quotable, provocative, and useful. Before he was done with them, he realized that they could be gathered into a volume of their own, "a sort of comprehensive manual or *vade-mecum*," though he shrank from the idea of writing a preface to his prefaces; such a collection finally appeared only in 1934, edited by R. P. Blackmur and called *The Art of the Novel*. James's acolytes in succeeding generations would often go too far in systematizing his principles, trying to make his practice into a set of laws for fiction as a whole. But no novelist has left a more sustained account of his own creative process.

Not everyone liked them. A Cambridge friend found them too "self-occupied," and believed that James's attempt to show how he had managed it all destroyed any sense of fictional reality. Some reviewers used his criticism of his own work to club him down; look, even he had said that *The Princess Casamassima* wasn't what it should be. Many readers thought, moreover, that in revising so heavily James had committed a kind of crime, and resented any alteration to the books they had known and loved for years. Yet the New York Edition soon presented him with another and bigger problem. Its separate volumes sold for $2 apiece, the same price as the 1881 American edition of the *Portrait*, but committing oneself to the series as a whole did make it expensive, and many potential customers already had his work on their shelves; the prefaces alone weren't enough to tempt them. Scribner printed 1,500 copies of the first volumes, and hoped to sell them as a set. By the end of 1908, however, the American sales were still below 600, and Macmillan took just 100 for distribution in England. Nor were those figures his only trouble. James had as always hoped for a good market, and had worked so hard and so exclusively on the edition that his income from periodicals had virtually disappeared. Now he learned that his proceeds would be eaten up by Scribner's obligation to pay his other publishers for the use of their copyrights, and in October 1908 his first royalty statement showed that he was due a derisory £7 14s 2d. Even a year later and with the edition complete, he was owed only $600. He told Pinker that the news delighted him; but by that time the damage had been done.

There are many explanations for the depression into which James fell at the end of 1909. He had long practiced an odd, faddish way of eating called "Fletcherizing" in which he chewed his food into liquid, but it now left him feeling undernourished and exhausted. He was periodically lamed by gout and believed he had begun to suffer from a heart condition like the one that would soon kill his brother William. And he had a family history as well, from his father's "vastation" of the 1840s on to William's own periods of despair in the years after the Civil War and Alice's sense of perpetual dusk. Those things all contributed, but we cannot discount what he saw as his own professional disaster, a catastrophe that struck him even more powerfully than his earlier one in the theater. Then he had believed that he could go back to the novel, that he had in fiction a retreat and a future, but it now seemed that the years he had spent on his great edition had led only to the utter absence of an audience. James was in no danger of poverty; the income from the family properties in Syracuse would take care of his needs. Nevertheless, his royalty figures mattered as a mark of the value, in the broadest sense of the term, that readers placed upon his work: a mark of attention, esteem, and permanence, and one that counted all the more now that he could only manage the occasional story. Like many people suffering from depression, he persisted in denying it and claimed that his illness had a purely physical cause. In October he wrote to William that he believed himself over the trials of his recent months, but at the New Year he could no longer get out of bed, and knew that he had entered a "black and heavy time."

It was so black, indeed, that William James sent his oldest son, the novelist's namesake, across the Atlantic to look after him. "Harry" James had trained as a lawyer and became both a successful businessman and a trustee of the American Academy in his uncle's beloved Rome. And it is this third

Henry James who has left the most affecting record of the novelist's illness. For one night in March 1910 the old man simply broke, sobbing and stammering for hour after despairing hour while his nephew held his hand. He spoke of his own death, and of his sister Alice's lingering illness, an illness that he feared might be his own fate as well. And he spoke too of his own failure, believing that he had lived to see "the frustration of all his hopes and ambitions." The future could only grow worse.

The young man's report was so alarming that his father decided that he must go over himself, ill though he was. The years since the turn of the century had brought William an unbroken chain of intellectual success, even as his heart grew ever more fluttery and weak. In 1900 he went for his first course of treatment at Bad Nauheim, the German spa that specialized in cardiac cases. He had needed regular injections of digitalis to get through the series of Edinburgh lectures that became *The Varieties of Religious Experience*, and yet his retirement from teaching only seemed to increase his pace. He filled lecture halls at one university after another, he turned his essays into such crucial volumes in American thought as *Pragmatism* and *A Pluralistic Universe*, and he enjoyed every minute of this belated flowering. But by the beginning of 1910 his disease kept him from his desk and made him plan another stay at Nauheim, though there was little that the period's doctors could do for him. His son's report was disturbing enough to make him sail early, however, and a note his wife wrote in Rye that June speaks to the family's condition: "William cannot walk and Henry cannot smile."

James's pocket diary for that spring records his own series of "Bad day[s]—bad, very, very bad . . . after bad night." He needed Veronal to help him sleep, and wrote to Edith Wharton that he was "wholly unfit to be alone." He wanted only to cling to his family; to cling so much, in fact, that he not only went to join William in Nauheim but also decided to return for a time to America. For he knew that William himself was hopelessly weak. He knew that these days would be the last they would ever spend together, and his notes on William's health soon began to supplant the ones he made on his own. They sailed in mid-August for Quebec, and then traveled by car over the difficult irregular roads of the day to William's summer house in New Hampshire, a farm surrounded by the lakes and pine forests of the White Mountains. The philosopher had wanted to see it once more, but by now he could hardly sleep or breathe, and he lived on a cocktail of morphine and milk. It could not last, and he had been at home for just a week when he died. "His extinction changes the face of life for me," James wrote. He had been the elder brother always, and the novelist had never ceased to look up to him as "my protector, my backer, my authority and my pride." Of course, that wasn't the whole truth. William had remained jealous of his younger brother's quick path to fame, while James was always anxious about the older man's response to his work, wanting his approval and knowing that he wasn't usually going to get it. Yet their competition was a form of companionship, and the novelist never forgot that, though desperately sick himself, his brother had come to see him through the darkness.

That knowledge gave James a new sense of purpose, and in the terrible empty winter that followed, he realized, as he sat with William's Alice in Cambridge, that he must now commemorate the family of which he was the last survivor. Intending at first merely to collect and annotate his brother's letters, he soon found himself seized by the "ramification of old images and connections" and planning a final "difficult & unprecedented & perilous" work. *A Small Boy and Others* and *Notes of a Son and Brother* are the last books he completed; there was a third memoir unfinished on his desk when he died. I have drawn liberally from them in my own early chapters: his recollections of early childhood, his account of Florence and the Boott family, and his memoir of Minny Temple. The second volume ends with her death, but James did not maintain a strict chronology. Instead he wandered as freely in time as Faulkner or Woolf, and in dictating to Theodora Bosanquet he would interrupt the flow of a year to anticipate a later relation or fall back into a newly remembered past. "I recover it as for ourselves a beautifully mixed adventure"; the words describe his schooling in France but they might indeed stand for it all. So long-forgotten Albany cousins grow as vivid on the page as Ralph or Isabel; Henry Sr.'s sudden changes of plan make him look as capricious as Daisy Miller herself; and modest antebellum Newport becomes the paradise his whole family has lost.

James was seventy when the second of these volumes appeared, however, and his age told. His heart troubles of 1909 had been imaginary, but now he did suffer the shooting daggers of angina. He recognized too that he could not again risk a lonely winter in Rye, and took a final London apartment on Cheyne Walk in Chelsea. Nevertheless, these last years did bring a share of the triumph that the New York Edition had not. The advance he received for his memoirs was justified by their sales, and a group of his admirers commissioned John Singer Sargent to paint his portrait. James sat for nine days in his friend's Tite Street studio, wearing a high collar and a dark suit relieved by the gold chain of his watch. He felt embarrassed by how much he liked the result, but it is in fact one of the painter's greatest works, and iconic in its depiction of the novelist's shrewd judicious authority. Sargent refused to accept his fee, and James accepted the painting only in trust; it hangs today in London's National Portrait Gallery. And a March 1914 letter to the ever more sardonic Henry Adams suggests how open and curious his sensibility remained. The historian had written to complain that the two of them were the last of their generation, with "the past that was our lives . . . at the bottom of an abyss." Yet to James that was no reason not to take an interest in what remained, in the "reactions—appearances, memories" of consciousness itself. He still enjoyed observing his own mind at work, and with the bitter wit of Adams's letter before him, he suspected that his old friend did too.

That buoyancy could not last. In that same year the lights went out across Europe, and he saw the proud tower of his seemingly stable civilization topple. The guns began to flame on the Continent, their report heard across the Channel in Rye, and in August 1914 he wrote that the start of the Great War seemed to "*undo* everything . . . in the most horrible retroactive way." The long peace had made him believe that such a wreckage had become impossible, but that faith now lay in ruins, and this sink of blood stood revealed as "what the treacherous years were all the while really making for and *meaning*." His autobiographies brought back the past in one way. The war reproduced it in another. James likened the German invasion of Belgium to the Confederate shots on Fort Sumter, and he soon became an obsessive visitor to military hospitals, walking down the long wards and trying to give what comfort he could. It wasn't much, just cigarettes and conversation, but it made him recall Whitman's visits to the wounded during the Civil War; and he must also have remembered his brother Wilky, lying broken in the hallway of their house in Newport. Yet though James tried to draw some comparison between the poet's war work and his own, he did not himself do Whitman's hard physical labor of nursing, and he could not shake a sense of his own futility. All he could do was write, and at least the essays he wrote about Belgian refugees and the need for more ambulances did help to raise money for their causes.

Then in 1915 he reached a final decision. James had sat out his own war, while believing in its cause, and he knew that however hapless a soldier he might have become, he had missed something that other men in his generation had known. Now he found himself repelled by his homeland's isolation and inaction. Washington might warn Berlin against destroying American shipping, but the country seemed bent on neutrality. James believed that America and Britain had the same fundamental interests. He had staked his life upon that, upon America's connection to Europe's common culture, and was appalled by Woodrow Wilson's refusal to join the Allied cause. That culture now mattered to him more than any accident of origin, and he therefore applied for naturalization, after almost forty years of residence, determined to demonstrate his "attachment and devotion to England, and to the cause for which she is fighting." The application required some sponsoring witnesses, and among them, along with Gosse and Pinker, was H. H. Asquith, his new nation's prime minister. James surrendered his passport, and on July 26, 1915, he became a British subject. Many years before, the newspapers of his birthplace had been outraged by *Hawthorne's* account of all that the New World lacked. Now they again accused him of disloyalty; but the future would confirm his conviction.

It was the last significant act of his life. Just a few days later he fell ill, and his letters now carried word of a "bad sick week . . . a regular hell" of gastric troubles and chest pains that confined him to his flat along the Thames. On December 2 in Italy, where a boy named Ernest Hemingway would later drive an ambulance, the Fourth Battle of the Isonzo came to an indecisive end. All that day it remained quiet in the trenches of the Western Front, and in London, Henry James had a stroke. He lay on his bedroom floor, his left side numb, but with voice enough to call for his servants. He dictated a telegram to William's family, and Alice immediately left for England, fulfilling a promise she had made to her husband. A second stroke followed, though James's mind remained steady for a few days more. Then he began to wander.

At times he thought he was in Ireland, at others in California, and he refused to listen to a barber who told him they were in London. He asked Bosanquet to move her typewriter into his room, and dictated a few brief troubled pages about his own "sketchy state of mind" and the "damnable . . . boring" business of trying to get better. Later he addressed a letter to his "most esteemed brother and sister," but he now believed that he was Napoleon, and the note concerned the imperial apartments in the Louvre. Once he told the gray authoritative Alice not to interrupt him. He improved slightly as the new year began. As a British citizen, he was now eligible for honors, and he both understood and enjoyed the news that he had been awarded the Order of Merit, a distinction more valued than any knighthood.

James lingered in the winter-darkened city while the Gallipoli campaign ended in defeat, and the United Kingdom introduced conscription. He recognized the people he saw, and spoke when he could, but though his phrasing remained forceful, the stitching was gone. On February 23, 1916, he asked Alice to tell William that he would soon be leaving, and on the 27th his consciousness fled. Henry James died at six the next evening. His sister-in-law, who would take his ashes back to Cambridge, said that in his last weeks his hand sometimes moved "over the counterpane as if writing."

I sabel starts up from her pillow toward dawn, believing that there is someone by her bed, "a dim, hovering figure in the dimness of the room." She had once asked if Gardencourt had a ghost, and Ralph had told her it did—a ghost no happy person had ever seen. Yet by now she has suffered enough, as the novel enters its last chapter, now the apparition can come to her, and the ghost has a name. For it looks as if Ralph himself is standing there, and as she stares into the gray light, she sees "his white face—his kind eyes; then she saw there was nothing." She isn't afraid but she knows that something has happened, and when she goes to his room, she finds that the doctor has just placed his dead hand by his side.

To Isabel, Ralph now looks like his father, and she remembers that six years earlier she had seen the older man "lying on the same pillow." The novel has made a circle. James has brought both her and us back to where we began, and his account of Ralph's funeral only increases that impression, attended as it is by all the living characters of the book's first chapters. Lord Warburton is there, and Henrietta Stackpole, and even Caspar Goodwood. Isabel is surprised to see him; he had visited her in Rome, but she had assumed he was now back to America. The only people missing are those who entered the book with Mr. Touchett's last illness and death, and of them Isabel thinks as little as possible, "postponing, closing her eyes," as though she were hiding in Gardencourt's shade. Still, she recognizes that her cousin's death means that her mission is over. She has done what she left Osmond to do and knows she must soon face the choice that both Ralph and Henrietta have asked her about. She knows too that no matter which path she takes her choice will not be happy. Osmond may be dreadful but marriage imposes "certain obligations," and Isabel stands condemned either to the mortifications of the Palazzo Roccanera or at the bar of her own judgment. And at this point James's readers grow fearful. The whole weight of the book sits in our left hand, and just a few thin pages remain on the right. George Eliot liked to kill off her heroines' unsatisfactory husbands, but James had already put on record his dislike of last-minute rescues. Isabel's return seems inconceivable, and yet as we read, our imagination of her future, of what might happen next, hits the same blank wall that she does.

A week after the funeral she sees Warburton coming up the drive. She has heard of his engagement to a "Lady Flora, Lady Felicia—something of that sort," and when they meet, he seems embarrassed, both eager for her approval and yet aware that he has something to explain. Afterward she wanders away across the lawn and eventually finds herself by a bench beneath a stand of great oaks. Isabel recognizes the spot as one where "something important had happened," though it takes her a minute to remember that it's where she had read Caspar Goodwood's letter of complaint on her first visit to Gardencourt, and then looked up to find Warburton preparing to propose. She has indeed circled back to her past, and sits down as she had long before, remaining there with a "singular absence of purpose" as the twilight grows thick in the trees. Then the past echoes once more, and she realizes that Goodwood himself is standing just a few feet off.

What follows is one of the most startling and in fact violent scenes that James ever wrote, one matched only by the end of *The Turn of the Screw*. And its storm will continue—it will extend to what James does to his readers, and to their sense of a proper conclusion, in the novel's last sentences. That violence does not, however, lie in the proposition Goodwood now makes to her, his plea that Isabel abandon her husband and come away with him. He has guessed what her marriage is like, he knows the price Osmond will make her pay for her journey, and asks her to turn to him instead of falling back into "that ghastly form." She has no children to hold her and they may go wherever they like, do absolutely what they please. They are free, as free to choose, in his version of things, as Isabel had once thought herself, for "the world is all before us—and the world is very large." Goodwood's words are themselves an echo. They recall the moment in which Isabel, in the first enjoyment of her wealth, had walked through London in an enchantment with possibility itself. But they also and more importantly summon up the ending of *Paradise Lost*, when after tasting the apple and being thrust from the garden, Adam and Eve must step forth into the fallen world before them. That is the world in which Isabel knows she must live: a world of constraint and necessity, in which her possibilities are limited by her past. Isabel knows, now, that we are never free to do absolutely as we please, and she knows as well that she cannot stay at the aptly named and Edenic Gardencourt. Yet Goodwood himself remains an innocent even as

Endgame 327

he invites her into adultery, and all too American in his faith in the world's unbounded promise.

"The world is very small," she says in reply, but James writes that she talks at random, unaware of what she means, and in fact she feels something different. For Isabel has learned something here. She tells Goodwood that one reason for returning to Rome will be simply "to get away from you," but even as she speaks, she recognizes a new truth. His force and his passion make her understand "that she had never been loved before. It wrapped her about; it lifted her off her feet." The world is very small, and yet it has never before seemed so huge: an ocean, and fathomless. She had wanted help, some light by which to steer through the murk of her life. Goodwood's offer makes it seem as if that help has come in a torrent, and a part of her deepest self now sinks into a sense of rapture. Her feet beat against the ground, as though treading water, and for a moment she wants to let herself drown in his arms. Nevertheless, she resists. She knows that "the confusion, the noise of waters, and all the rest of it, were in her own head," and in recognizing that, she manages to recover herself and begs him to leave. But before he does, she feels his arms wrap tight "about her, and his lips on her own lips. His kiss was like a flash of lighning; when it was dark again she was free."

He is gone; and Isabel runs back to the house as quickly as she can. She had not known what to do, where to turn, what choice to make, "but she knew now. There was a very straight path." Before we can follow her down it, though, we need to look at this scene once more. Women in James do kiss one another, as a sign of—often duplicitous—friendship. Madame Merle kisses Isabel when she hears the news of her fortune, and Maggie Verver will kiss her husband's mistress in *The Golden Bowl*. But men and women almost never do, and rather pointedly we have not been given such a scene between Osmond and Isabel. Goodwood *takes* this kiss—an assault, a hot illuminating crackle. So we have to ask just what it lights up, and unfortunately the 1881 version of the novel doesn't tell us. That kiss may show Isabel her path, but James doesn't say why. The second version of this scene does, however, and it stands as one of the most comprehensively reworked moments in the entirety of the New York Edition. By 1906, James had been living with Isabel for twenty-five years. He was no longer the same writer or the same man as the one who had first created her, and the changes he made to this scene allow us to measure the ways in which the person who had written both *The Golden Bowl* and those letters to Hendrik Andersen had changed himself.

"She had never been loved before." So James had written, but now he added something more. Isabel had believed herself loved, but "this was different; this was the hot wind of the desert," and it no longer simply lifts her off her feet but instead forces her teeth open as if with the taste "of something potent, acrid, and strange." She has never before been loved, not by Warburton and not by Osmond, has never known its consuming force. It burns her up—it sets her reciprocally aflame. She fears its power, and the next moment only confirms that fear, for Goodwood's kiss is no longer a simple flash of lightning but instead

> a flash that spread, and spread again, and stayed; and it was extraordinarily as if, while she took it, she felt each thing in his hard manhood that had least pleased her, each aggressive fact of his face, his figure, his presence, justified of its intense identity and made one with this act of possession. So had she heard of those wrecked and under water following a train of images before they sink. But when darkness returned, she was free.

It is the most frankly sexual moment in all of James's fiction—frank in its emotion and its language alike. He could not have written it in 1881; perhaps no novelist in English could have. Hardy has moments of bawdry, and also of an age-old symbolism, like the sword drill that Sergeant Troy performs in *Far from the Madding Crowd*, with his blade darting around Bathsheba Everdene's body. But he gives us nothing like this. Nor for that matter does Zola: nothing like the sublime and spreading flash this kiss produces, nothing like the heightened inner life that James presents as induced by the very power of Isabel's physical reaction. She feels, as she takes that kiss, as if each fact of Goodwood's being were realizing itself in the act of pressing up against her, as if he has now become more himself than ever. She may not like them, but she does now understand the purpose of "his face, his figure, his presence." Still, she continues to feel his separateness even as he devours her; even as she loses herself in the waves of what he has forced upon her.

At this moment Isabel seems both entirely responsive to sexual passion and afraid of it in equal measure—afraid because responsive, because the strength of Goodwood's emotion has turned the key of her own, and she discovers how entirely capable she is of losing herself. We remember the fear with which she regarded the likelihood of Warburton's proposal, and her sense of the uncertain ground that Osmond's declaration produced, her imagination halting before it could go too far. We remember too her belief that if a certain light ever came she could give herself entirely. Now that light has come indeed, and with a force that makes Isabel sink and gasp not for breath but for thought. Goodwood's kiss clouds her head even as she thrills with perception, and it is exactly her presence, her independence, of mind that she most fears to lose. It's what she had to fight for with Osmond, who wanted to deck her inner world in his own genius for upholstery. But she had saved herself. She sat before the fire and puzzled out her life, she came to a clear understanding of the forces that had shaped and trapped her, and she learned the nature of her own blindness. She set herself free, even before leaving to sit by Ralph's bed. Now she might lose it all, but then Goodwood releases her, the darkness returns, and she knows what to do.

James's revisions suggest the reason for the decision Isabel now makes; reasons that seemed obscure to many readers of the first edition and maybe even to the author himself. She returns to Rome. She leaves Gardencourt as quickly as she can, and the news comes to us as a punch, a kick, a stab. Rome? For what, and why? Once again James pulls away from Isabel at a moment of decision—he did not show her in the act of choosing Osmond, and he does not show her here. Once more he staggers us with a *fait accompli*. This second decision had, however, seemed undermotivated in 1881, as though Goodwood's kiss had simply shown her where her duty lay. The later version gives us something much more complicated, and we can begin to understand it by taking literally the words she speaks at random. She goes to Rome to get away from Goodwood, not only from the "aggressive fact" of his presence but also from her own desire. She goes because she recognizes that the most valuable thing she has is a free mind, and Goodwood challenges that freedom as Osmond no longer does, threatening the autonomous self she has fought so hard to regain. She chooses, knowing what she doesn't want, and she goes because at this point nothing forces her to; her choice is an active one, and she goes because she can. She goes, finally, because to stay would require her to accept an illusion. She would have to believe, with her own earlier self, that an unfallen world does indeed lie all before her.

The younger James had neither the language nor the emotional experience to write about that. The older one did, and he used it to show us just why Isabel makes this final choice. It's not that she's afraid of sex per se, as some readers have always thought, but that she refuses to grant it the power she now knows it could have. She will not allow her fate to be determined by desire. Whether James is *right* about this, whether he could or should have allowed her something more—well, that's another question. In Maggie Verver he created a woman whose independence of mind is sharpened by that same desire, and in creating her he learned what he needed to know in looking at Isabel once more. He was himself a different man by then, and the world of the novel was different too. Stephen Crane had already given us his own Maggie, that girl of the streets, and Edith Wharton would soon bring a mathematical precision to seduction in *The Reef*; D. H. Lawrence would begin to work, and Proust as well. The printed page had started to admit what everyone talked about. But James was right about it for this character, for Isabel. In the New York Edition he could show, as he could not in 1881, just why she behaved as she did, and yet in doing so kept both the character and her novel within the boundaries he had first defined. She isn't different in the later version; but he does know more about her.

The news that Isabel has returned to Rome comes on the book's last page; the novel did not begin with Isabel, and it does not end with her either. Our heroine disappears from the text, vanishing into the smoke and the steam of a southbound train, and leaving Henrietta behind to give Caspar Goodwood the news. He turns away when he hears it, but Henrietta then grasps his arm and tells him to wait. On which, in the last words of the first edition, "he looked up at her." *Finis*.

B ut what kind of ending is that? It is so fast, and so startling, that we seem to plunge as deeply into the waters as Isabel herself, a confusion in which our feet have no bottom to find. Many of James's first readers felt troubled by it, and wondered just what, exactly, Goodwood was meant to wait for. The *Spectator*'s R. H. Hutton thought that the novel finished on the verge of what it dared not describe, and that Isabel's straight path led directly to a "liaison with her rejected lover." In *Blackwood's*, Margaret Oliphant acknowledged James's usual way of teasing his readers "with an end which is left to our imagination," but her own imagination joined Hutton's in seeing some "future stain" on the heroine; a suggestion she refused to abide. And James himself took pains to clarify those last sentences. His notebooks are explicit: Isabel now "feels the full force of [Goodwood's] devotion—to which she has never done justice; but she refuses." He did recognize his readers' puzzlement, though, and at a Boston dinner party in 1883 he told the table that Henrietta's words merely offer the man a note of encouragement about life itself. Not that he takes it, as the 1906 revisions make clear. There, Goodwood looks up at her "only to guess, from her face, with a revulsion, that she simply meant he was young." No reader of that later version can entertain Hutton's fear; even Goodwood himself no longer believes that Isabel might turn to him.

Still, that fear is instructive. It reminds us of how sharply sudden the book's last words are, of how disconcertingly little we're told about what's going to happen next. We suffer from the absence of news, and that suggests both how much we have come to care about Isabel and the strength of our need for a conclusion. Not just an end. Endings may be bitten off or cut short, as this one is, and what we want instead is some final disposition of the characters' lives. George Eliot lets her widowed Dorothea remarry and have a baby, and she also orders Lydgate's early death; Anna Karenina disappears beneath the wheels of a train, and Levin, having decided not to kill himself, walks home with his wife and child. These separate fates may delight or trouble us, but what really matters is that we know. Their lives are settled, and when we shut the book, we can leave them in place. Yet about Isabel we know nothing, as though James's protagonist herself were but a loose end. He stops with her en route to Rome, and we can't really predict what will happen when she gets there. Some of us may even grasp at the straws of what he *doesn't* write. We know she has "started for Rome," but James doesn't say that she's returned to her husband, and we can find ourselves clutching at the ambiguity.

James thought about the problem of winding things up for the entirety of his career. In his notebooks he recognized that the "obvious criticism" of the *Portrait* would be that it wasn't finished, that he hadn't "seen the heroine to the end of her situation—that I have left her *en l'air.*—This is both true and false. The *whole* of anything is never told; you can only take what groups together." And twenty-five years later he returned to that idea in the preface to *Roderick Hudson*: "Really, universally, relations stop nowhere, and the exquisite problem of the artist is eternally but to draw . . . the circle within which they shall happily *appear* to do so." Human life spills out of form, and another episode is always possible. The novelist needs to acknowledge that and yet also to ignore it, and one of the ways James draws his circle is by drawing a circle in fact. The book returns to where it began—the same house, the same people, even the same bench, and that proto-modernist patterning offers a reassuring sense of wholeness, like the couplet at the end of a sonnet. It helps us accept that jagged stump of a last page. For James took a gamble here, and the response of his readers suggests that in 1881 it wasn't entirely successful. Many of them couldn't accept a heroine who seemed to have one foot over the edge of the unknown, couldn't accept uncertainty. We are used to open endings now, and in part because of novels like this one; because James has turned us into the kind of readers who can be trusted to work things out for ourselves, and don't need a final chapter of dessert and ices.

James wrote in his notebooks that Isabel's departure for Italy stands as the story's climax—not Ralph's death, and not even the kiss. Those incidents work instead to produce that climax, one in which the book narrows itself down to a decision between two starkly different futures. It presents us with a simple binary in which she must either stay or go, and once she makes that decision, in full knowledge of the forces that have shaped her, the novel is of necessity over. And we cannot say what will happen to her now; what would happen, if she were real. James seems to have thought of giving the *Portrait* a sequel, writing in his notebooks that what he had done was "complete in itself," but adding that "the rest may be taken up or not, later." He never did, and in 1898 answered a friend's question about the chance of one by saying that it was "all too faint and far away." No record survives as to what he thought might happen after the end of the last page—if indeed he thought anything at all. For one of the wonderful things about this clipped and disconcerting ending is that Isabel seems to travel into a future that lies outside her author's own knowledge. Some readers want her to take up Pansy's cause, and others believe that she goes home in defeat. Maybe she will suffer on in a place where others have suffered before her; maybe Osmond will take her money, and let her go. The lives we choose for her say more about us than they do about the character herself; in my own next installment her new awareness makes her formidable, and she goes home only to fight. Isabel's future will have more possibilities in it than anyone can know when she steps onto that train, simply by virtue of being a future, but this chapter of her imaginary life is now closed.

"Nothing is my *last word* about anything." The statement comes from a letter in which James answered a reader's objection to one of his stories, and anyone trying to reach some final sense of a man who wrote so many millions of words should bear them in mind. Yet a last word we must have, and so let it be here. James enjoyed looking at pictures, and while visiting the London galleries in the early summer of 1882, he found himself drawn to a portrait that appeared to "raise the individual to the significance of a type," one that made a khaki-clad reporter named Archibald Forbes seem the epitome of the globe-trotting Englishman. His own great picture was just a few months behind him, and we may take his words as an account of what he had tried to do with it. Another self-description comes in the lines he wrote a few years later about Sargent, when after considering such already-famous works as *Madame X* and *The Daughters of Edward Darley Boit* he warned the painter against his own facility. For while "there is no greater work of art than a great portrait," the truly magnificent ones unite a sharp immediate perception with some quality of "lingering reflection." The artist must be patient with his subject, must live with it and into it and learn to see beyond its surface. Only then can he humanize its formal problems.

Henry James did that with Isabel Archer, and with the novel that contains her. He did it twice, in fact, seeing ever more deeply into the slim shade of a young girl who had once stood there all alone in his mind, ready to affront her destiny. He built a house for her, and ever since, readers have wanted to live in it, wandering through its hallways and looking out of its windows, hoping for a cup of tea with some of its inhabitants and wishing we could warn her against others. Some of those readers may want to give the lady one more room of her own, and for all of us a sense of her being flows out beyond the ending, as though Isabel had some life beyond the words that fix her to the page. That too was a part of James's ambition, and one he paradoxically fulfilled by refusing to tell us everything we might wish to know about her. We want her to go on—but let me borrow his words once more, and offer you the last sentence of the preface he wrote for her: "There is really too much to say."

ACKNOWLEDGMENTS

I first read *The Portrait of a Lady* during the fall of 1977, in a class at Amherst College taught by John Cameron. He did not often let himself refer to James's biography, still less to the details of the novel's publication. But I learned most of what I know about the rhetoric of fiction from him and from my other teachers at Amherst, and my education there sits in judgment on each sentence I write.

A fellowship from the John Simon Guggenheim Memorial Foundation made it possible for me to spend the academic year 2007–08 at work on this book's opening chapters. Smith College has been characteristically generous with sabbatical leave, travel grants, and other research funds, and I am grateful to the provost's office and in particular to Susie Bourque for that material support. Earlier, a grant from the Mellon-8 Consortium administered by Smith encouraged me to spend a summer putting together a detailed proposal, a narrative of what I wanted this book to do. And at the other end, I finished this book in Paris, where Columbia University's Institute for Scholars at Reid Hall graciously provided me with an office.

My agent, Steve Wasserman, found me the perfect editor in Bob Weil. Bob pushed me into paradox, pushed me to be at once tighter and yet more expansive, and my every page is stronger because of his work on it. At W. W. Norton and now Liveright I am indebted as well to Drake McFeely, Phil Marino, Peter Miller, Will Menaker, Devon Zahn, and Fred Wiemer.

Christopher Benfey, Ruth Bernard Yeazell, and David McWhirter read the entirety of the manuscript and saved me from many mistakes. Several colleagues at Smith deserve special thanks: Rick Millington and Michael

Thurston served as my guides to the American nineteenth century; Nancy Mason Bradbury did the same thing in a far more literal way in Florence. I owe a particular debt to Greg Zacharias and Pierre Walker for making available the transcripts of James's unpublished letters from 1880 and 1881. Many other people had the generosity to answer my questions; my gratitude to John Auchard, Michael Anesko, John Pemble, David Ball, Philip Horne, Cornelia Pearsall, Fred Kaplan, Larzer Ziff, James Shapiro, Rosella Mamoli Zorzi, Franco Zabagli, Sara Philo, Sheldon Novick, Lyndall Gordon, Carol Osborne, Paul Saint-Amour, David J. Supino, and Joseph Donohue. Sir Julian Rose arranged for my visit to Hardwick; Piers Plowden and Francesca Rowan, the current tenants of Lamb House, allowed me a glimpse of James's bedroom and upstairs study.

Yale's Beinecke Library and Harvard's Houghton Library allowed me to use their holdings. At Smith I am grateful to Karen Kukil and Martin Antonetti of the Mortimer Rare Book Room, while Susan Barker in the College archives and Henriette Kets de Vries at our superb museum gave me their help with the photographs. Catharina Gress-Wright and Stephanie Friedman, my undergraduate research assistants, have worked with skill and care.

Most rigorous of critics and best of traveling companions, Brigitte Buettner has had to listen to far too much about Henry James for far too long. Our daughter Miriam has yet to read a word of him. But she did enjoy the garden at the Lamb House.

SOURCES AND NOTES

The literature on Henry James is enormous and ever-changing. The biographies are rich; the criticism both helpful and provocative; and the documentary evidence pertaining to his life, his work, and his world can seem unending. I have benefited from everything I have read but have kept my references to a minimum. These notes indicate the sources of my quotations and mark a few specific debts, but they are not intended to summarize the terms of scholarly debate.

I have used the Library of America volume of James's *Novels, 1881–1886* as my source for the 1881 text of *The Portrait of a Lady*; for the novel's revised version and preface in the New York Edition, I've drawn on the relevant entry in the series of Oxford World's Classics. A complete and newly authoritative edition of James's letters is under way from the University of Nebraska Press, but many of the important ones are already in print, and some of them several times. For quotations from letters I therefore give the date and the recipient, and note whether it remains as of 2012 unpublished, but do not cite any one source for those now available. Interested readers should consult the on-line *Calendar of the Letters of Henry James* (jamescalendar.unl .edu) about where to find any particular piece of correspondence.

References to standard works—*The Prelude, Middlemarch*—are given by either line or chapter number but are not keyed to particular editions; in the case of some short poems and essays, I have simply supplied the date. Canny readers may notice that at times I work in close paraphrase of a Jamesian text, or even include the occasional ventriloquized phrase, an unmarked or buried quotation. A good example can be found on my prologue's first page—"taken possession of it, inhaled it, appropriated it," words adapted from a letter to his family of 1 November 1875. I have given references for some of these in the notes below, but not all.

All italics in quotations appear in the original.

ABBREVIATIONS FOR SOURCES FREQUENTLY CITED

A—Henry James, *Autobiography*. Edited by F. W. Dupee. New York: Criterion Books, 1956.

CS—Henry James, *Complete Stories*. 5 vols. New York: Library of America, 1996–99. Reference given with number added (e.g. CS1) to indicate volume.

CTW—Henry James, *Collected Travel Writing*. Vol. 1: *Great Britain and America*. Vol. 2: *The Continent*. New York: Library of America, 1993.

E—Leon Edel, *Henry James*. 5 vols. New York: Lippincott, 1953–72.

LC—Henry James, *Literary Criticism*. Vol. 1: *Essays, American and English Writers*. Vol. 2: *European Writers and The Prefaces*. New York: Library of America, 1984.

LFL—Michael Anesko, *Letters, Fictions, Lives: Henry James and William Dean Howells*. New York and Oxford: Oxford University Press, 1997.

N—Leon Edel and Lyall H. Powers, *The Complete Notebooks of Henry James*. New York and Oxford: Oxford University Press, 1987.

P—*The Portrait of a Lady* (1st American ed.), in Henry James, *Novels, 1881–1886*. New York: Library of America, 1985.

PLHJ—Lyndall Gordon, *A Private Life of Henry James: Two Women and his Art*. New York: W. W. Norton, 1999.

PNY—*The Portrait of a Lady* (New York Edition; revised 1906, published 1908) Oxford: Oxford World's Classics, 2009.

WJL—*The Correspondence of William James*. Edited by Ignas K. Skrupskelis and Elizabeth M. Berkeley. 12 vols. Charlottesville: University Press of Virginia, 1992–2004.

PROLOGUE: AN OLD MAN IN RYE

xiv—**He blotted**: These pages do not survive in their entirety; those that do can be found at Harvard's Houghton Library. The best study of them is in Philip Horne, *Henry James and Revision* (Oxford: Clarendon Press, 1990).

xiv—**"last manner"**: CS4, 350.

xv—**"would pretend to date"**: Virginia Harlow, *Thomas Sergeant Perry* (Durham, NC: Duke University Press, 1950), 305.

xv—**"curiosity and fastidiousness"**: P, 242.

xvi—**"selective as well as collective"**: To J. B. Pinker, 6 June 1905, unpublished.

xvi—**"frank critical"**: To Charles Scribner's Sons, 30 July 1905.

xvi—**"delicate vessels"**: George Eliot, *Daniel Deronda*, ch. 11.

xvi—**"the surprise of a caravan"**: PNY, 16.

xvi—**"an American writing"**: To William James, 29 October 1888.

xviii—**"that which people know"**: LC1, 63.

xix—**"a wedge of brown stone"**: PNY, 43.

xx—**"the British maiden"**: To Alice James, 5 January 1880, unpublished.

xx—**"which we find"**: LC1, 401–2.

xx—**"swarming . . . pretty girls"**: CTW1, 707.

xx—**"vacancy"**: CTW1, 698.

xxi—**"mildly pyramidal hill"**: To Mrs. William James, 1 December 1897.

xxii—**"extraordinary precocity"**: See B. R. McElderry, Jr., "Hamlin Garland and Henry James," *American Literature* 23.4 (January 1952), esp. 442–43.

xxii—**"wistfully an American"**: Ibid.

xxii—**"room began to sway"**: WJL3, 311–12.

xxiii—**"hugely *improved*"**: To J. B. Pinker, 10 June 1906, unpublished.

xxiv—**"single small"** ... **"her destiny"**: PNY, 9.

xxiv—**"organizing an ado"**: Ibid.

PART ONE: A PREPARATION FOR CULTURE

CHAPTER 1: THE GIRL IN THE DOORWAY

3—**"tall girl"**: P, 204.

3—**"a shrewd American"**: P, 194.

4—**"discovered"** ... **"independent"**: P, 201.

4—**"square and spacious"** ... **"shade"**: PNY, 9.

5—**"not one"** ... **"slit-like"**: PNY, 7–8.

5—**"the consciousness"**: Ibid.

5—**"Under certain circumstances"**: P, 193.

5—**"It is a truth"**: Jane Austen, *Pride and Prejudice*, ch. 1 (1813).

6—**"Oh, I hoped"**: P, 205.

6—**"there will be"**: P, 200.

7—**"Miss Brooke had"**: George Eliot, *Middlemarch*, ch. 1 (1871–72).

7—**"nineteen persons"**: P, 224.

7—**"many oddities"** ... **"accident"**: P, 211.

7—**"You must be"**: P, 216.

8—**"no mark"**: *New York Sun*, 27 November 1881. The review appeared under the initials MWH, since identified as Mayo Williamson Hazeltine; it can most easily be found in *Henry James: The Contemporary Reviews*, ed. Kevin J. Hayes (Cambridge and New York: Cambridge University Press, 1996).

8—**"taken up her niece"**: P, 212.

8—**"continuity between"**: P, 225.

8—**"so entertaining"**: P, 218.

8—**"so held her"**: PNY, 42.

8—**"glimpse of contemporary aesthetics"**: P, 225.

9—**"with her theory"**: P, 214.

9—**"almost anything"**: P, 218.

9—**"physiognomy had an air"**: P, 226.

9—**"general air"**: P, 232.

CHAPTER 2: A NATIVE OF NO COUNTRY

12—**A manifest handed**: Information about the *China* can be found at www .immigrantships.net/v7/1800v7/china18680508.html.

12—**"always round the corner"**: A, 8.

14—"**divorced from you**": To William James, 15 July 1878.

14—"**Leisured for life**": Quoted in R. W. B. Lewis, *The James Family* (New York: Farrar, Straus & Giroux), 30.

14—"**vastation**" . . . "**room**": Lewis, 51–53.

15—"**Say I'm a philosopher**": A, 278.

15—"**opportunities had been**": P, 223.

16—"**interested in almost**": A, 36.

16—"**a native of the James family**": In a letter to their sister Alice, WJL6, 517.

16—"**breathed inconsistency**": A, 124.

17—"**paying**": A, 126.

17—"**a firm grasp**": Quoted in E1, 171.

18—"**moral equivalent**": The title of a 1906 speech, most readily found in William James, *Writings, 1902–1910* (New York: Library of America, 1988).

18—"**so much manhood**": Quoted in Alfred Habegger, *The Father: A Life of Henry James, Sr.* (New York: Farrar, Straus & Giroux, 1994), 422.

18—"**I had done**": A, 415.

18—"**exacerbated by**": E1, 183

18—"**during**" . . . "**history**": A, 414–15. Edel's biography offers as close a reconstruction of the event as possible; the most suggestive interpretation is that of John Halperin in "Henry James's Civil War," *Henry James Review* 17.1 (1996).

19—"**muscular weakness**": Edmund Gosse, *Aspects and Impressions* (London: Cassell, 1922), 27.

19—"**Fortunately he has**": P, 392.

19—"**tented field enough**": A, 417.

19—"**seeing, sharing**": A, 461.

19—"**sense of what**": A, 460.

19—"**through our great**": Quoted in Louis Menand, *The Metaphysical Club* (New York: Farrar, Straus & Giroux, 2001), 268.

20—"**Harry has become**": Quoted in Harlow, *Thomas Sergeant Perry*, 249.

20—"**secret employments**": To Thomas Sergeant Perry, 18 April 1864.

20—"**Come now**" . . . "**chose**": A, 107.

21—"*scenic* **method**": N, 167; the notebook entry is for 21 December 1896.

21—"**afraid of nothing**": A, 509.

21—"**for what he called**": Habegger, 137.

21—**William's most recent biographer**: Robert D. Richardson, *William James: In the Maelstrom of American Modernism* (Boston: Houghton Mifflin, 2006).

22—"**the most delightful**": A, 508.

22—"**that I had no**": A, 508.

23—"**unwritten history**": CS1, 34.

23—"**published me**": LC1, 507.

24—"**we seem**" . . . "**other**": LFL, 471–73.

26—"**smiling aspects**": From an 1886 essay on Dostoevsky. See Howells, *Selected Literary Criticism, 1886–1897* (Bloomington: Indiana University Press, 1993), 35.

26—**"he joined us"**: LFL, 472. See also Carol Holly's essay in David McWhirter, ed., *Henry James's New York Edition: The Construction of Authorship* (Stanford, CA: Stanford University Press, 1998).

27—**"of pulmonary weakness"**: PLHJ, 377.

28—**"I wish I were"**: Minnie's surviving letters to James appear in Robert Le Clair, "Henry James and Minnie Temple," *American Literature* 21 (March 1949), 35–48.

28—**"reeling & moaning"**: To William James, 30 October 1869.

28—**"somehow too much"**: To Henry James, Sr., 19 March 1870.

29—**"more strange"** ... **"painfully?"**: To Mary James, 26 March 1870.

29—**"reach & quality"** ... **"dead"**: To William James, 29 March 1870.

29—**"the death of"**: Edgar Allen Poe, "The Philosophy of Composition" (1846).

CHAPTER 3: A SUPERSTITIOUS VALUATION

31—**"the more I see"**: To Thomas Sergeant Perry, 18 July 1860.

31—**"is obliged to deal"**: N, 214.

31—**"we can deal"** ... **"culture"**: To Thomas Sergeant Perry, 20 September 1867.

32—**"Wendell"** ... **"moonshiny"**: To Charles Eliot Norton, 4 Febuary 1872.

33—**"neatness and coquetry"**: To William James, 22 September 1872.

34—**"rattling big"**: To Elizabeth Boott, 27 January 1875.

35—**"there is no shadow"**: Nathaniel Hawthorne, *The Marble Faun* (1860), preface.

35—**"texture of American life"** ... **"one may say"**: LC1, 351–52.

35—**critic Robert Weisbuch**: My argument in this chapter is indebted to Robert Weisbuch's *Atlantic Double-Cross: American Literature and British Influence in the Age of Emerson* (Chicago: University of Chicago Press, 1986). See also his "Dickens, Melville, and a Tale of Two Countries" in the *Cambridge Companion to the Victorian Novel*, ed. Deirdre David (Cambridge and New York: Cambridge University Press, 2001).

36—**"It takes a great deal"**: LC1, 320.

36—**"that we very soon"**: LC1, 327.

36—**One classic account**: See "Novel and Romance" in Richard Chase, *The American Novel and Its Tradition* (Garden City, NY: Doubleday, 1957).

36—**"asked but little"**: LC1, 341.

36—**"do New York"**: To Edith Wharton, 17 August 1902.

37—**"not from the sweet"**: In M. A. De Wolfe Howe, *Memories of a Hostess: A Chronicle of Eminent Friendships Drawn Chiefly from the Diaries of Mrs. James T. Fields* (Boston: Atlantic Monthly Press, 1922), p. 120.

38—**"the appearance, the manner"**: To his parents, 16 November 1873.

38—**"could do more work"**: WJL4, 452.

38—**"set of desultory"**: WJL4, 458.

38—**"as a matter"**: WJL1, 230.

40—**"before him, soliciting"**: PNY, 5.

40—**"youth of genius"**: To Grace Norton, 26 September 1870.

40—**"in every day at dusk"**: *The Correspondence of Henry James and Henry Adams*, ed. George Monteiro (Baton Rouge: Louisiana State University Press, 1992), 4.

40—**"unutterably filthy"**: To Theodore Child, 17 February 1880.

41—**"a fraud"** ... **"people"**: *The Letters of Henry Adams*, ed. J. C. Levenson et al., vol. 2 (Cambridge: Belknap Press of Harvard University Press, 1982), 392–93.

41—**"not at all crazy"**: To Elizabeth Boott, 22 February 1880, unpublished.

41—**"conspiracy to undervalue them"**: LC1, 435.

42—**"gentlemen's society"**: CS2, 246.

42—**"high time Harry James"**: Monteiro, *Correspondence of Henry James and Henry Adams*, 5.

42—**"big"**: To Henry James, Sr., 30 March 1880.

42—**"the portrait of the character"**: To William Dean Howells, 2 February 1877.

42—**"to which the American"**: To Mary James, 4 May 1877, unpublished.

44—**"open window"**: To Henry James, 30 March 1880.

CHAPTER 4: ALONG THE THAMES

45—**"far-away-from-London"**: To Mary James, 10 January 1881.

46—**"infusion"** ... **"as it were"**: To Grace Norton, 28 December 1880.

46—**"going to do"** ... **"her own"**: P, 254–55.

46—**"stood there"** ... **"her destiny"**: PNY, 9.

47—**"gruel and silence"**: A, 525.

47—**"a view"**: To J. B. Pinker, 14 June 1906.

47—**"a good deal bruised"**: P, 194. See also the entry for Hardwick in Nikolaus Pevsner and Jennifer Sherwood, *The Buildings of England: Oxfordshire* (New Haven: Yale University Press, 1996).

48—**"no more beautiful"**: *Country Life*, 21 July 1906.

49—**Family tradition.** See the family entry in Burke's *Peerage and Baronetage*; but note too that the biographies of Grahame himself do not confirm this identification.

50—**"shut out"**: P, 228.

50—**"an uninteresting"**: P, 229.

50—**"conscious observation"**: P, 231.

50—**"looked in at"**: P, 254.

50—**"to pass through"**: P, 251.

51—**"young, happy"**: P, 238.

51—**"in the thick, mild air"**: P, 245.

51—**"always want"** ... **"choose"**: P, 259.

52—**"Whoso"** ... **"always may"**: Ralph Waldo Emerson, "Self-Reliance" (1841).

52—**"proof that a woman"**: P, 243.

53—**"I like to be treated"**: P, 288.

53—**"cultivated"**: Quoted in Alan Trachtenberg, *The Incorporation of America* (New

York: Hill & Wang, 1982), 153. Parkman's article, "The Failure of Universal Suffrage," originally appeared in the *North American Review* (July–August 1878).

54—**"alienated"**: P, 278.

54—**"than one gives up"**: P, 282.

54—**"well-ordered privacy"**: P, 245.

PART TWO: THE MARRIAGE PLOT

CHAPTER 5: HER EMPTY CHAIR

57—**"I have just heard"**: To John W. Cross, 14 May 1880.

58—**"which your wife"**: Ibid.

58—**"aghast at"**: WJL1, 183

59—**"I knew he"** ... **"the wall"**: To Henry James, Sr., 14 May 1880, unpublished.

60—**"Aren't you sorry?"**: To Grace Norton, 19 August 1880, unpublished.

60—**"empty chair"**: To Alice James, 30 January 1881.

60—**"thoroughly ill"**: Quoted in Gordon S. Haight, *George Eliot: A Biography* (Oxford: Oxford University Press, 1968), 544.

60—**"a Reticence"**: Quoted in John Rignall, ed., *The Oxford Reader's Companion to George Eliot* (Oxford: Oxford University Press, 2000), 26.

61—**"Johnnie had"**: Gordon S. Haight, ed., *The George Eliot Letters*, 9 vols. (New Haven: Yale University Press, 1954–78), vol. 7 (1878–80), 285.

61—**"I had my turn"**: To William James, 1 May 1878.

61—**"to attend service"**: In Haight, *George Eliot: A Biography*, 454.

62—**"underlying world"**: To Henry James, Sr., 10 May 1869.

62—**"take them ... visitor"**: A, 583–84.

63—**"we of the ... comparison"**: A, 573–74.

63—**" 'Middlemarch ... whole"**: LC1, 958.

63—**"two suns"**: LC1, 962.

64—**"without loss ... monsters"**: LC2, 1107–8.

64—**"deep-breathing economy"**: Ibid.

64—**"sets a limit"**: LC1, 965.

65—**"marriages and rescue"** ... **"happy art"**: LC1, 1004.

65—**"aesthetic teaching"**: The statement comes in a letter to the Positivist thinker Frederic Harrison and can be most readily found in George Eliot, *Selected Essays, Poems, and Other Writings*, ed. A. S. Byatt and Nicholas Warren (London: Penguin, 1990), p 248.

65—**"commissioned herself"**: LC1, 965.

66—**"special case"**: LC1, 1003.

66—**"generalizing instinct"**: LC1, 965.

66—**"have less"**: To Grace Norton, 5 March 1873.

66—**"In these frail"**: PNY, 10.

66—**"mind and millinery"**: In George Eliot, *Selected Essays, Poems, and Other Writings*, 140.
66—**"scientific criticism"**: P, 242.

CHAPTER 6: PROPOSALS

68—**"husbands, wives"**: LC1, 48.
69—**"Millions of"**: PNY, 9.
69—**"all-in-all"**: PNY, 11.
69—**"We women"**: George Eliot, *Daniel Deronda* (1876), ch. 13.
69—**"flood and field"**: PNY, 15.
69—**"the centre"**: PNY, 11.
70—**"must not fall"**: P, 201.
70—**Isabel's resistance to the plot**: My argument in this chapter is indebted to Millicent Bell's indispensable account of *The Portrait of a Lady* in her *Meaning in Henry James* (Cambridge: Harvard University Press, 1991).
70—**"a woman ought" ... "completely"**: P, 243–44.
70—**"It's just like"**: P, 205.
71—**"a most formidable ... fear"**: P, 272–73.
71—**"cold and dry"**: PNY, 65.
71—**an alternate line of criticism**: See esp. Nina Baym's "Revision and Thematic Change in *The Portrait of a Lady*," which locates the character in her historical moment. (*Modern Fiction Studies* 22.2, Summer 1976; repr., in 2nd Norton Critical Edition of the novel, ed. Robert D. Bamberg [New York: W. W. Norton, 1995].)
72—**"May I not"**: P, 293.
73—**"such a thumper"**: P, 300.
73—**"some people"**: P, 304.
73—**"it cost her"**: Ibid.
73—**"I'm afraid"**: P, 301.
73—**"personage"**: P, 295.
73—**"what one liked"**: P, 296.
74—**"Imagine one's belonging"**: P, 248.
74—**"old-fashioned distinction" ... "certain way"**: LC1, 54–55.
75—**"psychological reasons"**: LC1, 60.
75—**"few things"**: LC1, 61.
75—**"she could do better"**: P, 296.
75—**"Who was she"**: P, 304.
76—**"Do you know ... lord!"**: P, 303.

CHAPTER 7: AN UNMARRIED MAN

77—**some representative titles**: Van Wyck Brooks, *The Pilgrimage of Henry James* (1925); Marius Bewley, *The Complex Fate: Hawthorne, Henry James, and Some Other*

American Writers (1952); Leon Edel, *Henry James: The Conquest of London, 1870–1881* (1962).

78—**That emphasis suited**: See Michael Anesko, *Monopolizing the Master: Henry James and the Politics of Modern Literary Scholarship* (Stanford, CA: Stanford University Press, 2012).

78—**"a smile"**: CTW2, 338–40.

78—**"dim sense"**: Fred Kaplan, *Henry James: The Imagination of Genius* (New York: Morrow, 1992), 300.

78—**"a most tender" ... "friendship"**: To Alice James, 24 May 1876.

78—**"strange" ... "oddity"**: LFL, 471.

78—**"verbal passion"**: Kaplan, 300.

79—**"undersized . . . men"**: Theodore Roosevelt, "What Americanism Means." Quoted in Edmund Morris, *The Rise of Theodore Roosevelt* (New York: Coward, McCann & Geoghegan, 1979), 480.

79—**"separate, not unworkable"**: Philip Larkin, "The Importance of Elsewhere" (1955).

79—**"the deepest thing"**: To W. Morton Fullerton, 2 October 1900.

80—**"Londonized"**: To Charles Eliot Norton, 17 November 1878.

80—**"Mrs. James"**: To William James, 1 May 1878.

80—**"as if it were"**: To William James, 23 June 1878.

80—**"of all the men"**: E. S. Nadal, "Personal Recollections of Henry James," *Scribner's Magazine*, July 1920, 94.

81—**"This last report"**: To Mary James, 31 October 1880.

81—**"generally felt ... all to myself"**: To Grace Norton, 7 November 1880.

82—**"the gospel"**: CS2, 865.

82—**"most objectionable"**: CS2, 886.

83—**"poor S.'s wife"**: N, 25.

83—**"the innermost" ... "covert"**: To Edmund Gosse. 9 June 1884.

83—**"somdomite" [*sic*] . . . "vicious"**: See Graham Robb's *Strangers* (New York: W. W. Norton, 2004), an exemplary synthesis of research in the field, albeit one that concentrates on the lives and situations of the articulate and the intellectual. Its accounts of Symonds and Wilde are especially useful.

84—**"band of the emulous"**: To Edmund Gosse, 7 January 1898.

84—**"mild cultured man"**: To William James, 28 February 1877.

85—**"who love"**: To J. A. Symonds, 22 February 1884.

85—**"unclean beast"**: E3, 31.

85—**"He was never"**: To Edmund Gosse, 8 April 1895.

85—**"a position in society"**: Nadal, 90.

85—**"being what I am" ... "second best"**: *The Memoirs of John Addington Symonds*, ed. Phyllis Grosskurth (New York: Random House, 1984), 184–85.

86—**"She made"**: P, 782.

86—**"always based"**: Tzvetan Todorov, "The Secret of Narrative," in *The Poetics of Prose* (1971), trans. Richard Howard (Ithaca: Cornell University Press, 1977), 145. Both this essay and its companion piece in the same volume, "The Ghosts of

Henry James," are among the most suggestive things ever written about James's work.

87—"name for everything": Sigmund Freud, "The Uncanny" (1919). The standard translation is by James Strachey.

88—"loved his friends": Theodora Bosanquet, *Henry James at Work* (1924; repr., Ann Arbor: University of Michigan Press, 2006, ed. Lyall H. Powers), 48.

89—"darlingest Hugh!": E5, 409.

89—"I can't!": See the introduction to Leon Edel, *Henry James Letters*, vol. 4, 1895–1916 (Cambridge: Belknap Press of Harvard University Press, 1984), xix. Edel presents the story as a form of urban legend, with Walpole telling it to Somerset Maugham, who told it to everyone.

89—"a horror" . . . "physical love": Leon Edel, *Henry James: A Life* (New York: Harper & Row, 1985), 724–25.

89—biographer Sheldon Novick: See his *Henry James: The Young Master* (New York: Random House, 1996), 109–10.

89—*L'initation première*: N, 238.

89—"regret a single": To Hugh Walpole, 21 August 1913. L4 680.

90—"supposed that he was" . . . "visible the face": Gosse, *Aspects and Impressions*, 42–43.

91—"oasis" . . . "*distingué*": To William James, 25 April 1876. The novelist always referred to his friend by the French version of his family name—Joukowsky. On their relations, see, in addition to Novick, Peter Brooks's *Henry James Goes to Paris* (Princeton: Princeton University Press, 2007).

91—"extreme purity" . . . "him": To Alice James, 24 May 1876.

92—"musical séance" . . . "failure": To Henry James, Sr., 11 November 1876.

92—"peculiar": To Henry James, Sr., 30 March 1880.

92—"sturdy, thickset": Cosima Wagner, *Diaries*, ed. Martin Gregor Dellin and Dietrich Mack, trans. Geoffrey Skelton (New York: Harcourt Brace Jovanovich, 1978–80) vol. 2, 432.

92—"rescued": Wagner, 439.

93—"opposed to those" . . . "nothing else": To Grace Norton, 9 April 1880.

93—"vileness" . . . "immoralities": To Alice James, 25 April 1880.

93—Kaplan suggests: See pp. 223–24 of his biography.

94—"*Non ragioniam*": N, 216.

CHAPTER 8: A LONDON LIFE

95—"murky metropolis": To Mary James, 6 August 1877.

95—"and Paris was": N, 215.

95—"if I sometimes": CTW2, 720.

96—"I don't like": To William Dean Howells, 28 May 1876.

96—"*say nothing*": To William James, 13 October 1876.

97—"beyond expression": To Mary James, 24 December 1876.

98—**Lionel Trilling**: "The Princess Casamassima," in *The Liberal Imagination* (New York: Viking Press, 1950).

98—**"came to know"**: N, 218.

99—**"better sort"**: This is the title James gave to a 1903 collection of stories.

99—**"conversing affably"**: To William James, 29 March 1877.

99—**"agreeable" . . . "form of life"**: N, 217–18.

100—**"You can do"**: Letter of 28 October 1885. In *The Letters of Robert Louis Stevenson*, ed. Booth and Mehew (New Haven: Yale University Press, 1985), vol. 5, 143.

100—**"the traces"**: CTW1, 118.

100—**"the dingy, British"**: CTW1, 296.

100—**"modern conversation"**: CTW1, 190.

101—**"cabinets and parties"**: Bosanquet, 52.

101—**"insidious, perfidious" . . . "good deal"**: To William Dean Howells, 18 April 1880.

101—**"himself . . . too hard"**: To Mary James, 4 July 1880.

101—**"tremendous material bribe"**: WJL5, 121.

101—**"inscrutable"**: WJL5, 105.

102—**"dinners and parties" . . . "few points"**: WJL5, 121.

102—**"transitory" . . . "show them"**: To Mary James, 4 July 1880.

103—**"the whole of"**: To William Dean Howells, 20 July 1880.

103—***"tant bien"***: N, 219.

103—**"for a sniff" . . . "to work"**: To Alice James, 9 October 1880, unpublished.

104—**"with such tact"**: To Mary James, 28 November 1880.

104—**"steadily, but very slowly"**: N, 220.

CHAPTER 9: THE ENVELOPE OF CIRCUMSTANCES

105—**"strictures on" . . . "so much"**: To William Dean Howells, 5 December 1880.

106—**"entertainment of seeing"**: P, 344.

106—**"whether this or that"**: P, 418.

106—**"stubbornest fact"**: P, 309.

107—**"remember what"**: P, 357.

107—**"She had done"**: P, 359.

107—**"You are drifting" . . . "immoral novel"**: P, 361.

107—**"I shall have"**: P, 374.

108—**"if certain things"**: P, 377.

108—**"never prevaricated"**: P, 374.

108—**"Daddy" . . . "miss you"**: Ibid.

109—**"cloven foot"**: The *Spectator*'s review was by R. H. Hutton and appeared on 26 November 1881; reprinted in Roger Gard, *Henry James: The Critical Heritage* (London: Routledge & Kegan Paul, 1968).

109—**"I take" . . . "veiled acuteness"**: P, 378.

109—**"to marry for a support"**: P, 379.

109—**"immoral"**: P, 381.

109—"see her going": P, 380.

109—"hovered before him": PNY, 5.

110—"to see what": P, 378.

110—and bank stock: See Elliot M. Schrero, "How Rich Was Isabel Archer?" *Henry James Review* 20.1 (1999).

111—"should so strongly": P, 368.

111—"I am Madame Merle": P, 369.

111—"deeply recognises": PNY, 15–16.

111—"woman of ardent impulses": P, 371.

111—"too perfectly": P, 388.

112—"to see what": P, 384.

112—"preposterous": P, 396.

112—"yours was" ... "his house": P, 397.

112—"When you have lived": P, 397–98.

113—"I think just": Ibid.

113—"What she wore": In the Pevear and Volokhonsky translation (New York: Viking Penguin, 2001), 79.

114—"of a new adventure": R. W. B. Lewis, *The American Adam* (Chicago: University of Chicago Press, 1955), 5.

114—"to leave the past": P, 222.

114—"the supremacy of the individual": LC1, 383.

114—"you think" ... "called I": Emerson, "The Transcendentalist" (1841). Like both "History" and "Self-Reliance," it forms a chapter in Emerson's *Essays: First Series.*

115—"ripe unconsciousness of evil": LC1, 254.

115—"no special providence": Quoted in Gordon Wood, *Revolutionary Characters* (New York: Penguin, 2006), 181.

115—"*a man's Me*": The passage comes in Chapter XII. See *William James: Writings, 1878–1899* (New York: Library of America, 1992), 174–75. I am grateful to Bill Brown's *A Sense of Things: The Object Matter of American Literature* (Chicago: University of Chicago Press, 2003) for making this connection between the work of the two brothers.

116—"the self as known" ... "as knower": *William James: Writings, 1878–1899,* 174.

116—"empirical aggregate" ... "be an aggregate": *William James: Writings, 1878–1899,* 208.

116—"Whatever I may": *William James: Writings, 1878–1899,* 174.

PART THREE: ITALIAN JOURNEYS

CHAPTER 10: BELLOSGUARDO HOURS

121—"well spoken of": *Baedeker's Northern Italy,* 5th ed. (Leipzig: Karl Baedeker, 1879), 342.

122—"If you're an aching alien": CTW2, 403.

122—**"big enough"**: Nathaniel Hawthorne, *Letters, 1857–1864* (Columbus: Ohio State University Press, 1987), 150–51.

122—**"a little grassy" . . . "front"**: P, 423.

123—**"colored a dull"**: From *Roderick Hudson* in Henry James, *Novels, 1871–1880* (New York: Library of America, 1983), 455.

123—**"peeping up"**: CTW2, 520.

124—**"incommunicative" . . . "no eyes"**: P, 423.

124—**"We are a wretched" . . . "anywhere"**: P, 392.

125—**"He is Gilbert" . . . "no anything"**: P, 393.

125—**"American absentees"**: P, 408.

125—**"can you get"**: P, 411.

126—**"unsatisfactory life"**: Nathaniel Hawthorne, *French and Italian Notebooks*, ed. Thomas Woodson (Columbus: Ohio State University Press, 1980), 437.

126—**"sombre kind"**: Ibid., 442.

126—**"hardly spoken to"**: To Grace Norton, 14 January 1874.

127—**"had been exactly" . . . "unemployed"**: CTW2, 396–97.

127—**"a rounded pearl"**: To William James, 27 December 1869.

128—**"the clatter of"**: LC2, 1043.

128—**"easy, friendly"**: To Catherine Walsh, 3 May 1880, unpublished.

128—**"one is liable"**: To Alice James, 25 April 1880.

128—**"an unconventional"**: PLHJ, 151.

129—**"my true country"**: Leon Edel prints the four surviving letters from Woolson to James in vol. 3 of his edition of James's letters. See *Henry James Letters*, vol. 3 (Cambridge: Belknap Press of Harvard University Press, 1980), 551.

129—**"if your sentence"**: "Miss Grief," in *Lippincott's Magazine*, May 1880. Repr., in Constance Fenimore Woolson, *Selected Stories and Travel Narratives*, ed. Victoria Brehm and Sharon L. Dean (Knoxville: University of Tennessee Press, 2004), 209.

130—**"amiable, but deaf"**: To Alice James, 25 April 1880.

130—**"authoress" . . . "intense"**: To Catherine Walsh, 3 May 1880, unpublished.

130—**"horrible ignorance"**: Letter from spring 1880 to a Mrs. Crowell, in *Five Generations, Part Second—Constance Fenimore Woolson*, arranged and edited by Clare Benedict (London, 1930), 188. This is a privately printed collection of letters and papers from Woolson's extended family, compiled by her niece.

130—**"likes to be"**: From "A Florentine Experiment," in Woolson, *Selected Stories*, P. 228.

131—**"the two destroyed"**: *Henry James Letters*, vol. 3, 524.

131—**"that sweet young American"**: Ibid., 545.

132—**"you said, in answer"**: Ibid., 539.

CHAPTER 11: MR. OSMOND

133—**"pass for anything"**: P, 425.

133—**"for the consideration"**: P, 463.

133—"**not to strive**": P, 462.

134—"**approached each other**": P, 437.

134—"**I know plenty**": P, 437.

134—"**it seem more**": P, 445.

135—"**as if, once**": P, 451.

135—"**to types which**": PNY, 459.

135—"**studious life**" . . . "**fatherhood**": P, 476.

136—"**she is a little**": P, 464.

136—"**that man**": P, 474.

136—"**coarse imputation**" . . . "**by selfishness**": P, 504.

136—"**wilful renunciation**": P, 462.

137—"**good humour**": P, 502.

137—"**are perfect**": P, 439.

137—"**for a cabinet**": CTW2, 360.

138—"**mental constitution**": To Alice James, 25 April 1880.

139—"**Italianate bereft**" . . . "**Gilbert Osmond**": A, 522.

139—"**traditionary**": P, 425.

139—"**as the only**": P, 439.

140—"**looking very well**": P, 437.

140—"**the girl is not**" . . . "**sacrificed**": P, 483–84.

CHAPTER 12: *STRANIERI*

141—"**passing travellers**": Augustus Hare, *Walks in Rome* (New York: George Routledge & Sons, 1873), 1.

142—"**the fresh, cool**": P, 485.

143—"**a young lady**": *The Letters of Henry Adams*, vol. 1: *1858–1868*, ed. J. C. Levenson et al. (Cambridge and London: Belknap Press of Harvard University Press, 1982), 135.

143—"**as if it were Clapham**": P, 490.

143—"**I have first or last**": To William James, 9 April 1873.

143—"**a double ruin**": *Journals of John Cheever*, ed. Susan Cheever (New York: Knopf, 1991), 72.

144—"**palpable imaginable**": LC2, 1177.

144—"**what the grand**": Henry James, *William Wetmore Story and His Friends*, 2 vols. (Edinburgh and London: Blackwood, 1903), vol. 1, 341.

145—"**cleverness**" . . . "**is greater**": To Charles Eliot Norton, 31 March 1873.

145—"**precursors**": *William Wetmore Story and His Friends*, vol. 1, 3.

145—"**consciousness of the complicated**": Ibid., 6.

146—**The historian John Pemble**: These figures, and Pemble's explanation, come from personal correspondence, an email of 23 September 2007.

146—**travel writer Bayard Taylor**: See *Life and Letters of Bayard Taylor*, ed. Marie Hansen-Taylor and Horace E. Scudder. 2 vols. (Boston: Houghton, Mifflin, 1895), vol. 2, 490.

146—**"Americans Abroad"**: *Lippincott's*, May 1894, 679.

146—**Murray and Baedeker**: The picture of the Anglo-American business commu-
nity here is a composite drawn from the following editions: *A Handbook of Rome and
Its Environs*, 5th ed. (London: John Murray, 1858), 11th ed. (1872), 12th ed. (1881);
Central Italy and Rome, 9th ed. (Leipzig: Karl Baedeker, 1886).

147—**"remarkably ugly"**: To Alice James, 10 February 1873.

148—**"at all regret"**: To Henry James, Sr., 4 March 1873.

148—**"I doubt that"**: To William James, 9 April 1873.

148—**"in the position"**: To Mary James, 24 March 1873.

149—**"without relations"**: To Mary James, 26 January 1873.

149—**"curl up, like"**: *Letters of Henry Adams*, vol. 5, p. 524.

149—**"It seems stupid"**: Edith Wharton, *The Age of Innocence*, ch. 24.

150—**"with its economical"**: CTW2, 392.

150—**"the ruins of"**: P, 723

151—**"imported"** ... **"moral responsibility"**: LC1, 363.

152—**"dingy drollery"**: CTW2, 416.

153—**"a terrible game"**: CTW2, 421.

153—**"I made no vows"**: *The Prelude*, Book IV, ll. 341–42.

153—**"close seat"**: To Mary James, 24 March 1873.

153—**"the very source"**: CTW2, 440.

153—**"unbroken continuity"** ... **"one else."**: CTW2, 444.

CHAPTER 13: AN UNCERTAIN TERRAIN

155—**"I didn't come"**: P, 493.

155—**"good fellow"** ... **"he's not"**: P, 495.

156—**"Does she"** ... **"horribly"**: PNY, 298.

156—**"qualified herself"**: P, 501.

157—**"one ought to"**: P, 507.

157—**"that I find"**: P, 509.

157—**"immense sweetness"**: P, 509.

157—**"ought to have"**: Ibid.

158—**"the sharpness of the pang"**: PNY, 310.

158—**"behind bolts"**: P, 222.

158—**Matthew Arnold**: "The Buried Life," ll. 84–85.

158—**"everything that's proper"** ... **"itself"**: P, 511.

158—**"agitation"** ... **"treacherous"**: P, 512.

159—**ellipses in its narrative**: I borrow this word from Millicent Bell, and my argument is indebted to her account of Isabel's resistance to and acceptance of plot.

160—**"individual technique"**: Graham Greene, "The Dark Backward," in *Collected
Essays* (1964; repr., Penguin, 1970), 56.

161—**"the dark shining"** ... **"she chose"**: P, 522.

162—**"I would rather"**: P, 528.

162—"I had no idea": P, 543.
162—"You are going": P, 543.
162—"more importance": P, 545.
162—"soaring . . . sailing": P, 546.
163—"a man to whom" . . . "of any sort": P, 548–49.
163—"his very poverties": P, 550.
164—"I hope it may never": P, 547.
164—"disjoined": P, 551.
164—"detestably fortunate" . . . "envying someone": P, 498–99.

CHAPTER 14: A VENETIAN INTERLUDE

165—"the temperature ferocious": To Thomas Sergeant Perry, 24 January 1881.
165—"quietly bring my": N, 220.
165—"Frenchified" . . . "digestion": To Fanny Kemble, 24 February 1881.
166—"dusky light": N, 220.
166—"virtually finished": N, 221.
166—Baedeker for 1879: Venice then had 128,000 inhabitants.
166—"painfully large": CTW2, 289.
167—"be lived in": CTW2, 329.
167—"awful": CTW2, 330. For the gondoliers' strike, along with much else about the nineteenth-century city, see Margaret Plant, *Venice: Fragile City, 1797–1997* (New Haven: Yale University Press, 2002).
167—"battered peep show": CTW2, 292.
167—"the most beautiful": CTW2, 314.
168—"*una bellezza*": N, 221.
168—"simpler pleasure[s]": CTW2, 289.
168—"one of those things": N, 221.
168—"sentient": CTW2, 291.
169—"craved more to possess": Quoted in Rosella Mamoli Zorzi et al., *Gondola Days: Isabella Stewart Gardner and the Palazzo Barbaro Circle* (Boston: Isabella Stewart Gardner Museum, 2004), 255.
171—"like a camel's back": CTW2, 297. On this point see Zorzi's "A Knock-Down Insolence of Talent," in *Sargent's Venice*, ed. Warren Adelson et al. (New Haven: Yale University Press, 2006).
171—"in the fruitless": NPY, 3.
171—"even the brightest": CTW2, 298.
171—"The creature varies": CTW2, 291.
172—"between the niece": CTW2, 296.
172—"be a sad day": CTW2, 287.
172—"you renounce all": CTW2, 305.

CHAPTER 15: FENIMORE

174—"sky-parlor": *Henry James Letters*, vol. 3, 557.

175—"Poor Isabel!": Ibid., 533.

175—"I suppose there": Ibid., 540.

175—"a woman": Ibid., 352.

176—"immense power": To Elizabeth Boott, 18 October 1886.

176—"thought the carriage": PLHJ, 199.

176—"hide": To Francis Boott, 26 November 1886.

176—"promiscuous, polygot": To Sarah Butler Wister, 27 February 1887.

176—"making love to Italy": To Edmund Gosse, 24 April 1887.

178—"local tone": LC1, 664.

178—"that the old lady": N, 33.

178—"in obscurity": CS3, 228.

179—"publishing scoundrel": CS3, 303.

179—"an out-of-the-way canal": CS3, 228.

179—"make love": CS3, 235.

179—"get out of it": CS3, 314.

180—"Henry is somewhere": PLHJ, 231.

181—"giving up being": PLHJ, 248.

182—"to Miss Woolson": To Ariana Curtis, 14 July 1893.

182—"whether the end": *Henry James Letters*, vol. 3, 550.

182—"alone and unfriended": To William W. Baldwin, 26 January 1894.

182—"sudden *dementia*": To Francis Boott, 31 January 1894.

182—"sills overlooking": PLHJ, 276.

183—"*After* such an event": To Francis Boott, 31 January 1894.

183—"too many and too private": To William W. Baldwin, 2 February 1894.

184—"all her precious things": PLHJ, 286.

185—"and they came up like balloons": PLHJ, 289. This is the most readily available source for the anecdote; one can also find it in *Gondola Day*, 145. Gordon draws the story from a 1956 radio interview with Mercedes Huntington, whose words are quoted here. Her family owned the Villa Castellani, and she claimed to have heard it as a young woman from James himself; a transcript of the interview is available at Harvard's Houghton Library. But sources closer to the period attest to it as well; see *Gondola Days*.

185—"never failed" ... "behaviour": CS3, 230.

185—"If her depression": Kaplan, *Henry James: The Imagination of Genius*, 383.

187—"to whom nothing": CS5, 540.

187—"The Beast in the Closet": See the chapter of that title in Eve Kosofsky Sedgwick, *Epistemology of the Closet* (Berkeley: University of California Press, 1990).

188—"have appreciated": CS2, 295.

PART FOUR: SEX AND SERIALS, THE CONTINENT AND THE CRITICS

CHAPTER 16: MAUPASSANT AND THE MONKEY

191—"**suggestive of**" . . . "**sun-bonnets**": The piece originally ran in the *Galaxy* for June 1875. It's reprinted in Henry James, *The Painter's Eye*, ed. John L Sweeney (Cambridge: Harvard University Press, 1956), 96–97.

192—**Some Victorian commentators**: See Kate Flint's analysis in *The Woman Reader, 1837–1914* (Oxford: Clarendon Press, 1993), ch. 4.

192—"**bring a blush**": Dickens, *Our Mutual Friend*, ch. 11. On blushing, see Ruth Bernard Yeazell, *Fictions of Modesty* (Chicago: University of Chicago Press, 1991), ch. 5.

193—"**Two ladies from the country**": From George Moore, "A New Censorship of Literature," *Pall Mall Gazette*, 10 December 1884.

193—**after a one-day trial**: See the trial transcript, "The Ministry of Justice Against Gustave Flaubert," trans. Bregtje Hartendorf Wallach in the Norton Critical Edition of *Madame Bovary*, ed. Margaret Cohen, 3rd ed. (New York: W. W. Norton, 2005).

193—"**no English author**" . . . "**to read?**": James Fitzjames Stephen, "*Madame Bovary*," *Saturday Review*, 11 July 1857.

194—"**cleanliness**" . . . "**Expurgatorius**": Margaret Oliphant, "Novels," *Blackwood's*, September 1867.

194—"**the novels of her**": Ibid.

194—"**into the hands**": See Cohen, ed. "*Madame Bovary*," 333.

195—"**between that which**": LC1, 63.

195—"**Candour in Fiction**": *New Review*, January 1890. Hardy's comments are on p. 20.

195—"**there is a terrible coercion**": *Adam Bede*, ch. 29.

196—"**rather shy**": LC1, 63.

196—"**I would rather**": P, 558.

196—**French verb is** *branler*: See any complete edition of the Goncourt diary; this section is available in an English translation by Robert Baldick, *Pages from the Goncourt Journal* (1962; repr., New York: New York Review Books Classics, 2006), 212–14.

197—"**Le petit Maupassant**": Ibid.

197—"**right mental preparation**": To Edmund Gosse, 17 October 1912.

197—"**as if her sky**": From Henry James, *Parisian Sketches: Letters to the New York Tribune, 1875–1876*, ed. Leon Edel and Ilse Dusoir Lind (London: Rupert Hart-Davis, 1958), 40. This passage comes from a piece itself called "Parisian Sketches," his letter for December 28, 1875.

198—"**rather embarrassed**": To Henry James, Sr., 20 December 1875. On James's Parisian experiences, see Peter Brooks, *Henry James Goes to Paris*.

199—"**editor of the austere** *Atlantic*": To William Dean Howells, 3 February 1876. James records Howells's reply in a letter of 4 April, and the Goncourt Diary lets us date the conversation to Sunday, 30 January; see Baldick, 220.

200—"with astronomy" ... "well-written": LC2, 1014.

201—"the subscriber": Ibid.

201—"more totally" ... "or catches": LC2, 892–93.

201—"misery, vice" ... "disagreeable". LC2, 861–62.

202—"nature ... as a combination": LC2, 866.

202—"poverty of ... consciousness": LC2, 327–28.

202—"English system": LC2, 869.

202—"than the effort": To William Dean Howells, 21 February 1884.

202—"I have to hide": Howells, *Selected Letters, 1882–1891* (Bloomington: Indiana University Press, 1980), 12. The letter is to John Hay.

202—"when Nana raised": Émile Zola, *Nana*, trans. George Holden (London: Penguin, 1972), 44.

203—"foulness": LC2, 867.

203—"her sexual parts": *Nana*, 385.

203—Henry Viztelly: On his editions of Zola, and the novelist's reception in England, see Anthony Cummins, "Émile Zola's Cheap English Dress: The Viztelly Translations, Late-Victorian Print Culture, and the Crisis of Literary Value," *Review of English Studies* 60 (2008), 108–32.

203—"l'âge ingrat": The phrase comes two pages in to *Nana*'s third chapter; Holden (75) translates it as "awkward."

204—"'good' talk?": LC2, 1125.

204—"old castles" ... "ancient monuments": CS2, 247.

205—"a great deal": CS2, 246.

205—"clever little reprobate": CS2, 291.

205—"old enough" ... "should like it": CS2, 275.

206—"portrait of a gentleman": Wharton, *The Age of Innocence*, ch. 14. Elizabeth Ammons's "Cool Diana and Blood Red Muse" points out the nominal relation between Wharton's protagonist and James's own. See the Norton Critical Edition of the novel, ed. Candace Waid (New York: W. W. Norton, 2003).

207—"mustn't think": Ibid., ch 16.

207—"at Florence with": Ibid., ch 20.

CHAPTER 17: THE MAGAZINES

208—"stifling *calidarium*": N, 223.

208—"I am afraid": To Houghton, Mifflin & Co, 13 July 1881.

208—"*probably* not less": To William Dean Howells, 23 August 1879.

209—The two were: See George J. Worth, *Macmillan's Magazine, 1859–1907* (Farnham, UK: Ashgate, 2003); and Ellery Sedgwick, *The Atlantic Monthly, 1857–1909* (Amherst: University of Massachusetts Press, 1994). On the economic necessity of serialization, see Howells, "The Man of Letters as Man of Business" (1893).

211—"next *long* story" ... "remember this": To William Dean Howells, 14–15 July 1879.

213—"devoured in the American papers": To Frederick Macmillan, 28 December 1880.

213—"stretch of months": To William Dean Howells, 5 December 1880.

213—"been explicit as": To William Dean Howells, 11 November 1880.

213—"strangely vague": To William Dean Howells, 5 December 1880.

213—"after Isabel's marriage": N, 13–14.

214—"to be settled later": Ibid.

214—"process and progress": Linda K. Hughes and Michael Lund, *The Victorian Serial* (Charlottesville: University Press of Virginia, 1991), 243.

215—"steady development": Ibid., 275.

218—"no magazine": Joseph Conrad, 6 January 1908. In *Collected Letters of Joseph Conrad*, vol. 4: *1908–1911*, ed. Frederick R. Karl and Laurence Davies (Cambridge: Cambridge University Press, 1990), 9–10.

219—"slow, sure growth" ... "whole": Hughes and Lund, 230.

219—James's income: See Michael Anesko's meticulous *"Friction with the Market": Henry James and the Profession of Authorship* (Oxford: Oxford University Press, 1986), Appendix B.

220—"nothing can be": *The Spectator*, 6 November 1880.

220—"considerably the most important": *The Nation*, 24 March 1881.

220—"the reader feels": *The Nation*, 18 November 1880.

220—"quite too lifelike": *The Examiner*, November 6 1880.

221—"the author evidently": Ibid., December 4, 1880.

221—"One afternoon, toward dusk": P, 559.

CHAPTER 18: THE ROCCANERA

222—"will perhaps": P, 559.

223—"if her husband": P, 562.

223—"who died two": P, 564–65.

224—"years had touched": P, 570.

225—"these people": P, 567.

225—"genius for upholstery": P, 588.

225—"high house": Ibid. P, 566.

225—"stern old Roman": Ibid.

225—Palazzo Antici-Mattei: See Charles S. Anderson, *Person, Place, and Thing in Henry James's Novels* (Durham, NC: Duke University Pres, 1977), 292. See also Harry Brewster, *A Cosmopolite's Journey* (London: Radcliffe Press, 1998), 182, a memoir by an expatriate of another generation who spent a part of his childhood there.

225—Mattei family: On their ownership of work by Michelangelo Merisi da Caravaggio, see Jonathan Harr, *The Lost Painting* (New York: Random House, 2005).

226—"a row of": P, 566–67.

226—"traditionary": P, 425.

227—"reflective reader": P, 592.

228—"there's the difference" ... "leading one?": P, 603–4.

228—"received an impression": P, 611.

228—"make him the reparation": P, 617.

228—"play the part": P, 618.

229—"The moment you": P, 625.

229—"It lies in": P, 626.

229—"has all the vivacity": PNY, 16.

230—"service her husband had" ... "terrors": P, 628.

230—"he could change": P, 630.

230—"stream of consciousness": William James, *Writings, 1878–1899*, 152.

231—"make-believe" ... "no retrospect": *Daniel Deronda*, ch. 1.

232—"oblique view" ... "impression of it": LC2, 1322.

232—"He had told her": P, 633–34.

233—free indirect discourse: See, for starters, Dorrit Cohn, *Transparent Minds: Narrative Modes for Presenting Consciousness in Fiction* (Princeton: Princeton University Press, 1978); Franco Moretti, "Serious Century," in *The Novel*, vol. 1 (Princeton: Princeton University Press, 2006); James Wood, *How Fiction Works* (New York: Farrar, Straus & Giroux, 2008).

233—"dark, narrow alley" ... "one by one": P, 629.

234—"everlasting weight": P, 638.

234—her life go undramatized: See Bell, *Meaning in Henry James*, 116–17.

234—"solidity of specification": LC1, 53.

235—"the different *pace*": William James, *Writings 1878–1899*, 987.

235—"like one who should say": Ibid., 164.

235—"defeated": To William James, 21 April 1884.

235—"chamber": LC1, 52.

236—"luminous halo": Virginia Woolf, "Modern Fiction," in *The Common Reader* (New York: Harcourt, Brace, 1925), 154.

236—"It is obviously": PNY, 16.

237—"anxiously and yet ardently": PNY, 423.

238—"was not a daughter" ... "at all": P, 636.

238—"indecent": P, 637.

238—"her husband and Madame Merle": P, 639.

CHAPTER 19: THE ART OF FICTION

239—Macmillan released: For these bibliographical details, see Leon Edel and Dan Laurence, *A Bibliography of Henry James*, 3rd ed. (Oxford: Clarendon Press, 1982), and David J. Supino, *Henry James: A Bibliographical Catalogue of a Collection of Editions to 1921* (Liverpool: Liverpool University Press, 2006). The Robert Frost Library at Amherst College made its copy of the Macmillan edition available to me;

for the Houghton, Mifflin, I used the copy belonging to the Mortimer Rare Book Room at Smith College.

240—**Mudie's**: The standard work remains Guinevere L. Griest, *Mudie's Circulating Library and the Victorian Novel* (Bloomington: Indiana University Press, 1970), to which I am indebted throughout this chapter.

241—**"gains in its"**: W. C. Brownell, *The Nation*, 2 February 1882.

241—**The *New York Sun***: 27 November, 1881; *Californian*, January 1882; both in Hayes, *Henry James: The Contemporary Reviews*. Horace Scudder's review appeared in the *Atlantic* for January 1882, and Margaret Oliphant's in *Blackwood's* for March 1882. Both appear in Bamberg.

242—***Lippincott's***: See *The Contemporary Reviews*.

243—**"your talent, your style"** . . . **"like it"**: *Henry James Letters*, vol. 3, 528–35.

244—**"new school"** . . . **"Thackeray"**: Reprinted in Gard, 126–35.

244—**"at the exploits"**: Margaret Oliphant, "American Literature in England." *Blackwood's*, January 1883, 137.

244—**"principle that"**: L. L. Jennings, "American Novels," *Quarterly Review* (January 1883), 225.

245—**"The indictment"**: To William Dean Howells, 27 November 1882.

245—**"as thick as blackberries"**: To William Dean Howells, 20 March 1883.

245—**"bright, troubled"** . . . **"conscience"**: Robert Louis Stevenson, "A Gossip on Romance," *Longman's Magazine* (November 1882), 189–90.

246—**"Boston Mutual Admiration Society"**: Jennings, 251.

246—**"to edge in"** . . . **"extent opened"**: LC1, 44. James's essay first appeared in *Longman's Magazine* for September 1884. Besant's own lecture was published together with James's in 1884 (Boston: Cupples, Upham & Co.) and appeared separately in 1902 (London: Chatto.) It is excerpted in Stephen Regan, *The Nineteenth-Century Novel: A Critical Reader* (London and New York: Routledge, 2001).

247—**"course of dessert"** . . . **"impossible"**: LC1, 48.

247—**"psychological"**: LC1, 61.

248—**"a living thing"**: LC1, 54–55.

248—**"What is character"**: Ibid.

248—**"A Humble Remonstrance"**: *Longman's Magazine*, December 1884.

249—**"That is the highest"**: E. M. Forster, *Aspects of the Novel.* (New York: Harcourt, Brace, 1927), 45.

249—**"shallow optimism"**: LC1, 65.

249—**"on the principle"**: To William Dean Howells, 21 February 1884.

250—**Child wrote**: "Contributors' Club," *Atlantic* (May 1884), 724–27.

250—**"evaporate"**: To Auguste Monod, 17 December 1905.

250—**"had as yet"**: "Contributors' Club," 726.

250—**"galley-slaves"**: To Thomas Bailey Aldrich, 13 February 1884.

250—**"tepid soap"**: To William Dean Howells, 21 February 1884.

250—**Mario Vargas Llosa**: See his *Perpetual Orgy: Flaubert and Madame Bovary*, trans. Helen Lane (1975; repr., New York: Farrar, Straus & Giroux, 1986), 220.

251—**"moral passion"**: LC1, 63.

251—**"the great American"**: To William Dean Howells, 21 February 1884.

251—**"brutal indecency"**: LC2, 861.

252—**"timidity"**: LC2, 880.

252—**"hard and fast"**: LC2, 549.

252—**"carnal side of man"**: LC2, 548.

253—**"the constant world-renewal"**: LC1, 107.

253—**"deeply in the quiet"**: LC1, 109.

253—**"impeded by the"**: Virginia Woolf, "Professions for Women," in *The Death of the Moth* (London: Hogarth Press, 1942); the essay originated as a talk given to the National Society for Women's Service in 1931.

253—**"falsify the total show"**: LC2, 964. See also David McWhirter, "Saying the Unsayable: James's Realism in the Late 1890s," *Henry James Review* 20 (1999).

PART FIVE: PUTTING OUT THE LIGHTS

CHAPTER 20: THE ALTAR OF THE DEAD

257—**"Darling old father"**: WJL5, 227.

258—**"worn and shrunken"**: N, 229.

258—**"ought to be"**: N, 216.

259—**"hand to its"**: N, 225.

259—**"old world—my choice"**: N, 214.

260—**"have ceased to suffer"**: To Mary James, 29 January 1882.

260—**"all that has gone"**: N, 229.

260—**"sweetness and beneficence"**: N, 229.

260—**"neither ideal or ethereal"**: E3, 38.

261—**"the most supremely"**: Letter to William James of 30 July 1891; in Ruth Bernard Yeazell, ed., *The Death and Letters of Alice James* (Berkeley: University of California Press, 1981), 186.

261—**"tensions and emotions"**: E3, 38.

261—**"obscene bird of night"**: Henry James, Sr., *Substance and Shadow* (Boston: Ticknor & Fields, 1863), 75.

262—**"beneficent hush"**: N, 232.

262—**"a way of his own"**: To Mrs. Francis Mathews, 13 February 1882.

262—**"Here lies a man"**: From the entry for 24 June 1891 in *The Diary of Alice James*, ed. Leon Edel (Boston: Northeastern University Press, 1999), 217.

263—**"softening of the"** . . . **"almost natural"**: To William James, 26 December 1882.

263—**"heard somewhere"** . . . **"my belief"**: To William James, 1 January 1883.

264—**"feeling somewhat unprotected"**: WJL5, 228.

265—**"let her off easy"**: CS4, 217.

265—**"complete appreciation"**: LC1, 1333.

265—"a past which is": LC1, 233.

265—"When the mortal": LC2, 1006.

265—"an air of": LC2, 1016.

266—"I bade him": LC2, 1026.

266—"ruled by a": CS4, 450.

267—"do something great": N, 233.

CHAPTER 21: "I WAS PERFECTLY FREE"

268—"in small pieces": P, 654.

268—"enough to do": P, 653.

269—"visibly happy": P, 705.

269—"direct opposition" ... "of marriage": P, 667.

269—"I can't publish": P, 694.

269—"have to take": P, 667.

269—"that had once": P, 724.

269—"old Rome into": P, 723–24.

270—"through the veil": Ibid.

270—"I was perfectly": P, 694.

271—"free and separate": Iris Murdoch, "Against Dryness," *Encounter*, January 1961.

272—"when one is": P, 721.

272—"Let him off": P, 723.

272—"mocking voice" ... "destiny": P, 720.

272—"Who are you" ... "Everything": P, 723.

273—"the man in the world": P, 725.

273—"that the worst": P, 726.

273—"the great historical": P, 725.

274—"aim high": P, 689.

274—"in the old way": P, 555.

274—"a chance for": P, 736.

274—"It's dishonourable": P, 744.

275—"malignant": P, 743.

275—"pure mind": P, 749.

275—"some one else's wife" ... "property": P, 750–51.

276—"I have watched": P, 752.

276—"no longer the lover": P, 751.

277—The critic Arnold Kettle: See his chapter on the *Portrait* in *An Introduction to the English Novel*, vol. 2 (London: Hutchinson's University Library, 1953).

278—"a high door": P, 756.

279—"dull un-reverenced tool": P, 759.

279—"your cousin" ... "match": P, 766.

CHAPTER 22: WORKING IN THE DARK

280—"despite the constant": N, 232.
281—"local" ... "New England": N, 19.
281—"down to the deep": *Diary of Alice James*, 230. See Jean Strouse's *Alice James: A Biography* (Boston: Houghton Mifflin, 1980) for details of her relationship with Katherine Loring.
282—"dishabituated to the": CS2, 246.
284—"inexplicable injury": To William Dean Howells, 2 January 1888. For James's earnings, see Anesko, *Friction with the Market*.
284—"anyone to be": E3, 211.
285—"shrinking opportunity": CS4, 337.
285—"last manner": CS4, 350.
285—"second chance" ... "of art": CS4, 355.
286—"flooded with light": To William James, 9 March 1886.
286—"of about the length": To William James, 1 October 1887.
287—"half a dozen": N, 52. Edel's biography remains the best source for details of James's theatrical career; see also his edition of the *Complete Plays of Henry James* (1949) with its introductions to each work.
288—"pure situation": N, 53.
289—"dip my pen": N, 77.
289—"the quantity of tailoring": E4, 26.
290—"repulsive and fatuous": To Isabella Stewart Gardner, 23 January 1882.
290—"clumsy, feeble" ... "a success": To Mr. and Mrs. William James, 2 February 1895.
290—"the *last*" ... "y'are": E4, 78.
291—"audible defeat": Ibid.
291—"an abominable quarter": To William James, 9 January 1895.
292—"need say" ... "I will": N, 109.

CHAPTER 23: THE SECOND CHANCE

294—"*march of an action*": N, 167.
295—"denounced": To Edmund Gosse, 28 August 1896.
296—"long-unassuaged desire": To Mrs. William James, 1 December 1897.
296—"not too-delusive": Ibid.
297—"wide, sheep-studded greenness": E4, 160.
298—"come back next": To Hendrik Andersen, 7 September 1899.
298—"without thinking": Ibid.
298—"their bellies and bottoms": To Hendrik Andersen, 31 May 1906.
299—"squalid violence": To William James, 26 April 1895.

299—"**absolutely** *holding*": To W. Morton Fullerton, 2 October 1900.

300—"**pendulous**" . . . "**two stockings**": Max Beerbohm, "The Mote in the Middle Distance," in *A Christmas Garland* (London: Heinemann, 1912).

301—"**It wasn't till**" . . . "**great decorated surface**": *The Golden Bowl*, in Henry James, *Novels, 1903–1911* (New York: Library of America, 2010), 733. My account of James's late style is indebted to Ian Watt's classic "The First Paragraph of *The Ambassadors*," *Essays in Criticism* (1960), and Ruth Bernard Yeazell's introduction to the most recent (2009) Penguin edition of *The Golden Bowl*.

302—"**apertures and outlooks**": Ibid.

302—**Many critics**: F. O. Matthiessen, *Henry James: The Major Phase* (1944); Dorothea Krook, *The Ordeal of Consciousness* (1962); Laurence Holland, *The Expense of Vision* (1964).

302—"**people's moral scheme**": LC2, 1312.

305—"**hugely and ingeniously**" . . . "**molehill**": To Sarah Butler Wister, 21 December 1902.

306—"**steel-souled**": CTW1, 418.

306—"**expensively provisional**": CTW1, 420.

306—"**distressful, inevitable waste**": CTW1, 540.

306—"**the moral identity**" . . . "**point of view**": CTW1, 525–26.

307—"**triumph of the superficial**": CTW1, 736.

307—"***Do New York!***" . . . "**waits for**": To Edith Wharton, 20 August 1902.

307—"**Would You Care**": Quoted in Home, *Henry James and Revision*.

308—"**as to expression**" . . . "**native city**": To Charles Scribner's Sons, 30 July 1905.

CHAPTER 24: ENDGAME

309—"**rushing hotels**": CTW1, 689.

309—"**hot-looking stars**": CTW1, 710.

310—"**filthily**": To Brander Matthews, 24 March 1915.

310—"**fit for appearance**": Bosanquet, *Henry James at Work*, 40.

310—"**values implicit**": Ibid., 42.

310—"**incapable of stupidity**": PNY, 183.

311—"**she grew impatient**": P, 777.

311—"**nervous and scared**": PNY, 560.

311—"**wide brown rooms**": P, 777.

311—**in the first systematic study**: F. O. Matthiessen, "The Painter's Sponge and Varnish Bottle," in *Henry James: The Major Phase* (Oxford: Oxford University Press, 1944). Reprinted in Bamberg.

311—"**private thrill**": PNY, 263.

311—"**time and the weather**": LC2, 1045.

312—"**a few buried**": LC2, 1046.

312—"**latent**": LC2, 1335.

312—"**the march of**": LC2, 1329.

312—"the inner life": Nina Baym, in Bamberg, 620.

313—"Are you going" . . . "is over": P, 785.

313—"a scene that": P, 773.

313—"life would be": P, 769.

314—"very bad" . . . "of me": P, 781–82.

314—Kant's idea of the categorical imperative: The standard account of Kant's relevance to the novel belongs to William Gass, "The High Brutality of Good Intentions," *Accent* 18 (Winter 1958). Reprinted in Bamberg. My quotation from the philosopher is drawn from Gass.

314—his secondary characters: See Alex Woloch, *The One vs. the Many: Minor Characters and the Space of the Protagonist in the Novel* (Princeton: Princeton University Press, 2003).

316—"have all eternity": P, 783.

316—"lost all her shame": P, 784.

316—"I never thanked": P, 784.

316—"that was not" . . . "ruined": P, 785.

317—"I shall be": P, 784.

318—"a sort of": To William Dean Howells, 17 August 1908.

318—"self-occupied": LFL, 422; the friend in question was Charles Eliot Norton's daughter Sally.

319—October 1908 his first royalty statement. James notes the figure in a letter to J. B. Pinker, 1 April 1909.

319—"black and heavy": To William Dean Howells, 27 May 1910.

320—"the frustration of all": E5, 440.

320—"William cannot": E5, 442.

320—"Bad day[s]": N, 314–15.

320—"wholly unfit": To Edith Wharton, 10 June 1910.

321—morphine and milk: For details of William's death, see Richardson, *William James*, 520.

321—"His extinction" . . . "pride": To Thomas Sergeant Perry, 2 September 1910.

321—"ramification of old": To Henry James III, 16 July 1912.

321—"difficult & unprecedented": To Mrs. William James, 13 November 1911.

321—"I recover it": A, 207.

322—"the past" . . . "memories": To Henry Adams, 21 March 1914.

322—"*undo* everything": To Rhoda Broughton, 10 August 1914.

322—"what the treacherous": To Howard Sturgis, 4 August 1914.

323—"attachment and devotion": To H. H. Asquith, 28 June 1915.

323—"bad sick week": To Edmund Gosse, 25 August 1915.

323—"a regular hell": To Hugh Walpole, 13 November 1915.

324—"sketchy state" . . . "sister": For what is called the "Deathbed Dictation," see N, 581ff.

324—"over the counterpane": E5, 559.

324—"a dim, hovering" . . . "nothing": P, 787.

325—"lying on": Ibid.

325—"postponing, closing" ... "obligations": P, 789.

325—"Lady Flora": P, 780.

326—"something important" ... "purpose": P, 794.

326—"that ghastly form": P, 797.

326—"the world is all": P, 798.

327—"The world is very small": Ibid.

327—"to get away" ... "feet": P, 797.

327—"the confusion" ... "free": P, 799.

327—"but she knew": Ibid.

328—"this was different" ... "strange": PNY, 580.

328—Goodwood's kiss is no longer: PNY, 581. The best account of Isabel's relation to sexual passion, and of the novel's conclusion as well, belongs to Dorothea Krook. See also Tessa Hadley, *Henry James and the Imagination of Pleasure* (Cambridge: Cambridge University Press, 2002).

331—"he looked up at her": P, 800.

331—"liaison with her rejected lover": Hutton in Gard.

331—"with an end": Oliphant in Bamberg.

331—"feels the full force": N, 15. James's 1883 words about the ending were recorded in a copy of the novel by its owner. See Supino, *Henry James: A Bibliographical Catalogue*, 135.

331—"only to guess": PNY, 582.

332—"started for Rome": P, 800.

332—"obvious criticism": N, 15.

332—"Really, universally": LC1, 1041.

333—"complete in itself": N, 15.

333—"all too faint": To A. C. Benson, 11 March 1898.

333—"Nothing is my": To Jane Hill, 15 June 1879.

333—"raise the individual": Henry James, "London Pictures," in *The Painter's Eye*, 213.

334—"there is no greater": "John S. Sargent," in *The Painter's Eye*, 227–28.

334—"There is really too much to say": PNY, 17.

INDEX

ABOUT THE AUTHOR

Michael Gorra is the Mary Augusta Jordan Professor of English at Smith College, where he has taught since 1985. His books include *After Empire: Scott, Naipaul, Rushdie*; *The Bells in Their Silence: Travels through Germany*; and, as editor, the Norton Critical Edition of William Faulkner's *As I Lay Dying*. He has received fellowships from the Guggenheim Foundation and the National Endowment for the Humanities, along with the Balakian award of the National Book Critics Circle for his work as a reviewer. He lives in Northampton, Massachusetts, with his wife and daughter.